Risen from Ruins

Stanford Studies on Central and Eastern Europe

Edited by Norman Naimark and Larry Wolff

Risen From Ruins

The Cultural Politics of Rebuilding East Berlin

Paul Stangl

Stanford University Press

Stanford, California

Stanford University Press
Stanford, California

Printed in the United States of America on acid-free, archival-quality paper

Library of Congress Cataloging-in-Publication Data

Names: Stangl, Paul, author.
Title: Risen from ruins : the cultural politics of rebuilding East Berlin / Paul Stangl.
Description: Stanford, California : Stanford University Press, 2018. |
Series: Stanford studies on Central and Eastern Europe | Includes bibliographical references and index.
Identifiers: LCCN 2017034427 (print) | LCCN 2017035711 (ebook) | ISBN 9781503605503 (epub) | ISBN 9781503603202 | ISBN 9781503603202 (cloth : alk. paper)
Subjects: LCSH: City planning—Germany—Berlin—History—20th century. | Socialist realism and architecture—Germany—Berlin—History. | Communism and architecture—Germany—Berlin—History. | Berlin (Germany)—Cultural policy—History—20th century. | Berlin (Germany)—Politics and government—1945–1990. | Architecture and state—Germany (East)
Classification: LCC NA9200.B4 (ebook) | LCC NA9200.B4 S73 2018 (print) | DDC 720.943/155—dc23
LC record available at https://lccn.loc.gov/2017034427

Typeset by BookMatters in 11/13.5/26 Adobe Garamond

Contents

Illustrations

Acknowledgments

THIS BOOK is the culmination of a project with roots extending back to my years in graduate school. I would like to thank the Department of Geography and Environment at the University of Texas–Austin, which first supported my research on Berlin. In particular, Kenneth E. Foote provided crucial guidance and continues to do so. Karl Butzer and Robert Mugerauer provided encouragement and insights that helped to shape my initial research. Additional thanks to Bill Doolittle and Gregory Knapp. Special thanks to Anton Nelessen of Rutgers University, whose support and instruction guided me in establishing a foundation in urban design that informs all of my research. The publications of Maoz Azaryahu proved invaluable when I was first sorting through an immense literature on Berlin's urban landscape and struggling to structure my research. Maoz has since become a helpful colleague and valued friend. Finally, I would like to thank the extremely supportive staffs of the Bundesarchiv, Landesarchiv Berlin, Staatsbibilothek zu Berlin, Stiftung Preußische Schlösser und Gärten, and Stadtmuseum Berlin.

Abbreviations

ACC	Allied Control Council
BA	Bundesarchiv
BM	Berlin Magistrat
BZ	*Berliner Zeitung*
CDU	Christian Democratic Union
DA	*Deutsche Architektur*
DBA	Deutsche Bauakademie (German Building Academy)
FDJ	Freie Deutsche Jugend (Free German Youth)
FIAPP	Fédération Internationale des Anciens Prisonniers Politiques du Fascisme (International Federation of Former Political Prisoners of the Nazi Regime)
GDR	German Democratic Republic
GEHAG	Gemeinnützige Heimstätten-, Spar- und Bau-Aktiengesellschaft (Benevolent Housing, Building, and Savings Association)
KPD	Kommunistische Partei Deutschlands (Communist Party of Germany)
LAB	Landesarchiv Berlin
MfA	Ministerium für Aufbau (Ministry of Building)
ND	*Neues Deutschland*

NSDAP	Nationalsozialistische Deutsche Arbeiterpartei (National Socialist German Workers' Party)
SAPMO-BA	Stiftung Archiv der Parteien und Massenorganizationen der DDR im Bundesarchiv
SED	Sozialistische Einheitspartei Deutschlands (Socialist Unity Party)
SKK	Sowjetische Kontrolkommission (Soviet Control Commission)
SMAD	Soviet Military Administration
SPD	Sozialdemokratische Partei Deutschlands (Social Democratic Party of Germany)
TR	*Tägliche Rundschau*
VVN	Vereinigung der Verfolgten des Naziregimes (Association of Those Persecuted by the Nazi Regime)

Risen from Ruins

Introduction

> Men make their own history, but they do not make it as they please; they do not make it under self-selected circumstances, but under circumstances existing already, given and transmitted from the past. The tradition of all dead generations weighs like a nightmare on the brains of the living.
>
> —Karl Marx, 1852

LITTLE MORE THAN ONE MONTH after the founding of the German Democratic Republic (GDR), the new building minister, Lothar Bolz, declared the rebuilding of Berlin after the Second World War "a lever to activate the entire population of Germany and... to raise the social consciousness of the entire population."[1] Bolz, a student of Soviet socialist-realist theory, viewed architecture above all as an art in service of the practical and emotional needs of humans. In the ruins of Berlin, with its severe housing shortage and devastated architectural heritage, Bolz saw opportunity. The city would not be reconstructed. Instead, a "new building up" (Neuaufbau) would win the support of the people and help guide their transformation into socialists. Optimism would displace despair. With revolutionary fervor, a "New Berlin" would emerge in a "New Germany," "risen from ruins," as the GDR's national anthem proclaimed.

This book examines city building in East Berlin from the end of World War II on May 8, 1945, until the construction of the Berlin Wall on August 13, 1961—a period of great interest in reshaping the city to express new political ideals. After centuries of growth, Berlin's destruction during the war confronted political and cultural leaders with myriad decisions about what to demolish, what to restore, what to reconstruct, and what to build. Throughout the postwar era, German Communists would exert the greatest influence in this regard, due to their immediate influence in the administration of Berlin and the fact that after the division the historic core of the city lay in East Berlin. The center of Berlin might have been completely restored, or it might have been totally razed in favor of a sanitized modern city. Something between these extremes occurred, however, as decision-makers operated within the constraints of existing cultural, political, and economic frameworks. Their approach to city building was shaped by their worldviews and political ideologies, beliefs about the relationship between urban form and society, political strategizing at municipal, national, and international levels, and assessments concerning the deployment of limited resources. These motives were further complicated by the great political, ideological, and theoretical instability and change during this era. The imprint of the decisions made throughout these years are evident all over Berlin today. These same issues had similar effects on hundreds of cities across central and Eastern Europe during the Cold War.

Between 1870 and 1945, a mere seventy-five years, Berlin had been the capital of three strikingly different states: the constitutional monarchy of the German Empire, the parliamentary democracy of the Weimar Republic, and the dictatorship of the Third Reich. Although many Germans genuinely embraced Nazism, it had only been the official ideology for twelve years when the Nazi state ended catastrophically and the victorious Allies initiated denazification efforts. This immense historical rupture provided fertile ground for innovative ideological developments, which the victorious powers sought to shape according to their interests. The urban landscape would play a vital role in this process. Most of Berlin's historic core was less than 150 years old, but its buildings, streets, and squares had been inscribed with a complex mosaic of identities to be enlisted in the ideological battle.

Examining the process by which Berlin's urban landscape became embroiled in cultural politics raises a series of questions. How was meaning borne in the urban landscape? Were there fundamental differences in the communicative nature of different landscape elements—that is, historic architecture, vernacular building, monuments, and public space—or did they all bear meaning in the same fundamental ways? Did the technical and political elite feel free to impress structures and places with an unlimited range of meanings, or did they perceive a field of opportunity and constraint? Ideology and theory provided a comprehensive framework for interpreting the landscape, but were these taken as steadfast guides for decision-making or were other factors influential? The answers to these questions center on how key actors understood the relationship between society, cultural memory, and urban form. At times, key actors and groups—the Soviet Military Administration (SMAD), German Communists, and the German cultural elite—viewed these relationships differently and thus took varied approaches to the cityscape. They often relied on ideology and theory for guidance, but other factors were influential, including pragmatic issues, concern for political consequences, and the idiosyncratic tastes of powerful individuals. Furthermore, complex place-based meaning could cloud the clarity of a beautiful theory.

This book contributes to a sizable literature on the relationship between cultural memory, politics, and the urban landscape, often focusing on monument and memorial construction, commemorative practices, and political spectacles.[2] Related scholarship has examined similar issues regarding street names, architecture, public spaces, historic preservation, and city planning.[3] Because of extensive debates over meaning in its urban landscape, Berlin has been a hotbed for these studies. Yet English-language publications on Berlin have given limited attention to the early GDR, with the exception of Maoz Azaryahu's work on street names.[4] German-language monographs have provided insight into politics, identity, and the urban landscape during the entire Communist era, often focusing on a building or a site, a street ensemble, or theoretical issues.[5]

This book shares commonalities with these works but differs from them in significant ways. First, it examines Communist politicization of all facets of the urban landscape, including memorials, toponyms, historic monumental and vernacular architecture, as well as new city plans and architectural designs. This broader perspective brings into focus the distinct approaches to the built environment taken by the major groups involved and identifies changes over time. Second, this book is grounded not only in architectural and planning theory but also in geography, with space, place, and representation as central concepts. This provides a standard for examining the interpretation of such diverse components of the city, revealing similarities and differences in how these features were seen to bear meaning and uncovering factors that complicate theoretical directives. Finally, the book demonstrates how debate was shaped by inherited ideologies and traditions, which Marx may have seen as nightmare but which also provided the conceptual building blocks for a new city and society.

The Urban Landscape

There are many approaches to studying memory and the urban landscape. One of the key distinguishing factors of this book is its analysis of the spatialization of memory. For instance, Rudy Koshar examines how human agents engage "highly resonant parts of a memory landscape" and "themes and symbols that are the raw material of the framing devices and meanings themselves."[6] This book spatializes the approach through an additional layer of analysis to examine how themes and symbols are expressed through landscape elements, and why this impacts their use in cultural politics.

Meaning is posited to reside in a triad of representation, spatial/formal characteristics, and place-based associations. Representation includes text, symbols, and icons that are inscribed in physical media—that is, sculpture, bas-relief, banners, flags, and so on with recognizable themes and symbols.[7] The messages may vary greatly in their degree of clarity, ambiguity, or polyvalence—an aspect strategically seized upon at times by Soviets and German Communists. Spatial and formal characteristics are considered in the broadest sense. Spatial characteristics such as the degree of enclosure, the nature of the ground plane and bounding surfaces (materials, pattern of articulation, nature of adjoining space and transitions), presence and nature of objects within the space (trees, benches, monuments, small structures), and nonvisual sensory qualities (smells, sounds, and tactile aspects) all define a space. Spatial relations between physical aspects such as size, proportion, distance, direction, and pattern can be a constitutive element of expression, equivalent to syntax in language. Humans may perceive and attribute value to different aspects of form and space at a given site. Two of these aspects were often important to cultural and political leaders in East Berlin. First, the spatial capacity of buildings and plazas to hold persons or objects, a strictly utilitarian value, was often very important to cultural and political leaders during this era. Second, architectural style is defined by the formal and spatial properties of buildings. At times style is attributed substantial symbolic value, including being taken as an expression of national identity.[8]

Finally, place-based meaning may be imposed through representation but acquires depth from social activities, from mundane routines to spontaneous, dramatic events, and ritualistic ceremonies. Reportage of meanings and events contributes to this process. According to Edward Relph, place is distinguished from space, in that places are "constructed in our memories and affections through repeated encounters and complex associations. Place experiences are necessarily time-deepened and memory-qualified."[9] The resulting link between cultural memory and a particular site is complex, ambiguous, and changing. Over time, the connection may grow stronger or weaker, be forgotten and recovered. Multiple themes may be associated with the same site. Even when an enduring, dominant association is evident—for example, the Berlin Palace and "Prussian monarchy"—this may be valued in widely divergent ways by different groups or by the same group in different eras. Yet place-based meaning can be very resilient, as even over time the physical effacement of a site may fail to wipe out the public's identification with the site (i.e., pilgrimages may continue even after a memorial is demolished).

Vernacular spaces acquire place-based meaning from the patterns of everyday life of their inhabitants. This occurs at various scales and for various types of space: cafe, street corner, park, or neighborhood. Meanings shared by individuals provide building blocks for local identities, which on occasion become quite prominent. Berlin's working-class district Wedding became known as "Rote Wedding" (Red Wedding) during the 1920s because of the large number of socialists residing there. The entire medieval town of Rothenburg ob der Tauber became a romanticized national icon during the late nineteenth century.[10] In contrast, monumental spaces are built to aggrandize and memorialize; they possess place-based meaning from the outset. They express cultural memory in a durable form that can be directly experienced by current and future generations. Hence, intentionally and unintentionally, the urban landscape acts as a repository of collective memory, playing an important role in cultural reproduction.[11] The process is dynamic as a society seeks to sustain or reshape cultural memory, vernacular sites become memorialized and monumental sites are effaced.

For these reasons the urban landscape would become embroiled in politics in the postwar era. While there was contestation among political parties during the early postwar years, the division of the Magistrat von Berlin (Berlin Magistrat), and more so the founding of the GDR, allowed Communists to fully engage the cityscape for their ends. Political socialization of the masses was carried out by the Sozialistische Einheitspartei Deutschlands (SED, the Socialist Unity Party) using all means available, for in accordance with Marxist-Leninism the state and Party must control all information to ideologically develop the population.[12] The urban landscape, like traditional means of mass communication, was crucial because of its ability to convey cultural and political content. It was an arena of contestation over cultural identity, in which group identities could be added, removed, or transformed. It was an effective instrument, because the most symbolic places were recognized by all Berliners, and often, all Germans. The construction, reconstruction, renaming, and reinterpreting of buildings, monuments, streets, and squares, as well as their use in public ceremonies, became media of state expression. Press reports on each of these activities would convey propagandistic messages throughout the territory.

Pathways of Memory

There is another layer to the story. Cultural memory does not reside in a contained past, a bank vault of themes and symbols awaiting withdrawal. The past permeates the present in living traditions, ideologies, and unarticulated worldviews. This is true even for broken or discredited traditions such as Nazi ideology, endured as a negative force, a no-go zone for public discussion. When East German political and cultural leaders deployed themes and symbols from cultural memory into urban space, they were guided by enduring structures of thought and practice. Both wittingly and unwittingly, they interpreted the urban landscape through a series of explanatory frameworks inherited from the past—and none of these dominated. Their attempt to create a new city and a novel society did not neatly mimic the Soviet model, and it did not emerge in a creative flash. Rather, they selectively applied existing discourses based on their personal knowledge, beliefs and preferences, assessments of contemporary political and material conditions, and a view to long-term development. Novelty would arrive in how they combined these elements, and how some frameworks were adapted over time.

In 1945 political and cultural leaders had varying degrees of awareness of and investment in different discourses. Members of key groups often displayed great similarity at a given time but operated in a climate of intense political pressure and capriciousness that conditioned how they applied what they believed and prompted changes in approach; ideologies and theories were adopted and abandoned due to political shifts. The main groups involved include the Soviet Military Administration (SMAD, which after 1949 was known as the Soviet Control Commission, SCC), German Communist politicians, and German cultural elites. Within these groups, key individuals could play prominent roles, including Walter Ulbricht (general secretary of the Kommunistische Partei Deutschlands [KPD], later SED), Wilhelm Pieck (the first president of the GDR), and Otto Grotewohl (the first prime minister of the GDR) as well as key architects and planners, and, on occasion, representatives of the Soviet military. After World War II the urban landscape was of immediate interest to these leaders for both its cultural and political symbolism and the importance of decimated neighborhoods to everyday life. Memorials and monumental architecture expressed identities and inculcated cultural memory and political values in the populace. Plans and efforts to restore or build anew the vernacular city were seen as proof of political efficacy and an expression of the values of the regime. Thus actions on the urban landscape were attributed the potential to increase support for politicians and political parties in the short term and to assist with political indoctrination in the long run.

The occupying powers and new German administrators were well aware of the sharp contrast between the recently established political system and the existing political culture, which had been formed by experiences of twelve years of a Nazi state, preceded by fifteen years of highly unstable democracy, preceded by decades of a constitutional monarchy that heavily favored the latter.[13] Although totalitarian theory suggests that the East German state was held together by Soviet military might and that the beliefs of East Germans were irrelevant, recent research has begun to explore variations in compliance, acquiescence, dissent, and opposition—variations that cannot be explained entirely by force as a means of supporting statehood.[14]

Moreover, the society-state dichotomy that underlies this approach breaks down in the GDR, where approximately one in five citizens participated in one of the "manifold organizations and institutions of the state" on a voluntary basis. Mary Fulbrook would not go so far as to accept the GDR's self-designation of "democratic centralism" but suggests that it functioned as a "participatory dictatorship." This did not require the inner conviction of the bulk of the population but outward compliance with the state order was essential. In this regard, the transformation of the urban landscape expunged cultural memory opposed to state ideals and imposed a vision expressive of the new order—part of a comprehensive overhaul establishing a public realm in which citizens would occupy their proper places. A tiny cadre of dedicated Communists facilitated these changes and a number of left-wing antifascists welcomed them as expressive of their worldview. Many citizens viewed these as an imposition yet came to accept them as "rules of the game," adherence to which led to personal rewards. Public discussion and the popular press informed them of the official view on matters so that they could position themselves accordingly.

Conformity, regardless of conviction, turns the gears of state. Yet a number of East Germans were indoctrinated into a socialist worldview, as later recollections testify. In light of recent wartime destruction and suffering, restoring the city and building a better future had great appeal.[15]

Hence the problem of political socialization was especially acute at this time. East German leaders were heavily invested in the idea that efforts to reshape the city were an essential component of their cultural political strategy. Nonetheless, East German planning and city building did not emerge as a unified vision derived from Marxist-Leninist ideology, contrary to Western perceptions of a monolithic socialist state. Rather, planning and building traditions emerged in fits and starts based on competing notions of how to build upon prewar German and international cultural developments and a changing political and economic landscape. These shaped how particular themes and symbols and ways of shaping cities were regarded.

Existing discourses are crucial to cultural politics as they provide bases for interpreting the world and acting upon it. These pathways of memory are neither static nor protean, but transform within limits, rise and fall in social prominence, and at times support and conflict with each other. As such, they provide crucial background for the material covered throughout this book. They are discussed individually, but they cannot always be neatly separated as they are currents in a stream of cultural development. The following provides an overview of the evolution of the pathways that were most significant for cultural developments in postwar Berlin. These include preservationism, *Heimatschutz* ("homeland-protection," a movement centered on local and regional conservation), science, German exceptionalism, humanism, Marxism, Marxist-Leninism, modernism, and socialist realism.

Preservationism. The preservationist movement in Germany has been traced back to the late eighteenth century, although it came to national prominence in the early nineteenth century in response to the widespread destruction of monuments by Napoleon's troops.[16] In the late nineteenth century the harmful impacts of rapid industrialization significantly strengthened the movement, which posited that historic structures and townscapes were vital to the spiritual and cultural health of the nation.[17] Thus preservation became entwined with the conservation of entire cultural landscapes, including agricultural and "natural" areas, and the built environment in the *Heimatschutz* movement.[18]

Heimatschutz. This traditionalist movement took a virulently nationalistic turn in the Nazi era, with prominent *Heimatschutz* leader Paul Schulze-Naumberg "becoming the most vocal spokesman for the Nazis in architecture," which would not be forgotten after the war.[19] However, many traditionalists and preservationists were not involved in Nazi politics and advocated for preservation and restoration of traditional urban form. The nationalist element of postwar preservationist discourse would be relatively muted and often avoided using the term *Heimatschutz*, but basic beliefs about culture and historic urban form remained intact.[20] Preservationists would remain highly active after World War II, but they possessed very limited political power.

Science. The scientific tradition (or traditions) and ideas about its relation to technological progress are important to this study for several reasons.[21] Science both contributed to the birth of ideologies and theories and became a component of these same ideologies and theories. Nineteenth-century scientific developments and industrialization endowed considerable importance to scientific and technological endeavors, inspired numerous scientisms, and gave birth to two "scientifically based socio-religious cults": Saint Simonianism and socialism.[22] Marx and Engels espoused a formal ideology of "scientific socialism," and Lenin endowed Soviet socialist thought with Western ideas about scientific management and technological development as crucial for economic development. During the early 1950s, Communist theories of culture emphasized the impact of artistic expression on the public, attributing science and technology a supporting role. However, by the mid-1950s a surge in enthusiasm for the power of technology inspired Soviet and German Communists to retheorize the significance of science for economic and social progress. This fervor was a crucial factor driving a paradigm shift in East German architecture and urban design, and it infused cultural expression with a veneration of technological power: a cultural high modernity similar to that in America but not the same.[23] Soviet leader Nikita Khrushchev perhaps encapsulated the spirit of the times when he menaced Western diplomats by suggesting he would keep his teeth sharp using "science and technology."[24]

German Exceptionalism. Theories of German exceptionalism (positing fundamental differences from the rest of the West) have appeared in various forms over the ages. Some have positively assessed Germany's alleged distinctiveness, such as the claims about the authenticity of German culture versus the superficiality of French civilization following the Napoleonic Wars. Yet negative assessments have appeared more frequently and can be traced back as far as the Roman writer Tacitus. They surface in the writings of Marx and Engels regarding the role of the Prussian Junkers, and Engels went so far as to warn that "the Reich is brought into deadly danger by its Prussian foundation."[25] In the late nineteenth and early twentieth centuries, writers from several nations, especially Marxists, developed variations on these ideas, asserting shortcomings of the Prussian elite and a disjuncture between German economic and political conditions. After the Second World War, authors in the East and West argued that Nazism arose due to failures in Germany's cultural and/or political development process. Some traced this deviation as far back as Luther, but they held that the key divergence from "proper" modernization came with the failure of the bourgeois revolution in 1848.[26] This view was codified in Communist historiography in Der Irrweg einer Nation, written by Alexander Abusch while exiled in Mexico and reprinted in Germany in 1947.[27] The book portrayed direct lineage from Prussian King Friedrich II to Prussian statesman Bismarck to Hitler, casting a pall over Prussian-German heritage, and seems to have been a widely held view among German Communists.[28]

Humanism. The centuries-old humanist tradition has been multifaceted and ever changing. Continuity is nonetheless found in humanists' enduring focus on human experience and human rights, the liberation of creative power through education and individual freedom, and the great value of ideas and critical reason. Nineteenth-century humanists witnessed the transformative effects of industrialization with some ambivalence, but many believed the new wealth would ultimately improve the welfare of all humans, which along with nationalist and democratic challenges to the old order would contribute to social progress.[29] Humanism is primarily of interest in this book for its relation to Marxist thought. Marx was deeply engaged with the impact of these same technological changes. He entered a humanist phase in the early 1940s, positing that the achievement of true democracy with unrestricted voting would enable emancipation, and the elimination of all conditions that degrade humankind to attain a form of socialism based on a liberated human community. He championed individual difference and freedom to develop one's full talents, in opposition to the Communism of Proudhon and Fourier with its decided leveling effects confounding individuality.[30]

Humanism was abandoned by Marx in favor of "scientific socialism," but it was reembraced by Soviet theorists in Marxist-Leninism. Here, humanism was defined in accordance with stages of world historical progress, resulting in separate definitions of classical humanism, bourgeois humanism, and finally socialist humanism. "Bourgeois humanism" was viewed as a flawed but progressive cultural movement that transitioned into "socialist humanism," which created the conditions necessary for true human liberation.[31] In the Potsdam Agreement of 1945, the Allies agreed that the German people must be denazified, demilitarized, and democratized, and, fittingly, Communist cultural policy in the early postwar years aimed at restoring the German, humanist cultural tradition to assist in these efforts. It had immediate political currency as shared German culture and would serve as a long-term, educational strategy to bring the population closer to socialism.[32]

In public speeches and press reports Communists in postwar Berlin employed a framework for interpreting the national situation that pitted humanism and democracy against past Nazism. As the Soviets were the first to occupy the city, they established a German-run local government for the whole city, including an administrative branch, the Berlin Magistrat, and an executive branch, the Senat (hereafter, the City Council). This government would assume normal municipal functions and guide the reconstruction effort, although the occupying powers would retain significant influence. The Soviets attempted to portray this government as democratic but placed Communists in key positions to control important decision-making. To appear independent of the Soviets and comply with denazification, Berlin's government stressed its self-definition as an "antifascist, democratic front" of all political parties opposed to the fascist past—in other words, all permitted parties.[33] This strategic separation of Nazism from the German people was devised by Communists who had spent the Nazi era as exiles in Moscow. Following the Battle of Berlin, on May 4, 1945, Wilhelm Pieck addressed the city through Radio Moscow, declaring: "Berlin is free from the Nazi mob that will and must be completely annihilated. However, our German people will live on. It is valid now to undertake a fundamental cleaning. Their shameful past must be concluded. This has to do with a new birth of our people, with a new beginning in their entire thinking and acting. New people, a new Germany must come about, in order to live in peace and friendship with other peoples and to guarantee the German People against a repetition of the aggression from the German side."[34]

Electoral politics soon became reality, and the most popular parties to emerge included the Christian Democratic Union (CDU), the Communist Party of Germany (KPD), and their historic working-class rival, the Social Democratic Party of Germany (SPD). In April 1946 the KPD forced a merger with the SPD in the Soviet sector and, to win over its members, emphasized the "nineteenth-century humanist roots of the socialist movement" rather than twentieth-century Leninism.[35] In sum, German Communists viewed the humanist tradition as an essential component in the reeducation of the German people and deployed it as propaganda for short-term political gain.

Marxism. Marx emerged from his humanist phase when he determined that given the communal nature of humankind, liberation was possible only through class struggle and the end of class exploitation. He embraced socialism but abandoned its advocates' arguments based on justice for an allegedly scientific understanding of the laws of history. In this determinist view the individual's only free choice was whether to follow the forces of history or to work against them in vain—a view incompatible with humanism. The result (nineteenth-century German Marxism, or "scientific socialism") is the version of Marxism evident in the Communist Manifesto and most familiar throughout the world. Many German Communists returning to Berlin after the war adhered to this ideology and were unfamiliar with cultural theory developed under Lenin and Stalin. Grounded in materialism, German Marxist teleology foresaw a trajectory of world historical progress based on economic development and class conflict generating revolutions that would culminate in a Communist world order. Progress toward Communism would unfold through the eradication of inequality—that is, through the elimination of private property, state control of credit and means of production, and so on.[36] When Marx proclaimed, "From each according to their ability, to each according to their need," individual freedom was curtailed in favor of an egalitarian society. Yet Marx would continue to struggle to reconcile egalitarianism with individual freedom throughout his life.[37]

Scientific socialism offered a clear perspective on housing reform and raised questions about the very structure of the living arrangements it was intended to serve. Liberal and conservative housing reform efforts, from the 1840s on, held up the single-family home as the ideal form of housing for the health and morality of the family, which was the building block of the nation.[38] This traditional Germanic form of housing was set in opposition to multifamily housing, a product of Latin culture that could "lead us all to the barracks of socialism."[39] The Communist Manifesto asserted that bourgeois and conservative reform efforts were a means of securing their continued existence (preventing revolution). It lumped "improvers of the condition of the working class" with "organizers of charity, members of societies for the prevention of cruelty to animals, temperance fanatics, hole-and corner reformers of every imaginable kind."[40] Engels later elaborated on Marx's ideas in a series of articles. The bourgeois fringe active in housing reform could only "superficially palliate [the housing shortage's] most terrifying consequences," while the government, as "the organized collective power of the possessing classes," was only interested in preserving the existing order.[41]

The Communist Manifesto even called into question the idea of the family, and later socialist theorists posited alternatives. August Bebel condemned marriage and the family as oppressive institutions, suggesting that in the Communist future equal rights and equal opportunities for women would allow sexual freedom and public provision of child care and household labor.[42] This would require communal facilities for many household tasks, thus a rethinking of housing design. Yet even socialist politicians ignored these ideas, which were apparently too radical to enjoy broad support.

When the housing crisis became acute in the 1870s, Social Democrats denounced the situation as evidence of market failure and resolved that the only solution was the creation of a socialist state in which all land is held as communal property. They condemned the market for leaving the working classes crammed into unsanitary apartments, a form of "killing by neglect." Failure to pay rent regularly led to evictions of entire families, who were left homeless. They contrasted this situation with the large sums of money spent on monumental architecture to aggrandize the wealthy (bourgeois apartments) and the state (a new city hall).[43] Despite increased supply, housing conditions remained dismal for the working class. By the 1890s Social Democratic politicians had entered the Reichstag, and in consideration for the well-being of their constituency, many began to rethink Engels's position. They brought forth a series of failed housing bills that were vehemently opposed by propertied interests.[44]

Marxist-Leninism. Marxist-Leninism resulted from Lenin's efforts to build upon Marxism to address essential contemporary issues, including "imperialism and proletarian revolutions... the disintegration of colonialism and the victory of national liberation movements... the transition of humanity from capitalism to socialism and the construction of Communist society."[45] Lenin's theories of economy and state were crucial in shaping Soviet government and, with some alteration under Stalin, would become the bases for governmental structure and decision-making in the GDR. His view of the nation-state as the contemporary vehicle of social progress conflicted with the Allied Control Commission's (ACC) insistence that German nationalism was taboo immediately after World War II. For the first few years German Communist cultural policies downplayed nationalism and centered on the German humanist tradition, appearing to follow the commission's directive.[46]

Yet, as East-West tension grew during the late 1940s, this policy changed. In city elections of October 1946, the SED obtained just 20 percent of the vote, compared with 49 percent for the SPD, which now controlled the City Council. The Soviets initiated a campaign of terror directed at Berliners supporting the Western allies, with thousands disappearing from the streets of East and West Berlin.[47] Tension escalated further in June 1947 with the announcement of the Marshall Plan and the Soviet veto of anti-Communist Ernst Reuter's (of the SPD) election as mayor of Berlin. The SED gradually began employing subtle methods of developing class consciousness and increasingly overt presentations of elements of socialist ideology. By 1948 the SED had abandoned the "antifascist front," in favor of depicting itself as the leader of the "battle for German unity" fighting against the efforts of the Western allies to split the nation.

East-West tensions exploded in June 1948 with the introduction of a new Western currency and the Soviet response, the infamous blockade. The Western Allies responded with the famous airlift to keep West Berlin from collapsing and coming under Soviet control. In September, Communist demonstrators disrupted meetings of the local government, which relocated to West Berlin, and a duplicate government was established by Communists in East Berlin. In May 1949 the Soviets called off the blockade, but division was imminent. On May 24 the West German state was founded, and on October 7 the East German state was founded. Wilhelm Pieck became the first president of the GDR and Otto Grotewohl the first prime minister, but Walter Ulbricht, as first secretary of the SED, held ultimate political authority. The mayor of Berlin, Friedrich Ebert, initially exerted a great deal of influence over city building issues, but his role was soon constricted by the state leadership. Propagandistic activity was stepped up considerably and focused on "winning" the young generation.[48] The new state described its system as "democratic centralism" and emphasized its "democratic" nature in the press, downplaying its "socialist" identity. Stalin restrained the German leadership in this regard as he attempted to negotiate with the West for a united, neutral, unarmed Germany.

Nonetheless, Marxist-Leninism was now the foundation for all cultural policy, while "humanism" and "democracy" endured as key tropes in public discussion.[49] The Politburo determined that "extraordinary weaknesses" were present in cultural work, because large numbers of intellectuals and a portion of the SED still didn't recognize its importance.[50] Soviet Marxist-Leninism had returned to humanist Marxism to establish a role for culture in shaping society, rather than viewing it a superstructure blossoming from a material base as typical of German Communists.[51] The details of this view had been developed in socialist-realist theory in the 1930s, which had tremendous consequences for city building in Berlin. The SED was finally permitted to openly declare the "construction of socialism" in July 1952 after the Western allies rejected the Stalin Note, which proposed a united, neutral Germany. Stalin died in March 1953, and Khrushchev gradually consolidated power and initiated a de-Stalinization process that included a more open cultural atmosphere. Economic reforms sought to improve the standard of living, and in 1958 the SED's Fifth Party Congress (held under the motto "Socialism wins!") set the goal of overcoming West Germany in per capita consumption of major consumer goods.

Modernism. The modernist cultural movement developed as a reaction against tradition and its alleged culmination in the tragedy of World War I. During the Weimar era, leading German architects played a key role in the development of modernism. In particular, the Bauhaus school with Walter Gropius, Ludwig Mies van der Rohe, and others attained worldwide renown.[52] In 1933 the Congrés Internationaux d'Architecture Moderne (CIAM, International Congresses of Modern Architecture) formulated the primary theory of modernist architecture and planning, the Athens Charter.[53] This charter is a classic product of the technocratic approach to planning marked by a "faith in progress through science and rationality tied to the constructive use of power in the form of the plan" and a belief in a "unitary public interest that experts of goodwill can identify and maximize."[54] Technical specialists engaging in rational planning could improve the quality of human life by mediating between communal and individual interests to harmonize the form of the urban environment with the lifeways of its residents. Although some landmarks would be deemed worthy of preservation, there were no qualms about clearing most structures to make way for the new. Architecture was to be designed in a contemporary style and not imitate the past or attempt to conform to a historic district. These last tenets set modernists in direct conflict with traditionalists.

During the housing crisis that followed the First World War, modernism became the dominant style for new social housing projects. With Berlin firmly under SPD rule, government policy spurred the construction of more than 140,000 new dwelling units by trade unions, cooperatives, benevolent associations, and local government. The largest of these in Berlin, the Benevolent Housing, Building, and Savings Association (Gemeinnützige Heimstätten-, Spar- und Bau-Aktiengesllschaft, GEHAG), was founded by unions and building cooperatives upon the initiative of Martin Wagner, Berlin Housing director. GEHAG was the first union organization established with funding from the Reich and constructed ten thousand units from 1924 to 1933. Wagner and other adherents of the "Neues Bauen," (international modernism) dictated the form the expanding city, the "New Berlin." As a remedy for old Berlin's "rental barracks," the city housing program would "restore the lost link between people, their house and nature, and give residents the opportunity to be at least partially self-sufficient."[55] Lack of fresh air and light were not the only ways that rental barracks had separated residents from nature: "Children who grew up here did not know a sandbox, sports facilities or indoor swimming-pools. A survey of Berlin grade-school children revealed that in 1905, of 100 children, 70 could not picture a sunrise, 49 were not familiar with a frog, and 87 did not know what a birch tree looks like."[56]

The solution lay not in incremental changes to the city but in defying traditional urban form with new, large-scale, residential projects on the urban periphery. Wagner called for standardized building components and rationalized construction process to increase affordability. Based on scientific analysis of spatial needs, modular, ornament-free row houses and walk-up apartments overlooked ample green space and were detached from the street where possible. Each housing unit was provided considerable light, air, and views of greenery. GEHAG's Hufeisensielung, still today a symbol of modernist apartment building, established a prototype for other projects to follow. Leading architects such as Bruno Taut, Walter Gropius, Hans Scharoun, and others designed modernist housing settlements that received international acclaim.[57]

The National Socialist German Worker's Party (Nationalsozialistische Deutsche Arbeiterpartei, NSDAP) initially rejected modernism for its ties to avant-garde revolutionary thought and because Berlin's large housing estates were products of left-wing state intervention in the failed Weimar Republic. NSDAP housing policy adopted the cottage as the ideal home for the family unit, now part of antiurban, "blood and soil" ideology. In Berlin suburban Kameradschaftsiedlung exemplified this approach with one-third detached houses and two-thirds rental units in small buildings.[58] Yet, given the practical advantages of modernism, the 1940 "Führer's Decree for the Preparation of German Housing Construction after the War" initiated a paradigm shift toward a mass-produced "social housing" program that "came very close to propounding the same theories advanced by the vilified Bauhaus."[59] Multistory townhomes on curving streets open to light, air, and greenery would provide a healthy environment for breeding a stronger German race. Traditionalist ideas regarding the incorporation of regional building styles were blended into the theory but were lacking in practice.[60]

By the end of World War II, several decades of practice meant that this dominant strain of modernism, now known as the "international style" was an established tradition. Modernist architects returned to Berlin and assumed positions of power but would soon find themselves embroiled in political conflict as Soviet ideas about culture were adopted by the state. Another variant of modernism began appearing in different countries after World War II, midcentury modernism. This style departed from 1920s international modernism's rigid rules of composition in favor of organic forms, often futuristic in appearance. In this regard, the style would seem a natural fit for the high modernist enthusiasm for advancement in science and technology during the late 1950s, when it became a matter of contention in East Germany.

The Soviets also had embraced modernism early in the twentieth century, although it was short-lived. Following the October Revolution, Soviet modernism drew global attention, and throughout the 1920s both modernists and traditionalists competed for projects. By the mid-1920s a competition for political support was under way. In the early 1930s traditionalists attained full control over theory and practice with Stalin's support. Over the next years the traditionalist approach was developed into an official doctrine of socialist realism. Modernism was written off as misguided approach.[61]

Socialist Realism. The Marxist-Leninist theory of art, socialist realism, was developed in the Soviet Union during the 1930s, providing a comprehensive perspective on culture, politics, and urban form. Adjustments were made in the development of plans to rebuild Moscow, and the result provided the exemplar of this approach, which adapted traditionalist architecture and city planning to suit contemporary needs.[62] Modernist German architects who emigrated to the Soviet Union for work during the 1930s were confronted with this new orthodoxy and had to adapt if they wanted to find employment. Many were disillusioned and returned, while a few, such as Kurt Liebknecht, remained and assimilated socialist realism.[63] After the war most German architects remained dedicated modernists, which was also true of those who had been exiled in the Soviet Union. Thus, in December 1949, the minister of building, Lothar Bolz, a longtime Moscow exile, convinced the prime minister of the GDR, Otto Grotewohl, to send leading architects on a "Trip to Moscow" to learn from the "most progressive" examples of city building. The trip took place in April and May of 1950 and initiated the forced indoctrination of design professionals into the Soviet approach.[64]

Socialist realism presented a rather complex view of historic architecture and tradition to which it was deeply connected. The style held architecture to be both a functional object and an art form. As an art form, it was a reflection of society, which conversely could shape society, inspiring the individual with its beauty and educating through its function and imagery. The purpose of this edification was political, and in Marxist-Leninism the nation-state was the necessary vehicle for social progress for the capitalist and socialist eras. Thus progressive art appeals to national consciousness and is built on national traditions. As all nations contained both progressive and reactionary traditions, architectural styles could be progressive (i.e., classicism) or regressive (i.e., late-nineteenth-century eclecticism). Progressive architecture could be sponsored by the Prussian monarchy, as its design and production by premiere German architects and laborers made it national cultural heritage. Historic buildings considered progressive were to be preserved as "living witnesses to these traditions from which everyone learns" and would be given a content appropriate to the new society. Architecture was viewed dialectically as a unity of form and content. Content, in turn, was held to be a unity of theme, which is similar to function or pragmatic purpose, and idea, an expression of societal values or ideals. Existing buildings were to maintain a continuity of theme, adapted to express the societal ideas of the German Democratic Republic.[65]

Socialist realism, like traditionalism, emphasized the continuity of inherited building practices and the preservation of monumental architecture, but only given adaptive reuse of a "progressive" nature (e.g., restoring a former Arsenal as a museum presenting German history from a Marxist-Leninist perspective). In contrast, vernacular buildings in working-class neighborhoods were seen as products and symbols of capitalist oppression, a view compatible with modernist creative destruction and in conflict with *Heimatschutz*. Although vernacular structures were largely devalued as architecture, the historically evolved structure of the city was considered crucial to its further development. In this regard, socialist realism paralleled Western developments opposing modernism, as elaborated by Saverio Muratori and his followers, who outlined issues in urban morphology that theorists and designers continue to struggle with in the contemporary world.[66] The dominance of this approach was short-lived as Khrushchev ordered a shift to industrialized construction in 1954 that was soon carried into the GDR. Socialist realism remained official theory, but debate raged over the nature of the new construction aimed at creating a "socialist architecture." Tradition and "German architecture" faded from discussion.

In 1945 most German Communists knew little about these Soviet theoretical developments in art and architecture. With no ideological basis to approach the built environment, they retained a traditional Marxist view, which held urban design to be superstructure and buildings to be direct expressions of their patrons, who indelibly imbued them with their own sociopolitical ideals. Thus they viewed many of Berlin's most significant memorials and monumental buildings as symbols of monarchy, militarism, and the Prussian state. This, along with their negative view of German exceptionalism, in which Prussia's "aberrant" modernization led the German nation to reactionary politics and militarism, resulted in disdain for these structures. In word and deed, they were dedicated iconoclasts. Though never theorized, the resulting Communist iconoclasm was evident in numerous statements and actions regarding urban heritage in the late 1940s.[67]

These various discourses were crucial in shaping political and cultural elites' interpretation of Berlin's urban landscape and hence decisions made regarding its future. Yet their influence was not always straightforward. To apply them always involved an act of interpretation. At times, individuals appeared to negotiate between conflicting ideas inherent to a well-detailed ideology or theory. Sometimes individuals deviated from an established or official approach for personal reasons. Complexities in place-based meaning—essentially issues that emerge when relating cultural memory attributed to a site with contemporary concerns—also precluded straightforward application of seemingly clear ideological direction in certain cases. Changes in political and economic context further shifted the status of discourses—some fell out of favor, others became official doctrine. They provided essential frameworks for interpreting the world, but none was absolute.

The Beginning: Ruins and Rubble

Romantic contemplation of ruins has a long history in Europe. Eighteenth-century German noblemen were especially enthusiastic in decorating their estates with artificial ruins.[68] Hitler believed monumental architecture should be built to endure thousands of years as beautiful ruins to reawaken the nation after a period of weakness.[69] Following the unprecedented devastation of World War II, neither of these ideas resonated for Europeans, who saw their homes and cities destroyed. During the war 6,427 acres of Berlin were destroyed by bombing raids. Approximately 40 percent of the city's buildings were destroyed, along with 10 percent of its underground infrastructure. However, the damage was distributed unevenly. Many outlying districts were untouched, whereas destruction was almost complete at the center of Berlin, where the bombing and ground fighting had been the most intense. The Soviet sector was hit especially hard. In the Mitte district 67 percent of all apartment buildings were destroyed, in Friedrichshain more than 50 percent, and in Prenzlauer Berg over 20 percent.[70]

The prognosis for Berlin's recovery was grim, as many writers noted at the time.[71] One correspondent reported:

> Wrecked and burnt-up streetcars and vehicles of every sort lay all around on the streets. Pieces of the streetcar's power lines were hanging down, a quarter of the subway system was flooded, and all of the city's gas and electric lamps (approximately 100,000) were destroyed. Of the 225 bridges in the city, 140 were destroyed, blocking the city's waterways. . . .
>
> Hordes of refugees passed through our city from north to south, from east to west, and vice versa; lugging their few rescued possessions along, tired and numb to their surroundings, an image of misery, not knowing if they will find their home or their relatives again.[72]

Most Berliners now faced lives of toil and hardship to survive. Personal memories of the city and experience living with ruins and rubble while rebuilding provided a relatively fixed set of core meanings that allowed little room for Romantic introspection. At war's end many resided in crammed air-raid shelters, shacks, and "caves" in the rubble. Those able to occupy apartments lived with broken and damaged furniture, ubiquitous debris and dirt, and often, exposure to weather and the view of outsiders. The stench of dead bodies rotting under rubble provided a counterpoint to prewar memories of family life in their apartments and bustling neighborhood streets. Faced with desolation, some Berliners employed gallows humor proclaiming: "Berlin ist die Stadt der Warenhäuser; hier war'n Haus und da war'n Haus" (Berlin is the city of warehouses, here was a building and there was a building).[73] In light of these experiences, it is apparent that the reconstruction would have great meaning to Berliners, and Communist leaders were well aware of its political potential.

Though radical planning proposals suggested that Berlin should be abandoned and a new city constructed for residents, these overlooked the tremendous value of streets, intact buildings, and their foundations below rubble as well as the immense amount of undamaged infrastructure below ground. The only economical option was to rebuild the city in place, which was fraught with practical difficulties. There was insufficient labor and means of transport to remove all rubble from the city limits. To spread it evenly across the surface of the city center would raise it 5 meters (about 16 feet), burying functional streets and infrastructure. The remaining possibility was to salvage as much usable material as possible from the rubble (especially desirable given the extreme scarcity of many building supplies), to reconstruct damaged buildings and infrastructure, and, where necessary, to remove excess rubble to parks and outlying disposal sites.[74]

On May 25, 1945, the Magistrat approved a resolution allotting RM 6 million (reichsmarks) credit to the Department of Building and Housing for demolition and rubble removal. Berlin residents would provide the necessary labor to demolish ruins and remove rubble for daily wages and as volunteers.[75] By years' end, men employed in demolition had taken down more than a thousand ruins.[76] Women made up a sizable portion of the tens of thousands workers who removed rubble, inspiring the iconic image of the Trümmerfrauen (rubble women).[77] From 1945 through 1946 an estimated 4.7 million to 6.5 million voluntary workdays were completed, and 23,000 to 33,000 paid workers were engaged in rubble clearance.[78] At this early stage, much of the work was performed by hand due to a lack of machinery and an emphasis on the recovery of building materials. By the end of 1945 millions of bricks and stones had been scraped of mortar by hand and neatly stacked for future construction.[79] After removing impurities and valuable buildings materials, much rubble was machined into cement powder and aggregate for concrete, bricks, and much needed roof tiles.[80] One article boasted that a machine on Potsdamer Platz could crush 20 cubic meters of rubble per day to be sieved and made into roof tiles on site.[81]

Despite recycling efforts, immense amounts of debris remained that had to be disposed of throughout the city in diverse ways.[82] Ruins adjacent to passable waterways allowed for easy transport by barge to outlying lakes that became dump sites.[83] A range of creative uses were developed for disposing of rubble near its site, particularly in more dense central districts. In Tiergarten a courtyard interior was filled 1.5 meters high (almost 5 feet) with rubble, covered with soil and planted.[84] In Mitte a canal was filled-in and greened.[85] In Pankow rubble was used to pave dirt roads.[86] In Tempelhof, 10,000 cubic meters of rubble were used to raise damaged park paths, thereby sparing greenery while improving walkways.[87] An admittedly incomplete map of rubble disposal sites has recently been compiled, indicating only a degree to which rubble was dispersed throughout the city.[88]

The immense physical task of clearing vernacular ruins and rubble was a focal point of public discussion, and at times East Berlin politicians and the press would highlight the cultural and political content of this endeavor. In 1946, Prime Minister Grotewohl (of the SED) led a nonpartisan meeting to initiate planning for the reconstruction of Berlin, setting an encouraging, apolitical tone that would dominate press reports on rubble removal and the recovery of building materials.[89] Progress reports with upbeat headlines provided a sense that the ruinous old Berlin was receding into the past but offered little to indicate the nature of the new life that was emerging.[90] Nonetheless, the Communist press subtly incorporated some political content. Corresponding with the Party line developed during the war, the German people were separated from Nazism, and culpability for the ruinous cityscape was attributed to Hitler and the Nazi Party. Mayor Arthur Werner declared, "Hitler made Berlin into a city of ruination; we will make Berlin into a city of work and progress."[91]

The following day, the Berliner Zeitung (hereafter BZ) reported on the meeting, directly linking this policy with reconstruction enthusiasm and the German humanist tradition: "Above the speaker's podium in letters visible from far off, the slogan 'Antifascist unity—the pledge of rebirth of the German people!' . . . A festive assembly in the middle of the ruin. In a hall that is almost entirely restored. This is not a coincidental surface appearance—it works as a symbol. Involuntarily, Schiller's words penetrate the memory, 'And new life blooms out of the ruins.'"[92] Occasional reminders linking ruins, the war, and Nazi rule would have powerful effects as they tied into Berliners' everyday life experiences among ruins.[93] Blaming Nazi leaders rather than the people would avoid stirring up potential resentment that could detract from the cohesiveness of the "antifascist, democratic front."[94] This apparently was driven by political opportunism rather than conviction, as German Communist leaders openly attributed blame to the entire German people in Neues Deutschland, the organ of the Communist Party, the KPD.

While ruin reportage focused on practical steps to a better future, and secondarily on the national past, the present political situation generally remained implicit. In the spirit of the "antifascist, democratic front," comparisons of progress in rubble removal was largely among German cities, and differences between the sectors of Berlin were initially ignored.[95] An article providing a rare link between past, present, and future declared that the NSDAP-ruined city was being restored in the new German "democracy" through cooperation among antifascist parties, "especially the SED"—a victory for the working people. The superiority of Soviet administration is implied, but there was still no direct comparison with the western sectors. After Communist defeat in the Berlin elections of December 1946, East-West tension increased. Soviet sector press no longer shied away from direct comparisons between East and West, albeit they were still neutrally worded in comparison with later, Cold War commentary: "In the Soviet Sector, rubble has disappeared from streets, reusable stones piled up, doors and window openings sealed, and in the British Sector one stumbles, as before, through rubble-filled streets. It looks like it was under attack yesterday."[96]

In 1948, Berthold Brecht wrote the "Building Song of the Free German Youth," which proclaimed, "away with the old, on to the new State" before closing with its refrain, "away with the rubble." When the GDR was founded in October 1949, *Berliner Zeitung*, in the language of *Heimatschutz*, noted that "Hitler-barbarians have left the once proud capital of our fatherland in a rubble heap" and praised "the men and women of our home city [*Heimatstadt*]" for their hard work to restore the city after the war.[97] The sounds of hammers, saws, and shovels were lauded as the "appropriate music for the birth of the true democratic republic that corresponds to the will of the entire nation." In fact, the East German state encapsulated the moment in the opening line of the national anthem: "Risen from ruins, and facing the future, let us serve you for the good, Germany, united fatherland."[98] As May 8, 1950, approached, German surrender became "Liberation Day," in which the Soviet Army as "friend and helper" provided for Berliners' basic needs, enabling them to "literally dig their home city [*Heimatstadt*] out of the debris with their hands."[99] In Ulbricht's speech at the opening of the Deutsche Bauakademie (DBA, the German Building Academy) in December 1951, he declared that the "old Germany" of fascism, militarism, and war had left Berlin in ruins, but these were being removed through the construction of "Berlin, capital of Germany," a "new Germany" of peace, democracy, and progress—an oft repeated narrative in the GDR's early years.[100]

How Berliners would rise up to rebuild their city of ruins would be heavily shaped by decisions made by cultural and political leaders from Germany and the occupying powers in light of cultural, political, and economic factors. Berliners too would have their influence, often small, but on occasion great. The remaining chapters of this book examine these dynamics as they played out in Berlin between the end of the battle of Berlin in May 1945 and the construction of the Berlin Wall in November 1961.

Organization

The first two chapters of the book have a thematic focus, whereas the latter four are place-based, centering on significant streets or squares. Chapter 1, "Landscapes of Commemoration," examines the purge of symbolic elements of Berlin's urban landscape incompatible with the views of the new regime; also explored is the rapid development of spaces of commemoration honoring the Soviet military and German Communism. Chapter 2, "City Plans," examines the development of plans for Berlin and the shift from a modernist to a socialist-realist paradigm and finally to an eclectic mix. Politicians and planners seized upon the extreme semantic flexibility of modernist city plans, associating them with a wide range of political and cultural claims but these possibilities were notably constricted with socialist realism, because it was closely associated with the Soviet Union and socialism.

The remainder of the book focuses on representative architecture and urban design in key locations across the city. Chapter 3, "Unter den Linden," illustrates the role of worldview and ideology in the redevelopment and use of an ensemble of representative architecture, monuments, and public spaces on the iconic street. Though guided by larger frameworks of understanding, at times place-based meanings greatly complicated decision-making. Chapter 4, "From Royal Palace to Marx-Engels Square," uncovers a conflict between socialist-realism and German Communist worldview regarding cultural memory and the urban landscape. Ultimately, Ulbricht's personal ideas resulted in the neglect and demolition of the Berlin Palace in favor of a new square for state-orchestrated parades. Chapter 5, "Wilhelmstrasse," examines the former center of German government, where the same factors examined on Unter den Linden assume significance in strikingly different combinations. Chapter 6, "Stalinallee," depicts the attempt of architects and politicians to solve the century-old housing question in the face of dire economic conditions, while creating a new ceremonial axis extending east from the city center.

Throughout the period of study, Communist leaders continued to believe in the vital importance of the cityscape for the social and political lives of its citizenry. Through political and economic changes and the adoption of new theories of city building, this did not waver. As the largest city in Germany, the historic capital city, and the cultural center of twentieth-century German cultural life, Berlin and its reconstruction would inevitably speak volumes of its rulers. How the cultural and political elite engaged the urban landscape emerged from changing dynamics involving formal ideologies and informal discourses, personal views, political maneuvering, cultural memory, accrued place-based meaning, and spatial idiosyncrasies.

Some general trends in how different groups approached meaning in the urban landscape can be observed. From May 1945 through the summer of 1947, German Communists emphasized the rejection of the fascist past and the creation of a "new Berlin." While all political parties agreed on purging symbols of Nazism and Prussian militarism, debate emerged over the extent of iconoclasm and the selection of replacement street names. The Soviet Military Administration (SMAD) and the Communist Party of Germany (KPD) planned memorials to inscribe their own narratives of their past in Berlin. An immense effort to remove rubble and restore heavily damaged vernacular buildings was initiated. The Eastern press generally depicted ruins as an inheritance from Hitler and exonerated Berliners. Planners rejected everything about this past, envisioning a new Berlin transformed according to modernist principles.

Politicians of all parties welcomed the proposals, viewing nineteenth-century workers' housing as unfit for contemporary living. Though planning was largely seen as a technical matter, it was attributed a range of political contents that changed as time passed. Monumental architecture in the historic core was largely left to decay, as German Communists occupying key government positions viewed these buildings as symbols of the hated Prussian monarchy and military. Planners, preservationists, and non-Communist politicians recognized their artistic and historic value, appealing in vain for emergency repairs. The SMAD was only interested in the spatial capacity of buildings for exhibitions, educational plays, and office space. This allowed for repairs to some larger structures, including a few Nazi buildings after iconographic purges.

The summer of 1947 through October 7, 1949, was marked by increasing political turmoil. A series of tension-raising events reached a boiling point in 1947, when Berlin's City Council nominated staunch anti-Communist Ernst Reuter in June, and a Soviet veto in the Allied Control Council (ACC) in August blocked his appointment.[101] The SED began to portray itself as the party of national unity and increasingly appealed to nationalism. This new political climate resulted in major changes in the interpretation of the urban landscape, some legal jostling, and a few building projects. The SMAD was able to realize its primary war memorial in Treptow. German Communists' efforts to build a memorial and promote extensive iconoclasm remained embroiled in political wrangling.

Efforts to restore residential fabric continued, and the Eastern press began comparing progress in the Soviet and Western sectors of Berlin to assert the greater efficiency of the Eastern administration. In 1949 the SED stepped up planning efforts and, to win popular support, depicted these as populist and humanistic rather than socialistic, occasionally employing the language of *Heimatschutz*. German Communists continued to display disdain for monumental buildings that they saw as expressions of Prussian-German monarchism or militarism. The SMAD remained largely disinterested in Berlin's architectural heritage, although they ordered the destruction of Hitler's Chancellery, which had already been cannibalized. When the Social Democratic Party attained control of the municipal government, the SMAD commandeered several buildings for their own use and even renovated one historic structure as a House of Soviet Culture for the edification of Berliners.

The founding of the East German state on October 7, 1949, marks the most severe rupture in political and cultural practice during the period of study. The state-founding meant Marxist-Leninism would guide all educational and cultural activity, and leading architects and planners were soon forced to accept socialist-realist theory. The German national past was now divided into progressive and reactionary traditions, and national identity was central to all cultural work. The GDR provided a political-economic base for an extensive building program, one of the major focuses of state activity. The new government swept away street names associated with the Prussian monarchy and military and constructed a Socialists' Memorial designed by President Pieck. This memorial and the war memorial in Treptow became sites for major ceremonies on key state holidays—one commemorating deceased Communists, the other celebrating "liberation" by the Soviet Union. Efforts to construct new memorials in the city center to honor fallen socialist leaders were held up by disputes over their design.

Given the bifurcation of the world order, Germany, and Berlin itself, the East German press no longer attributed the ruinous cityscape to Hitler, but to English and American bombs. The GDR's remedy, the National Building Program, concentrated on Stalinallee, bringing the cult of Stalin into Berlin's cityscape. This state-orchestrated effort—depicted as populist, democratic, and humanistic—was intended to win support in both East and West Berlin as well as throughout Germany by demonstrating the capability of the GDR to provide exceptional housing for the average citizen. The architecture was heralded for its roots in national and local tradition, which were apparent at several scales, although Soviet socialist-realist and some modernist influences were evident in others.

In accordance with the dictates of socialist realism, plans were developed for a representative city center, including a large central square for state parades and rallies. Ulbricht, obsessed with maximizing the size of these demonstrations of obeisance to state, assured that it drove the planning process to the detriment of other aspects of socialist-realist theory. This included unnecessary disregard for historic preservation as the Berlin Palace was demolished to create an extensive square. Despite extensive protest from cultural and political leaders, Ulbricht's iconoclastic impulse held sway. In contrast, historic buildings on Unter den Linden were restored, with a little prodding from Soviet advisers. On Wilhelmstrasse many historic structures were left to decay and were eventually demolished, suggesting the endurance of iconoclastic tendencies and perhaps a modernist devaluation of the past on sites other than the showcase, Unter den Linden.

The final period considered in this book began on November 30, 1954, at the All-Union Conference of Builders, Architects, and Workers in Moscow. In the face of continued housing shortages, Khrushchev proclaimed that building costs must be decreased and productivity increased by removing ornament and rationalizing construction. Ulbricht brought the message to East Germany in April 1955 at the First Building Conference of the GDR. Though socialist realism remained official theory, this allowed the return of many principles of modernist design. Housing was seen as a consumer good and the press focused on the quantity of units produced, rather than qualitative or place-based attributes of design that had dominated in the early 1950s. Although Stalinallee would showcase industrialized building, most housing would be constructed in large estates on the urban fringe to maximize economic benefits. Despite this drive toward the new, a secondary component of the National Building Program financed residents and cooperatives to rehabilitate damaged vernacular structures and complete minor infill projects with traditional methods. This program had been continued since the 1953 Uprising due to its effectiveness and popularity. Regardless of building technique, the press emphasized the quantity of apartments produced, although it gave top-billing to articles on industrialized construction as a demonstration of technological power.

In response to the West Berlin Internationale Bauaustellung (IBA), the German Democratic Republic hosted its own competition for the socialist redesign of the GDR capital. The winning designs tended to follow socialist realism in providing an enclosed central square adjoined by a government high-rise, and some included classical architectural elements. However, many designs included modernist architecture similar to that of the 1920s, while others included more expressive forms comparable to Western midcentury modernism. The latter were frowned upon by political leaders and the jury, who recognized that these designs could not be built with standardized components. Historic preservation continued on Unter den Linden, but significant architecture was demolished on Wilhelmstrasse and adjoining the new central square. Vernacular structures fared poorly as well with the demolition of the Fischerkietz, including the nationally renowned Sperlingsgasse, to create open space along the Spree River.

This periodization of the cultural politics of city building demonstrates that diverse features of the urban landscape were impacted by changes in political conditions and the status of key discourses. Conversely, some inconsistency was evident within each period for several reasons, most notably the power of key individuals to exert their personal views and complications stemming from place-based meaning. The remaining chapters of the book examine the bases for continuity and change, consistency and inconsistency, and conflict and cooperation in the reconstruction of East Berlin.

1

Landscapes of Commemoration

On today's Fifth Anniversary of the German People's liberation from the dictatorship of Hitler-fascism through the famous armies of the Soviet Union, the Government of the German Democratic Republic sends you, and through you the Government of the USSR, the Soviet Army and the entire Soviet People, feelings of eternal thankfulness from the democratic and peace-loving Germany.

—Otto Grotewohl, Prime Minister of the GDR,
Telegram to Joseph Stalin, May 7, 1950

IT IS NOTEWORTHY that the symbolic dimension of the urban landscape became a focal point of activity immediately after World War II, given the dire need for housing and the impending cold winters. The collapse of the German state and denunciation of Nazi ideology created an opening for radical change, and the new power holders viewed this as a pressing need. The impetus for specific changes came from different groups for varied purposes. All allies and German political leaders agreed to a denazification process that would include the citywide removal of monuments and iconography testifying to a tainted past. This effacement of Nazi memorials and iconography was just the start, as Communist historiography traced the roots of Nazism into the depths of the Prussian/German past. This, and the need to find replacement street names that would express contemporary ideals, elicited more debate.

The construction of memorials by Communists at this time may have raised more eyebrows considering the "scientific socialist" prioritization of material needs over cultural superstructure. The Soviet Military Administration (SMAD), in accordance with the tradition of memorializing foreign veteran's cemeteries, constructed three war memorials in Berlin. The most elaborate of these not only honored the Soviet fallen but imposed a history of the war from the Soviet perspective. While the Soviets had a free hand in the memorial's design, they apparently mediated the narrative to consider its reception by the German population. At the same time, newly empowered German Communists set out to restore the burial grounds of those fallen in the Revolutions of 1848 and 1918. These sites of oppositional memory had been effaced by the Nazis, and the opportunity was at hand to resanctify the sites and establish a narrative of working-class struggle fitting for the postwar era. The effort was soon impacted by political gestures toward the Social Democratic Party (SPD) and political wrangling within the city government. Thus, in different ways, all three efforts to reshape cultural memory inscribed in the urban landscape were influenced by immediate political concerns.

The Purge

Along with the reconstruction of vernacular buildings, purely symbolic elements of Berlin's urban landscape were given immediate attention after the war. Toponyms and memorials bore testimony to a tainted past that had no place in the "new Berlin." The former could be replaced for a minimal investment, and the latter could be destroyed with little or no loss of utilitarian value. Yet the line between the reactionary past and acceptable heritage was not always easily identified. "Nazism" was rejected wholesale but discourse on "Prussia" was multifaceted and changing.

The Western Allies viewed Prussia as the center of German militarism, thus it was dissolved as a political entity in 1947.[1] Many Germans shared this view, including such conservatives as Konrad Adenauer. German Communists were especially critical of Prussia's role in German history, displaying continuity from Friedrich Engels's observation that "the Reich is brought into deadly danger by its Prussian foundation."[2] This view was codified as history in *Der Irrweg einer Nation*, written by Communist-exile Alexander Abusch in Mexico and reprinted in Germany in 1947.[3] This narrative of German exceptionalism portrayed direct lineage from Prussian king Friedrich II to Prussian statesman Bismarck to Hitler. In East Germany this view was abandoned in 1952 with the shift to "national history writing," which established that not everything to do with the military is militaristic; this led to the rehabilitation of some Prussian military leaders.[4] The shift aligned German Communist historiography with Marxist-Leninist ideology by granting approbation to people and events deemed progressive for their era, rather than the nondialectical, wholesale rejection of a culture's past. The following discusses changes in

Berlin toponyms, the effacement of memorials, and the construction of new memorials.

Toponyms

Place-names play a unique role in urban landscape symbolism in that they are seen as a necessity, they are immediately present in the everyday lives of residents, and they tend to be taken for granted as part of the natural order. Hence they are ideal vehicles for political socialization, and when history is rewritten, place-names can be quickly changed for a modest expenditure. In the early weeks after the collapse of the Nazi Party's regime, street signs associated with Nazism were removed with broad support from German political parties and the occupying forces. As revealed in Maoz Azaryahu's work, there was less consensus about the removal of toponyms associated with the Kaiserreich and about the new names that would replace them.[5]

At the first meeting of the Berlin Magistrat on May 24, 1945, Mayor Arthur Werner (unaffiliated) considered returning the names of streets honoring Nazis to their previous names but indicated a preference for avoiding political content—a view shared by representatives of nonsocialist parties. "Nazi" street signs were soon removed and replaced with cardboard signs, later with wooden ones. In June the Magistrat placed the mayor's first deputy, Karl Maron (KPD), in charge of street renaming. Maron also served as chief of police, a position historically given jurisdiction over streets in Berlin. He granted district administrations authority to propose new street names, except for "especially representative streets and squares, which the Magistrat must reserve for the names of significant personalities."[6]

"Bourgeois" political parties tended to favor a limited purge with politically neutral replacement street names, as in the middle-class Zehlendorf district where all the new names were taken from the fields of mineralogy, geography, and botany. In contrast, Communists favored an extensive renaming effort replacing "reactionary" names with politically charged "progressive" names under the slogan "New time—New names!" The *Berliner Zeitung* (hereafter *BZ*) called for a more vigorous effort to expunge names expressive of militarism and Prussian imperialism and replace them by names appropriate to the "democratic, antifascist" ideals of the "new German state." The article suggested that one in ten Berlin streets should be renamed, as they represent Prussian militarism, German imperialism, and Nazism. At a Magistrat meeting the following day, Maron presented criteria for renaming streets, prioritizing the removal of fascist names, then militaristic and imperialistic names. No criteria were provided for determining new names, indicating that this was not a priority. Given the scope of the project and Magistrat control over key names, there was no need to micromanage the districts.[7]

The Magistrat renamed only a limited number of streets during this time. Two streets were named for early socialist leaders August Bebel and Franz Mehring to highlight the common heritage of the Social Democratic Party and the Communist Party, and a square was named for Soviet Commandant Besarin after his death in a motorcycle accident. The coordinating role of the Magistrat proved essential on a practical level as renamings undertaken by the districts were not always recorded on official maps and confused the public and higher levels of government. Maron had expected the districts to submit street names by March 1946, but the lists were not finalized until September. The list slated 1,795 streets of a city total of 9,000 for renaming. Political neutrality carried the day, with "576 geographical names, 346 names of artists and scientists, 242 political names, 44 pre-Nazi era names, and 485 'other' names." The inner-city districts were more prone to commemorating victims of fascism, especially Wedding and Reinickedorf, which had Communist mayors. Yet, in general, eradicating names associated with Nazism and militarism and replacing them with largely "apolitical" names reveals a lack of consensus regarding the identity of the "new Berlin." Maron did not express concern about the new names, true to his goal of purging reactionary names, yet he decided to wait until after upcoming municipal elections for their enactment.[8]

After the SPD's electoral victory in the autumn of 1946, a new commission was established to review the list of proposed street names. The list was reduced by 90 percent (151 streets) and primarily removed Nazi names, ostensibly as the cost of RM 2.5 million was too high. Some "militaristic" and "dynastic" street names were also removed. Thirty-four names given during the Weimar era were restored, and thirty-five new names commemorated founders of German social democracy and communism, along with socialist victims of fascism. After the division of the city administration in 1948, little street renaming activity occurred. Possibly this resulted from a desire to appear "democratic" rather than "socialist" in the quest to maintain national unity, which was not officially abandoned until mid-1952.

Yet Walter Ulbricht quietly worked to reinforce an enduring socialist, East German state, and in the spring of 1951, 159 streets were renamed in East Berlin in preparation for the World Festival of Youth. Names removed included those directly associated with the Prussian monarchy, dynasticism (e.g., Kronprinzstrasse), Prussian generals, German war heroes, and names referring to means of warfare (e.g., Artilleriestrasse), as well as symbols of victory against France in 1870 (e.g., Sedanstrasse).[9]

The 1952 shift to national history writing transformed Prussian generals of the War of Liberation from symbols of "Prussian militarism" into "patriots." The names of Scharnhorst, Gneisenau, Lützow, Körner, and York soon returned to the streets of Berlin. This dialectical view of history saw victory over Napoleonic rule as enabling independent national development, the nation-state being seen as the necessary vehicle for progress from monarchal rule to bourgeois rule and ultimately toward socialism. That Russia and Prussia had been allies certainly enhanced the appeal of this war as venerable history.[10]

Monuments and Memorials

Many memorials in Berlin, like street signs, bore testimony to a tainted past. Unlike street signs, memorials ranged greatly in size—from those small enough to be removed by a single person in a few minutes to those substantial enough to require considerable time, labor, and machinery to remove. Although the reconstruction of infrastructure, housing, and public facilities strained the supply of labor, equipment, and materials, purely commemorative structures attracted considerable debate and resources.

In October 1945 an SPD initiative in the Magistrat called for the removal of all images of representatives of the "Prussian dynasty," the "militaristic caste," and "National Socialists" from public buildings. KPD officials supported the move, and Hans Scharoun was tasked with compiling a list of memorials to be eliminated. No follow-up report appeared, likely as Scharoun and his office were heavily engaged with pressing housing and planning issues. In February 1946, Hans Jendretsky (KPD) returned to the issue, calling for the removal of all Prussian monuments, singling out the equestrian statue of Friedrich the Great on Unter den Linden. At the next meeting the Magistrat approved a proposal by Scharoun for classifying memorials and guiding decisions regarding their fate:

1. National Socialist memorials, which would all be removed.
2. Memorials from the Wilhelminian and pre-Wilhelminian eras, which for the most part would be removed.
3. Memorials that artistically reflect a specific epoch and possess cultural value, which therefore should be preserved in place or in a museum.[11]

Before action was taken, the Allied Control Council (ACC) intervened with Directive No. 30, "Liquidation of German Military and Nazi Memorials and Museums," slating for removal any monument that "tends to preserve and keep alive the German military tradition, to revive militarism or to commemorate the Nazi party, or which is of such a nature as to glorify incidents of war." Exceptions for utilitarian and architectural value would be granted if "objectionable parts" were removed or "memorial character" could be eradicated. Military authorities in each zone designated German officials to inventory memorials and enabled them to request exemptions for "exceptional artistic value." In contrast to the initiatives of the two socialist parties, only "militarism" and "incidents of war" subsequent to August 1, 1914, would be considered, thereby exonerating the entire pre–World War I Prussian monarchy and Prussian military.[12]

SPD and especially KPD members of the Magistrat driven by disdain for Prussia as the font of German militarism and Nazism went well beyond the required categories to target for removal memorials to Prussian generals, kings, and statesmen, both before and after 1914. A committee including members of the Department of Housing and Construction and the Department of Education developed a register of monuments, which City Councilman Otto Winzer (SPD) presented to the Magistrat. Memorials were now classified according to their destiny: (1) those to be destroyed; (2) those to be removed and preserved in museums; and (3) those that would remain in place. Winzer explained that this approach would free Berlin from "all Nazi and militaristic memorials, while simultaneously preserving artistically valuable memorials, so as not to press ahead with blind iconoclasm."[13] All Nazi memorials and Wilhelminian and pre-Wilhelminian memorials deemed militaristic were to be destroyed. Category 3, a small group of "historic memorials," would be allowed to remain in place "without great reflection," presumably honoring apolitical figures noted for cultural or scientific achievement. Category 2 provoked the most reflection to determine "if and to what extent these memorials can be displayed to the public, or only serve as study objects for scientists and artists." The basis for such decisions would be worked out in the future.[14]

More than forty memorials spread throughout the city were marked for destruction. Considerable debate centered on memorial at the Great Star intersection in Tiergarten. An ensemble of marble statues of Prussian monarchical and military figures spaced evenly along the periphery of this traffic circle formed the start of Victory Avenue. At the center of Great Star, the looming 220-foot Victory Column commemorated Prussian victories over Denmark in 1864, Austria in 1866, and France in 1871 (figure 1.1). Originally located on Königsplatz (in front of the Reichstag), these monuments were relocated here during the Nazi era to extend their *via triumphalis* from Unter den Linden in the city center. Nazi parades along this route asserted a link between Prussia, the German Empire, and Hitler, which undoubtedly drew the committee's attention. During the war many of the statues were severely damaged, and some were totally destroyed. A few statues were to be spared due to "artistic value." Initially, a figure of Bismarck was to be left in place for this reason and because of its inconspicuous position between trees, evident discomfort with the chancellor mitigated by an inconspicuous location. However, Communists protested, viewing Bismarck as a key link in the German path to fascism, and the statue was sent to a museum.[15]

Although the Victory Column is an iconic symbol of Berlin, the committee decided that "it is not artistically valuable enough to remain standing in such a conspicuous position."[16] Scharoun argued against the proposal, warning of an enormous financial burden (estimated at RM 2.3 million) and demand for three hundred laborers for one year. City Councilman Ottomar Geschke (SED) offered to appeal to Berlin workers and unions to voluntarily destroy the memorials, and Arthur Pieck (SED) suggested that the rubble from memorials in certain locations (such as the Siegessäule) could be left in place for some time. Geschke, Maron, and Paul Schwenk (all SED) proposed additional cost-saving measures, evidencing their strong aversion to Prussian militarism. The resolution stipulated that the work be carried out by August 15, 1946, and was passed with minor changes. *Tägliche Rundschau* (hereafter *TR*) ignored the issue, apparently in anticipation of a hostile public reaction. The Victory Column and Victory Avenue were left intact for a time, likely as Scharoun was assigned with a task he opposed. Five months later, the SPD won a majority in the City Council and although the Magistrat was still under Communist

FIGURE 1.1. Victory Column. This monument to Prussian military victories over Denmark, Austria, and France laid the groundwork for Bismarck's top-down unification of Germany. In this 1946 photo the French flag waves atop the monument. BA, Digital Picture Database, Image 212-138, Sammlung Ugo Proietti, July 1946.

control, it was no longer solely a direct subordinate of the Allied Commandant but was subject to the SPD-controlled City Council.[17]

Discussion of the Victory Column ended, although Victory Avenue became a matter of contestation between the Magistrat and City Council in the summer of 1947. The Magistrat sought to remove all the statues, sending those still intact to the Märkisches Museum and others into storage for later use of their marble. The director of the Magistrat Division of Memorial Preservation, Hinnerk Scheper, reasoned that the memorials were not part of a "natural sense of tradition" but of Kaiser Wilhelm II's "dynastic exaggerated self-confidence," and therefore they are not "testimonies to historical events, but exclusively embody the Wilhelminian Era and its exaggerated need for imposing public display." Scheper's assertions about true "history" and "natural tradition" reveal an essentialist view common among German preservationists since the nineteenth century, when they established themselves as stewards of the cultural nation.[18]

In late July the City Council "requested" that the Magistrat account for its work on memorials and establish a formal structure for decision-making regarding the demolition and construction of monuments and historic architecture. In November the Magistrat approved a resolution presenting two lists of memorials to be removed and establishing clear jurisdiction over decisions about monuments, including a special commission under the chairmanship of the mayor, who would become involved in "cases of special cultural significance." The Magistrat also requested that the City Council accede to its resolution to dismantle Victory Avenue. The conflict took on a familiar form: Communist anti-Prussian iconoclasm exceeding Social-Democratic understanding of Prussian militarism. The Magistrat provided an account of its work through: (1) a list of existing memorials and an estimation of their condition provided by the Office of Historic Preservation, and (2) a list of the memorials, emblems, and so on proposed for demolition as well as a list of memorials that have been removed since the end of the war. Most of the memorials were in outlying districts and Western sectors, probably because the city center had been largely destroyed during the war and the most offensive symbols had already been effaced there. Although the Magistrat tactically avoided condemning the prominent and artistically valuable equestrian state of Friedrich the Great on Unter den Linden, it strove to remove less significant memorials to the monarchal and military past, including statues of Field Marshall Count Wrangel on Leipziger Platz and "historically trivial" members of the House of Orange on the Palace terrace. The memorial to Kaiser Friedrich III near the Brandenburg Gate was also targeted, though he had displayed progressive tendencies that were checked only by the brevity of his rule; German Communist iconoclasm left little room for nuance.[19]

Monuments dedicated to the Prussian monarchy and military leaders continued to disappear until 1952, when an official shift to "national history writing" upgraded many Prussian leaders from "representatives of reaction to patriots."[20] The change was made public in *Neues Deutschland* on May 31, 1952. A distinction emerged between "military" and "militarism," opening the possibility that an armed force could be progressive, depending on the social context and their political goals. The following day, *Neues Deutschland* (hereafter *ND*) proclaimed the generals of the Wars of Liberation—Gneisenau, Yorck, Blücher, and Scharnhorst—to be the greatest men of Prussia. In the present era their names would be invoked in the battle for national unity and independence against the "treasonous Adenauer gang." This created an "ideological opening for a future GDR army" with Prussian military leaders as heroes and models; as one SED leader indicated, a socialist army has nothing to do with militarism.[21] In Marxist-Leninism, militarism is a product of capitalism, whereas the "military politics" of socialist states is in accordance with the "interests of the People."[22] Recognition of this ideological point and the generals' rehabilitation were in fact both responses to political change: the directive to establish a military had already been sent from the USSR in April, and the Council of Minsters approved the formation of the People's Police in Barracks on July 1, 1952. This transformed police units into a paramilitary force, preceding the formation of the National People's Army by approximately four years.

An Emerging Memoryscape

Soviet occupation and German communist empowerment brought about a purge of militaristic and monarchal memory throughout Berlin, but it also allowed for creation of new sites celebrating formerly marginalized and alien memory: that of German socialists and Soviet conquerors.

Soviet Memorials

As German authorities purged Berlin of Nazi and militaristic memorials, the Soviet Military Administration (SMAD) began constructing veterans' cemeteries and memorials in all occupied territories to honor their fallen and arguably to emphasize the indebtedness of liberated lands to the Red Army or, in other accounts, to mark conquered ground. This wave of Soviet military commemoration initiated the "Cult of the Soviet War Dead," a "conscious attempt to draw meaning for the rituals of the present from the vast reservoir of past suffering," which permeated all aspects of Soviet life.[23] Almost immediately after the war, the first major Soviet memorial was built in Tiergarten near the Reichstag, marking the remains of twenty-five hundred Soviet soldiers who died in the Battle of Berlin. In a design competition for a larger Soviet memorial held in 1946, winning entries were chosen for construction in cemeteries in parks in Pankow and Treptow.[24] German architects were invited to participate, likely as a diplomatic gesture, and a Soviet duo, including one of Stalin's favorite sculptors, Jewgeni Wutschetitsch, designed the winning entry, which would be built in Treptow. The designers acknowledged advice from the SMAD in Berlin, and it is probable that Stalin himself was involved.[25]

The Pankow site included the remains of more than thirteen thousand Soviet soldiers, compared with approximately five thousand Soviet soldiers for the Treptow Park site, yet the latter would become the primary memorial. German Communists had already constructed a small memorial stone at the site in Treptow to thank their liberators, and Soviet sources later indicated that Wilhelm Pieck convinced the SMAD to locate the main memorial there because of its "revolutionary tradition."[26] Historically, Treptow Park was indeed a major site for socialist rallies, but more likely Pankow was excluded for its insufficient size relative to the plan and its position nearly adjoining the sector boundary.

The Treptow memorial placed what would become the primary "temple" in the "cult of the Soviet War dead" on German soil, in the former *Reichshauptstadt* (the imperial capital), raising political concerns that would require mediating the Soviet war narrative used at home with the version used in Germany. Soviet historiography and press reports were closely controlled for propagandistic purposes, hence as a substitute for historical research, a collection of Stalin's speeches was published as *The Great Patriotic War of the Soviet Union*. Soon a series of formulas for interpreting the war were developed by tailoring elements of Stalin's postwar speeches to the political situation.[27] Soviet society was depicted as a "monolithic unity" transcending all social differences, victory in war due in part to the army and the people, even more so the Party, and most of all Stalin, whose flawless leadership guided the effort.[28] This cult of personality deviates from Marxist-Leninism, in which society is transformed by structural forces not by great leaders. The Soviet press depicted the German people as evil incarnate during the war, but the image was softened for policy reasons near the end of the war. This also conflicted with Marxist-Leninism, which views imperialist states as the enemy rather than entire peoples, which always contain progressive and reactionary forces.[29] This willingness to tailor the message for political aims would carry into the German occupation.[30]

For a mix of ideological and diplomatic reasons, Soviet discourse in Germany emphasized humanism and liberation, rather than socialism and victory. The Soviet occupiers downplayed their socialist identity and, in accordance with Marxist-Leninist ideology, called for the reeducation of the German people on the basis of humanism as a prerequisite to learning about socialism. Confronting the German population with "socialism" and "communism" would only hinder their receptivity to the German Communist Party or the SMAD.[31] Thus initiatives in the Soviet sector of Berlin were consistently associated with the term "democratic." Stalin was recognized as the Soviet head of state but not hailed in a cult of personality until the founding of the GDR, when he was recognized as the "pioneer and standard-bearer of peace throughout the world." The German people were not burdened with guilt as in the USSR; they had been "liberated" thanks to Stalin, the Soviet army, and the Soviet people.[32]

For Soviets the memorial in Treptow heralded victory over a mortal enemy in the capital of the former Reich and would serve as a primary symbol in war commemoration. Yet for its accessibility to German audiences, the memorial was designed to simultaneously serve a subtle diplomatic mission by distinguishing the German people from Hitler and Nazism and by positioning them as potential allies. The memorial was designed according to socialist-realist principles, drawing from several traditions (figure 1.2). Classicism would be most apparent to the visitor in the design of triumphal arches, sarcophagi, and other elements, which include a plethora of textual and iconic references to the Soviet Union and the Red Army. However, the diagonal entry axes terminating at a focal point and the turns of the stairs could be related to the baroque. The section from the pylons to the far end of the memorial has strong parallels to gothic cathedrals (narthex, nave, aisle, chancel, and ambulatory). The sarcophagi, with a narrative emphasizing sacrifice, suffering, and burial, set along the side aisles bear similarity to the Stations of the Cross.

The entry is marked by a triumphal arch bearing Soviet iconography and an inscription acknowledging "heroes" who died liberating the "socialist homeland." The path leads from the arch to a modest sculpture, *Motherland*, representing a mother mourning for a son lost in battle. At *Motherland*, the route turns ninety degrees and proceeds up a gradual incline to pass be-

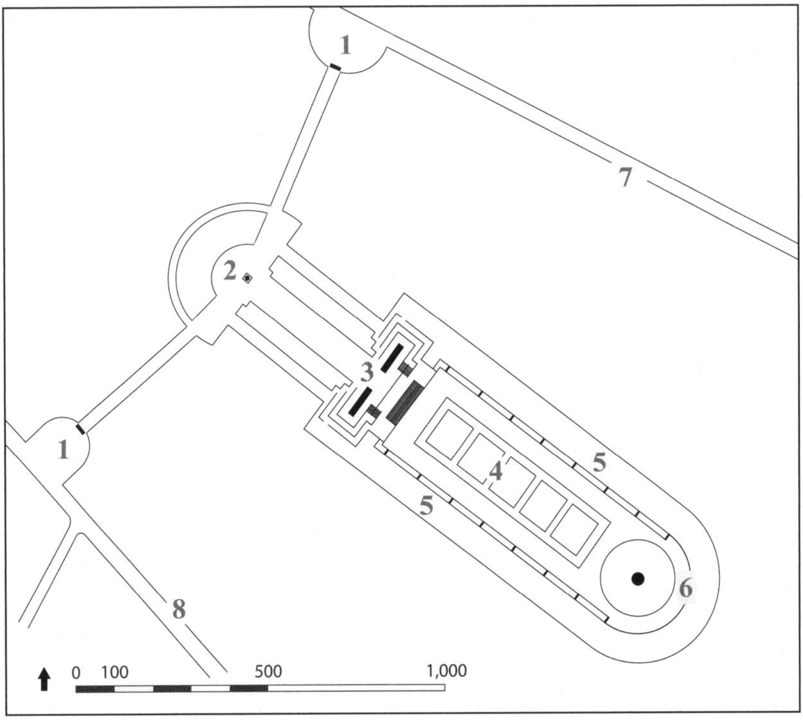

FIGURE 1.2. Map of Soviet Memorial in Treptow. The memorial's immense scale and formal sequencing of spaces are evident in this plan: (1) triumphal arches, (2) *Motherland* sculpture, (3) pylons (lowered flags), (4) central lawn, (5) rows of sarcophagi, (6) kurgan and statue of soldier, (7) Puschkinallee, and (8) Am Treptower Park. Map adapted from Google Earth image. Cartography by Paul Stangl.

tween two massive granite pylons representing lowered Soviet flags—stone used in the pylons, throughout the memorial, and in the Tiergarten memorial was removed from Hitler's Chancellery. A bronze statue of a Soviet soldier kneels in front of each pylon, facing the central axis. The view between the pylons extends across a lawn-covered plaza, terminating in a huge statue of a Soviet soldier. Stairs descend to a walk between the central lawn, which contains the soldiers' remains, and a flanking series of sarcophagi, depicting the course of the war in relief and text through quotes from Stalin: Hitler's Germany (*Hitlerdeutschland*) invades the peaceful Soviet Union, which mobilizes its army and people to heroic fighting to achieve liberation; in conclusion the fallen soldiers are honored (figure 1.3).

The narrative elaborates on a past that is symbolized in various ways

FIGURE 1.3. Soviet Memorial Sarcophagus. Blind students on field trip to the memorial in March 1961 aside the sarcophagus depicting partisan resistance. Each sarcophagus includes a relief and quote from Joseph Stalin, inscribed in gilded letters. The same narrative is presented on both rows of sarcophagi, the reliefs are duplicates, the text in one row is German, the other Russian. BA-Digital Picture Database, Image 183-81481-0004, *Allgemeiner Deutscher Nachrichtendienst-Zentralbild*, Eva Brüggmann, March 21, 1961.

throughout the complex, thus upon arrival at the sarcophagi, the visitor has already moved through a ritualistic space, encountering imagery of Soviet triumph, mourning, and veneration. Finally, the axis terminates at an immense statue of a Soviet soldier—one hand gripping a lowered sword resting atop a smashed swastika, the other bearing a small girl (figure 1.4).

FIGURE 1.4. Ceremony at Soviet Memorial. View from position in front of the pylons across central lawn to the kurgan with statue of Soviet soldier. At this ceremony, held during the month of Soviet-German friendship, visitors lay wreaths to honor the Soviet fallen. BA-Digital Picture Database, Image 183-12488-0010, *Allgemeiner Deutscher Nachrichtendienst—Zentralbild*, Shack, November 7, 1951.

The figure is set upon a tall pedestal containing a mausoleum, which rests upon a steep hill, representing a kurgan, an ancient Russian burial mound. The soldier completely dominates the space. A seemingly unequivocal symbol of Soviet victory, the statue leaves room for changing interpretations: the soldier can represent either the Soviet army or the Soviet people, the swastika either the Nazis alone, the German state, or even the entire German people; the child could refer to future generations of the Soviet Union alone, include East European nations as well, or even the Germans. If the German nation was included, was it simply liberated from Nazism or born anew into Communism? These symbols allow for interpretation from a variety of political perspectives and were used to clarify some issues while obscuring others.

Text and images on the sarcophagi provided a detailed narrative of the war, yet remained silent on the issues left ambivalent by the statue. Soviet society is depicted as a monolithic unity, concealing discord between ethnic groups; between state, army, and people; and between partisan and resident.[33] This corresponds with the formula used in the Soviet press with a few key differences. The Party and socialism were largely omitted in the memorial, in favor of the state, which appears several times. Stalin, continually hailed in the Soviet press as the great wartime leader of the Soviet peoples, is unmentioned, although he is cited for the texts on each sarcophagus. Stalin, continuing his role as (alleged) author of anything authoritative, paid respect to the army and the people, inverting the usual relationship.[34] These changes correspond with Soviet discourse in the German context. This narrative of Soviet progress from fascism through liberation to "freedom" and "equal rights" with no direct references to "socialism" or flattery of Stalin, presents a vision of a humanist future as intended by the designers: "In order to explain the enormous historic role of the Soviet army in the liberation of humanity from the danger of enslavement through fascism and to show our army as a new type of army, as a liberation army, as an army of peace, progress and humanism, we strove to depict the course of the Great Patriotic War in concrete episodes."[35] Nonetheless, a Soviet or German Communist could on the basis of their Marxist historical perspective complete the image of world historical progress through humanism to socialism. The memorial's ambiguity allowed for these multiple interpretations.

The German people are not mentioned as perpetrators or victims. Instead, "Hitler's Germany," "Hitler's rouges," and the "Hitler-fascist ideology" guided the German military in an unprovoked invasion of Soviet territory. The war drove the enemy from the Soviet Union, and thankful Eastern European peoples appear among the liberated.[36] Germans do not. Contemporary historiography continues to examine the extent to which the German people supported Hitler and Nazism, but indeterminacy was not a factor here.[37] Clear perspectives on the German people had already been expressed. Soviet wartime discourse condemned all Germans as perpetrators and the treatment of the German population made clear that they were not counted among those liberated from Nazism.[38] In contrast, the Soviet-controlled press in Germany separated the actions of Hitler and a small group of leading capitalists from the German people.[39] Stalin emphatically granted the Germans liberation in the Soviet-controlled press in Germany: "Hitlers come and go, however, the German people and the German state remains."[40]

An examination of commemorative activity illuminates the dual Soviet and German influences. German Communists invited to speak at

Soviet Victory Day celebrations (held at the Tiergarten memorial before 1949) spoke directly about the German people, including them among the liberated (like Stalin) and sometimes chastising them for having supported Hitler.

In contrast, Soviet Army speakers counted the "Soviet Union," "Europe" and/or "humanity" among the liberated, while Germany and the Germans were rarely mentioned. They were reticent to exculpate the German people when commemorating their fallen at the primary sacred space of the Soviet military, yet for diplomatic reasons they avoided incriminating them, presaging the narrative used in the Treptow memorial.[41]

The memorial's narrative is based on the Soviet narrative, especially regarding the role of the Soviet people and army but deviates in the absence of the German people, socialism, and the Party, and the reduction of Stalin's significance. The design of this Soviet site of memory in Berlin mediated sometimes conflicting historical perspectives with a well-structured ambiguity, enabling interpretations to vary for key audiences: non-Communists would see humanism where Communists saw a socialist future; Germans could view themselves as liberated, while Soviets could evade such recognition.

The Treptow memorial was dedicated on May 8, 1949, the fourth anniversary of the "victory over fascism." A procession of Soviet and German delegations laid wreaths on the Kurgan. General-major Kotikow, the Soviet commandant of Berlin, delivered the keynote speech, and Otto Grotewohl, cochair of the Socialist Unity Party of Germany (Sozialistische Einheitspartei Deutschlands, SED), spoke on the significance of the memorial for the German nation. The political situation had crystallized since the last Victory Day celebration, and on this same day the Basic Law was approved in Bonn, establishing a West German state. In the face of heightened political tension, the ceremony became overtly politicized with direct support for Soviet policy and animosity toward the West. The Soviet Union was now designated "socialist" and the vanguard of world historical progress. Kotikow stated: "It is a symbol of the battle of the world's people, led by the Soviet Union, for the sovereign rights of the nations, for socialism and democracy, and against slavery and the arbitrary use of power, and against the arsonists of a new war."[42]

The "arsonists of a new war" (meaning the Western powers) are grouped with the other opponents of the Soviet Union, those who inflicted slavery on European peoples—that is, according to the text on the sarcophagi, the old, fascist Germany. The East German press reiterated this role of the Soviet Union in a headline: "The Protectors of the Freedom of Nations [*Völker*]."[43] Kotikow went so far as to state "Germany itself suffered under fascism," yet he avoided mentioning the Germans as oppressors or liberated. Following established German Communist discourse, Grotewohl elaborated on the meaning of the memorial for the German people, who "owe thanks to the Soviet Union, the Soviet army, for being liberated from fascism."[44] He also tied German liberation to the historic progression toward socialism, although the SED itself had not yet publicly proclaimed this goal.

In 1950, Victory Day was renamed Liberation Day, a national holiday in the newly founded GDR; the German people were officially ranked among the liberated. Soviet and East German national anthems were performed, German leaders laid wreaths with ribbons proclaiming the German people's thanks to their Soviet liberators, and the East German People's Police (*Volkspolizei*) replaced Soviet troops on honor guard, which "Berlin Mayor Friedrich Ebert . . . referred to as a special sign of trust."[45] The East German state had assumed responsibility for the memorial, basing its origin myth in an act of liberation by the Soviet Union. An annual pilgrimage of the East German state leadership and state-organized groups of East Berlin's residents would demonstrate that "Berlin workers" and "German people" were grateful for their liberation, "the turning point in German history," and as an expression of friendship between the German and Soviet peoples. Laying wreaths on the kurgan beneath the feet of the Soviet soldier became an act of obeisance to the Soviet army. This tradition built an origin myth to serve in East German state building, which faced a significant legitimacy deficit among the population, because it was product of geopolitical competition between the superpowers lacking even the free elections of West Germany.[46] The GDR claimed to represent the entire German nation in opposition to imperialist forces from the West, as part of an effort led by the Soviet Union. The imposed Soviet ritual commemorating the Great Patriotic War was intended to affirm this bond of friendship.

In the early 1950s commemoration was heavily politicized as thousands of East Berliners participated in mass processions, laying wreaths at the base of the kurgan and carrying banners with political slogans. The press asserted this to be a demonstration of the "deep thankfulness" of Berliners to the "fallen heroes of the Soviet army," even a "vow to defend our democratic achievements."[47] This "support" was contrasted with statements about West Berlin police interrupting ceremonies and beating those attempting to visit the Soviet memorial in Tiergarten. The wartime love/hate schema was now being applied to the new German governments. Berlin residents were encouraged to love the GDR and its Soviet liberators and hate the "West Berlin Senate" and its supporters.

Khrushchev's denunciation of Stalin in March 1956 initiated a process of de-Stalinization, which included the release of purge victims from gulags, some cultural liberalization, and the demise of the "cult of Stalin." The official Soviet narrative of the Great Patriotic War was altered accordingly: Stalin's role was severely reduced and credit was spread among all of Soviet society. As part of the process, streets honoring Stalin were renamed and Stalin statues were removed from public space throughout the Soviet sphere of influence, although this did not occur in Berlin until 1961.[48] Despite these changes, the memorial in Treptow remained unaltered, arguably because it was already largely in line with the new Soviet narrative: Stalin was not directly honored, as his name only appeared in citations, and considerable attention was focused on the role of the Soviet people. As long as the GDR endured, the narrative remained essentially intact: the Soviet army liberated the German people from fascism and the nations were now bound in friendship.

German Revolutionaries' Cemeteries

The martyrdom of opposition leaders in the Revolutions of 1848 and 1918 and their subsequently established burial sites would be contested between rulers and opposition throughout the nineteenth and twentieth centuries. During National Socialist Party rule, these sites were effaced, thus after World War II, German Communists began efforts to restore them. This required some intricate maneuvering to work through the complex trajectory of events while considering consequences for political relations with the Social Democratic Party. The history of these sites extends to the Revolution of 1848, when oppressed workers and a powerful middle class rose up against monarchal rule.[49]

In Berlin the revolution began on March 18, when after a few days of minor street-fighting, demonstrators assembled before the Berlin Palace to petition the Prussian king. Shots were fired into the crowd, barricades went up throughout the city, and fighting ensued. The following morning the king withdrew his troops from the city and was forced to make concessions, although the monarchy gradually managed to nullify the reforms.[50] The revolutionaries brought some of the 270 fallen to the palace courtyard on stretchers decorated with flowers, twigs, and laurel leaves. After calls from the crowd, the king appeared on the balcony and removed his hat in a gesture of recognition. A public funeral ceremony took place a few days later: "The Revolution's victims were brought . . . along Unter den Linden, past the Palace, across Alexanderplatz and through Landesberg Gate [later Leninplatz] to Friedrichshain, where they were ceremoniously interred."[51] Now sanctified, this cemetery at the periphery of Berlin became the destination of an annual pilgrimage by Berlin workers to honor those who died in the revolution.[52]

According to Marxist-Leninist historiography, the Revolution of 1848 was Germany's "bourgeois-democratic revolution," a major step in the progression of the German nation toward socialism, though less important than the Revolution of 1918, which was taken as the socialist revolution.[53] The first socialist political parties in Germany emerged in the 1860s and were merged in 1875 to form the Socialist Labor Party, which later became Germany's Social Democratic Party (SPD). Socialist splinter groups formed in opposition to World War I, including the radical Spartacists. Led by Karl Liebknecht and Rosa Luxemburg, the Spartacists followed the Soviet model of socialism, which included internationalism, revolution, and "dictatorship of the proletariat." In contrast, the SPD remained nationalist, reformist, and in favor of parliamentary democracy. In 1918 a sailors' mutiny inspired nationwide uprisings, strikes, and the collapse of the war effort, which led to the resignation of the Kaiser and declaration of a new German republic. Conflict between the SPD and socialist splinter groups shaped the effort to design the new government, with battles in the political arena and on the streets. The Spartacists formed Germany's Communist Party (Kommunistische Partei Deutschlands, KPD) in January 1919 and instigated a large uprising in March. The ruling SPD allied itself with militarists, who then subdued the uprisings, resulting in more than twelve hundred deaths, the arrest of numerous Communist leaders, the murder of Liebknecht and Luxemburg, and a seemingly unbridgeable gap between the SPD and the KPD. In August 1919 the new constitution was ratified and the Weimar Republic was founded as a parliamentary democracy.[54]

Soon after the November Uprising some of the deceased were buried in the Cemetery of the March Revolution. After the events of March 1919, the KPD requested permission to bury Liebknecht and Luxemburg there too, but this was declined by the Magistrat. At this point, Wilhelm Pieck, one of the founders of the KPD, began his long-running involvement with the cemeteries. He would go on to represent the KPD in German parliament from 1928 until the National Socialists (Nazis) assumed power in 1933, when he went into exile in Moscow. Pieck, and other KPD leaders, personally brought the issue to the attention of Berlin's mayor, who claimed that there was no more space available in the cemetery. Instead, the Magistrat allocated a plot in Friedrichsfelde, then located beyond the city boundaries.[55] The Social Democratic Party, viewing itself as heir of the 1848 revolution in a lethal conflict with the Communist Party since the revolution of 1918, could only balk at the prospect of interring Communist martyrs alongside the "democratic" martyrs of 1848. Relegating the fallen revolutionaries to the urban edge reduced their significance in the city's symbolic landscape.

The decision to construct a memorial for Luxemburg, Liebknecht, and other martyrs was made at the end of 1923 by KPD leaders, including Pieck.[56] He laid the cornerstone for the Revolutionsdenkmal (the Memorial of the Revolution) on June 15, 1924, the fifth anniversary of Luxemburg's burial. According to Communist sources, the police interfered with the procession to the cemetery at various points and only small delegations were permitted entry. A few hundred participated in the ceremony, and Pieck buried a capsule including a statement vowing to avenge the fallen heroes of the revolution.[57]

The Mies van der Rohe–designed memorial, completed in April 1926, built of brick with black mortar, was modernist in form with asymmetrical, intersecting planes. Stretching 12 meters (40 feet) long, 4 meters (13 feet) wide, and 6 meters (20 feet) high, "the memorial awoke a gloomy, but... massive impression. Rising up defiantly from the memorial was a long flagpole, upon which a red flag waved. On the right side of the memorial a large Soviet Star was fastened."[58] The words "Ich war— ich bin— ich werde sein" (I was—I am—I will be), attributed to Rosa Luxemburg writing on revolution, appeared on the memorial.[59] The wall-like form of the memorial was to recall the "wall of Federalists" against which the Paris Commune was shot in 1871. The masonry blocks were to symbolize the power and massiveness of the working-class movement.[60] Thus the Communist tenets of "internationalism" and "revolution" were central to the design and manifest in several ways. The memorial monumentally asserted the role of German Communist martyrdom in world historical progress toward socialism, a distinctly Communist perspective inscribed on the edge of Berlin, where it was tolerated by the state.

The memorial was unveiled on June 13, 1926. Pieck delivered the keynote speech, depicting the Social Democratic Party as the accomplice of reactionary forces and calling for the organization of a revolution to overthrow the Weimar Republic; according to Marxist-Leninist teleology, this was necessary for historical progress toward true socialism.[61] Every January thereafter, until the Nazi seizure of power, the KPD organized a march to the memorial, where a ceremony was held. The event, which came to be known as the L-L-L Celebration in honor of Lenin, Liebknecht and Luxemburg, was deeply etched in the memory of Communist Party members. Pieck spoke at the ceremony every year he was able until the Nazi's seizure of power.[62]

The KPD and the SPD remained adversarial throughout the Weimar era. On occasion, the Communist Party collaborated with their arch-enemy, the Nazis, in actions to undermine the Social Democratic Party and the Republic. In the November 1932 elections the Nazis received the most votes, but the combined votes of the two socialist parties was larger, a fact that would not be forgotten after the war. Hitler was appointed chancellor in 1933, and soon members of both the KPD and SPD were arrested, tortured, and murdered. The National Socialist Party sought to wipe out communism and began to efface sites of Communist memory. Iconography and text, as the most explicit and easily removable expressions, were targeted first: the Soviet star and the words of Rosa Luxemburg were removed from the memorial. Visitors regularly came to the cemetery but were either driven off or were "arrested, interrogated and usually sent to prison or a concentration camp."[63] In 1935 the Nazis dismantled the memorial, exhumed the graves of socialists, and interred newly deceased civilians. The sarcophagus containing Liebknecht's remains was buried at an unmarked site where it survived the war, but Luxemburg's remains were never recovered.[64] Although not directly targeted, the Cemetery of the March Revolution was neglected and in a state of disarray by the end of the war. In Nazi state history the 1848 Revolution "appeared outwardly as the bourgeoisie revolution" but "in reality represents the beginning of the battle for internationalism, parliamentarism, and capitalism, therefore the world domination of Jewry."[65]

The tragic events of the Nazi era provided impetus for members of the Communist and the Social Democratic parties to pursue unity after the World War II. Walter Ulbricht (of the KPD) initiated a "clarification process" to develop a common platform as a basis for unification. The SPD soon began losing enthusiasm for the effort as their complaints about Soviet Military Administration (SMAD) favoritism toward the KPD went unattended. After the Communists' disastrous showing in Hungarian and Austrian elections in autumn 1945, the SMAD and the KPD began a coercive unification process, including "a ban on [SPD] assemblies, support for proponents of unity, and massive intimidation and arrest of opponents of unity."[66] The KPD and the Eastern Zone SPD were forcibly merged to form the Socialist Unity Party on April 22, 1946, while the SPD in the Western Zones remained independent after voting down the merger.[67] Animosity between the Western SPD and the SED continued throughout the life of the German Democratic Republic.

On May 28, 1945, just nine days after being established by the SMAD, the Berlin Magistrat resolved that "a grove of honor will be erected to the honor of all deceased pioneers and as an exhortation to all citizens of the new Berlin," initiating postwar planning regarding the revolutionaries cemeteries.[68] It is clear from Pieck's file notes that all correspondence on the project was directed to him and that he was in charge of the project.[69] This is logical, given the depth of Pieck's emotional attachment to the site and the issue as he was a personal friend of many Communists buried in Friedrichsfelde and could easily have been among them.[70] Pieck surveyed the site on December 6, 1945, and wrote to Karl Maron (deputy mayor of Berlin and member of the SED's Central Committee) calling for a Magistrat resolution to reconstruct the memorial.[71]

Pieck suggested combining the graves of the "old socialists" (the Social Democrats from before 1918 who had not been buried at the memorial) with those from the 1918 Revolution. He also suggested turning the Cemetery of the March Revolution into a memorial site. A few weeks later, the Magistrat passed a resolution with Pieck's suggestions. The basis for reconstructing the memorial was to make the living generation aware of the sacrifices made by the socialist movement to battle feudalism, imperialism, and fascism, and the continuation of this battle in the present day, against the remnants of fascism.[72] Social Democratic sympathy for Liebknecht and Luxemburg was evident at this time, making them suitable rallying points for unification. For instance, a 1946 issue of *Tagesspiegel* (published in western Berlin) ignored Communist ceremonies but recalled the orchestration of Liebknecht and Luxemburg's murder by "monarchistic officers" in a path of history leading to the concentration camps.[73] Socialists and Communists may have shared this view of the past, but agreeing on the present or future proved more difficult. The "antifascist, democratic front" as a common cause of opposition to feudalism and fascism was easier to define than a clear vision of the future, or even a present identity, beyond "democracy"—a term used to bestow legitimacy on innumerable forms of government.[74]

In January 1946, Pieck used the L-L-L Ceremony as a platform to prepare for the upcoming unification of the Social Democratic Party and the Communist Party, or more aptly, the absorption of the former into the latter. Pieck, speaking near a wooden replica of the original memorial, explained: "The goals of Reaction . . . were supported by the disastrous division of the KPD and SPD. That we both stand united here at the graves of the victims is a sign that we have learned. We do not want to repeat the mistakes of 1918 and want to vow that we will not rest until unity has been established."[75] This assertion of reconciliation would be symbolically demonstrated by combining the graves of heroes recognized by the Social Democrats (the "old socialists") with Communist martyrs, creating a unified place of commemoration. However, the Communist content of the original memorial in Friedrichsfelde, strongly hinted at the future identity of the unified workers' party, and the addition of the bodies of "old socialists" to this reconstructed memorial suggests they were part of a linear progression leading to communism—a co-optation of memory.[76]

The forced merger of the socialist parties to form the SED in April 1946 and the SPD's dramatic electoral victory in Berlin in October 1946 increased tensions between Communists and non-Communists. The announcement of the Marshall Plan and the Soviet veto of Ernst Reuter's (SPD) election as mayor of Berlin in the summer of 1947 aggravated the situation. The SED soon changed its self-depiction from a member of the "antifascist front" to the leader of the "battle for German unity," fighting against the efforts of the Western allies to split the nation. In November 1946, Pieck continued his efforts to move the project forward and proposed changes to the resolution from 1945 in a letter to Mayor Arthur Werner (unaffiliated).[77] Furthering his concept, Pieck called for a combination of graves from the 1848 Revolution, the "old socialists" (of the Wilhelminian era), those from the Revolution of 1919, and some "prominent Communist and Social Democratic leaders murdered by Hitler."[78]

Thus the memorial would display a complete historical representation of working-class martyrdom for social progress. Pieck presented a layout, including a "memorial sculpture" in the center of a large circle, and he did not specify any hierarchical treatment of the martyrs of different eras. Political overtones are evident in the shift in interest from reconstructing the Memorial of the Revolution to this new design; it was less overtly Communist, less tied to Communist tradition, and thus less alienating to former Communist Party members, whom the SED was especially interested in winning over after the poor electoral showing. Pieck expressed hope that a new resolution would not be necessary to implement this plan as it would be subject to the approval of the SPD-controlled City Council.[79] Two days later, the issue of combining the graves "on a worthy site" was brought to the Communist-controlled Magistrat, which decided that a new resolution was not necessary. Pieck developed a design program, including a large space for ceremonies, separate entrance and exit paths to accommodate "flowing demonstrations," and a "massive grandstand in front of the memorial between the paths."[80] While Pieck was attempting to appeal to the SPD in terms of symbolism, an overt gesture, the functional layout of the complex (spatial order) was intended for one of the key Communist tools of indoctrination, the "demonstration" or political rally, a more covert content.

On December 5 the new City Council elected Otto Ostrowski (of the Social Democratic Party) as mayor of Berlin, and the project disappeared from the files for a few months. During his speech at the L-L-L Ceremony in January 1947, Pieck brought the issue to the public. He established the antifascist credentials of the German working-class movement and designated the Communist Party as the "most progressive part" of the movement, thereby maintaining a common heritage for the KPD and the SPD, while granting the former primacy. He also described some basics of his plan: a site near the entrance of the cemetery and the inclusion of socialists from three eras in a common grave site.[81]

In March the Magistrat turned its attention to Friedrichshain, resolving to "lay a wreath" at the cemetery on March 18 and to renovate the cemetery for next year's hundredth-anniversary celebration. The existing form was to be closely followed: memorial slabs lying strewn about were to be returned to the raised central area and grouped as a central element to express unity, and the narrow path would be widened to accommodate large delegations.[82] *Neues Deutschland* reported on the ceremony, describing the neglected condition of the cemetery and questioning whether the fighters of the 1848 Revolution had been forgotten, before declaring that the Socialist Unity Party had not, as evidenced by their ceremony. The SED was depicted as the true representative of the German working class and German nation: the heirs of the Revolution of 1848. It was an attempt to co-opt the cemetery and its associated heritage. The article concluded by pointing to the physical neglect of the cemetery due to war and Nazism, asserting that its restoration is the duty of the Berlin Magistrat and all democratic organizations.[83] The western *Tagesspiegel* did not report on the event.

In June, Mayor Ostrowski called for a design competition for the memorial, although the site had not yet been determined. Pieck had been in contact with Ostrowski over the issue and presented him with some sketches for the design of a memorial.[84] The Magistrat and the SED reached an agreement for the design competition with a jury comprised of two members of the Magistrat, one person from each of the two socialist political parties, an architect, a landscape architect, a representative of the unions, and the mayor of the district Lichterfelde.

The politics of the memorial location proved quite interesting. A document in Pieck's files dated December 1, 1947, reported on the advantages of the Friedrichshain site, including less extensive grave transferal, greater architectural possibilities, and, foremost, "crowds of people could march onto this area without hindrance."[85] These latter two advantages were a result of the large undeveloped space in the park around the cemetery. The next day Pieck wrote to Karl Maron of his interest in the construction of "Project No. 2" in Friedrichshain and requested that he reach an agreement with the Social Democratic Party regarding the matter.[86] Pieck was willing to abandon his plan to return to the site of the Memorial of the Revolution for this site, because of its spatial advantages, the reduction of conflict surrounding disinterment, and the opportunity for SED members to exert influence on the design of one of the SPD's sacred sites, rather than giving the SPD jury members a chance to influence the shape of the Communists' sacred site in Friedrichsfelde.

The design competition was held for the site in Friedrichsfelde, which given Pieck's stance was likely the result of SPD influence. The jury met on February 15, 1948, but failed to reach an agreement on the basic nature of the memorial. With political tensions running high, disputes among jury members fell along predictable lines. Pieck called for a "grandiose memorial… that provides a frame for impressive commemorative ceremonies" and claimed that none of the entries satisfied this requirement.[87] Ernst Reuter countered, stating that the Magistrat's original goal was to create a "place of silent reflection, whose calm and simplicity should not be disturbed, in which one's feelings would be moved."[88] Pieck desired a spatial form enabling the site's place-based meaning to be linked with social activities of political indoctrination, whereas Reuter consciously sought a spatial form that excluded these social activities. Architect Heinrich Tessanow pointed out that the decision could only be based on criteria stated in the competition guidelines. A decision was ultimately reached, primarily on aesthetic grounds.

While the competition was under way, the Magistrat's Department of Building and Housing began renovating the cemetery in Friedrichshain in preparation for the upcoming hundredth anniversary of the 1848 Revolution.[89] A simple stone block less than 2 meters high (scarcely 6.5 feet) was placed in the center of the cemetery, set in a slightly sunken quadratic block bearing the inscription:

> To the deceased of 1848/1918
> The memorial you have erected yourselves
> This stone speaks just one serious exhortation
> That our people never forgo that for which you died
> —to be united and free
>
> —Peter A. Steinhoff

The SPD-controlled City Council exerted its authority to assume control of the ceremony as council chair Otto Suhr (of the Social Democrats) presided. As common among Western politicians of the time, he emphasized the importance of freedom, stating that Berlin must "fight for its most elementary rights." Suhr insinuated that basic rights are not respected in the Eastern sector, thus the SED is heir to the reactionary monarchy, not the revolutionaries.[90] Neither the Soviet commandant nor leading East German politicians were present. The SPD tapped the place-based meaning of the cemetery as a site of Social Democratic martyrdom for democracy and the right of self-determination, while excluding Communist memory.

East-West tensions began to rapidly increase in June 1948, culminating in the Soviet Blockade of Berlin and the Allied airlift. As these larger issues occupied all attention, the project in Friedrichshain was tabled. The

Berlin government split into East and West administration in September 1948; the West German state was founded in June 1949, and the East German state in October 1949. After the division of the Magistrat, with both memorial sites falling in the East, the SED-controlled Eastern Magistrat had a free hand to take up the project without interference. It would now impose the official historical narrative of working-class progress in the landscape without compromise. In February 1949 a Politburo proposal called for a tombstone for Liebknecht and Luxemburg, and the construction of a memorial for the "deceased of the workers' movement" across from the cemetery in Friedrichshain, mainly for advantages in holding mass demonstrations.[91]

However, Pieck decided to shift the memorial to Friedrichsfelde, further evidence that his previous interest in the Friedrichshain plan had emerged from political jostling with the SPD. Pieck wrote to the new mayor of the Eastern Magistrat, Friedrich Ebert (SED), requesting another resolution for the memorial, as the winning design from the competition would not accommodate "large memorial rallies." He urged the speedy implementation of the project. Pieck included a sketched plan for a memorial in Friedrichsfelde and reiterated many of the basic design features he had developed in 1946. The location would be the site of the original memorial, requiring the removal of approximately two hundred graves from the Nazi era, which would no longer be a problem. He stated that the representatives of various departments within the Magistrat and district Friedrichsfelde had agreed to his suggestions, "subject to its artistic execution."[92] Ebert consulted members of the Magistrat and decided that the memorial should be built on a more accessible site near the entrance of the cemetery, an idea that was apparently accepted.[93] In March 1949, Ebert wrote to Pieck of an imminent Magistrat resolution and the need to find a new group of artists, as the competition-winning team had "declined to alter their plans in accordance with [Pieck's] proposal."[94]

In early 1950, East German historical research institutions compiled lists of murdered antifascists for the SED's Central Committee.[95] Yet Pieck maintained authority over the project. In fact, one letter warned that no list of "deceased socialists" was to be used before obtaining Piecks approval.[96] His concerns about large-scale ceremonies emerged again in a letter to Ebert in September 1950, when he demanded that a chapel and several trees be removed, because the path needed to be widened.[97] Pieck also maintained exacting control over all inscriptions, his detailed list of plaques providing detailed categories for the victims.[98] The inner circle around the memorial stone was to be reserved for Communist martyrs of 1918 and the Nazi era, whereas the "old socialists" were to be placed in the outer circle. This hierarchical layout contrasts with Pieck's previous design, in which with no graves were placed inside the circle.

A twenty-ton stone was placed in the center of the memorial, bearing the inscription, "The deceased admonish us" (figure 1.5). Commemorative plaques were placed around this stone for Liebknecht, Luxemburg, and Franz Mehring (another martyr of the 1918 Revolution) and for four Communist martyrs murdered during the Nazi era. Years later, the three leading figures in the founding of the East German state were buried in the inner circle: Pieck, Ulbricht, and Grotewohl. Thus the focal point of the memorial linked Communist martyrdom with the founding of the Communist state. A walkway encircled this central area and was itself encircled by another series of graves, including leading Communist and Social Democratic leaders from all eras up to the founding of the GDR. Finally, a 4-meter-high wall surrounded this outer circle and contained urns with the remains of more Communist and Social Democratic leaders. The spatial accommodation of large ceremonies was grounded in long-standing German Communist practice and was in line with socialist-realist ideas, as were the simple, rectangular grave stones and plaques; however, the rough-hewn stone at the center belongs to an international tradition of neomegalithic nationalist and military memorials (such as the Battle of the Nations monument in Leipzig, constructed in 1913).[99] In sum, this memorial was Pieck-esque eclecticism.

In January 1951 the memorial was dedicated at the annual L-L-L Ceremony, which remained one of the largest state ceremonies in East Germany. Large, front-page articles typically reported mass marches of the Berlin working class to the site (150,000–200,000 participants), where they lay wreaths and flowers at the memorial. Leading Communist functionaries would then deliver speeches on the significance of the 1918 Revolution for the development of socialism and the contemporary political situation.[100] The remonumentalized site was now being used to transmit the most rigid, teleological, and totalizing of histories; Communist memory and (East) German state history thus came into alignment. The memory of the March Revolution faded in significance. Ceremonies were held at the cemetery in Friedrichshain in 1949 and 1950, although reportage was brief.[101] Thereafter, March 18 was removed from the commemorative

FIGURE 1.5. Socialists' Memorial. This wreath-laying ceremony was held on the Memorial Day for the Victims of Fascism in September 1956. The large stone in the center bears the inscription, "The deceased admonish us." BA-Digital Picture Database, Photo Image 183-41269-0002, *Allgemeiner Deutscher Nachrichtendienst—Zentralbild*, Hans-Günter Quaschinsky, September 8, 1956.

calendar—the “bourgeois revolution” was too closely associated with the West. A brief flourish of attention arrived in 1960, when a statue titled *Red Sailor* was placed near the entrance, to acknowledge that some of the martyrs of the November Revolution were buried there; this reinforced the link between the democratic revolution of 1948 and the socialist revolution of 1918.

A Testimony Transformed

After World War II, occupying powers and Berlin’s municipal government directed a great deal of attention and effort at reshaping the symbolic dimension of the urban landscape, despite the immense demand for housing and infrastructure in the decimated city. This is especially noteworthy in the case of German Communists, whose materialist worldview would seem to prioritize the latter. In 1946, Western Allies ordered the removal of symbols of Nazism and Prussian militarism from the public realm. German Communists, adhering to a negative view of German exceptionalism that situated Prussia as the font of German militarism, expanded the scope to include the Prussian monarchy. Debates ensued within the Magistrat over the future of specific toponyms, iconography on buildings, and statues, with German Communists displaying the strongest iconoclastic tendency. The Allies’ policy focused on symbolism, or representation, regardless of location, yet in a few cases on Victory Avenue, spatial and place-based attributes were seen as contributing to the overall message. Also, the specific medium had some impact on decision-making, as changes to toponyms were influenced by the suitability of replacement names, while the effacement of some memorials involved weighing artistic merit against political taint. In 1952 the Prussian military was rehabilitated, due to political concerns that prompted the remilitarization of the German Democratic Republic. This terminated a purge that may well have included some of the city’s more significant public art. For instance, once in power and with greater resources, German Communist attempts to demolish the iconic Victory Column might have succeeded.

While the construction of memorials on veterans’ cemeteries on foreign soil is a common phenomenon, the Soviet War Memorial in Treptow is distinctive for its sprawling scale, extensive artwork, and use in heavily politicized ceremonies. An early application of socialist realism in Berlin, its monumentality, traditional forms, and formal sequence of spaces provides the impression of an outdoor cathedral for secular purposes. As Soviet sacred space in the heart of the former Reichshauptstadt, its message was carefully tailored to consider its dual Soviet and German audiences by omitting certain themes and retaining ambiguity for others. In 1950 the Soviet's annual "Victory Day" celebration was renamed "Liberation Day" in the GDR, establishing a founding myth for the East German state that would be celebrated with ceremonies in Treptow each May.

In contrast to the recent origins and clear-cut decision-making regarding the Treptow site, the revolutionaries' cemeteries in Berlin evolved through a century-long contestation of meaning that became embroiled in postwar politics. No significant memorial remained in either cemetery, but their deep and complicated place-based meaning made them focal points for German politicians and architects. Conflict emerged due to differences in how Communists and Social Democrats interpreted the German revolutionary past. The KPD, adhering to Marxist-Leninist teleology, viewed both memorials as testimony to a narrative of world progress culminating in Communism. The Social Democratic Party recognized the 1848 Revolution as a step toward democracy and the 1918 Revolution as a failed putsch. The KPD hoped a new memorial would assist the two socialist parties in overcoming their embittered past and unite, emphasizing the humanist roots of socialism and the importance of antifascism. For much of the late 1940s, proposals were altered in the face of political jockeying and changing East-West relations. With the political division of Berlin, Wilhelm Pieck was able to impose his unique vision for a new socialists' memorial in Friedrichsfelde. Both Communists and SPD members remaining in the East would be presented with the Communist version of their history each January through annual L-L-L ceremonies at the new memorial.

2

City Plans

Naturally there will be people of little faith . . . but the great majority of the population of Berlin will show great enthusiasm and interest for reshaping Berlin [*Neugestaltung*]. No suggestion, no thought that could lead to an improvement to the General Plan is so small that it should not be expressed.

—Friedrich Ebert, Mayor of East Berlin, 1949

KATERINA CLARK indicates that the reconstruction of Moscow in the 1930s fits the nationalist tradition in which the capital city represents the state, but with very high stakes as Moscow would proclaim socialist values to Russia, Europe, and the world. Modernism was abandoned, and classical precedent was espoused and reworked for the contemporary situation. The new city would display care for people, in contrast with their exploitation in capitalist cities. It would contribute to the creation of a new human, efficiently serving his needs and leading him to a higher level of consciousness, thereby contributing to the construction of socialism. This was part of a broader cultural turn, involving a shift from pure materialism to humanistic Marxism.[1] Planning for Berlin would also begin with modernism and shift to socialist realism, not as a result of internal politics but as a foreign imposition. Though these theoretical imperatives were imposed in Berlin, their application was less straightforward and provoked considerable debate.

After World War II, demolitions, repairs, and rebuilding efforts were carried out in piecemeal fashion, while the Berlin Magistrat worked on a comprehensive plan to guide reconstruction. Several plans were produced within a few years, all proposing extensive transformation of the city in accordance with modernist design principles to remedy the ills of the nineteenth-century city. Each iteration was less idealistic, more realizable, and more politically charged. After the founding of the German Democratic

Republic, modernism was abandoned in favor of socialist realism, which mandated a return to traditional urbanism, respect for historic structure, and emphasis on the city center as a political space. A Central Axis Berlin design competition was proposed but never undertaken. In the mid-1950s the Soviet Union led the East German state to rationalize and industrialize construction to maximize labor productivity and economic efficiency. Although socialist realism remained the official theory, many interpreted these changes as a return to modernism, and a 1958 design competition left designers to mediate between paradigms. The new plans combined principles of socialist realism and modernism and manifest a technological optimism deriving from high modern enthusiasm for progress through science and technology.

Past City Plans and Planning Traditions

Berlin's medieval core grew in an organic pattern around the Berlin Palace. In the seventeenth century, the first planned urban extensions, Luisenstadt and Friedrichstadt, were mapped out to the west of the city walls. The monarchy strictly controlled urban design and foresaw a central tree-lined boulevard (Unter den Linden) adjoined by a grid of streets framed with buildings of great architectural unity.[2] Early nineteenth-century urban growth prompted renewed planning efforts, including the 1830 Building Plan for the Periphery of Berlin and the more extensive Lenné Plan of 1840. The king's landscape architect, Peter Josef Lenné, sought to employ baroque urban design to draw the city into a unified whole at a time when rapid, piecemeal development, notably industrial buildings and railroads, were fragmenting the city. Lenné expressed concern for beauty, efficiency, and social issues; the tree-lined promenades were intended as recreational spaces for workers. However, the king no longer possessed the money or the power to implement such a vast plan. By the late 1850s city planning had degenerated into an effort to reconcile the spatial requirements of public infrastructure with those of private land development. In response, the 1862 Hobrecht Plan integrated rail transportation with a hierarchical street network fit to the new sanitary sewer plan. Large blocks (about twelve acres or four block faces of about 730 feet) were intended to enable interiors to be used for industrial workshops or gardens, overcoming the unhygienic conditions of the cramped inner city. Instead, rental barracks with narrow courtyards were built throughout the city, whether the blocks were large or small.[3]

These limited-scope nineteenth-century plans have been characterized as "extension plans" in contrast with twentieth-century "comprehensive planning."[4] In contrast, the 1908 competition for a greater Berlin plan and resulting 1910 exhibition engaged multidisciplinary "comprehensive planning" as the remedy for the ills of the industrial metropolis. The project area included the entire Berlin region, yet there was no metropolitan government to implement it. Hence it was not the Royal Academy of Architecture but professional architects' associations that had drawn the City of Berlin and numerous surrounding municipalities into the design competition. Many submitted plans included an extensive municipal railway system, a park network, the breaking open of rental barrack courtyards, and suburban expansion through garden cities. Though not prescribed by the guidelines, some entries included a monumental core intended to express either national power or democratic municipal life similar to American City Beautiful civic centers.[5]

In 1920 the Greater Berlin Act consolidated municipalities around Berlin into a single metropolitan government. A metropolitan plan was produced with a focus on transportation and housing. Significant results were obtained for the latter, with the design and construction of large, suburban housing estates, inspired by the Garden City movement and international modernism. These were understood to be part of broader urban visions being developed throughout Europe that became codified in the Athens Charter in 1933. The Athens Charter proposed that "town planning is a science" that could remedy the "disturbances" industrialization imposed on urban life: crowding, pollution, poor sanitation, exposure to unfavorable natural conditions and lack of access to favorable ones for the poor; places of work and leisure disconnected from residential areas and outdated transportation networks. The solution, shaping urban form to fit the daily needs of residents, demanded a reconfiguration of spaces of work, residence, leisure, and transportation, and the deployment of "the full resources of modern technology."[6]

At the smallest scale, the *Wohnzelle* (a "cell for living" or "residential cell") referred to a dwelling. These would be organized into a group forming an appropriately sized "habitation unit" (essentially a neighborhood) containing various community facilities in a low-density setting. A hierarchy of roads, classified by type, would connect each of these functions, with nonstop, high-speed automobile thoroughfares at the top. The separation of housing from industry and traffic through strict zoning would reduce pollution in residential areas adjoined by green spaces, and apartment building design would ensure sufficient air, sunshine, and views into green space. This required cutting new transportation routes through the city, clearing slums, and transforming land uses into a linear pattern of monofunctional "bands" containing industry, green space, transportation, or residences—the latter separated from industry by the greenbelt.[7]

The Nazi era greatly empowered urban planners, who developed a range of projects. Well-known are Albert Speer's plans to reconfigure Berlin as a monumental capital city of a "Thousand Year Reich" centered on a grand north-south axis cut through the city center. Less attention has been given to urban renewal and new town planning in many German cities at this time. Dense housing would be constructed along the outer portions of Hitler's monumental axis. However, as in modernist planning, the bulk of the city would have reduced density, block interiors would be opened, and urban expansion would be concentrated in low-density suburbs and new towns with land uses segregated in ribbons following landscape contours. The leading theoretical work, *Die neue Stadt*, called for decentralizing the population into small garden cities and breaking existing cities into "cells"—residential neighborhoods around which the needs of daily life would be planned. Strong similarities between Nazi-era city planning and the Athens Charter stem from a common planning tradition, continuity in staff, and a concern with similar planning issues. Underlying beliefs about public health, community, and a connection to nature were also shared, although Nazi ideas and vocabulary on race peppered their plans. Finally, after bombing raids began, the idea that low-density worked as a defensive strategy gained considerable traction, and some planners suggested returning parts of cities to nature.[8]

This vignette reveals a long-standing view that planning could enhance the city's functional efficiency and improve the lives of Berliners including the working classes.[9] Planning efforts were initiated by the monarchy (in the 1840s through the 1860s), bourgeois professionals (in 1910), a Social Democratic administration (in the 1920s), and the National Socialist state (in the 1930s). Despite radical differences in political orientation and stages in the city's development, Berlin's planners displayed continuity of belief in the value of low-density development with a strong connection to nature for public health and social welfare. Similarities between planning carried out under the Nazis and their leftist enemies from the Weimar era demonstrate that a particular style of planning cannot be an essential expression of political ideology. Also, many of the plans formed in Germany during these eras were similar to, or even adapted from, paradigms developed in other countries. Thus claims about political values or national identity and planning styles remain somewhat tenuous.[10]

The Modernist "New Berlin"

In the years between the end of World War II and the founding of the German Democratic Republic, several plans were developed for Berlin. The Magistrat's chief planner, Hans Scharoun, was an experienced modernist who had worked with Walter Gropius in the 1920s.[11] Scharoun led a team of modernist architects and city planners, later known as the *Planungskollektiv* (Planning Collective) to develop the first major postwar plan for Berlin. Their *Kollektiv Plan* (Collective Plan) was presented in the exhibition *Berlin Plant* (Berlin Plans) in 1946, along with a parallel exhibit, *Berlin im Aufbau* (Berlin under Construction), reporting on construction progress in the Soviet sector. After the election of an SPD-controlled City Council in late 1946, Scharoun was replaced by Karl Bonatz, but modernist ideals continued to guide planning, culminating in the Bonatz Plan (1948), which shared features of earlier efforts but required far fewer changes to the city structure. After the division of the Magistrat in 1948, the new Eastern Magistrat's chief planner, Wils Ebert, began work on yet another modernist plan, the *Generalaufbauplan 1949* (General Building Plan 1949).

Scharoun delivered a speech on the fundamentals of city planning in April 1946. Borrowing from the Athens Charter, he pointed to the failure to plan for the explosive growth of the nineteenth century, when society focused on increasing the performance of machines instead of "planfully deploying machines" for human purposes.[12] Berlin's density would be dramatically reduced, while maintaining its urban character—a necessity as the city exercised actual and symbolic power throughout the nation and the world. In discourse presaging that of Communists at the time of the state-founding, Scharoun declared that Berlin was to "reflect the unity of Germany" and that the "forces of division, which represent an evil in the cultural development of the occident as a whole, and are playing a political role in German lands today for reasons of comfort, short-sightedness, or opportunism, must be opposed by a creative synthesis, which—in this connection—finds its expression in the City of Berlin, the German City."[13] The city would contribute to national unity through socioeconomic and cultural functions and representationally as a symbol of the nation.

The first postwar plan for Berlin, the Collective Plan, was presented in the exhibition, *Berlin Plans* in the White Hall of the Berlin Palace in August 1946.[14] Scharoun's emphasis on urbanity and the identity of Berlin as bulwark against foreign forces of division are difficult to connect to the plan, which fully embodies the tenets of modernism. His modernist perspective was reinforced by a personal view involving traditionalist urban planning and German exceptionalism. Scharoun condemned the use of "axes," essentially boulevards in the baroque tradition, asserting that they had led to "marching"—the development of parade grounds "and finally under Hitler to the parade-axis."[15] These were to be eliminated from planners' imaginations and replaced by transportation systems designed according to physical conditions (geology and topography recurring in his statements), technical possibilities, and the needs of everyday life. For nearly a century, German planners had proposed cutting wide, straight streets through cities, primarily as means of improving traffic circulation, increasing the availability of light and air in cities, and creating a monumental aesthetic.[16]

Since the 1890s, opponents argued against boulevards for aesthetic reasons (a return the picturesque), respect for existing property lines, and even health reasons (dubious assertions that they acted as dust conduits). Yet Scharoun's recent experience with Nazi military parades overwhelmed any memory of this debate. His plan eschewed the axis, monumentality, and ceremonial space as expressions of a dark past. The Athens Charter would shape the plan's organization and content; the flaws of the nineteenth-century city were to be overcome through rational planning engaging twentieth-century technology.[17]

Prewar Berlin had a population density of thirteen hundred people per hectare (about 525 per acre) in the city center and fifty people per hectare (about 20 per acre) on the periphery. The plan called for a relatively even distribution with no more than 250 people per hectare (about 100 per acre) and large green spaces distributed throughout the city center. Land uses and major transportation corridors were organized in "bands" corresponding to the course of the Spree River and the city's underlying geology, which presumably offered greater efficiency for transportation and land use than the existing radial network. This reconfiguration would require radical modification of the existing city. New streets would be cut through blocks, and existing streets widened to create freeways set in immense greenways (200 meters or about 650 feet wide), with overpasses and cloverleaf interchanges enabling free-flowing traffic while demanding more land and adding considerable expense.[18] Many other streets would be turned into cul-de-sacs, pedestrian paths, or bikeways (figure 2.1).[19]

The areas between freeways would be restructured into one or more *Wohnzellen* ("residential cells"), each containing four thousand to five thousand residents with basic community facilities in high-rises, walk-ups, and/or single-family houses. The surviving rental barracks of Eastern Berlin were marked for extensive reconfiguration: interior buildings would be torn down so that the entire center area could become one green space, and a few buildings on the streetfront would be removed, allowing access from the street and increased air circulation.[20]

Museum Island and the monumental boulevard Unter den Linden would be preserved for cultural and historic reasons, although the latter was clearly a reactionary axis in Scharoun's view. Peter Friedrich, who designed the network of freeways to crisscross the city, criticized suggestions that the Brandenburg Gate be moved or razed to enhance traffic flow along Unter den Linden. Instead, diverting through-traffic would maintain the architectural character of Pariser Platz and make Unter den Linden into a "quiet promenade" and "retail street." Unter den Linden and Museuminsel together would form the "cultural center" of the "new Berlin."[21] The Athens Charter called for the preservation of architectural heritage, even if traffic required rerouting. Nonetheless, when considered as a whole, the plan proposed radical changes that would result in great financial expenditure and legal issues surrounding property ownership. Drastic restructuring was unrealistic without massive political reforms enabling large-scale sequestration of property, a considerable loss of existing infrastructure, and an extremely long-term construction effort.

Public discussion of the plans and rebuilding effort were framed in a language of humanism and democracy to gather support from residents, architects, and politicians of all political persuasions. Nevertheless, Communists inserted their perspective on the reconstruction at times. The exhibitions *Berlin Plans* and *Berlin under Construction* (on rubble clearance and construction progress in the Soviet-occupied districts of Berlin) were jointly opened in a formal ceremony attended by public figures from Berlin and Germany, including the occupying powers. Mayor Werner gave an introduction, Scharoun spoke about the new plan, and Karl Maron (SED), deputy mayor and future minister of the interior in the GDR, spoke on the significance of the exhibition *Berlin under Construction* in light of the contemporary political situation.[22] Maron wrote the foreword

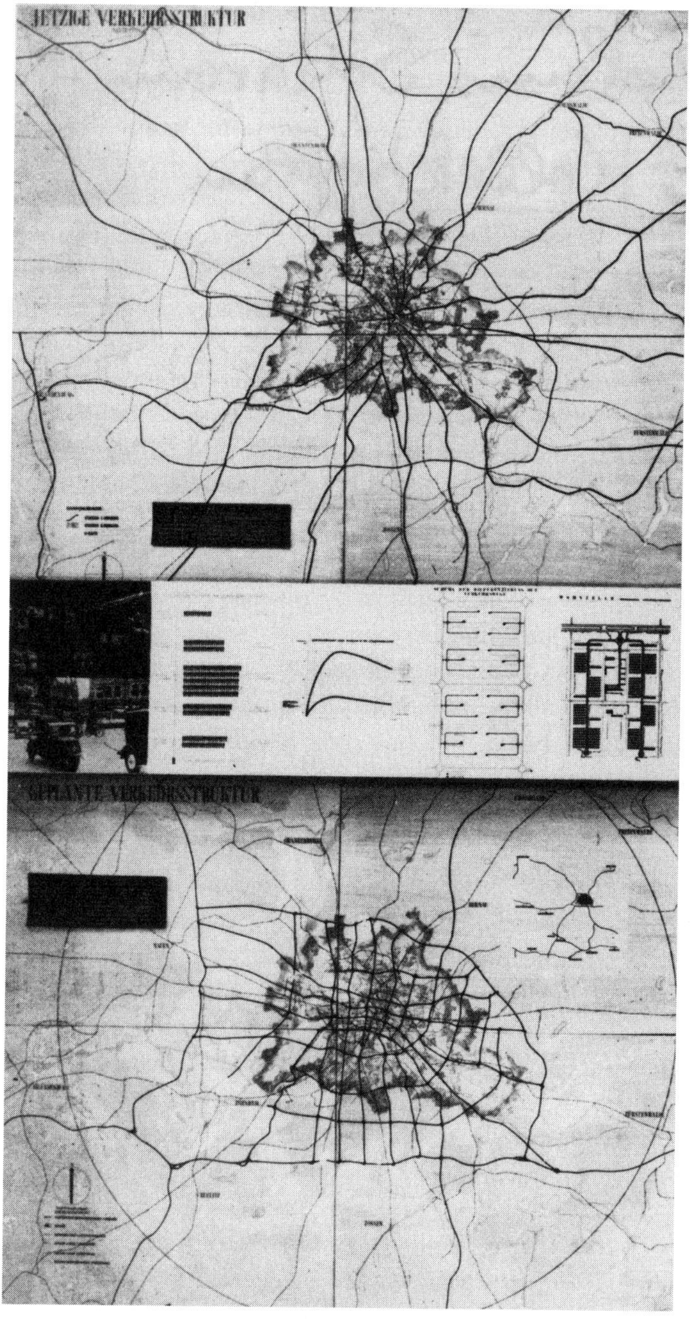

FIGURE 2.1. *Berlin Plant* Exhibition, 1946. The existing radial network of major roadways (above) would be converted to a grid at the city center (below) based on calculations to determine the most efficient circulation pattern. Akademie der Künste, Scharoun, 3781F.162/6.

to the exhibition's catalog and co-opted the language of the *Heimatschutz* tradition, undeterred by its recent association with Nazism.

The foreword, "Our Berlin," declared that the overwhelming majority of Germans wanted to return to their home, whether a village or city, as "love of home [*Heimat*] is one of the strongest feelings."[23] Berliners were tied to their city like a "tree to its soil," declining opportunities to move into housing in other districts, and they remained living in a "cellar or half-destroyed apartment on 'their' street." The old political, socioeconomic order resulted in inadequate living conditions for the working class, which would be rectified through the new building effort. This subtly introduced the issue of class relations but avoided explicitly socialist content. Love of home provided the motivation to work to build the new city, with sufficient light, air, sun, green spaces, theaters, and cinema for everyone. Along with its motivational role, the language of *Heimatschutz* glossed over the fact that modernist plans would transform most of Berlin beyond recognition.[24]

When the exhibit opened, *Tagesspiegel* (a West Berlin daily) praised Scharoun for his nonpartisan handling of planning issues and named him the "Rescuer of Berlin."[25] While planners in the "Anglo-Saxon lands," specifically Frank Lloyd Wright, remedied the ills of the capitalist city through an antiurban approach, Scharoun incorporated some their ideas but avoided the "dissolution of the city." The destruction of Berlin is attributed to bombs, without mention of Hitler or Nazism. Maron's report was praised. The exhibition on Soviet-sector reconstruction, *Berlin under Construction*, was ignored.

Tägliche Rundschau (the Soviet paper in East Germany, first published after the war) was more partisan. Most of this article was devoted to Maron's speech, criticizing the West in unusually harsh terms—a stark contrast with his essay for the catalog. Maron stopped short of proclaiming socialist goals, while applying its theoretical bases to attack the West. He condemned those "sowing malicious claims and suggestions behind the stage front of democratic freedom of expression"—that is, the Western occupying forces. They misused the words "democracy" and "*Aufbau*, to camouflage [their] dark work" in service of the "egotistical, profit-greedy goals of a small minority of the people [rather] than the rights of the productive people, the majority of the people [*Volk*], to have apartments, school rooms, and places for production, culture, and recreation."[26] The ruined city, "inheritance from Hitler," was being cleared through the initiative of the "nameless, simple people" or the "working people," because they believed "that the newly emerging Berlin will be the capital of a real democracy"—presumably unlike those in the West: "We want to build a new Berlin! This city should be built, not just from the elements of the architecture, but its future appearance should be developed according to the basic rights of productive citizens. Under the concept 'new Berlin,' we also include the genuine democratization of life in Berlin as a whole. These new houses shall be inhabited by new human beings."[27]

The goal was a "new Berlin as capital of a new, democratic Germany." Recognition for work accomplished would produce confidence for coming tasks, hence the exhibition advanced these aims. The term "new Berlin," which would come to appear frequently in the Communist press, had been employed in the Weimar era by modernist architects and city planners, usually Social Democrats, who rejected the city building techniques of the past. Maron linked his "new Berlin" to a "new Germany" that rejected the unjust political and economic systems of the past. While the creation of "new human beings" is central to Marxist thought, here it is couched in terms of democracy to increase popular appeal.

As the election campaign for the City Council heated up in September, the Western media sharpened criticism of the exhibition. One article, "The Magistrat's Building Exhibition: Position of the SPD—Utopian Plans Cause Confusion," deemed the plan infeasible and criticized the imposition of a freeway network dividing the city into zones arbitrarily assigned residential or commercial.[28] Allegations of incompetence were intended to raise questions about the city administration. As the plan "leads in the wrong direction politically and economically," the responsible authorities should be "put to a vote of confidence." Another article criticized the Magistrat's work and suggested that Berliners vote the SED out of office in October elections. Hans Scharoun's personal notes contain a rebuttal defending the plan and arguing that political attacks on a technical issue were criminal.[29] This view was shared in the West by renown journalist Margret Boveri, an advocate for German unity. Boveri pointed out that the future of Berlin and Germany was in the hands of the occupying powers, whose ideological differences were also evident among Germans. Hence planners' apolitical, technical work produced a plan that the opposing camps all approved, giving hope to those visiting the exhibition.[30]

Competing claims regarding the identity of Berlin and the interests of Berliners expressed by the plan reveal a range of perspectives. Curiously,

Maron initially cloaked the plan's modernist metamorphosis of Berlin with *Heimatschutz* vocabulary and later fused modernist and Marxist concepts in a message about overcoming class exploitation through democracy—a new Berlin as a step toward a new Germany. Scharoun embraced change, claiming that Berlin and German identity would be expressed through the transformation of the vernacular city and the preservation of monuments and historic architecture on Unter den Linden.[31] Boveri saw an apolitical planning process as a contribution to German unity. Another Western report reversed the relationship, however, with the political future of Germany a prerequisite to determining the role of Berlin and the development of city plans. Impending changes in local government would send the planners back to the drawing board.

A Social-Democratic majority was elected to the new City Council in October 1946, and at their first meeting in December they appointed Karl Bonatz to replace Hans Scharoun. Bonatz criticized the Collective Plan as unrealistic because of the plan's disregard for the value of existing infrastructure and reparable buildings in the face of urgent housing needs and limited financial capacity.[32] The imposition of a rectangular network of freeways enclosing swaths of land (cells) in a series of parallel bands ignored the value accrued though eighty years of urban development, in favor of improved transportation efficiency and a desire to shape the city to a glacial valley that is no longer perceptible.[33] Furthermore, cutting "race tracks" (freeways) through the city was unnecessary and would blight adjacent areas, exposing firewalls, backs of buildings, "and other horrible images."[34]

With the political and economic future of Berlin in limbo, Bonatz's primary planning objective was to provide a modicum of guidance for decisions about rubble clearance and building restoration. The "New Plan" synthesized a simplified version of the Collective Plan's freeway network with that of the Zehlendorfer Plan (developed by planners in that district), which used a network of boulevards rather than limited-access freeways to improve traffic flow. The plan was presented uneventfully in the exhibition *Berlin Plant/Zweite Bericht* in December 1947. The *Berliner Zeitung* offered little criticism, suggesting it be recognized as another in a series of city plans, perhaps too modest but worthwhile as a launching point for debate about the future.[35]

A visit from Walter Gropius prompted a debate about the future that appeared in professional journals in early 1948. These efforts culminated in the *Plan Berlin 1948*, also known as the Bonatz Plan, which was displayed in an exhibition in West Berlin in September and October 1948. This plan followed the premises of Scharoun's work but required far fewer incisions into the urban fabric: density would range from 400 residents per hectare (about 160 per acre) in central areas, while areas with gardens for each apartment would fall as low as 75 residents per hectare (about 30 per acre). The plan arrived at an inopportune time. The Western currency reform had recently been initiated, and the division of the city government soon followed. Bonatz became director of city building in West Berlin.[36]

A few months after the division of Berlin's government, in April 1949 the mayor of East Berlin, Friedrich Ebert (of the SED), launched an initiative to develop a new plan for the city. The Planning Collective had retained a number of key personnel except for Scharoun. The introduction to its program for the *Neuplanung der Stadt Berlin* (New Planning of the City, Berlin), while not overtly Marxist, applied its philosophy, dialectical materialism, explaining that "wartime destruction is only the surface reason for replanning Berlin. The deeper reason: the contradiction between content and archaic form, changed social relations. The main point of view for the planning: the working person stands at the center."[37] Thus city form should reflect contemporary social conditions, which were not yet socialist but had progressed beyond capitalism. The framework for approaching the plan was rooted in the "old Berlin"—"new Berlin" dichotomy. "What is revealed by a critical examination of the old Berlin?" and "How should the new Berlin be created?"[38] The "new Berlin" described in the program was very similar to the one proposed in recent plans: decentralization, homogeneous density, bandlike spatial order following the course of the river, continuous green space, "residential cells" containing five thousand residents, and cultural facilities as the smallest planned unit. The completed plan was presented to the public in July 1949. Johann Friedrich Geist and Klaus Kürvers aptly characterize the plan as "a version of the plan from 1946, revised and adjusted to fit the actual possibilities" (figure 2.2).[39]

The SED claimed this plan would represent the interests of Berliners and all Germans, although it only modestly differed from the Bonatz Plan that the Party had ignored. The Magistrat approved the sale of DM 100 million in bonds throughout Germany with the motto "reconstruction of the capital of Germany."[40] Mayor Ebert presented the plan and invited public input. *Berliner Zeitung* headlines declared: "Berliners will build a new Berlin: Mayor Ebert puts the Berlin Aufbauplan up for Discussion."[41]

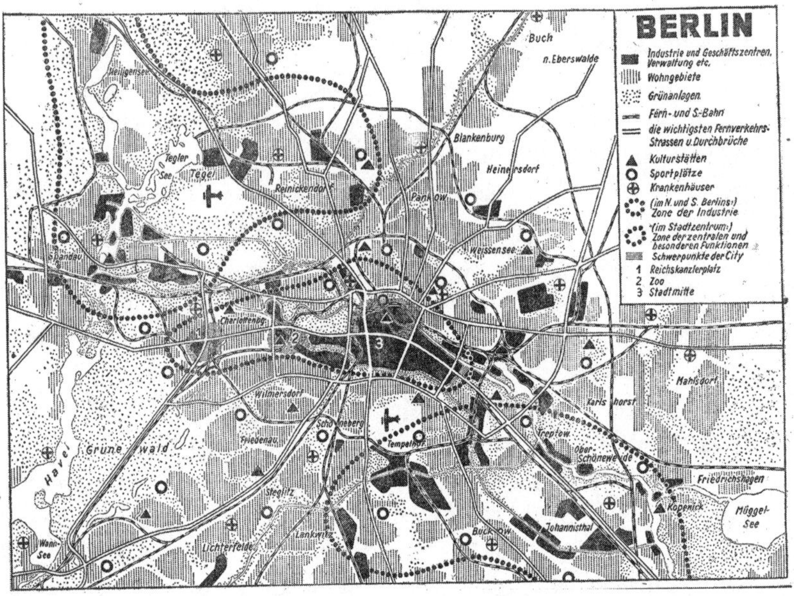

FIGURE 2.2. General Building Plan, 1949. Though reliant on the same premises as the modernist plan from 1946 plan, the new plan was considerably modified to respect existing conditions for practical reasons. "Plan für Berlin," *Berliner Zeitung*, July 27, 1949.

Compared with the program, this characterization of the plan appeared less Marxist and more humanist. Ebert remained focused on overcoming the past: "Today we are laying the foundation stone for the work, which future generations will have to continue building upon, until the results of the Hitler-crimes have been overcome." Practical benefits for everyday life were highlighted, and no reference was made to "socialism," the "new Germany," the "new human," "democracy," or "reunification."

Wartime destruction was claimed to have been only the "surface reason" for replanning, but unlike the program, a deeper reason was not mentioned. Great care was being taken to maintain political neutrality for this populist appeal, calling all citizens of Berlin to participate in the planning effort regardless of class, sector, political affiliation, or any other distinction.[42] He asserted that previously in German society, as elsewhere, urban design remained in the hands of detached financial and technical elites interested in profits, but the Eastern Magistrat empowered Berliners interested in the "destiny of the citizenry and their grandchildren" in shaping "their *Heimat*." The combination of populism and love for *Heimat* was offered as evidence of "true democracy," avoiding explicit Marxism while remaining compatible with Marxist thought. After several weeks of public discussion, the plan was hardly altered. It was technocratic, produced by elite planners in isolation from popular influence.

Neues Deutschland articles omitted populist rhetoric and provided SED members with the Party's perspective on the plan's political significance. Images of the nineteenth-century industrial city as a product of capitalist speculation were contrasted with the new plan for Berlin, which places "the working person [*werktätige Mensch*] at its center." Quotes from Hans Jendretsky, chair of the Berlin SED, indicated that the solid economy would enable the "democratic Magistrat" to realize this plan, in contrast to the administration in the west sectors, "which speak of future plans but never once pay their debts and cannot fulfill [their] obligations to the population"—a cynical comment less than two months after the end of the Blockade of West Berlin.[43] The plan expressed "the entire unlimited confidence of our people [*Menschen*] in a better future for our fatherland, the unshakeable trust and the conviction that this fatherland can only be a united Germany, which Berlin will worthily represent as capital. And that is exactly why this is not a plan for just Berlin or just our zone, but rather a plan for all Germany, a plan whose realization concerns all Germans."[44]

A series of points and counterpoints are evident: German cities were chaotic, products of capitalist speculation in the industrial era, but this plan would bring order, shaping the city for livability. This plan was realistic, while Western plans were not. This plan would result in a suitable capital for a united Germany, while Bonn was trying to split the nation. Whereas news aimed at all Berliners depicted the planning effort as nonpartisan and tending to *Heimat (Berliner Zeitung)*, news aimed at Party members depicted the effort as a part of a battle for the national future (Neues Deutschland).

The Political Content of Modernist Plans

The plans developed during this period were all based on modernist principles, intended to improve the functional efficiency of the city and improve the quality of life of Berliners. They differed only modestly—the latter plans requiring fewer alterations to the city. Despite this, public discourse portrayed great differences between the plans, asserting that they provided evidence of government competence or incompetence, expressed and influenced social values, and impacted larger political issues including the national question.

Regarding government competence, the Collective Plan was initially well received in the Eastern and Western press, but as political tension rose, it was criticized in the West for being utopian, the product of incompetent government. The Plan Berlin 1948 was held up in the Western press as a product of the new Social Democratic–run government, and the General Building Plan of 1949 was hailed in the Eastern press as a demonstration of real democracy and effective governance. Regarding planning and social values, Scharoun believed the formal order specified by urban plans could support regressive national cultural and political traditions or reject these, as did the Collective Plan. Maron depicted this plan as a contribution to the construction of a new society. In 1949, Communists viewed the General Building Plan as prioritizing the needs of the working person, because it reflected a transformed society. However, they presented the plan to Berliners as conserving their *Heimat* and used a populist appeal for democratic participation. Regarding plans' impacts on political issues, in 1945 Scharoun expressed a belief that a new plan could work to support German national unity, and in 1949 the Communist press made the same assertion.

These wide-ranging claims raise the question as to whether the political content of plans was groundless rhetoric. The issue of government competence relates to the effectiveness of plans in improving everyday urban function and is directly subject to expert and popular opinion in this regard. The plans' symbolic significance and role in inter-German and international politics is less straightforward, however. The attempt to redress inadequate conditions created under past political and economic systems through the rejection of traditional approaches to urban form left considerable leeway for interpretation. Was this an expression of humanism or socialism, love of *Heimat* or nationalism, or even "democracy"—a word itself rich with ambiguity?[45] Were they tainted because planners working for the National Socialist German Workers' Party had employed a modernist paradigm in many locations? As for the plans' alleged contribution to national unity, their lack of impact is clear. While symbolic gestures and cultural politics can be effective, at this time Berliners' and Germans had little influence on the occupying powers that were determining the future of the city and the nation. This could hardly have been the intent; rather, nationalist rhetoric was being used for local politics, to help persuade Berliners of the merits of the SED.

Planning a Representative "Capital of Germany"

The founding of the East German State in October 1949 created a political and economic framework that enabled a massive building program. Yet with only part of the city falling under the control of the new state, plans for the entire city lacked effective means of implementation. This would in no way deter city planning efforts, which became even more politicized in accordance with theoretical guidelines imported from Moscow. Socialist realism rejected the modernist attempt to scientifically reinvent the city, instead informing their visions with a "scientific" understanding of traditional urbanism. Communist discussion of modernist plans was underlain with traditional Marxist materialism and lacquered with humanism and democracy. Socialist realism was not strictly materialist but posited that culture, including architecture and urban design, could also play a role in shaping society, a reengagement of humanist Marxism with profound consequences for city building.

The state-founding initiated a wave of institutional restructuring that transferred ultimate authority over planning and building from the Berlin Magistrat to the German Democratic Republic's newly created Ministry of Building (Ministerium für Aufbau, MfA) led by Lothar Bolz. During years of exile in Moscow, Bolz familiarized himself with debates over art and theoretical developments in planning and architecture.[46] In November 1949, a few days after the MfA was founded, Prime Minister Otto Grotewohl hosted a meeting with his adviser Tzschorn; the minister of building, Bolz; East Berlin's mayor, Friedrich Ebert; chair of the Berlin SED, Hans Jendretzsky; architects Hans Scharoun and Kurt Liebknecht; and others. Bolz expressed his view that the planning for Berlin is a national affair: "As the capital of the German Democratic Republic is the symbol of German unity, the reconstruction of the capital is the symbol for the reconstruction of all-Germany.... Above all, it must become a lever to activate the entire population of Germany and serve to raise the social consciousness of the entire population. For these reasons... the experience of the most progressive model that exists in this area must be used, namely, the experience of Moscow."[47] Bolz convinced Grotewohl that a delegation should be sent to Moscow and Warsaw to learn firsthand about principles of city planning being applied in the reconstruction of those cities. The MfA and the Magistrat would jointly plan the effort, although Bolz retained control as correspondent with Grotewohl, Ebert, and Ulbricht regarding the matter. While in Moscow for Stalin's seventieth birthday celebration in December,

Ulbricht met with the relevant professionals and arranged for the reception of a delegation.[48]

The Trip to Moscow during April and May of 1950 served as a turning point for Berlin planning from a modernist to socialist-realist paradigm. During the trip, Arkady Mordvinov, president of the Soviet Academy of Architecture, met the delegation. Bolz requested commentary on the "ideological battle in the field of architecture." Mordvinov outlined the architecture-society relationship. Architecture involved three categories: economic, technical, and artistic. The latest advances in technology were to be applied to architecture but only in service to artistic content, which was capable of social communication. Modernism had inverted the relationship through constructivism or "technology fetishism."[49] Bauhaus architects attempted to move architecture forward but were limited because they operated in the era of capitalism. They removed useless ornament and broke with the architectural tradition expressing feudalism but could not introduce a new idea.[50] Thus Mordvinov condemned the Bauhaus for falsely viewing building as a purely technical matter, as "an expression of the deepest pessimism."[51]

Later theoretical discussion posited formalism (an overemphasis on form) as the chief culprit, with constructivism and functionalism as subsets. Ironically, the functionalist Mies van der Rohe had warned against "formalism," meaning the subordination of function to form in the early 1920s.[52] The Soviet definition shares this root, but rather than a lack of concern with function, the chief problem is the loss of artistic expression of cultural content. Breaking with tradition in search of something "entirely new" inevitably "uproots national culture, destroys the national consciousness, promotes cosmopolitanism, and, as a result, directly supports the American imperialist's militarist policy."[53] Mordvinov clarified that in accordance with Lenin's Theory of Reflection, architecture and urban form must mirror society. Hence in socialist realism the content of each building—a combination of function and social meaning—determines its form.[54]

However, architecture and urban form not only reflect society, they possess the potential to shape society. Lenin's Theory of Reflection was taken to demonstrate how architecture, as an art form, conveyed an "idea" with social content and is therefore a means of education. A beautiful building or even a subway station could stimulate pride and affection. The combination of emotive and intellectual content is what made art and architecture especially effective.[55] As later summarized in an East German architecture journal: "A beautiful architectural creation instinctively awakens human interest. This feeling then transforms into love for a beautiful street, for a square, finally for the whole city and exercises a certain influence on the development of a patriotic feeling."[56] Love of place could be built upon through iconography and text, patterns of use that establish familiarity (everyday activities, formal ceremonies, speeches, tours) and secondary sources of information (books, magazines, newspaper articles, etc.). The government would provide the content, for art must contribute to world historical progress by expressing progressive ideas—the core of education in the Soviet Union was socialist indoctrination. Mordvinov recited fundamental principles of socialist realism to guide artistic development, stating, "How should art be? Socialist in content, national in form! For every architect, concern for the people and serving people (that is the socialist content!) is the highest law."[57] The nation-state was believed to be the vehicle for social progress in that era. Only with the establishment of Communism would nations lose significance and merge. Attempts to force this process would be counterproductive.[58]

A second thesis regarding the society-space relationship is that urban form influences social behavior. It could enhance or discourage political and cultural activity; however, the populace must be educated to properly use urban space. Urban densities and traditional streets and squares defined and enlivened by building facades along their edges were essential features. The proletariat had demonstrated in city streets and had formed urban mobs that fought for liberty, culminating in revolutions. With the establishment of socialist governments, state-run parades were depicted as the contemporary form of political demonstration in the street. In Moscow, broad, straight streets lined by multistory structures—a continuation of the baroque tradition—served this purpose and were contrasted with the narrow streets and cramped quarters produced under the czars' rule. Wiktor Baburov from the Soviet Ministry of City Building pointed out that the soul of the city is its center. The most important cultural and government institutions are located there along with a large square for demonstrations.[59]

Traditional urbanism stood in opposition to modernism's low densities and separation of traffic from buildings, to Scharoun's rejection of "axes" for fear of marching, and to Nazi-era ideas about low density as a defensive measure against air raids. Yet Baburov ignored these German planning precedents and blamed the West: "The English-American theory of the quality and economic viability of the 'dispersed' city. It is uneconomical, is not secure against air raids, and isolates the worker from political life and makes him into a petit bourgeois.... The street is a device for festive life.... The city and its people are not to be disturbed by auto-oriented streets. That is what we have to say to the Abercrombies, who decide for the auto."[60] Ironically, German architects had played a key role in the development of modernist planning ideas that were now being pigeonholed as English and American.[61]

Unsurprisingly, when the German delegation presented a revised version of the General Building Plan, the Soviets sharply criticized it as utopian (as had West Berlin press), for completely ignoring the cost of land with its low densities, and for being "outdated." The Soviets claimed to have learned about the shortcomings of modernist planning through their own experience and considered the idea that people need to live adjacent to work as "medieval."[62] Baburov considered the plan "cosmopolitan," lacking adherence to national tradition. He stated: "In urban planning, Germany has made great contributions to world culture. It has independently produced a lot, and has great national traditions. In this plan, however, there is nothing national."[63] Baburov asked, "Where is the idea of a capital city?... With the Berlin traffic solution, it is no longer clear what is central and what is suburban... Where do the demonstrations go? Where is the square for parades? Where are the streets for parades? Where are the government and cultural institutions? That is the center."[64] He suggested that "Unter den Linden and Tiergarten could be the center of Berlin... the one correct standpoint is the political." Soviet lectures on the matter were reinforced with direct experience at the annual May Day celebration. Walter Pisternik recorded that the impression was overwhelming, as millions marched past Stalin and the Party leadership, who observed from a grandstand in Red Square. While the International Congresses of Modern Architecture (CIAM) omitted the idea of an urban center, and Scharoun believed axes were inherently militaristic, these concepts formed the core of the socialist-realist approach.[65]

Regardless of their pre- or post-trip views on modernism, the members of the German delegation had no choice but to follow Bolz's lead and accept socialist realism. While in Moscow, they developed the GDR's official theory of architecture and planning, "The Sixteen Principles of City Building." These were approved by the government in July 1950, and became law guiding all reconstruction through the Council of Ministers' "Gesetz über der Städte in der Deutschen Demokratischen Republik und der Hauptstadt Deutschlands, Berlin" (*Aufbaugesetz*, or building law).[66] The importance of the urban environments for society and the state is apparent in the preamble: "The planning and architecture of our cities must give expression to the social order of the German Democratic Republic." The first principle elaborated: "The city is the most economically and culturally rich form of settlement for community life.... The city, in its structure and architecture, is the expression of the political life and national consciousness of the people [*Volk*]."[67] While Soviet emphasis on "socialist content" and "national form" was maintained in the initial draft of the Sixteen Principles. The Building Law stated that "architecture must be democratic in content and national in form," apropos the GDR's emphasis on democracy rather than socialism.[68] It was only at the SED's Second Party Conference in July 1952 that socialism was proclaimed, and thereafter the slogan was changed to "socialist in content, national in form."[69]

The sixth principle addressed the role of traditional streets and squares, which would be given inordinate attention in planning for Berlin. It stated: "The center forms the determinant core of the city. The center of the city is the political center of the life of its inhabitants. The most important political, administrative, and cultural institutions lie in the center of the city. Political demonstrations, parades, and celebrations on public holidays take place on the squares of the city center."[70] Nature was to be considered in the layout of cities, but the provision of light and air were given modest attention compared to historic, cultural, and economic factors—reversing the emphasis in the Athens Charter.

Upon returning to Berlin, Bolz and Pisternik were key figures in disseminating the Sixteen Principles to architects and public officials. Meetings were depicted as an opportunity to participate in "developing theory," and some attendees challenged the approach. Bolz stressed the importance of public life on the street and square, and the need to socialize the citizenry to properly use it as the center of political life. For the French, "streets and squares belong to life," the Russians had recently learned this, and Germans could too. He noted that during their Trip to Moscow they were amazed "that after the demonstration on the first of May ended, people remained on the street, the city belonged to them."[71] An architect challenged this view, asserting that one could demonstrate in green spaces, as had been traditionally done in Nordhausen.[72] Bolz rebuked this idea, asserting: "One of the reasons that fascism came to power is that the German workers' movement [the SPD and the Unions] held their demonstrations in green space... the task of the architects will be to shape the center so that the people of Nordhausen are drawn to it.[73]

In fact, Bolz was ignoring the complex history of German working-class use of urban space. Social Democratic strikes and demonstrations often involved locations at the workplace, in parks, on streets, and at key urban locations. Clara Zetkin's ideological rants about the imperative of action in the streets—stemming from the Communist Party's defeat in battles on the streets during the Revolution of 1918—made the concept central to German Communist' worldview. In fact, streets became the focal point for KPD action during the Weimar era, when it was in opposition to the SPD. Rather than rallying at the workplace, it shifted to mobilizing the legions of unemployed for demonstrations and fighting on neighborhood streets.[74] Bolz must have known this. As a lawyer, he defended antifascists during the Weimar era and had been a member of the KPD since 1929. When the NSDAP was elected, the battle for the streets ended. Perhaps personal memories of streets under reactionary control and Zetkin's theories clouded the memories of German Communists.

Some participants' modernist convictions were quite deep, and at times these became entwined with questions of national tradition and charges of reactionary nationalism. Henselmann embraced the idea of building on Berlin tradition, not through formal similarities with historic buildings but by appropriating the "real feelings that color the city."[75] Hans Hopp suggested that building materials, structural design, and social science were international and thus it was not important whether the building was in Berlin or Moscow. Bolz countered, suggesting that vastly different music is all made from the same notes, and the case was similar for architecture—that is, Hellenic architecture and Roman architecture were distinct despite common classical elements.[76]

At the next meeting, both Henselmann and Scharoun articulated favorable views of modernist architecture. Richard Paulick expressed concern that the Sixteen Principles would lead architects to rely on ornament to achieve a national aspect in their work, when differences should emerge in response to climate, geology, and landscape. Yet he also felt that Germany's small size did not allow a direct comparison to the Soviet Union, which consisted of seventeen republics. In outright confrontation, Paulick referred to the ornate attic stories of socialist-realist high-rises as "medieval fools' caps" and "Soviet kitsch." He condemned the use of traditional classicism in Germany as a return to Schulze-Naumburg and "blood and soil" doctrine—that is, tainted *Heimatschutz*. Furthermore, he challenged Bolz's depiction of modernist architecture as cosmopolitan, pointing to Gropius's book, *Internationale Architektur*, which maintained that modernism displayed "lively national differences."[77]

Bolz denounced these assertions as a "national-chauvinist embarrassment." He found it senseless that Soviet ideas could be tied to Schulze-Naumberg and accused the architects of an ethnocentric view that "the Russians have not undergone the same development that we have in the past century."[78] He implicated all Germans for nationalist views, an arrogant pride, "instilled in us Germans without individual guilt, through a century-old history through the schools and so on and so on.... We are discussing kitsch in Russian art with the typical German feeling that Russians are idiots. You don't see your own kitsch, so you can't discuss it."[79] He challenged those criticizing "Russian kitsch" to visit the Tretyakov-Galerie, as they would leave with a feeling of shame over the quality of their own work.

The meetings were never intended as a collaborative process but as an educational process to diffuse established principles and uncover opposition.[80] This would require an extensive and enduring effort, a multifaceted campaign run by the Deutsche Bauakademie (DBA, German Building Academy), "The Battle for a New German Architecture." Kurt Liebknecht worked out the guidelines for the program after a discussion with the SED's Central Committee. It would include an exhibition in the Sports Hall on Stalinallee, discussions at colleges and with professional architects, a Schinkel celebration, and translation of Soviet writings, among other strategies.[81] While the DBA focused its efforts on East German architects, it monitored West German responses, where one architectural journal asserted that the emphasis on national tradition simply followed the Soviet return to "classicism, which we have overcome, thank God."[82]

Planning the Center of Berlin

In June 1950 the Politburo ordered the development of guidelines for reconstructing the capital of the GDR. The socialist-realist paradigm was firmly entrenched, but there was considerable uncertainty over its application to Berlin. Walter Ulbricht, though not a student of socialist realism, had acquired some of its precepts through direct experience during his lengthy exile in Moscow. Most significantly, he witnessed impressive ceremonies on Red Square, and German Communists followed suit, staging May Day parades and other events in the city center in the beginning of 1946. Ulbricht's desire to have a large, representative space for these events would drive city planning in the early 1950s.

The Magistrat and MfA were assigned with "coordinating" planning for the capital, but the latter was given authority over the former.[83] Karl Brockschmidt (of the Magistrat) contacted Bolz regarding the need to bring scattered building projects together into a building program in light of the soon-to-be-approved Five-Year Plan that would finance its implementation.[84] Brockschmidt listed the fourteen most urgent projects, most of which were found in Dorotheen and Friedrichstadt (north and south of Unter den Linden). The government center would continue to be concentrated in the area between Prince Albrecht, Stresemann, Leipziger, and Wilhelmstrasse. Thälmannplatz sat at the top of the list, likely as Brockschmidt saw it as the future center of the government quarter (see Chapter 6).

Brockschmidt's list did not mention the area around the Berlin Palace, which had come into Walter Ulbricht's view as the city's center point and location for the new central square. Just two days prior to Ulbricht's speech launching the new building program at the Third Party Congress, Liebknecht's office produced a document, *Das Zentrum Berlins*, confirming that government functions were concentrated around "Reichs Chancellery Square" adjoining Wilhelmstrasse, yet the historic location for demonstrations in the city was the Lustgarten in front of the Berlin Palace.[85] *Das Zentrum Berlins* offered several possibilities for creating a central square for demonstrations without tearing down the palace. Likely, this was intended to convince Ulbricht to avoid demolishing the palace to create a square, although it is unknown whether any communication reached him on the matter.[86]

The official launching point for the reconstruction of Berlin was the SED's Third Party Congress in July 1950, which outlined a five-year-plan, including DM 4.12 billion for rebuilding fifty-three cities in the GDR.[87] On July 23, Ulbricht's speech "Prospects of the People's Economy" criticized recent planning efforts, indicated a need to incorporate lessons in "progressive city planning," and made public the shift in authority for planning Berlin to the Ministry of Building.[88] He declared that the thoroughfare from Stalinallee to the Brandenburg Gate would be the focus of reconstruction efforts and that the palace would be torn down to make room for a monumental square for demonstrations.[89] Absent a plan, Ulbricht spoke in general terms about the reconstruction, repeating socialist-realist ideas regarding the reconstruction of cities. The "new Berlin" was passé, the preferred term now being "Berlin, Capital of Germany," reflecting the GDR's "battle for German unity" against the West. Ruins were no longer attributed to "Hitler's war" but to "American imperialism"—a shift in culpability that would endure throughout the GDR's life. "The most important thing is that out of the ruins of the cities destroyed by American imperialists," Ulbricht wrote, "new cities arise, more beautiful than ever!"[90]

A group of architects under Kurt Liebknecht developed two designs of a "square for central rallies" and a proposed a building program for the city center, which were reviewed by Ulbricht on August 5, 1950.[91] The building program was developed into the *Plan des Neuaufbaus von Berlin* (Plan for the New Building of Berlin), approved at the Politburo meeting on August 15.[92] Descriptive guidelines and urban design plans centered on key areas around the city center, first and foremost, the "Main Thoroughfare: Stalinallee—Brandenburg Gate," specified by Ulbricht. While a plan for the entire city was infeasible, its symbolic core fell under control of the GDR, which would be reshaped as "capital of Germany." An attached "Demonstration Plan" estimated the capacity of the core for stationary demonstrations at 300,000 persons on a redesigned Lustgarten and for marching demonstrations at 160,000 persons per hour proceeding past a grandstand. The cost estimate and schedule indicated that the city center and Lustgarten were to be transformed in time for the parade on May 1, 1951.[93]

The budget included demolishing the Berlin Palace, establishing an open, paved area with a grandstand, and installing loudspeakers on the square and streets designated as the parade route. Ulbricht's fixation on reshaping the city center for parades was driving the planning process. Indeed, the only element in the plan not directly relevant to public ceremonies was the extension of Französiche Strasse from Wilhelmstrasse to Ebertstrasse to improve traffic circulation. The plan was approved by the Council of Ministers on August 25, with Grotewohl emphasizing that "the government will provide for the planned building of Berlin as the capital of Germany and that the implementation of this task is a matter for the entire German population" (figure 2.3).[94]

The MfA considered design competitions for Unter den Linden and

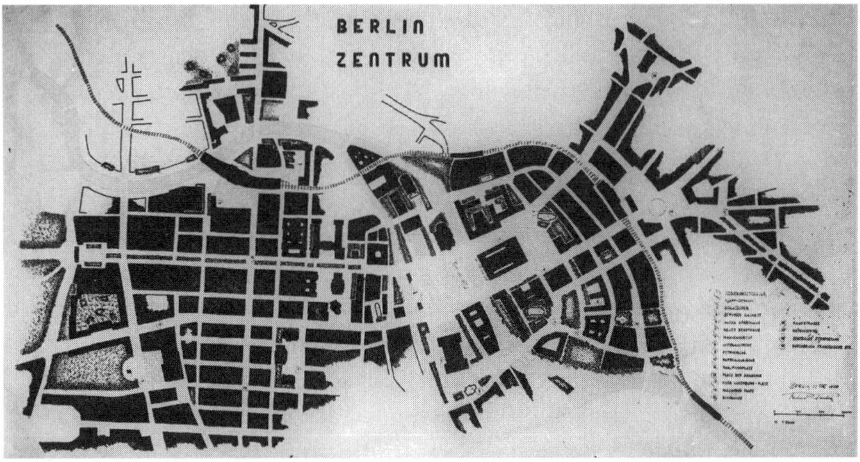

FIGURE 2.3. Plan for the New Building of Berlin, 1950. Major routes converge on the proposed Marx-Engels Square, the large white space at the center of the plan. The large black square to its right is the proposed government high-rise. BA-Digital Picture Database, Photo Image 183-R88645, *Allgemeiner Deutscher Nachrichtendienst—Zentralbild*, Schmidtke, August 1950.

the new Marx-Engels Square, but the Berlin Planning Commission convinced Bolz and Ebert to combine them in a "Competition Central Axis," announced in August 1951.[95] The political strategy was to retain East German control while asserting significance for all of Germany, an expression of the "antifascist democratic order" using the "design method" of socialist realism. All German citizens could enter the competition, but the jury included only East German politicians and architects. The goal was to design and build the center of "the capital of Germany, Berlin" with the involvement of "the entire German people" and an appeal to architects from "all of Germany to help fulfill this important task." Tradition figured in both historic preservation and the design of new buildings, which were to tie into Berlin architecture associated with "Schlüter, Knobelsdorff, Gilley, Schinkel, and Langhans," representatives of classical and baroque heritage. The "criminal Hitler war" had turned much of Berlin into a field of rubble, and the city was to be restored according to "natural and historic conditions."[96]

The Sixteen Principles advised consideration for nature in the layout of cities, but emphasized the urbanity of the city center. Aptly, the competition guidelines only considered nature in suggesting that the Spree should not be capped, and its banks and the square should be provided with greenery. In accordance with Ulbricht's view, Marx-Engels Square was described as the "traditional celebration and demonstration square of the working class," the "political and urban center point." A new high-rise on the square would terminate the Unter den Linden axis, architecturally dominate the silhouette of Berlin, and "be the most important political and social center of the capital and above and beyond this, all Germany."[97]

The competition "Central Axis Berlin" was never carried out, likely as Stalinallee demanded a total mobilization of resources and had become the focal point of the building effort. Marx-Engels Square was never completely ignored but remained of peripheral interest to planners, architects, and politicians until the late 1950s. In March 1954, Victor Baburov visited Berlin and largely approved of the plans. He agreed that the city should have "grandness and spaciousness in its facilities and squares (something like Paris), but on the other hand more humanity in overcoming 'Prussianness.'"[98] He emphasized the need for small squares around the city center and cited Berlin precedents such as the Chestnut Grove outside the Neue Wache and Gerndarmenmarkt. He called for idyllic, green spaces for pedestrians, in contrast to bourgeois, autocentric planning—a view that did not contradict the Sixteen Principles but stressed aspects he believed were neglected in the plan. In April, Herman Henselmann and Walter Ulbricht discussed the project and concluded that it may be possible to begin construction in 1960, but planning must be prepared beforehand. In October 1955 the MfA recommended a design competition for the center of Berlin, as the "architectural design of the city cannot go on without a plan for the entire center," but no action was taken.[99] Leading East German architects continued to produce new designs for Marx-Engels Square with a high-rise, although it was unclear what the building would contain.[100]

Socialist realism was accurately portrayed as a continuation of the neoclassical and baroque traditions, which have a long history in Berlin's urban planning. The preservation of historic architecture and streets, appeal to national traditions, and respect for place parallels the *Heimatschutz* tradition, which always had considerable support in Germany. Socialist realism provided the East German state a theory to engage cultural history and urban form in the service of state building, but its application to the city center plan, and other areas (discussed in the remaining chapters) raised complex issues that provoked considerable debate. East German claims that the plans were "democratic" or "German" rested on soft terrain as the approach was developed in the Soviet Union and imposed in Berlin. The proposed demolition of the Berlin Palace to create a square for demonstrations made an emphatic statement against preservation and local tradition. Moreover, the impact of new developments in construction technology and political change in the Soviet Union on city building would soon pose a challenge to fundamental tenets of socialist realism.

Competition for the Socialist Redesign of GDR's Capital

In September 1955, Konrad Adenauer outlined the Hallstein Doctrine to the West German parliament, asserting that the Federal Republic of Germany was the sole legitimate state representing the entire German people. A month later, parliament approved a "Capital City Berlin" design competition including both East and West Berlin, although the competition was not held until 1957–58.[101] The East German government responded with its own competition. East-West tensions had been increasing since the Soviets crushed the Hungarian Uprising, and Ulbricht, frustrated by the loss of refugees to the West, pressured the Soviet Union to take action on Berlin.[102] In contrast with Khrushchev's "peaceful coexistence," GDR politicians soon insisted that "ideological coexistence" between "capitalist and socialist architecture" was unacceptable. This, along with a continued desire to outperform the West in city building, made this an opportune moment to assert their own planning effort.[103] An early draft of the competition guidelines candidly stated: "The generous new shaping of the city center of Berlin will be a lively testimony to the entire German people of the superiority of socialism over capitalism."[104]

Unsurprisingly, the East German competition was designed with close consideration of the details of the West German competition. In July 1957 the meeting to set the groundwork for the competition noted that documents from the design competition of the "Federal Government and the Senate of West Berlin are in Mayor Ebert's possession."[105] The entire organization of the competition was set in relation to the West Berlin competition: "Schedule: the competition should run after the West Berlin competition, therefore after February/March 1958. (b) Participation:... open all-German competition planned... Special request for participation by experts from the GDR, Western Germany, foreign countries? Prizes? (Arrangement under consideration for the Western Berlin competition)."[106] Regarding the Cathedral, they questioned, "in West Berlin competition preservation or demolition?" Every detail was a potential point of contestation in an ideological battle. As the committee stated, "the political-ideological content of the competition must be clarified and formulated."[107]

Marked changes in city building practice and the political context resulted in considerable differences from the Central Axis Berlin competition. A shift toward industrialized building was initiated in the Soviet Union after Stalin's death. At the All-Union Conference of Builders, Architects, and Workers in Moscow in November 1954, Khrushchev denounced the excessive use of capital and labor to develop aesthetic buildings, while leaving the majority of the population in inadequate housing. Ulbricht followed suit in April 1955 at the First Building Conference of the GDR under the motto, "Build better, faster, cheaper." The goal was to quickly satisfy housing needs in an adequate manner, which would be achieved by reducing building costs through extensive standardization and industrialization of construction.[108]

Though socialist realism remained official theory, this shift in practice was greeted by many architects as an opportunity to return to modernism. Politicians and some leading architects rejected this possibility, suggesting that technologically advanced building techniques would be artistically employed to express social and national ideas. This required a deeper understanding of national tradition, studying not external form but the principles by which forms are developed. A period of confusion and competition ensued as professionals worked out the theoretical and practical details of socialist architecture and city building (see Chapter 6).[109] Efforts to clarify theoretical issues stimulated an "architecture discussion" in 1957. Richard Paulick maintained the importance of national heritage and insisted that Stalinallee was not a "detour," but rather a direct, if flawed, path toward an architecture that would reflect socialist society, a "socialist architectural style."[110] The claim is telling. The inability to theoretically reconcile national tradition with industrialized building, along with socialist state building, meant the "nation" would lose significance. At the Third Congress of the Bund Deutscher Architekten (BDA) in December, Ulbricht stated that the residential complex must reflect socialist living conditions.[111] While many architects believed industrialization would unify the architecture of East and West, the Congress concluded that socialist and capitalist architecture and city planning were incompatible.[112] Liebknecht framed the task of developing a new, industrialized architecture as a "component of our great plans for the Construction of Socialism" and "battle against the influences of anarchistic and formalistic building in the West."[113]

The quest for a New German Architecture had been displaced by the search for a "socialist architecture," whose defining characteristics would derive from standardization, industrialization, and technological progress. This emphasis was expressive of an emerging ideology centered on the power of scientific and technological progress. In fact, Gerhard Kosel's 1957 book *Produktivkraft Wissenschaft* had theoretically positioned science as a force of production, claiming to have recovered original Marxian postulates long forgotten by the Communist Party. In the book Kosel presented the "scientific-technical revolution" of the mid-twentieth century from a Marxist perspective, suggesting that under socialism the revolution would improve the relations of production, helping facilitate the transition to Communism. In 1961 the Soviet Communist Party adopted Kosel's formulation in its official ideological framework and resolved to place more weight on the role of science in the construction of Communist society.[114] Kosel's theoretical justification for industrialized building reflected a broader societal shift in which science and technology assumed a more central role in cultural discourse. Architects and engineers not only strove to harness these tools through industrialized construction but began to celebrate them in architectural form, displaying considerable similarity to Western midcentury (or organic) modernism. The professional and popular press distributed these images and highlighted the technical details of design. These cultural changes would be evident in the new plans for Berlin's city center and plans for Stalinallee (see Chapter 6).

In advance of the design competition, Kosel published in April 1958 a plan for the city center in *Deutsche Architektur*, proposing that a great work of architecture expressing the "victorious ideas of socialism" counter the "capitalist exploiter's world of 'bridgehead' West-Berlin" (figure 2.4).[115] Kosel maintained that clear direction was necessary to obtain good results from the upcoming competition and included five theses and a building program for the development of a Marx-Engels Forum. His plan embodied socialist-realist urban design, perhaps better than plans from the early 1950s. The city center would be marked by a central government high-rise with an extensive base, similar to Soviet designs, although the tower was simplified, modernist in appearance. The high-rise forecourt included a Marx-Engels Memorial and opened across the Spree to a large square on the former site of the Berlin Palace and a grandstand on the opposite side

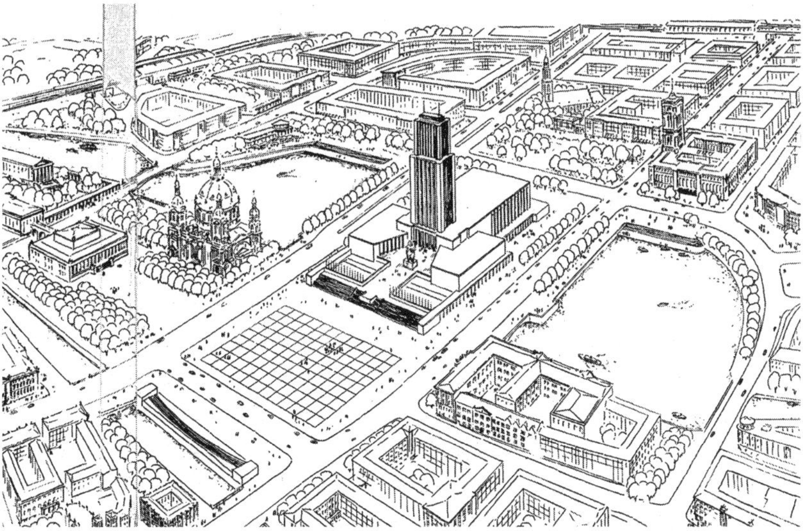

FIGURE 2.4. Kosel's Plan. Strong definition of streets and squares is maintained, although these forms would require conventional rather than industrialized construction. Demonstrators approaching from Unter den Linden (lower left) transition into the vast space of Marx-Engels Forum with the high-rise looming above them. The dominance of this government building is enhanced by widening the eastern arm of the Spree into a basin to its north and south and placing a park to its east. "Aufbau des Zentrums der Hauptstadt des demokratischen Deutschlands Berlin," *Deutsche Architektur* 7, no. 4 (1958): 180–181. Im Bestand der Staatsbibilothek zu Berlin—Preußischer Kulturbesitz.

of the Spree Canal. The Spree would be widened into pools in reference to the lakes of the surrounding landscape. A demonstration plan illustrated the accommodation of parade columns approaching and departing the central square. Nearby historic structures, including the Cathedral, Marienkirche, and the Schinkel-designed German Building Academy would be preserved. The main governmental and cultural buildings would enclose streets and squares, and monuments would honor Marx and great German socialists. The stretch of Stalinallee between Straussberger Platz and Alexanderplatz was shown to be lined with low-rise commercial buildings and residential slab buildings, making full use of industrial production. Further out, a ring of "dominants" would surround the area, just as the "seven sisters" ringed the Palace of Soviets in the plan for Moscow.[116]

Given Kosel's focus on industrialization, it may seem ironic that the strong street enclosure illustrated in the area surrounding the central square could only be realized through extensive use of traditional building methods (see Chapter 6), yet he maintained the need for an exceptional solution to the conditions of the center of the capital city in accordance with socialist realism. Henselmann saw the plan as an encroachment on his turf as chief architect of Berlin, however, and responded with a letter to Kosel (Ulbricht copied), rebuffing Kosel's narrow focus on the central square, which could only be effectively designed after the larger planning framework was established. Henselmann asserted that Berlin's planners had worked out the structure of the entire city, including a rational distribution of land uses, and these must be precedents for planning, rather than just "drawing little pictures" of the central square. The "socialist city center" would contrast with the "capitalist city" by having a much lower office density, a considerable residential population, only the most significant cultural institutions, and mass transit along with an expanded road network that could accommodate peak travel without difficulty. He condemned Kosel's architectural forms as a breach of socialist realism and Berlin tradition.[117] Henselmann published a plan for the section of Stalinallee between Straussberger Platz and Alexanderplatz, in which he criticized Kosel's plan as a "completely failed solution," suggesting that the necessary artistic mastery would emerge in the forthcoming design competition.[118]

In July 1958, with the Cold War under way, the SED's Fifth Party Congress was held under the motto, "Socialism Wins." The Party called for the "socialist redesign" of the city center, expressing not the nation but the new state and its ideals. City planning was to convince East and West Germans of the superiority of socialism and contribute to the construction of a successful, socialist state. Kosel drafted design guidelines that were approved by the Politburo on September 9, 1958. Core socialist-realist ideas from earlier planning efforts endured. The project area centered on the "central axis" from Unter den Linden to Stalinallee's Straussberger Platz. The competition was announced on October 7, the ninth anniversary of the GDR's founding. With increased political tensions and faded hopes for reunification in the short term, all-German aspirations and the "Battle for German Unity" receded. "Socialism" and posturing against the West came to the fore: "Socialism established all prerequisites for the constantly growing material and intellectual needs of the society to be given corresponding space and expression through the planned building of cities." The city center plan was to express "life as it is developing under socialism," in contrast to West German city centers which provided proof that rebuilding cities in the interest of the entire population is not possible in the "period of capitalist decay."[119]

The competition guidelines proclaimed Berlin the capital of the German Democratic Republic, not Germany. Architects and planners from the GDR and invited designers from "socialist countries" could participate, reflecting a demarcation from West Germany and identification with Soviet satellites. National tradition was never directly mentioned, although "the historically developed structure of the city [was] to be taken into consideration," and the existing differentiation of land uses in key locations was to be further pronounced.[120] Historic buildings on Unter den Linden would be preserved, and new construction on the street would respect the traditional 18-meter (about 59 feet) height limit. However, new architecture was not required to relate to tradition, even on Unter den Linden. Rather, the use of "newest technology and industrial building methods" was mandatory. Despite this, not any form of modernism would do. Ulbricht warned against the creation of a second Hansavierteil (Hansa Quarter), the product of the West Berlin competition.[121] Hansavierteil was comprised of showcase structures by leading architects set in a park-like surrounding. Heritage and place-based meaning were considered in the requirement for "a forum of the German working-class movement" that would accommodate 275,000 people. Working-class demonstrations and revolutionary activity on this site and current festivals of the East German state were presented as one continuous tradition that would inform the new design.[122] A Marx-Engels Memorial, grandstand for three thousand honored guests, and several key government and cultural institutions would be located there. Given the focus on developing a representative center, light, air, and green space were not addressed.

Fifty-seven entries were submitted before the jury's first meeting in August 1959. The degree to which these embodied socialist-realist or modernist principles varied considerably. Modernist structures were primarily simple rectangular buildings, fitting the international style. However, a technophilic, future-orientation manifest itself in several plans through slender towers ("steel-needles") and flying saucer–like structures, both condemned by the jury. These bore an uncanny similarity to Western midcentury modernism. For instance, Henselmann's plan (not part of the competition) included an assembly hall which seemed to anticipate the Theme Building (1961) at the Los Angeles Airport, proving his recent condemnation of Kosel's departure from socialist realism to be a political ma-

FIGURE 2.5. Henselmann's Plan (view from northwest). The jury noted that the attempt to give strength to the center of the capital with a technical apparatus (television tower) was unconvincing. The assembly hall, which resembled Western midcentury modernism, was ridiculed. Leibniz Institute fur Raumbezogene Sozialforschung, Abbildung A12-U11-004.

neuver (figure 2.5).[123] The jury panned Henselmann's structure as "absurd," "unfounded in its tectonic form," and disruptive of the ensemble. "Socialist architecture" would not follow this vein of modernism. Undeterred, Henselmann later requested to visit Brasilia, Brazil, where plans for a National Congress building had inspired Berlins' proposed "flying saucers." Ulbricht refused, as "we in socialist states develop our own architecture that does not stand in harmony with capitalist building."[124]

In accordance with Liebknecht's advice, there was no first prize. Second prize was awarded to Gerhard Kröber and his collective from Halle (figure 2.6). Two third prizes were awarded—one to a Herbert Schneider's collective from Dresden, another to Lüben Tonev's collective from Bulgaria (figures 2.7 and 2.8). The jury considered a wide range of the required criteria, and more, praising Tonev's incorporation of green space and promenades. However, comments on winning projects emphasized the composition of the central square, high-rise, and related structures. Kröber's winning entry stood out for a "grand scale" corresponding to the

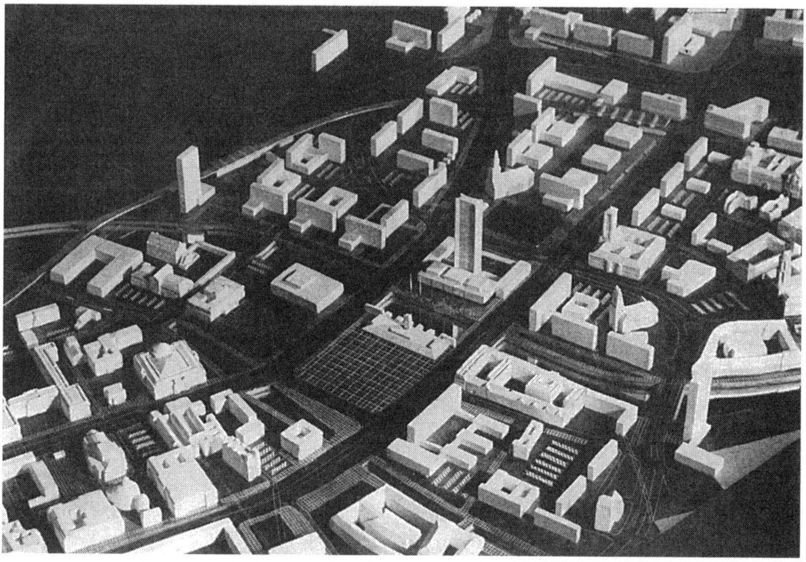

FIGURE 2.6. Kröber's Plan (view from southwest). The highest award given, second prize, went to Collective Gerhard Kröber from Halle. The jury appreciated the "grand scale" of the design as befitting socialism. The location of the high-rise east of the Spree and its orientation to Marx-Engels Square and to the east and west of Berlin were favorably noted. "Ideenwettbewerb zur sozialistischen Umgestaltung des Zentrums der Hauptstadt der Deutschen Demokratischen Republik, Berlin," *Deutsche Architektur* 9, no. 1 (1960): 9. Im Bestand der Staatsbibilothek zu Berlin—Preußischer Kulturbesitz.

"socialist development of Berlin," through a large open space combining Marx-Engels Square and the Lustgarten, the high-rise east of the Spree well connected to "Marx-Engels Square and the west of the city, as well as the east." The grandstand, to be erected for special occasions on the east side of Marx-Engels Square, across the Spree from the high-rise, was described as poorly related to that structure. Schneider's third-place winning design was considered "spacious," opening up the area between the S-Bahn and the central building by widening the Spree River into a broad basin providing passengers "an impressive view of the central ensemble." Tonev's third-prize winning design expanded Marx-Engels square seamlessly onto the Lustgarten by eliminating the Cathedral yet was criticized for placing the Council of Minsters building across its south end, which reduced the size of the space and blocked off Rathausstrasse. Neither Tonev's nor Alexander Naumov's central building were considered dominant enough. Naumov's and Kurt Leucht's central square failed to accommodate the simultaneous entry and exit of two separate columns, cutting the breadth of

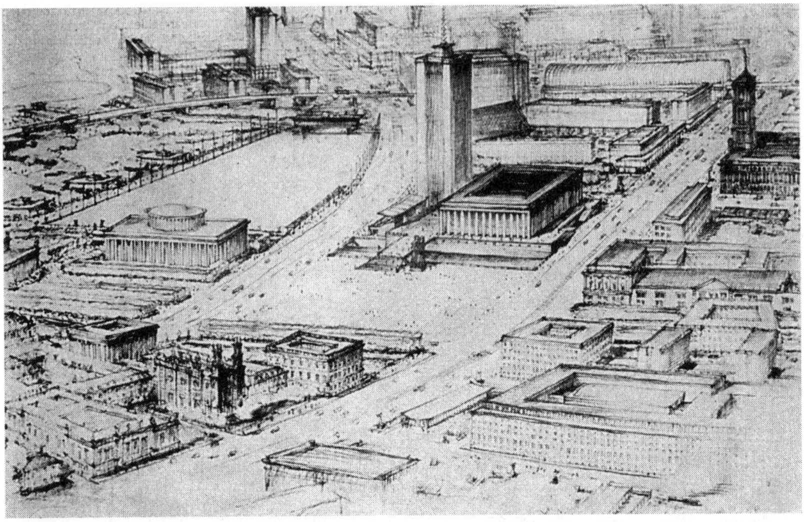

FIGURE 2.7. Schneider's Plan (view from southwest). The high-rise Council of Ministers building and the People's Chamber are grouped on the east side of the Spree. Their visibility from the S-Bahn across the newly created water basin was praised. A pedestrian bridge crosses the Spree to link these buildings to Marx-Engels Square, where a freestanding Marx-Engels Memorial is located. The jury found the strength of this connection to be insufficient. "Ideenwettbewerb zur sozialistischen Umgestaltung des Zentrums der Hauptstadt der Deutschen Demokratischen Republik, Berlin," *Deutsche Architektur* 9, no. 1 (1960): 10. Im Bestand der Staatsbibilothek zu Berlin—Preußischer Kulturbesitz. Permission obtained from Huss Verlag.

parade in half. Schneider was criticized for the poor relation of his Marx-Engels Memorial to the demonstrators, while Naumov was commended for its location in the center of the grandstand on axis with Unter den Linden. Its immense size would certainly have been considered as part of this equation.[125]

While many jury comments concerned socialist realism and traditional principles of urban design, modernist principles came to the fore in ways that left the plans suspended between paradigms. First, much of the architecture adjoining the central square was modernist. In Kröber's plan this was lauded for combining "Berlin's architectural traditions and the new conditions of industrial building," though the high-rise suffered from "arbitrariness," likely in reference to the use of metal poles as decorative elements near the top.[126] Second, in accordance with the requirement that Karl-Liebknecht Strasse and Rathausstrasse be built into traffic arteries, the resulting plans isolated the government center from its surroundings.

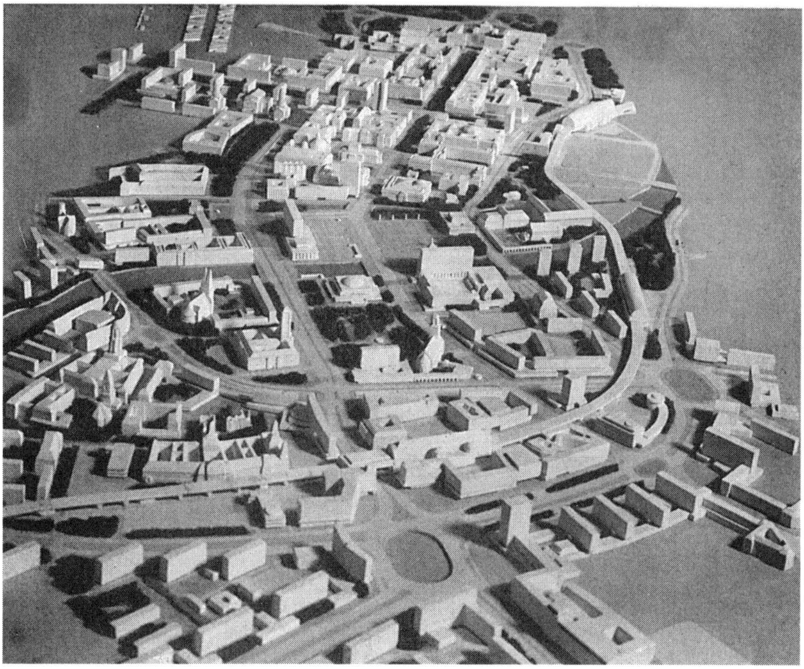

FIGURE 2.8. Tonev's Plan (view from east). The Council of Ministers building encloses the south end of Marx-Engels Square (left side of square in center), while the vertically dominant structure, the Marx-Lenin Institute, is located at the intersection of Unter den Linden and Marx-Engels Square (above center of square). The People's Chamber and assembly hall sit east of the Spree. "Ideenwettbewerb zur sozialistischen Umgestaltung des Zentrums der Hauptstadt der Deutschen Demokratischen Republik, Berlin," *Deutsche Architektur* 9, no. 1 (1960): 15. Im Bestand der Staatsbibilothek zu Berlin—Preußischer Kulturbesitz.

This is most pronounced in Schneider's design, in which an insular Marx-Engels Square is separated from the city on either side by a six-lane arterial road; the type of modernist incision that could hardly be justified as respecting the historic city, or the Eighth Principle of City Building, which stated: "[Traffic] may not tear up the city and be a hindrance to the population." Finally, some winning plans' demolition of the Cathedral and/or the Building Academy expressed modernist "creative destruction" better than socialist-realist respect for historic structure.

Neues Deutschland ran a full page on "The New Center of our Capital City" summarizing the jury's commentary and inviting the Berliners and residents of the entire Republic to view the models and provide their input, which it proclaimed "even more important than the work of the architects."[127] A month later, *Berliner Zeitung* published a similar public invitation, but the article only presented a Russian competition entry that, in recognition of the coming age of the automobile, planned streets adjoining Alexanderplatz that could carry ten thousand cars per hour. The key was removing the pedestrian, the "snails of street traffic," to an elevated pedestrian network similar to Norman Bel Geddes's urban vision from Futurama at the 1939 World's Fair.[128]

Helmut Hennig was assigned with evaluating public input. Naumov's futuristic design was chosen by 131 of the 420 visitors as their favorite, more than three times as many votes as the second most popular plan. Hennig claimed that many visitors found its grandness appropriate to socialism but disliked the "steel needle" and assembly hall that looked like a "flying saucer." In fact, *Berliner Zeitung* had already condemned Henselmann's similarly futuristic plan as utopian.[129] Whether this swayed public opinion or not, it revealed the official view. Hennig concluded that the public desired neither high-tech nor neoclassical but simple modernist structures; as one visitor commented, "neither a flying saucer nor a Walhalla." Yet he included among his "typical" comments, "With the exception of Naumov's and Henselmann's design, one does not detect anything of a vision for building in the age of communism and space travel."[130]

Some visitors missed small, intimate places, which Hennig interpreted as a misunderstanding of the significance of the city center for mass rallies. Nonetheless, Hennig was surprised that hardly anyone pleaded for the preservation of the Fischerkietz on the southern end of Spree Island. Though many of its small, premodern buildings had survived the war in good condition, most plans called for their demolition and replacement with large apartment houses.[131] Fischerkietz's intimate spaces and vernacular buildings from distant eras would have provided the type of connection to the past many Germans sought after the war.[132] In 1952 the preservationist Gerhard Strauss had pleaded on behalf of the Sperlingsgasse (Sparrow Alley) in Fischerkietz. This alley had been renown across Germany since the publication of Raabe's novel, *Chronic of the Sperlingsgasse* in 1856. Strauss argued that the alley was an irreplaceable part of Berlin's *Heimat* image, whose loss "would be seen by the German public as an intrusion in the national substance."[133] Yet the socialist-realist perspective on heritage centered on great works of architecture rather than the vernacular. This, and the site's location adjoining the very core of the new socialist city center, spelt its doom. Future planning called for the demolition of the Fischerkietz to create a "loosely" built and thoroughly greened area, befitting their goal of providing pleasant everyday spaces in the city center for residents and government workers.[134]

A selection of comments that aligned with the jury's conclusions were published in the press. They lauded the plans for creating a modern center and leaving the old city of rental barracks behind. Criticism was directed at plans preserving the Cathedral and those proposing structures previously denounced for excessive financial and technical demands. The implication is that industrialization depends upon standardization of parts, and the custom production of components for unique buildings would undermine the effort.[135]

In October 1959, Kosel presented Ulbricht with a revised version of the plan that he, Hopp and Mertens had previously developed for the city center. Nonetheless, the Politburo assigned the German Building Academy (Deutsche Bauakademie, DBA) with evaluating the competition results and formulating theses for the further development of the city center.[136] The jury's assessment of different aspects of each of the winning plans impacted the formulation of the theses. For instance, a lack of attention to the details of the entire planning area resulted in relatively detailed guidelines for different subareas. The specificity could be great, such as positioning the grandstand and Marx-Engels Memorial on axis with Unter den Linden. In this, and other ways, the theses took cues from Kosel's work, along with Henselmann's ideas about incorporating balanced land uses and Tonev's concept of a network of green space.[137]

To direct further planning, a Commission for Building the Berlin City Center was assembled, including politicians Paul Verner and Mayor Ebert (later Ulbricht and Grotewohl) and leading architects from the DBA and City of Berlin. Three collectives were formed to further develop plans, led by Hopp, Kröber, and Kaiser. In February 1960 three Russian architects—including Naumov, who had entered the design competition—submitted an expert opinion on the plans to the committee. They emphasized the importance of "organically combining new modern forms with the historically developed forms and structures of the city," creating a socialist ensemble of magnificent scale while maintaining the "old, traditional, German... national spirit." Their critique scrutinized the spatial composition of individual projects, condemned excessive demolition of historic urban fabric, and suggested that a dominant high-rise was inappropriate given the city's geographic and architectural structure (Naumov's plan had included a "flying saucer" and "steel-needle").[138]

In May 1960 the new plans were reviewed by the commission, which now included Grotewohl and Ulbricht, who offered a less nuanced view of spatial composition and criticized the architects for lacking political-ideological clarity. In contrast to Naumov, Ulbricht saw the absence of a high-rise in the new plan as a lack of insight into the "roll and perspective of the GDR," which "embodies the future of all of Germany... we are in the period of the victory of socialism and there can be no subordination to western Germany."[139] Ulbricht deduced that because West German firms are building high-rises, the "representative buildings of our Workers and Peasant's State" must be visible from far away. He concluded that a narrow group of qualified architects should continue the design effort. The architects presented their revised plan to the Politburo in April 1961 for discussion prior to approval by the City Council.[140]

Paul Verner introduced the plan, evidencing a continued devaluation of tradition and heightened emphasis on technological advancement and modern urban design. Verner's commentary on heritage was limited to a suggestion that "old valuable buildings must be incorporated into the urban design solution" and a recommendation that only the facade of Schinkel's German Building Academy be preserved and incorporated into a new building. The main principles behind architectural design were technological: "Construction activity must be carried out with the broadest application of industrialization in building, which results in new problems, which also have strong effects on architecture."[141] Concerns about insufficient technological development permeate Verner's report, most clearly regarding "modern technology for office buildings," of which Verner admitted, "America is the furthest," although the Soviet Union was quickly gaining experience. Scientific investigation of several aspects of construction (i.e., foundations, structural engineering, HVAC systems, etc.) was needed, although there "was a great deficiency of specialists and engineers in these areas." It went unmentioned that specialists such as these had been emigrating West in large numbers each year due to dissatisfaction with their situation under the construction of socialism. Verner made anecdotal mention of nature in the city in a characterization fitting modernist planning: "The new Berlin will be characterized by large squares, broad streets, a lot of green space and air in the center of the city." Otherwise, separating restaurants from office buildings would facilitate industrialized building and provide fresh air and exercise for office workers.[142]

Ulbricht commented on a range of topics, including the pressing need to establish standardized building types. The West remained a point of comparison. He called for a transportation system emphasizing subway and taxis rather than private automobiles; otherwise it may be faster to walk as in London, New York, and Paris. He demanded another solution be found for the roof of a building on Alexanderplatz, instead of copying American buildings. Finally, he emphasized that it is "absolutely necessary" that the high-rise bear the GDR state seal on all sides, illuminated at night. Moscow had embraced nighttime illumination of buildings as a sign of the modern city, yet the similarity to American corporate tradition seems ironic.[143] In 1962 conceptual design began for a forty-two-story government building with the state seal. Henselmann's sketches included a view from Charlottenburger Chausee, demonstrating its visibility from across the Wall, yet the plan was gradually forgotten.[144] With technological optimism ever-strengthening in the 1960s, an immense television tower was constructed near Alexanderplatz, taking a form reminiscent of Henselmann's condemned "steel needle" with a satellite-like sphere near the top.[145]

On April 21, 1961, *Neues Deutschland* reported on the new plan and building program for the city center recently approved by the City Council. Mayor Waldemar Schmidt explained the influence of the design competition and popular input provided during the exhibition, which occurred due to "Walter Ulbricht's demand." The West Berlin competition was described as an attempt to carry the Cold War into city planning and a "still-born child." The future center of Berlin would be "determined by us, the Berliners who love their city." The old city center was a "typical product of capitalistic-anarchistic development" destroyed by the "criminal policies of German imperialism and militarism." Unfortunately, individual works of "great master builders" and "our ancestors' hard work" were also destroyed—a clear denial of responsibility for the demolition of the Berlin Palace and the coming demolition of Schinkel's Building Academy. Several buildings on Unter den Linden would be restored according to their "historical character," including the Kaiser-Wilhelm-Palais, the "Kommode," and Prinzessinenpalais (Princesses' Palace). The program displayed an overwhelming future-orientation, emphasizing modern design, building technology, and a government center for an East German socialist state.[146]

On May 16, 1961, the *Berliner Zeitung* article "Starter's Gunshot for

Building the City Center" reported on the first excavations of the Haus des Lehrers (Teachers' Building) on Alexanderplatz and the coming restoration of the former Princesses' Palace as the Opera Cafe. An adjacent article, "700 Letters," reported on a City Council initiative to engage Berlin citizens, especially youth, in guiding planning efforts. Allegedly, seven hundred responses to a published draft of the plan for the city center demonstrated the "close relationship between the city council and the population, which the Schöneberger Rathaus [West Berlin] wouldn't dare dream of." The emphasis on youth assisting the "victory of socialism" continued an approach developed in the early 1950s. On May 21, *Berliner Zeitung* published a series of short interviews, expressing popular enthusiasm for the new building program. A twenty-three-year-old construction worker expressed pride in the quality of his work and the new buildings. He found it "great that our state puts so much trust in the youth," while older colleagues claimed that they never had any say in matters before. "When I go through our Berlin as a grandpa in 40 or 50 years, then I can say to my children and grandchildren, 'I helped make this. Our brigade, the youth brigade, poured the concrete slabs.'" Throughout the interviews the words "new" and "modern" are repeated and the only mention of historic Berlin was some criticism of "unhealthy apartments." Construction of the Berlin Wall had begun in April, a month before the "starter's gunshot." The GDR would indoctrinate the next generation into socialism in isolation from the West.[147]

The Politics of Ephemeral Urban Visions

A series of modernist plans were developed for the "New Berlin" between 1945 and 1949. In part, this occurred as most leading architects were dedicated modernists, but the paradigm appealed in other ways. The centrality of the functional necessities of daily urban life to this paradigm offered a radical remedy for the ills of the nineteenth-century industrial city and fit well with German Communists' materialist ideas about the path to a new human and a new society. Many Germans sought a break with the disastrous national past, and the style's radical break with traditional urban form physically manifest this, suggesting a newness, a New Berlin into which one could escape. While strongly associated with the Weimar era, the style was not without cultural baggage due to the National Socialists' development of modernist plans. Yet those plans were largely forgotten in the shadow of Albert Speer's neobaroque plans. Though not a blank slate, modernism remained less bound to cultural memory and more future-oriented than traditional planning, allowing considerable flexibility for the projection of cultural and political content. Hence the press attributed varied meanings to the plans, which were at times depicted as humanist, democratic, conserving *Heimat*, overcoming capitalist injustice, and contributing to national unity.

The shift to socialist realism in 1950 marked a return to well-established urban planning traditions in Berlin. For the theoretically informed, there was a hidden political utility. Socialist-realism's Marxist-humanistic foundation established architecture as an art that could educate citizens and shape society, thus politically advancing the rise of socialism through the language of local and national tradition. Yet by virtue of its Moscow origins, socialist realism bore specifically non-German associations. The plans even less so, as evidence of traditional urbanism was overshadowed by an exaggerated central square for demonstrations and dominant government building that were unmistakably Soviet. The "socialist" and "Soviet" origins were downplayed in the Eastern press, which depicted the plans as "antifascist" and representing the interests of the entire German nation. The city was heralded as the "capital of Germany" with the East German state leadership as its stewards. In this view, planning and construction of the capital was intended to win support for efforts to reunite the nation under an allegedly neutral government.

In response to West Berlin's efforts to host a design competition for Berlin, East German leaders organized a competition for the socialist redesign of the capital of the German Democratic Republic in the late 1950s. The shift to industrialized building and protracted theoretical debates drove many designers to mediate between socialist realism, modernism, the imperatives of industrialized construction, and in some cases their own technological optimism. Manifestations of the latter, expressed in architectural renderings of buildings shaped like flying saucers or "steel needles," were rejected by the state leadership but not because they fit the socialist-realist definition of "constructivism." The state esteemed technology for its contribution to productivity, and industrialization required the use of standardized building components. The unique structural components needed to build forms celebrating technological power diminished this capacity. Most plans were hybrids, but the degree of emphasis on one or more planning paradigms varied considerably. In contrast with the Communist press on modernist plans from the early postwar years, these were designated as "socialist" and expressions of the East German state rather than an advertisement for national reunification.

Throughout Berlin's history, planning was never separate from politics, as successive regimes believed it had utility in the pursuit of a range of social and political goals. It is unsurprising that effective planning could remain tied to claims of governmental competence, yet the endurance of an essentialist view attributing particular styles with inherent social or ideological values requires explanation. Radically different regimes—monarchal, Social Democratic, National Socialist, and Communist—proclaimed the same planning styles to be expressions of their values and sometimes shifted positions. City plans attract public attention briefly as new proposals, then fade from consciousness whether implemented or forgotten. Their impacts largely become part of the everyday world that were not identifiable as products of an abstract drawing from another era. Hence the public would have little awareness of past claims associated with plans. Even Berlin's architects, while familiar with the city and its history, evidenced only a brief time-horizon in their knowledge of planning history and politics, often extending no further than their professional careers. Regardless which paradigm was employed, throughout the struggle to resolve conflicting ideas about planning, many politicians and planners enthusiastically embraced the plans as an essential step toward building a new society.

3

Unter den Linden

Now representatives of the Soviet Control Commission have expressed . . . that the street, Unter den Linden, as principle street of the democratic sector of greater Berlin and as gateway from the western sectors, must be built up quickly and representatively.

—Lother Bolz, minister of construction, November 1950

THE BOULEVARD, Unter den Linden, evidences a centuries-long layering of Prussian-German architectural history. Its distinctive structures varied considerably in their size, architectural style, initial purpose, and subsequent use. On the one hand, the Socialist Unity Party (Sozialistische Einheitspartei Deutschlands, SED) viewed the boulevard as an urban design unit and at times made general policy statements regarding its future; on the other hand, they perceived immense differences in the meaning of key structures and dealt with them individually. After the war German Communists maintained iconoclastic views of the street's monumental buildings as expressions of monarchal rule, withholding emergency repairs as architecturally valuable structures decayed. With the introduction of socialist realism they were forced to accept these structures as architectural heritage and were pressured to consider them as architectural framing for the "central axis" parade route. Buildings that served cultural purposes were viewed most favorably and easily rehabilitated, while those that served military purposes were treated with more concern and reflection. Here more than anywhere, nuances of place, space, and representation were given detailed consideration.

Bridle Path, Via Triumphalis, Urban Center

In 1647, Friedrich Wilhelm, elector of Brandenburg, created a representative axis with six rows of lime and nut trees from the medieval city west to the Tiergarten. In ensuing decades, plans were developed to trans-

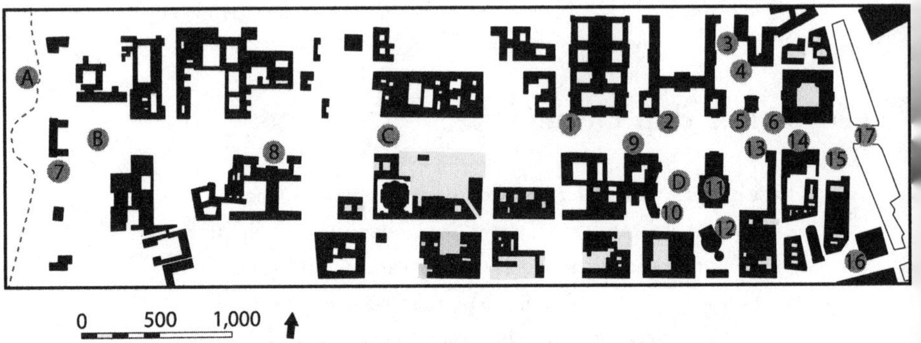

FIGURE 3.1. Map of Unter den Linden, late 1953. The considerable gaps between buildings on the west half of the street are mainly due to wartime destruction: (A) Sector boundary, (B) Pariser Platz, (C) Unter den Linden, (D) August-Bebel Square (former Forum Fridericianum), (1) Humboldt University, (2) State Library, (3) Singakademie, (4) Palais am Festgrabungen, (5) Neue Wache, (6) Arsenal, (7) Brandenburg Gate, (8) Soviet Embassy, (9) Kaiser Wilhelm Palace (Altes Palais), (10) Alte Bibliothek, (11) German State Opera, (12) Saint Hedwig's Cathedral, (13) Princesses' Palace (1963 Opera Café), (14) Crown Prince's Palace, (15) Site of demolished Neue Kommandantur, (16) German Building Academy, (17) Palace Bridge (across Spree to Marx-Engels Square). Map adapted from "Stadtzentrum der Hauptstadt Berlin, Bereich Straße Unter den Linden," *Deutsche Architektur* 10, no. 11 (1962): 637–638; "HistoMap Berlin" and "Berlin um 1953," both from http://histomapberlin.de/histomap/de/index.html. Cartography by Paul Stangl.

form this axis into a representative urban boulevard, as the centerpiece of an urban extension with adjoining secondary streets laid out in a grid, typical of late seventeenth-century Renaissance urban design.[1] Early in the eighteenth century, the Zeughaus (the Arsenal) and the Kronprinzenpalais (the Crown Prince's Palace) were constructed on eastern Unter den Linden (figure 3.1). Later that century, the city's defensive fortifications were demolished and a wall encompassing the new portions of the city was constructed as a customs barrier. The "Quarre" (later, the Pariser Platz) was built at the western end of Unter den Linden, and in 1791 the Brandenburg Gate was constructed. At the eastern end of the street, space opened by the removal of the old city walls was used to construct the Forum Fridericianum, which included the Deutsche Staatsoper (the German State Opera), Hedwig's Cathedral, and the Kommode (the Royal Library). Additional projects included a princely palace to the west of the Arsenal (now Humboldt University) and minor representative structures (figure 3.2).[2]

After the successful War of Liberation in 1815, the monarchy initiated a new round of construction transforming Unter den Linden into a *via*

FIGURE 3.2. Parade on Unter den Linden. President Paul von Hindenburg and others stand in front of the Neue Wache observing a parade down Unter den Linden in 1931. The corner of the Arsenal is visible along the left edge. Across the street from right to left is the edge of the Princesses' Palace, Crown Prince's Palace, the Neue Kommandantur (demolished 1946), and the Berlin Palace. BA, Digital Picture Database, B 145, Image P054274, Carl Weinrother, 1931.

triumphalis.[3] The wooden bridge connecting Unter den Linden to Spree Island was replaced by the representative Palace Bridge, including numerous classical sculptures. The Karl Friedrich Schinkel–designed Neue Wache (New Guardhouse) replaced an older nonrepresentative guardhouse and was flanked by statues of victorious Prussian generals. The construction of the Kaiser-Wilhelm Palace completed the basic form of the ensemble on eastern Unter den Linden. Nearby, the Singakademie was completed and the facade of the Crown Prince's Palace was built to its present form. In 1853 a height limit of four stories was established for new construction on Unter den Linden, to help maintain its architectural integrity.[4]

The founding of the empire in 1870 brought a construction boom to Berlin, adding commercial and industrial buildings of increased scale and eclectic architecture, primarily to the western and middle sections of Unter den Linden (by 1897, five stories were permitted). Variations among classical buildings had been quite minor in comparison to those rendered by this large-scale, historicist architecture, attributed to an increased bourgeoisie desire for self-representation. On eastern Unter den Linden the Deutsche Staatsbibliothek (the German State Library) was inserted in an architecturally appropriate manner.[5] There was little new construction during the Weimar Republic and the Nazi era. In the 1920s the Dresdner Bank, lining the rear of Forum Fridericianum (the Communist-era August-Bebel Square, now Opera Square) added two additional stories under protest from architects, planners, and art historians.[6] By the end of World War II, Unter den Linden's architecture was severely damaged, heaps of rubble blocked the street and in some places bomb craters extended down to subway platforms. The Brandenburg Gate, a crucial east-west connection, was blocked by a wartime barricade and rubble. Efforts to clear and restore the street and sidewalks would continue through 1945.[7] Decision-making regarding the fate of historic architecture lining the street would take considerably longer.

Effacement or Restoration?

Postwar, Berlin's planners and historic preservationists struggled with limited success to secure funding for provisional repairs to secure historic buildings against weather damage and looting. The Soviet Military Administration (SMAD) initially displayed little interest in the street's architecture regardless of its artistic or historic significance but brought buildings that could accommodate political activities into a usable state. Undertaking provisional repairs and renovations for utilitarian purposes rather than restoring architectural integrity, the SMAD was not applying a socialist-realist perspective. In the summer of 1947 the Soviets began taking an interest in architectural value in select cases, typically involving self-representation. Yet during this same period German Communist policy-making ensured the neglect and further decay of much national architectural heritage associated with the Prussian-German monarchy and military, because they viewed buildings as expressions of their patrons and held the Prussian monarchy to be the font of German militarism (see Chapter 2).

The founding of the East German State enabled the restoration of Unter den Linden's historic structures and spaces by establishing a political-economic framework capable of large-scale reconstruction and empowering a government interested in city building as a political tool. While many German Communists would have applauded the demolition of historic buildings, the adoption of socialist realism proved essential to their restoration. Observing its tenets, the East German political and cultural elite decided that state-run parades would proceed along Unter den Linden and culminate in the Lustgarten, which was to be expanded into a much larger Marx-Engels Square through the demolition of the Berlin Palace. The ensemble of historic buildings lining Unter den Linden would provide a frame for parades that associated the new state with German national culture. Hence the Plan for the New Building of Berlin, approved by the Politburo on August 15, 1950, designated numerous buildings on Unter den Linden for restoration.[8] Soon thereafter, the Berlin Planning Commission began searching for new uses for these structures, thus the symbolic value of their architecture as national cultural heritage was now primary, and their spatial capacity and potential future function was secondary.

Soviet representatives reviewed the new plans for Berlin in October 1950 and informed German planners that because Unter den Linden was "the principle street in the democratic sector of greater Berlin and gateway from the western sectors," it must be quickly built up in a "representative form."[9] Lieutenant-Colonel Martyshin emphasized the importance of providing evidence of the *Neuaufbau* from the sector border. The Soviets had been planning a replacement for their new embassy on eastern Unter den Linden near the Brandenburg Gate since 1947, and it was under construction before the GDR was founded.[10] Befitting its larger role in Berlin, the new structure would spread across several adjoining buildings. This first socialist-realist building in Berlin expressed its monumentality through the classical architectural tradition.[11] Soviet aggrandizement was perhaps a factor influencing their call for more building on Unter den Linden, but more broadly the embassy and all buildings on the street would contribute to the creation of a monumental government center. The Soviets had indicated the importance of Unter den Linden during the Trip to Moscow and now highlighted the importance of architectural framing on the new central square. While the GDR was left to reconstruct most of Unter den Linden, the Soviets maintained control over their embassy, which was omitted from discussions of Berlin planning.[12] The embassy was also largely absent in the East German press. The official view of Soviet-German relations was publicized through Liberation Day at the Soviet Memorial in Treptow, highlighting Soviet sacrifice rather than Soviet rule.

Although Bolz's primary interest was the reconstruction of Marx-Engels Square (the area of the former Lustgarten and the Berlin Palace) and Stalinallee, he acknowledged the political necessity of following this advice.[13] He proposed a design competition for Unter den Linden open to all Germans, East and West, and received Ulbricht's approval. Bolz informed East Berlin's mayor, Friedrich Ebert, that a competition announcement was required, emphasizing the need to take advantage of its propagandistic value.[14] In January 1951 the competition area was expanded to include the Brandenburg Gate and the Lustgarten.[15]

The draft for a competition "Central Axis Berlin" lay on Prime Minister Otto Grotewohl's desk in August 1951. Unter den Linden was divided into three sections, from west to east: (1) Pariser Platz to Wilhelmstrasse; (2) Wilhelmstrasse to Charlottenstrasse; and (3) Charlottenstrasse to the former Palace Bridge (the eastern end). The first section would include embassies, hotels, and administrative offices, and few existing structures were to be preserved; the Brandenburg Gate was to be restored, while Pariser Platz was to maintain an enclosed character. The second section would contain buildings for political organizations, "People's Own" businesses, upscale restaurants, hotels, travel agencies, and so on. The third section, which contained many of the oldest historic structures, would preserve all existing buildings.[16] The competition was never held. Resources and attention soon shifted to the massive Stalinallee development, where the National Aufbauprogram (the National Building Program) began constructing housing for workers on a monumental, mixed-use boulevard (see Chapter 6). However, restoration projects were regularly undertaken on Unter den Linden throughout the life of the GDR, often focusing on one key structure with considerable press attention. The processes leading to the reconstruction of key historic structures on Unter den Linden are analyzed below.

State Opera

The case of the State Opera (Staatsoper) illustrates the Soviet focus on the spatial capacity of buildings and the radical impact of socialist realism on the preservation of national architectural heritage after the founding of the GDR (figure 3.3). The State Opera was constructed between 1741 and 1743. Georg Wenzeslaus von Knobelsdorff designed the neoclassical structure with a prominent portico resembling a Greek temple. During the war the building's interior was heavily damaged, the exterior less so.[17] From a socialist-realist perspective, the building represents the best of Germany's progressive traditions in both form and content.

In the summer of 1945, at the behest of the SMAD, the Berlin Mag-

FIGURE 3.3. German State Opera. This photo of the State Opera was taken in 1951, just days before a resolution was passed to restore the structure. The decision was celebrated in the press as the opera was emblematic of "progressive cultural tradition" for both its architecture and function. BA, Digital Picture Database, Image 183-11116-0001, *Allgemeiner Deutscher Nachrichtendienst-Zentralbild,* Schmidtke, June 1951.

istrat began renovating the State Opera and several other theaters to facilitate the restoration of theater activity to reeducate the German population by restoring humanistic national traditions and to present a positive image of the Soviet Union.[18] German and Soviet classics, as well as works banned by the Nazis, would be presented. Most of the buildings were of modest architectural and historic value, chosen for their spatial capacity; there is no indication that the State Opera was thought of any differently. After the founding of the GDR, the Plan for the New Building of Berlin called for the full restoration of the State Opera. The Berlin Planning Commission developed a program to restore the building to its original form and function as a conservatory; the commission obtained approval from the Ministry of Building.[19] In June 1951, in the presence of "famous German composer Erich Kleiber," the government decreed that the building be reconstructed as an opera with extensive consideration for the original architecture.[20] A committee was formed to collect and examine the original plans, and a second group under architect Richard Paulick carried out the design work. The project was estimated at a cost of DM 21 million, far more than granted any project prior to the state founding.[21] Paulick described the restoration as "a culture-building [process that] documents most effectively our will to peace, our battle for peace, the will to preserve and care for our cultural heritage, in order to fill it with a new content and develop it further in new buildings."[22]

According to socialist realism, both the form and the content of the State Opera were models of "progressive" architecture, thus it was chosen as a showpiece of preservation. Although opera was considered a progressive cultural tradition, it began as a function of courtly salons, thus spaces housing opera were usually linked with palaces. Here, its location in a freestanding building adjoining the Forum Fridericianum was taken as an expression of a struggle, "to free [opera] from the servile role to which absolutist monarchy had belittled it."[23] The building's architecture was viewed as a "breakthrough to early classicism," preceding progressive changes in the opera itself, which would reveal "the opposition between the ascendant bourgeois against the dissipate life of the absolutist princes." Having simultaneously shown a "progressive content and a new form," it was an ideal choice for the new state's seminal restoration project.

Singakademie and Palais am Festungsgraben

In contrast to the State Opera, the restoration of the Singakademie and adjoining Palais am Festungsgraben marked the commencement of Soviet interest in Berlin's architecture for purposes of self-representation and the selective application of socialist realism as part of a cultural-political response to increased East-West tensions (figure 3.4). The Singakademie, a small neoclassical concert hall, was constructed between 1824 and 1826 for Berlin's choral society, a bourgeois alternative to the courtly opera.[24] Thus from a socialist-realist perspective this building, like the State Opera, represented a progressive tradition both in terms of its form and content.

The Singakademie was obliterated to near its foundations during the war, while the Palais am Festungsgraben escaped with moderate damage. In 1947 the SMAD commandeered and reconstructed both buildings, displaying an interest in Prussian-German heritage at a time when many German Communists preferred its effacement.[25] This new "House of Soviet Culture" opened a theater in May 1947, proclaiming it an "act of great significance for our cultural life and peaceful understanding between peoples."[26] The building's connection with German classical heritage was

FIGURE 3.4. House of Soviet Culture. This reconstruction of the former Singakademie would serve as the theater for a new "House of Soviet Culture." Like the State Opera, it neatly fit the socialist-realist understanding of progressive cultural tradition. BA, Digital Picture Database, Image 183-11844-0006, *Allgemeiner Deutscher Nachrichtendienst-Zentralbild*, Martin Schmidt, 11 September 1951.

indicated as a basis for its present use, which, according to one SMAD representative, included introducing the population of Berlin to the cultural life of the Soviet Union, thereby enabling them to receive a "truthful image of the country."[27] Soviet and German theater performances and art exhibitions would demonstrate their common classical heritage.

In June 1947 the Society for the Study of Soviet Culture (renamed the Society for German-Soviet Friendship in 1949) was established and given control of the building. After the founding of the GDR, control of the House of Soviet Culture was transferred to the new German state, as "proof of the generosity of the Soviet Union and its trust in strengthened German democracy."[28] The state seal was added to the tympanum on the facade of the theater building, demonstrating the new state's close association with the Soviet Union and respect for Soviet culture.[29] In socialist-realist terms the new use represented a continuity of theme as a venue for classical culture, while its societal idea was shifted to emphasize Soviet culture, to rectify popular bias.[30] This extension of Soviet interest to representative architecture was likely a response to increased East-West tension in the summer of 1947, as the hardening of sectoral boundaries provided greater incentive for long-term investment in cultural politics.

Neue Wache

Although subject to the same ideological and political forces as the previous cases, the Neue Wache's unique place-based and spatial qualities resulted in a considerably different path to restoration (figure 3.5). The Neue Wache was designed by Karl Friedrich Schinkel and is considered one of the most significant nineteenth-century classical buildings in Germany. Despite the efforts of planners and preservationists to restore the Neue Wache, it was left to decay during the early postwar years, ignored by the SMAD because it lacked spatial value and intentionally neglected by the Magistrat because it was associated with Prussian-German militarism. This later characteristic resulted in extensive debate over its restoration and especially its reuse after the founding of the GDR, when other historic structures faced little controversy.

Early History

The Neue Wache was built between 1816 and 1818 following victory over Napoleon in the War of Liberation. The upgraded status of militarism in Prussian society was evident in its design. Its form synthesized elements of a Roman castrum, four corner-towers and an interior courtyard, with a Greek temple, the entrance portico in the Doric order. Winged goddesses of victory appeared on the portico's entablature, Victoria as a conquering hero graced the tympanum, and statues of Prussian generals Scharnhorst and Bülow flanked the structure. Additional militaristic expression included a display of cannons looted by the Prussian army in the surrounding chestnut grove (expanded after the Franco-German war of 1870 and 1871) and the changing of the guard in front of the building, a popular attraction for Berliners.[31]

With the end of the German monarchy in 1918, the Neue Wache lost its function and various new uses were considered. In 1930 the Prussian government decided that it would be renovated as a national memorial for the fallen veterans of World War I, citing the significance of its role as a monument to the War of Liberation. A design competition was held calling for a simple, solemn design appropriate to the graveness of the

FIGURE 3.5. Neue Wache. Considerable damage is evident on the exterior of the building and the interior was burned out. In 1950 an additional section on the right side of the portico collapsed. To the right of the picture, a gaping hole is evident in the portico on the western facade of the Arsenal. BA, Digital Picture Database, Image 183-M1205-329, *Allgemeiner Deutscher Nachrichtendienst-Zentralbild*, Otto Donath, Autumn 1945.

time. Heinrich Tessenow's winning entry was implemented with minor changes. Interior partitions were removed to create a single room focused on a "large, dark, sarcophagus-like stone" bearing a gold- and platinum-plated oak wreath. This Gedächtnisstätte für die Gefallenen des Weltkrieges (Memorial for the Fallen of the World War) was dedicated on June 2, 1931. Once in power, the Nazis designated the memorial Ehrenmal für die Gefallenen des Weltkrieges (Memorial of Honor for the Fallen of the World War), marking a shift in emphasis from quiet remembrance of the dead to glorifying soldierly death. "Hero's Day" activities were centered there, and whereas two police officers surveyed the building during the Weimar Republic, a military watch was returned to duty. The Neue Wache was heavily damaged in World War II. The interior had been burnt out, and the far right side of the portico had collapsed.[32]

The Neue Wache after the War

For Berliners the Neue Wache remained a memorial as they continued laying flowers at the ruinous structure after the war. A preservationist assessed the damages and proposed provisional repairs to secure the building for a negligible expenditure, yet the Communist-controlled Magistrat did nothing. In 1949 suggestions from German Communist organizations included demolition, reconstruction as a Goethe-memorial, and reconstruction as a gateway to the House of Soviet Cultures. In contrast, Tessenow proposed leaving the building in its present condition as a historical reminder, a rejection of the militaristic past.[33]

In early 1950 a further section of the portico collapsed, but later that year the Plan for the New Building of Berlin marked the building for restoration.[34] Despite this, the Berlin Planning Commission continued to consider arguments for demolition, before acknowledging that it must be preserved.[35] The structure's newfound status as important classical heritage demanded its reconstruction and reuse, suppressing iconoclastic impulses but not dispelling reservations about the structure's militaristic associations. Initial repair work was of a provisional nature, employing inappropriate materials, removing sculptures from the tympanum and entablature, removing the flanking statues of Generals Scharnhorst and Blücher, and leaving the interior open to the sky.[36]

The Berlin Planning Commission considered possibilities for the building's future use, including the previously mentioned Goethe memorial and a gateway to the House of Soviet Cultures, along with an exhibition space/Schinkel museum and a memorial (*Denkmal*) for the victims of imperialistic wars.[37] Walter Pisternik of the Ministry of Building (Ministerium für Aufbau, MfA) reported on the meeting to Willi Stoph of the SED's Central Committee, favoring the memorial idea, while warning that it may "remind a portion of the people of the past purpose [but this could be remedied by covering] the preceding content over with the [new] content, 'victims of imperialistic wars.'"[38] Rudolf Michealis of the Magistrat's Department of Education also expressed concerns that certain uses would allow the public to continue to view the site as an *Ehrenmal*, elevating militarism, and suggested that the building become a "guardhouse of peace." As Unter den Linden is the "approach for parades heading to Marx-Engels Square, the political center of the capital of Germany," the Neue Wache would serve those fighting for peace now and in the future, rather than yesterday's victims, who could be honored in "one of Berlin's cemeteries."[39] The intention was to restore the original function for a new purpose, thereby providing an assembly ground for "peace-fighters" while preserving cultural heritage and acting as a "symbol of... national achievement." Michealis, who joined the SED with the hopes of propagating his deeply held anarchistic beliefs, was nonetheless in line with the Communist shift away from honoring victims to emphasizing martyrdom and the fight for socialism.[40]

Both the "memorial to victims of fascism and war" and "guardhouse for peace" were inconceivable prior to the introduction of socialist realism, which enabled planners to separate the artistic value of the Schinkel-designed structure from political content to preserve architecture as national heritage. In the former, the most recent theme, "war memorial," would be maintained, whereas the idea would change from glorifying the deaths of German soldiers to quietly remembering all victims of imperialistic wars. The latter concept reclaims the original theme of guardhouse, combined with a new societal idea: fighting for peace. The result is a symbolic guardhouse for peace, instead of an actual guardhouse defending the monarchy. Concerns about misinterpretation by the public rather than theoretical correctness were undoubtedly the basis for the indecision that followed, as the Berlin SED suggested further proposals be developed with "a content that represents our battle for peace in an appropriate form."[41]

The matter did not return until 1955, when Berlin's deputy mayor Fechner prompted the Historic Preservation Department to address the future use of the structure. This office determined that along with Schinkel's exterior, Tessanow's interior should be preserved for its artistic and symbolic value. This form necessitated its continued use as a memorial, and the following year, the Magistrat resolved that the Neue Wache be renovated as a "memorial (*Mahnmal*) for the victims of fascism and both world wars." In 1957 the shoddy renovations from the early 1950s were removed, and the building was reconstructed. Plans for Tessenow's interior were obtained from West Berlin, and the interior was restored with the original, partially melted granite block remaining in place. The Nazi-added cross on the back wall was replaced with a bronze plaque stating, "Den Opfern des Faschismus und Militarismus" (To the victims of fascism and militarism).[42] The restoration paralleled the establishment of memorials at concentration camps, which honored victims primarily to glorify the resistance fighter and victory over fascism and to relate this to present struggles and future achievement.[43] Thus the memorial could be as future-oriented as the "guardhouse for peace" with the advantage of co-opting victims' suffering to bolster its claims.

In December 1959, in light of the upcoming fifteenth anniversary of Liberation Day, the Politburo renamed it Memorial (Mahnmal) for the Victims of Fascism and Militarism and ordered minor modifications to the interior.[44] The restored statues of the "generals of the Wars of Liberation against Napoleonic foreign-rule," removed in May 1951, would be placed in the park next to the State Opera.[45] The turn to "national history writing" in 1952 meant that these generals were no longer part of a reactionary tradition, due to their roles in the progressive War of Liberation and were now suitable for display in public.[46] However, their original location was avoided due to fears that it would encourage militaristic interpretations of the memorial. As an additional safety measure, all iconological and rhetorical references to their identity were to be removed (including the Prussian Eagle) beyond the personal names as well as birth and death dates of the generals.[47] In February 1960 the Berlin Magistrat ordered the renovation of the Neue Wache according to the designs of the Politburo, although the *Berliner Zeitung* attributed the decision to the Magistrat.[48] The memorial was dedicated on Liberation Day, in a ceremony including Walter Ulbricht, Otto Grotewohl, and "many well-known personalities."[49] Deputy Mayor Schmidt called for the remembrance of "victims of two world wars who were driven to their deaths by German militarism"; he declared that this militarist legacy had been overcome in the GDR but needs to be realized in the "Western Zone."[50] Such use of the memorial as a storehouse from which to retrieve years of tradition in service of East German policy endured as long as the GDR.

In January 1969 the Politburo approved the renovation of the interior of the Neue Wache for the upcoming twentieth anniversary of the GDR. The melted granite block was removed and replaced with a prismatic glass block bearing an eternal flame just behind the tombs of the unknown soldier and the unknown resistance fighter, and the GDR's state seal was engraved on the back wall; remembrance of war was sanitized and placed directly in service of state.[51] The trajectory of the Neue Wache is illustrative of the complex dynamics of the society-space relationship during these years. During the early postwar years German planners sought restoration for architectural value, German Communists sought effacement of a symbol of Prussian-German militarism, and the SMAD remained indifferent due to its lack of spatial capacity. After 1949, socialist realism provided a theoretical basis for fully rectifying and restoring the building; however, continued concerns about its militaristic associations resulted in a considerable delay in finding an appropriate new theme and led to the spatial severing and iconographical cleansing of the statues of Generals Scharnhorst and Bülow.

FIGURE 3.6. The Arsenal on May Day. Parade participants proceed past the Arsenal and across the Palace Bridge on May Day 1952. The flag of the Free German Youth (FDJ) is visible in the lower-right corner. BA, Digital Picture Database, Image 183-14500-0098, *Allgemeiner Deutscher Nachrichtendienst-Zentralbild*, May 1, 1952.

The Arsenal

Like the Neue Wache, the Arsenal suffered from associations with the Prussian military tradition; however, it was rectified considerably earlier, due to an exceptional confluence of Soviet interest in its spatial capacity and representative value as well as the mobilization of key German cultural and political elites in Berlin. The Arsenal was built between 1695 and 1730 to store weapons and other devices of war (figure 3.6). In 1877, no longer suited to its original purpose, it became a historical museum for weaponry, artillery, and engineering as well as a storehouse of the trophies, uniforms, and personal effects of the royal house and famous military leaders.[52] The Arsenal survived World War II with moderate damage, including the destruction of many sculpted stone elements.

From Symbol of Prussian Militarism to Art Museum

Almost immediately after the war the future of the Arsenal became a subject of contestation. Key participants included the SMAD, Deputy-

Mayor Ferdinand Friedensburg (of the Christian Democratic Union, Christlich Demokratische Union, CDU), Dr. Iwan Katz of the Magistrat's Planning Department, and Professor Ludwig Justi from the Magistrat's Office of State Museums, formerly director of the National Gallery in Berlin.[53] In the summer of 1945 the SMAD, interested in the Arsenal for its spatial capacity, arranged for control of the building to pass to Katz and prompted the Magistrat to carry out minor repairs to make the ruinous structure habitable.[54] In October the Allied Control Council ordered that the contents of the museum be liquidated, that the building become a "symbol of peaceful reconstruction" and be made available for exhibitions.[55] In December the SMAD pressured the Magistrat to speed up their work so that the exhibition, *Products of Industry and Workshops in the Soviet-Occupied Zone*, could open on time.[56] The Magistrat financed the exhibition and completed some repairs yet lacked sufficient materials and left the Arsenal partially exposed for the winter.[57] Throughout 1946 the building continued to be used for exhibitions serving Soviet interests.[58]

In response to this neglect, Berlin planning and historic preservation staff members sought funding to effectively preserve the structure and argued for its full restoration. They lauded its architectural value and depicted the building as free from militarism, references to its significance thus tended to avoid the topoi "German" and "Prussian" in favor of "Berlin," "European," "international," and "world."[59] The Magistrat approved limited funds in September 1946, but building materials were lacking and it was claimed that an official Soviet command was necessary to receive preferential treatment in the distribution of material and labor.[60] In early 1947 a city staff member brought the Arsenal to the attention of Dr. Justi, who enlisted Mayor Friedensburg to argue for its use as a museum.[61] In July, Friedensburg convinced Soviet Deputy-Commandant Alexej Jelisarov to verbally order the building's transfer to the Magistrat's museum administration and have the SMAD assume responsibility for its reconstruction. On July 15, Friedensburg reported on this meeting to the Magistrat, and a conflict emerged between Justi and Katz, who preferred using the building for exhibitions and noted that the Soviets had reneged on several verbal agreements regarding the building over the past two years.[62] The Soviet organ, *Tägliche Rundschau*, published an essay on August 6, 1947, attacking the Planning Department's inability to restore the building and its inappropriate use for exhibitions, including its "desecration" with a rabbit exhibition.[63] Katz responded in the same newspaper, claiming to act in the interests of the working class. He asserted that only old men with an outdated Wilhelminian, militaristic view saw the exhibitions as a desecration and that their desire to return its "past character" was exactly what antifascists did not want.[64] A final response by the paper countered that the goal was not to restore its warlike character but to display art being stored in damp cellars.

In September 1947 the Magistrat approved a proposal requesting funds to weatherproof the building, the first of three phases to renovate the building as a "Central Museum of Berlin"—as specified at the July meeting.[65] The exhibit *Masterworks of German Sculptors and Painters* opened on October 20; however, four days later General Alexander Kotikow, commandant of the Soviet Sector of Berlin, transferred the building to the SMAD-controlled German Department of Education. Friedensburg protested the transfer to Kotikow and Jelisarov, who countered that building was "too important" to leave under the control of the Magistrat, because it was ultimately subject to the City Council, which they could not trust—as it was controlled by the western Social Democratic Party (SPD).[66] The building would now serve Soviet cultural political purposes by displaying "peaceful German art," thereby restoring progressive national traditions, and more directly political purposes, such as the 1948 exhibition on industrial production in the Soviet Zone.[67]

The German Historical Museum

Soviet intentions for the Arsenal took form in February 1948, when the German Education Administration in the Soviet Zone contracted the reconstruction of the Arsenal as a "house of culture," contributing to the development of "our entire people"—all Germans.[68] The building thus was commandeered into the proclaimed "battle for German unity" of the Socialist Unity Party (SED); it would be restored to its original form and include space for exhibitions and a variety of cultural activities including a theater. The Soviets were to be thanked that it was not being destroyed as a "symbol of Prussian Militarism." In 1949 rubble was cleared and the restoration of the exterior-sculpted stonework was initiated.[69] After the GDR's founding, the Ministry of Education assumed control over the project," now the "Museum of Cultural History," and restoration was slated to commence on June 1, 1950.[70] However, an interior pillar collapsed and it was determined that the vaulting would be replaced by a steel frame and modern interior in the Linden wing due to temporal pressure as the exhibition

History of the Revolutionary Workers' Movement was scheduled to begin in April 1951. The SED's Central Committee further developed the museum concept, and in September 1950 the project became a "Museum of German History," to present the new generation of Germans, East and West, with a Marxist-Leninist view of history.[71]

While architects and preservationists considered details of the restoration, Walter Ulbricht expressed concerns that the Arsenal protruded onto the course of parades headed for Marx-Engels Square; he ordered that work be broken off while plans were developed for setting the facade back.[72] The Planning Commission argued against this action on the grounds that the building's position was not a significant factor in determining the breadth of parades, and the move would not improve the view of the grandstand but would destroy the symmetry of the building, damaging its function enclosing the Lustgarten.[73] Ultimately Kurt Liebknecht, president of the German Building Academy, managed to convince Ulbricht to abandon his idea.[74] Work on the building was carried out in phases lasting until the mid-1960s. Examining the content of the building in terms of socialist realism, there existed a continuity in theme, as the building remained a museum; in accordance with the broader shift in societal ideas, it went from a museum of "Prussian and German military history" to a "Museum of German History" narrated from a Marxist-Leninist perspective.[75] Ulbricht's threatened alterations resulted from his disregard for socialist realism's valuation of architectural heritage, desire for personal aggrandizement, and fascination with parades witnessed in Moscow.

Like the Neue Wache, the Arsenal pitted German planners' aspirations for preserving architectural heritage against German Communists' will to efface Prussian militarism. In this case, however, the building's spatial capacity drew the SMAD to immediately order a few emergency repairs. In 1947 the SMAD responded to an intensive preservation effort by the German cultural elite as they recognized the potential use of the building's symbolic and spatial value in serving cultural policy. With the adoption of socialist realism, the concept of a German history museum with a Marxist-Leninist perspective was developed.

Additional Sites on Eastern Unter den Linden

Due to limited resources, a number of historic structures on eastern Unter den Linden were not restored until the late 1950s and 1960s, including Hedwig's Church, the Kaiser Wilhelm Palace, the Royal Library, the Crown Prince's Palace, the Princesses' Palace, and large sections on Humboldt University.[76] Socialist-realist respect for "progressive national tradition" was evident in several ways, though not always determinant. The Kaiser Wilhelm Palace, a severe neoclassical structure and therefore model of progressive architecture, quickly came under consideration for renovation, but other projects soon took priority and it was not restored until 1964.[77] Forum Fridericianum was renamed August Bebel Square and restored according to the original design intentions, which included removing the top two floors of the Dresdner Bank, which lined the rear of the square.[78] These floors had been added during the Weimar era under protest from architects, city planners, and art historians, so their removal provided a favorable point of contrast with city building under capitalism.[79] The Princesses' Palace was slated for restoration as a restaurant and cafe serving the adjacent State Opera.[80] A terrace would overlook the green space between this building and the State Opera. The green space was to remain "intimate and quiet" with sculptures dedicated to famous opera composers.

Buildings considered regressive according to socialist realism were effaced to make room for the progressive reshaping of the urban fabric, as two eclectic buildings from the Wilhelminian era were demolished to make space for a proposed structure forming part of the entryway to Marx-Engels Square.[81] The case of the Schinkel-designed Palace Bridge evidences enduring concern about militarism in Prussian history. Built between 1819 and 1821, as part of the renovation of Unter den Linden following victory over Napoleon, the bridge included a series of statues depicting "the development of a boy into a war hero as a 'monument of victory in general,'" based on Greek mythology.[82] Although a testament to classical origins built in a progressive historical era, associations with militarism may have influenced the decision to neglect the bridge beyond the application of concrete patches. It was only in the 1980s that matching sandstone was applied, and the statues were reconstructed.[83]

The equestrian statue of Friedrich the Great, Elector of Brandenburg, set in the middle of Unter den Linden near Humboldt University in 1851 (completed 1836) presents another case of public art and ambivalence toward early Prussian history. The statue marked a decisive shift from idealized to realistic representation in Berlin, and the sculptor, Christian Rauch, is considered one of the greatest German sculptors of the nineteenth century. The base of the statue bore a table listing seventy-four names of leading figures from the period of Friedrich's rule—one set of allegorical reliefs depicting ruler's virtues (strength, justice, moderation, and wisdom); another set of reliefs showed scenes from Friedrich's life.[84] Despite the statue's artistic merit and the fact that Friedrich is considered an enlightened despot, the statue was removed to Potsdam in the summer of 1950, prompting western protest. The move corresponds with the effacement of symbols of the Prussian monarchy and military from the city center, part of a decanonization of Prussian heroes, which was probably delayed until this period when hopes for maintaining national unity were deferred.[85] The desire to improve the flow of parades may have provided additional incentive for the statue's removal.[86] In 1952 a number of Prussian generals and symbols were recanonized, but others, including Friedrich the Great, were still considered reactionary. The statue was not placed on display in Potsdam until 1962 and was not returned to Unter den Linden until 1980, as part of a broader restoration of Prussian history.[87]

The Brandenburg Gate and Pariser Platz

The Brandenburg Gate had over time attained iconic status as a symbol of Berlin and thus was never threatened with effacement despite a clear association with the Prussian monarchy and military (figure 3.7). After the GDR's founding, a new interpretation of the monument eventually emerged, based on a claim to recover its alleged original meaning as a "Peace Gate." Despite some validity, this interpretation suppressed the designer's intended reference, which was reactionary according to Marxist-Leninist ideology.

Early History

The original Brandenburg Gate, a modest structure called Tiergarten Gate, was built on the Quarre (later Pariser Platz) between 1734 and 1738. This gate was flanked by a small guardhouse and customs house, and palaces were built around the square. The impetus to construct a new gate came from a customs reform in 1786, and the idea of modeling the gate after the Athenian propylaea allegedly originated with the king. The structure and crowning Quadriga were designed by the architect Carl Gotthard Langhans and further developed and constructed by the sculptor Johann Gottfried Schadow.[88]

The Gate included considerable iconography, bearing explicit sym-

FIGURE 3.7. The Brandenburg Gate. View from the southeast over rubble-strewn Pariser Platz to the Brandenburg Gate in May 1945. BA, Digital Picture Database, B 145, Image 00047258, *Presse- und Informationsamt der Bundesregierung–Bildbestand*, Puck Archive, May 1, 1945.

bols of war and peace, enabling a variety of interpretations, but with one intended reference, as indicated by Langhans: "The Quadriga standing on the attic, represents the triumph of peace, the bas-relief below signifies protection through righteous arms, granted by innocence. On the other side was to be set, how through these weapons, seven scattered arrows, are once again bound together."[89] The acknowledged referent was Prussian military intervention to restore the aristocratic House of Orange in Holland, which was threatened by a large-scale democratic uprising.[90] Other prominent iconography included heroic deeds of Hercules (foe of monsters and evildoers), a battle between Lapiths and Centaurs (civilization triumphing over barbarism), Athena (the protector of the state), and Ares (the god of war) sinking his sword into his sheath offering peace—all expressing the Prussian state's self-image as conqueror of evildoers and champion of civilization and peace in Holland.[91] With victory over the Prussian army in 1806, Napoleon's troops occupied Berlin and sent the Quadriga to Paris as loot. Napoleon was defeated in 1814, and the Quadriga was recovered and returned to its original place with the addition of an eagle perched on an oak wreath encircling an iron cross on the goddess's staff, thereby "reinterpreting the goddess of peace as a goddess of war."[92] The Quadriga was ceremoniously dedicated by the king on August 9, 1814, and the Gate became a multifunctional "national memorial" used as a background for public spectacles.[93]

The Brandenburg Gate after the War

The Battle of Berlin left the Brandenburg Gate heavily damaged, the Quadriga decimated, and much of Pariser Platz in ruins. Soviet troops raised their flag on the Gate and later replaced it with a red flag, the international workers' symbol. A few suggestions emerged for replacing the demolished Quadriga with a new sculpture, but no action was taken. In 1949 the Magistrat resolved to speed up rubble clearance on Unter den Linden and prepare for the restoration of the Brandenburg Gate, which would be left freestanding after surrounding buildings were demolished, allowing traffic to pass around the monument—typical modernist disencumberment that traditionalists opposed. Despite protest from the director of the National Gallery, several ruins along Pariser Platz were razed in preparation for a Communist-organized assembly involving East and West German youth in the summer of 1950, and by the end of the 1950s all ruins on Pariser Platz had been demolished.[94]

In December 1949 the Magistrat ordered the restoration of the Brandenburg Gate and the transfer of the heavily damaged Quadriga to a museum, but the Quadriga fell to pieces upon removal.[95] The Magistrat attempted to obtain the original Quadriga molds from the West Berlin Senate to reproduce the figure "without the iron cross and Prussian Eagle."[96] In April 1950 the Magistrat ceased efforts to obtain the molds and approved a design competition for a crowning element.[97] Nonetheless, the West Berlin Senate (originally counterpart to the Berlin Magistrat, now municipal government of West Berlin) soon approved funding for steps leading to the reproduction of the Quadriga.[98] The competition was never held, and in February 1951 the restoration of the Brandenburg Gate was drawn into the Unter den Linden competition.[99]

Restoration work began in early 1950, with much attention being given to damaged sculptures and reliefs as well as to the middle section, which was to be completed by the start of the World Festival of Youth in July 1951. In early 1951 a German sculptor proposed creating a 6- to 8-meter-high sculpture of Picasso's peace dove to replace the Quadriga so that the Gate would no longer be a "warlike symbol" but would express the idea of peace.[100] Bolz informed him of the intent to return the Quadriga and that there was no interest in a provisional solution.[101] Work on the Quadriga was discontinued in 1952, due to a shift of finances to Stalinallee, leaving a partially complete, shoddy restoration. Magistrat planners and preservationists attempted to obtain funding for measures to safeguard the building again in 1953, but they were unsuccessful.[102] The issue returned in August 1956, as the Politburo assigned East Mayor Ebert with "finding a copy of the Quadriga" and decreed that the red flag would remain on the Gate until then.[103] In September the Magistrat approved a "Beautification Plan for Democratic Berlin," calling for the restoration of the Gate and other sites located near major border crossings, train stations, and routes leading out of the city—apparently in response to the West Berlin Internationale Bauausstellung (IBA). Ebert approached the West Berlin Senate regarding the original molds for the Quadriga, setting off a media war, yet the Senate approved funds for a reproduction in January.[104]

Restoration work resumed on the Brandenburg Gate and much of the shoddy repair work from the early 1950s needed to be repeated. The topping-out ceremony was held in December 1957, and the flanking gatehouses were completed in April 1958. The new Quadriga was transported to Pariser Platz in August 1958, and after difficulty in the mounting process, it was taken to a nearby building for adjustments. The Western press sarcastically questioned if a red flag would be placed in Victoria's hand. Alterations were in store, as on August 31 the *Berliner Zeitung* asked for readers' opinions on a proposal to remove the iron cross and eagle, because they did not correspond to the original Schadow design and the symbols were "no longer usable," due to misuse by fascists. Most published responses rejected the Schinkel insignia as a breech of style and a symbol of war and suffering, which was later taken as evidence of Berliners' support for a Magistrat resolution on September 15, stating that there is no room on the Brandenburg Gate for "swastikas, iron crosses, and Prussian eagles." The iron cross and eagle were removed before the Quadriga was mounted on September 22, 1958.[105] Author Michael Cullen suggests that the reader opinions expressed in the *Berliner Zeitung* were genuine, as the horrors of war were recent and the manner of posing the questions was set to influence the results in the desired direction.[106] Moreover, the Politburo had already made the decision on September 9, 1958, and used the Magistrat as a cover, allegedly representing the people of Berlin.[107]

In a return to fictive origins, the Eastern press hailed the Brandenburg Gate as a "symbol of peace."[108] In the eighteenth century the triumph of peace symbolized by the Brandenburg Gate was a peace restored by a Prussian military action, crushing an antimonarchical uprising on foreign soil. Whether East German historians, journalists, and politicians were aware of this is not clear. The iconographical reference to the triumph of peace over war was maintained, severed from its specific referent, which in Marxist-Leninist thought represents the victory of reaction over progress. Instead, it was claimed that the semantic shift to a "peace gate" was a reflection of the establishment of the GDR, "where peace has found its home for the first time in German history," in contrast to the West Germany and West Berlin, where people still use iron crosses and demonstrate "that they have learned nothing from history."[109] On August 13, 1961, the Berlin Wall was constructed, running along the west side of the Brandenburg Gate, which was transformed from a gateway to a landmark at the border of East and West.

The Brandenburg Gate, as the most recognized symbol of the city of Berlin, could not be effaced without serious political repercussions. The Gate's lack of spatial capacity meant the SMAD had no pragmatic reason for repairing the structure, while preservationists apparently saw no immediate threat of additional decay. The introduction of socialist realism provided a theoretical framework for reinterpreting the monument, although in this case the "reactionary" aspects of its original meaning were lost or ignored.

From Symbols of Reaction to Cultural Heritage

Immediately after the war, German cultural elites displayed a traditional preservationist view of Unter den Linden's architecture as cultural heritage. They lobbied the Magistrat for funding and materials to carry out emergency repairs to the Neue Wache, the Arsenal, and other historic structures on Unter den Linden. The SMAD initially valued only spatial capacity, disregarded architectural value, and largely ignored political associations. For instance, they immediately ordered the renovation of numerous theaters with little architectural merit, along with the State Opera, but only for utilitarian space not architectural integrity. Similarly, they prodded the Magistrat to create exhibition space in the Arsenal, while remaining silent on the remainder of Unter den Linden's historic fabric. As the division between East and West deepened, however, the SMAD came to emphasize place-based meaning, symbolism, and architectural value, applying a socialist-realist perspective in key locations. For instance, in May 1947 the Singakademie was reconstructed in original form to serve as a "house of Soviet cultures," and in July 1947, after some lobbying by German cultural elites, the SMAD agreed on the restoration of the Arsenal.

In contrast, the German Communist political leadership initially emphasized the political significance of place-based meaning and representation through iconography and text and thus sought the effacement of historic architecture due to associations with Prussian-German monarchism and militarism—hence their refusal to approve paltry sums of money for emergency repairs to the Neue Wache, the Arsenal, and other structures on Unter den Linden. After the GDR's founding, the adoption of socialist realism prompted the valorization of monumental architecture as national heritage, leading to new interpretations of place-based meaning for key buildings. The Plan for the New Building of Berlin called for the restoration of all historic structures on eastern Unter den Linden and key structures along the entire length of the street, such as the Brandenburg Gate. Despite the theoretical approval of all edifices considered architecturally progressive, place-based meaning and symbolism brought the legacy of the past to the fore in ways that proved troublesome in certain cases. For example, the long-term use of the Neue Wache for purposes considered militaristic resulted in considerable debate and delay over its restoration and reuse as well as the removal and enduring separation of the statues of Prussian generals Scharnhorst and Bülow, which were integral to its architecture.

Finally, the adoption of a new, official ideology may not eradicate or constrain the expression of personal beliefs that are directly contradictory to it. Walter Ulbricht's desire to set back the Zeughaus facade, compromising the building's architectural integrity to broaden the path for parades, is illustrative in this regard. Ideology figured prominently into interpretation and decision-making with regard to the Unter den Linden but was one of a range of forces.

4

From Royal Palace to Marx-Engels Square

We do not need any cities, whose mid-point and entire plan are determined by a royal palace and its masters... rather the great social buildings of the productive people, which indicate that they are master of the political, economic, and social life in their home.

—Lothar Bolz, minister of building, March 8, 1950

THE CASE OF THE BERLIN PALACE is unique in that a hated symbol of monarchy was also the historic nucleus of the city, esteemed architectural heritage, and a skillfully composed urban design feature that mediated between adjoining areas of very different scale and style. As in the case of Unter den Linden, Communist political leaders initially saw only its symbolism and left the structure to decay despite the pleas of architects and preservationists. Similarly, both cases were impacted by the adoption of socialist realism following the state founding, as artistic value was to be separated from political associations. Yet, unlike the buildings on that street, the Berlin Palace was demolished. Socialist realism appeared to give contradictory directives in this case, as national cultural heritage should be preserved and a large square should be located in the city center. Walter Ulbricht insisted on its demolition, asserting a narrow interpretation of the latter point and claiming that the building's architectural value was destroyed in the war. He thereby concealed iconoclastic motives, as evidenced in the following discussion. A "scientific" effort to preserve artistically valuable components and document the building produced few results, as the state was primarily interested in hurriedly clearing the site for the coming year's May Day celebration. Planning efforts to shape a new Marx-Engels Square were soon under way, although debates over appropriate design and limited building resources ensured it would take decades to complete.

FIGURE 4.1. The Palace (aerial view from northwest). The palace occupies the center of the photo. Courtyard I, the Eosander courtyard, is to the right. Behind this (left) is Courtyard II, the older, more architecturally valuable Schlüter courtyard. Portal IV is located in the center of the northern facade (left) facing the Lustgarten. The Palace Bridge (lower left) and the Lustgarten (just above this) are partially visible. To the west (right) of the palace dome, on the bank of the Spree, is the National Memorial. Stadtmuseum Berlin, Aero Lloyd Luftbild GmbH, Luftaufnahme. "Das Königliche Schloß vom Lustgarten aus gesehen Richtung Waisenbrücke, Berlin," 1913/14, Photograph: Silbergelatine, Papier; 12 x 17.30 cm, Inv.Nr.: IV 85/445 V, © Stiftung Stadtmuseum Berlin.

Construction and Demise

The Berlin Palace was built over centuries, initially as the residence of the Elector of Brandenburg, later the king of Prussia, and finally the German Kaiser (figure 4.1). The resulting structure embodies the historic trajectory of north German architecture and the evolution of Prussian/German monarchal power from a medieval outpost to a nineteenth-century nation with global ambitions. The cornerstone of the original castle was laid on July 31, 1443. Among numerous additions and renovations accumulated over the centuries, the most meaningful was designed by Andreas Schlüter for the newly crowned king of Prussia around the turn of the eighteenth century. Schlüter was dismissed in 1707 and the project was completed by other architects, including Johann Friedrich Eosander von Göthe. In the mid-nineteenth century a prominent dome was added above the western entry. Apart from its function as residence, the palace housed administrative offices and, in the Staatsratsaal, the Prussian Staatsrat.[1]

The adjoining Lustgarten (pleasure garden) was given a formal layout in the 1600s. In the early 1700s, Friedrich Wilhelm I had it reconfigured as a parade ground for troops; he also commissioned the construction of the Berlin Cathedral on its northeast edge (the Neue Wache across the Spree River already defined the southwest edge). In the early 1800s landscape architect Peter Josef Lenné and architect Karl Friedrich Schinkel redesigned the space as a pleasure garden with neoclassical motifs. Buildings framing the Lustgarten were to represent the four pillars of the Prussian state: the crown (Palace), the church (Cathedral), the army (Arsenal), and culture (Royal Museum). The square was opened to formal strolling by the upper and middle classes, as were the palace courtyards in 1840. In the 1850s the square was revamped again, with a large central paved area for military reviews and an equestrian statue of Friedrich Wilhelm III replaced the fountain. By the late 1800s the Lustgarten was opened to the general public, hosting both Christmas markets and performances and events intended to facilitate state-building. Near the turn of the twentieth century, the cathedral was replaced by a much larger neobaroque cathedral.[2]

A number of noteworthy political events occurred in and around the palace. The Prussian Landtag opened in the White Hall in 1847 and the first German Reichstag in 1888, providing some association with the emergence of German democracy. The surrounding area was a hotbed of street-fighting during the Revolution of 1848, and on March 22, 1848, the kaiser was obliged to remove his hat before the funeral procession for those fallen in the revolution. During the German Empire the Kaiser delivered numerous speeches from the balcony on Portal IV, which faced the Lustgarten. During the Revolution of 1918 the palace was again a center of fighting and was "occupied, plundered, and fired upon," before Karl Liebknecht proclaimed a doomed, socialist republic from the balcony on Portal IV. A revolutionary People's Marine division occupied the palace, now "property of the people" until being forcibly removed on Christmas morning with considerable damage to the west facade.[3]

Following the establishment of the Weimer Republic, the Hohenzollern's palaces and castles were confiscated for residential and office space, and if culturally valuable, as museums. The Berlin Palace, under the directorship of Ludwig Justi, acquired the Kunstgewerbe Museum, a collection of European decorative arts that was combined with the palace art collection. The "historical residential rooms" of the royal family were also opened to

FIGURE 4.2. The Palace (northwest view). Two Soviet soldiers stand along the Spree River with the western facade of the palace parallel to the river in the background. BA, Digital Picture Database, Image 204-013, *Sammlung Henryk Gorovits*, May–June 1945.

the public, and on occasion, concerts were held in the Schlüter Courtyard. Some offices of the Administration of State Palaces and Gardens, created to maintain the property of the Prussian monarchy for "the entire people" due to its historic and artistic value, and remaining space was rented for use as offices.[4] The Lustgarten became a favorite open-air meeting place of the Berlin labor movement, in part as the government's protest-free zone (*Bannmeile*) began just to the west on Unter den Linden.[5] During World War II aerial bombing inflicted heavy damage, mainly to the palace interior, and street fighting further damaged the exterior (figures 4.2 and 4.3).

Preservation versus Iconoclasm

In the immediate postwar years, traditions in socialist politics, modernist architecture and planning, and historic preservation would shape debate on the future of the Berlin Palace. Traditions in historic preservation were particularly important to approaches taken by professionals dur-

FIGURE 4.3. Schlüter Courtyard. View of the Great Portal on the east side of the Schlüter courtyard after the war. Stiftung Preussicher Schlösser und Gärten, Berlin-Brandenburg, F0002966: Berlin, Schloss Berlin, Schlüterhof, nach der Zerstörung. Photographer unknown.

ing this time. In the late nineteenth century, historic preservation became a major force in German cities as a bourgeois response to rapid physical and social change. Planning for traffic, sanitary sewer construction, and disencumberment of monuments were seen as the primary threats to historic fabric. Preservationists opposed these forces, viewing themselves as apolitical stewards of the heritage of a cultural nation. Monumental architecture, gardens, and squares were valued as public symbols deriving from their historic associations and/or artistic merit. Monuments were believed to establish emotional connections between individuals and the nation, to serve as a "moral stabilizer," a source of inspiration, and a compass for the future. Vernacular environments, including old urban quarters and minor historic sites, became a secondary area of interest. These documents of the national past provided lessons for contemporary artisans and workers and could become "public symbols," in some cases icons of national identity, "unintentional monuments" as defined by Alois Riegl. Documentation was considered an important part of preservationists' work, and historic research, techniques of classification, and restoration were considered scientific.[6]

During the Weimar era many modernists repudiated history and tradition, questioning the very bases of preservation. Others provided more modest challenges—that is, asserting that monuments should not be viewed as belonging to just one nation. The Athens Charter called for the preservation of "fine architecture" and ensembles as expressions of earlier cultures, although nationalism was removed from the equation. Despite the modernist challenge, German preservationists' basic assumptions endured and palaces throughout Germany were preserved as aristocratic heritage and for their art-historic value. During the Nazi era, preservationists continued to view historic structures as documents of the cultural nation, but many imbued them with racist content and linked them with the state. The monumental urban core became center stage for state parades and political rallies. Nevertheless, many preservationists carried out their work independent of Nazi Party involvement and continued to view their labor as apolitical. After the war there would be considerable continuity in staff and perspectives on historic preservation.[7]

Debate over the future of the Berlin Palace quickly took shape after the war, pitting Hans Scharoun, director of Berlin's Department of Construction and Housing, against Communist members of the Magistrat. The efforts of Scharoun, a modernist architect, aligned with the Athens Charter's doctrine that exemplary historic architecture should be preserved and in some cases disencumbered of surrounding urban fabric. Scharoun brought three initiatives of increasingly limited scope for emergency repairs on the palace to the Magistrat between July and October 1945. At the session on July 23 he proposed to protect "irreplaceable cultural monuments" from "total decay."[8] Arthur Pieck and Edmund Noortwyck (both of the Communist Party, KPD) asserted the need to distinguish "real art" from "expressions of Hohenzollern imperialism." Scharoun indicated that the intent was to rescue works by Schlüter and Eosander, who rank among the greatest architects of Germany, but he withdrew the proposal at Mayor Werner's request.

Scharoun returned in August, requesting emergency roofing, weatherproofing, and security against break-ins due to the palace's architectural and urban design value.[9] First, this was "the most outstanding northern German baroque building and single surviving work of Schlüters." Though only a few "artistically notable portions of the interior" were still salvageable, the structure was "fundamentally intact" except for "a few deeply collapsed sections in the Eosander-part." If left exposed for another winter, "unique and irreplaceable" plasterwork would be destroyed. Second, the building provided a crucial link between the medieval city to the east and the Renaissance extension to the west. Third, due to its architectural value and spatial capacity, the palace should be used as a museum. Paul Schwenk (KPD) opposed the motion, as the need to construct housing for the coming winter was a matter of life and death.[10] Noortwyck (KPD) questioned the merit of preserving German culture, arguing that, "Because of the guilt of the Nazi criminals, a great part of German culture has come to its end." The motion was declined ten votes to eight.

In October, Scharoun requested that the White Hall of the palace be weatherproofed for use as a storage area for salvaged artworks. Mayor Werner supported his proposal because of the room's value as storage space and as the work of the greatest architect in the history of Berlin. Karl Böttcher, who later emigrated to the West, supported the proposal, as did Winzer (KPD), both recognizing the need to store art. Other Communists held firm, suggesting that numerous places could be found for storage, but the motion was approved.[11] Communist disdain for the palace and its symbolism, often implicit in previous meetings, was clearly articulated by Heinrich Starck (of the Socialist Unity Party, SED) in April 1946: "The fact, that Berlin remains not just the capital of Germany, but will also become a city of congresses, must be taken into consideration in light of the *Neugestaltung* of Berlin. One should, for instance, redesign the square next to the palace as a square of worker's uprisings. The palace was a symbol of a time that was unbearable for us. One should dispose of this thing."[12]

This prescient call for a central square for workers and first public appeal for the demolition of the palace were symbolic gestures to impose

Communist identity in the core. Starck, like other Communists, took an iconoclastic stance on the palace; its demolition was worthwhile regardless of the square. Schwenk, Karl Maron, and Starck again raised objections to spending on the palace rather than Berlin residents' pressing needs at a Magistrat meeting in May. Nonetheless, Maron concluded that there was no option but to finish the work using as little construction material as possible. The White Hall and the adjacent stairhouse were partially restored and the exhibition *Berlin Plans* opened in August 1946.

Communists used the housing shortage as a basis for withholding funds from the Berlin Palace several times during this period, continuing a utilitarian argument about spending on monumental structures that had been employed by Berlin socialists as far back to the mid-nineteenth century. Yet little utility could be found. First, only a few housing units could be constructed for the amounts Scharoun had requested. Second, Communists supported the far more cost-intensive renovation of theater buildings that were neither historically nor architecturally valuable but provided space for cultural political theater productions.[13] The rarely articulated statement condemning the palace as a symbol of the Prussian monarchy and Prussian militarism underlie their stance.

In April 1947 a few months after the Social Democratic Party (SPD) won control of the City Council, the Soviet Military Administration (SMAD) commandeered the Berlin Palace, due to its capacity for housing exhibitions and administrative offices.[14] In October 1947 the Magistrat asserted that only sections of the palace were worth restoring. The northwest portion was described as best preserved—ironically the very section Starck would soon attempt to have demolished as unsafe. The report also noted that in the southwest wing the "the large and representative [Staatsratsaal] has relatively little damage" and thus should be used for museumlike purposes. The report emphasized the spatial capacity of the palace, which was of interest to German Communists and the SMAD, but no action was taken.[15]

With the formation of separate East Berlin and West Berlin governments in fall 1948, German Communists attained absolute authority over the palace. The Building Inspector's Office (Baupolizeiamt Mitte) ordered parts of the palace to be cleared and access restricted, due to unsafe conditions resulting from weathering.[16] The Berlin Palace was closed off in March 1949, despite protests of those occupying the offices and insufficient evidence of structural instability—"73 year-old Justi [who] wouldn't be held back from climbing up directly under the dome, to inform himself of the extent of the damage."[17] Western journalists questioned whether the palace would be demolished and charged the "East Magistrat" with iconoclasm.[18] On July 15, Mayor Ebert presented the "General Building Plan 1949" and invited public input. The plan did not address the future of the palace, though *Neues Deutschland* continued the long-running socialist view of urban form as a superstructural expression of the conflict between the ruling class and the working class, perhaps intimating at its potential demise: "A showy, spacious, cold Palace in the style of Wilhelminian barrack-baroque, on the one hand, and narrow, slums crammed between smoking factory chimneys, on the other—that [capitalism's] mark! The plan, according to which the new Berlin will be shaped, will make a final break with this ignominious tradition."[19]

Nonetheless, there continued to be support within the Magistrat for preservation. In April 1949, Magistrat planner Wils Ebert developed a register of historic buildings to be preserved, including the Berlin Palace. For an estimated DM 11.9 million, the palace would be restored apart from destroyed sections viewed as reminders of the history of the Hohenzollerns. In July the Kulturbund, the leading German Communist cultural organization, formed a study group on the history of Berlin, which spoke out for preservation due to concerns that city planners would demolish the entire city center—a continuation of flare-ups between planners and preservationists that extended back to the nineteenth century. The Planning Collective conceded that the Schlüter courtyard should be preserved and eventually restored, while the allegedly unstable western portion should be torn down; the collective resolved to develop a proposal for the Magistrat. In November members of the Planning Collective attended a meeting of the Kulturbund, whose study group declared that the palace would last centuries as a ruin, and the only solution is to secure unstable pieces and reconstruct the entire palace at a later date for a democratic use, as in the Weimar era.[20]

Starck, now building director for the Magistrat, countered: "A reconstruction is not to be thought of, above all due to a shortage of resources. Apart from this, there are a number of people and institutions who support tearing down the front section. These plans demand a necessary parade forum, and at the present I cannot tell how much closer they have come. One thing is certain: the most valuable part of the Palace, the Schlüter courtyard, will, in any case, be preserved for posterity."[21] It is unlikely that Starck, the outspoken iconoclast, had suddenly discovered the cultural value of the Berlin Palace. He was informing preservationists of the intent to demolish part of the palace for a new parade ground without taking responsibility, assuring them that the section of greatest artistic value would be preserved.

In fact, a period of ideological confusion ensued with members of the SED expressing varying perspectives on the palace. Articles appearing in the Eastern press reported various proposals regarding the future of the palace, according to which the Magistrat planned to restore the Schlüter courtyard; planned to preserve the section built by Eosander; and, in response to letters pointing out the discrepancy, had not yet reached a decision but would strive to preserve the entire palace, as an artistically valuable building.[22]

After the founding of the GDR, the introduction of socialist realism complicated discussion of the palace. Prior to the Trip to Moscow, Lothar Bolz, who orchestrated the introduction of socialist realism in East Germany, viewed architectural heritage as an expression of its patrons and their social and political standing. Addressing the *Deutsche Bautagung*, Bolz stated: "We do not need any cities, whose midpoint and entire plan are determined by a royal palace [Königsschloss] and its masters... rather the great social buildings of the productive people, which indicate that they are master of the political, economic, and social life in their home."[23]

Soon Bolz would have to consider two pertinent principles of socialist realism. First, as Bolz knew from his experience as a Moscow exile, the city center should include an adequately sized square for large public ceremonies. Second, national cultural heritage should be preserved, great architecture being an expression of the people not their rulers—iconoclasm was not condoned. The apparent conflict only emerges if one makes the unfounded assumption that the palace must be the center and the location of the new square.

In terms of urban design, the Berlin Palace indeed occupied the pivotal position in the urban core; however, socialist realism spoke of a central area based on political criteria, including the location of governmental institutions, cultural facilities, a history of demonstrations, and the capacity of streets and open space to accommodate parades. Nothing suggested that an exact point had to be located as the existing and future center. Advice from Soviet advisers during the Trip to Moscow left considerable flexibility as to how the center of Berlin was defined and how the new government building and square related to it.[24] In Berlin the center of monarchal power had been the palace, but since the founding of the German Empire, many government institutions located in and around Wilhelmstrasse, such that the street's name had become a metonym for German government.[25] A short distance away stood the most important building of popular representation of the "bourgeois-democratic" era, the Reichstag, while Nazi power was overwhelmingly centered on the Hitler's Chancellery and nearby offices on Wilhelmstrasse (see Chapter 5). One could argue from a dialectical standpoint that either the Reichstag or the Chancellery on Wilhelmstrasse represented the most advanced state of bourgeois rule, and each was fronted by a square.

In terms of political activity in public space, Unter den Linden had been the Prussian and German states' main parade street for centuries, and the Victory Avenue in Tiergarten had been a secondary site since the late nineteenth century. During the Trip to Moscow, Soviet advisers hinted that Unter den Linden could be the city center (see Chapter 3). Over many decades the working class held rallies and demonstrations at numerous sites, although the right to demonstrate in public space was often contested. From the 1860s to the Weimar era, small decentralized marches took place on city streets in working-class neighborhoods, and larger marches and assemblies were located on Unter den Linden, in front of the Reichstag, in Tiergarten and Treptow Park.[26] Late-GDR historians listed sixteen locations as "rally squares," including less significant spaces in the core, such as Bülowplatz and Weberwiese. In 1848 and 1918 working-class revolutionary activity, a central component of Communist history, concentrated on the area around the palace, Unter den Linden, and Alexanderplatz, although Karl Liebknecht addressed workers on Victory Avenue too.[27] Socialist commemoration of the 1848 Revolution was focused on the cemetery in Friedrichshain, and after 1918 Communists honored Liebknecht and Luxembourg at the cemetery Friedrichsfelde.[28] During the Weimar era the SPD and the KPD held their largest May Day events on the Lustgarten, now permitted as there was no governmental power in the palace. Demonstrations of the National Socialist Workers' Party were held in front of the Reichstag, the actual center of power.[29] After the Nazi Party obtained control of government, they replaced the trees on Unter den Linden with pylons bearing swastikas to accentuate parades. Wilhelmplatz, across from the Chancellery, was their main space for political rallies, although many events were staged on the Lustgarten.[30]

For the SED the Reichstag was off-limits in West Berlin. Many of the other sites, such as the revolutionaries' cemeteries, were outside what could reasonably be considered the city center. The area around Wilhelmstrasse, Unter den Linden, the palace, and the Lustgarten remained available for consideration as an expansive "center." The site criteria and the history of these spaces do not mandate the Lustgarten as the central space. From a dialectical perspective a new, larger space could have been created on any range of locations within or adjacent to this central area. GDR theorist Gerhard Strauss later outlined an exemplary development process of this type in the 1801 extension of Karlsruhe and an unrealized plan from 1947.[31]

The personal experiences of Communists during the Weimar years offer strong clues regarding the choice of site. The most significant Communist celebration at that time, May Day, was celebrated in various locations, but its focal point was the gathering on the Lustgarten.[32] Communists seemed to view their march to the square as a form of appropriation. Enthusiastic participants annually exceeded one hundred thousand, spilling out to surrounding streets and spaces, which Ulbricht and leading Communists would have experienced in person.[33] After the war, Communists held rallies in the Lustgarten, erecting a grandstand on its north side as in the 1930s.[34] Ulbricht's poignant prewar memories, along with his iconoclastic views of architecture, likely precluded extensive ideological reflection and convinced him of the need for a larger central square.

Kurt Liebknecht, aware of the threat to the Berlin Palace and of socialist realism's theoretical implications, sought to discredit the iconoclastic perspective in a lecture in June 1950: "We have spoken with our Soviet friends about historic preservation. They said, 'We do not have the right to remove a work, because the patriarch under whom it was created had been unpleasant. That does not play a role. Who produced the building? People's committees.' One must still examine the Berlin Palace question [to determine] if it will be torn down. Schlüter, who belonged to the best German master builders, had worked on it."[35] To counter the idea that the palace must be torn down to create space for demonstrations, Liebknecht's office produced a document, *Das Zentrum Berlins*, arguing that the capacity of the new square would be sufficient without demolishing the palace. The current Lustgarten could hold 140,000 people. The demolition of the palace and cathedral would allow for 300,000 people but would eliminate the square's architectural frame. It could take ten years until the square was "architecturally shaped in such a way that it makes an impression on the demonstrators."[36] As an alternative, Liebknecht recommended flowing demonstrations as "on Red Square in Moscow." With the preserved palace in the background, 140,000 people per hour could march across a much larger square than the one in Moscow. Later, a still larger square to accommodate 700,000 people could be built to the east of the Spree, framed by new governmental buildings. Though unmentioned, the preservation of the palace made this an even more effective expression of socialist realism.

Ulbricht would not be deterred or delayed by a formal planning process. The day after *Das Zentrum Berlins* was produced, he delivered his oft-cited speech at the Third Party Congress in July 1950. The future of the palace was clear: "The center of our capital, the Lustgarten and the area of the Palace-ruin must become a great demonstration square, upon which the will of our people to fight and build can be expressed [tumultuous applause]."[37] Referring to the palace as a ruin skirted socialist-realist dictum on the preservation of heritage by asserting that the palace had already been lost to wartime bombing. Ulbricht's commitment to socialist realism only wavered when it conflicted with his elemental compulsion to iconoclasm.

Many leading East German architects and planners were aware of the emphasis placed on historic preservation during the Trip to Moscow and did not agree with Ulbricht's decision, but they would not publicly protest.[38] Prompted by Ulbricht's speech, a team of architects under Liebknecht began to translate the leader's words into urban design plans. Within days of Ulbricht's speech, Helmut Hennig (of the Magistrat) and Richard Paulick (of the Ministry of Building, Ministerium für Aufbau, MfA) each developed a plan for a "central square for demonstrations." Hennig's plan removed the palace and extended the Lustgarten across its site, whereas Paulick's preserved the palace and placed the new square to its east across the Spree. Paulick's team argued that "the preservation of the old form of the Lustgarten in its beauty, as designed by Schinkel is especially valuable in a city that is so poor in beautiful and memorable squares.... Carry forth the historic inheritance by including... the Palace."[39] As Werner Durth, Jörn Düwel, and Niels Gutschow have observed, the proposals were dominated by a preoccupation with mass-ceremonies and their "technical assumptions," centering on the quantity of persons involved in demonstrations. This was emphasized in Hennig's drawing by columns of demonstrators marching through the streets and across the new square. The proposals were presented and discussed until a conclusive meeting with Ulbricht and several leading architects and politicians on

FIGURE 4.4. Proposal for Marx-Engels Square. This model from the Plan for the New Building of Berlin reveals an expansive central square with a relatively weak sense of enclosure. At the far end of the square is the Altes Museum fronting the former Lustgarten. Moving clockwise from the top right is the cathedral (domed structure), the proposed grandstand, the Marstall, the proposed new state opera house (labeled 2), and the proposed FIAPP Memorial (labeled 3). The square-shaped building across the Spree from the FIAPP Memorial is the German Building Academy. BA, Digital Picture Database, Image 183-T00203, *Allgemeiner Deutscher Nachrichtendienst-Zentralbild*, Kümpfel, August 24, 1950.

August 5.[40] The first of fourteen points of the work program stated that "the Palace is to be torn down." Most of the points focused on the ceremonial spaces of the axis from Unter den Linden to Stalinallee, and the final point called for the development of a parade plan.

In short order, Hennig's plan was further developed into new plan for the city center (see figure 2.3). This Plan for the New Building of Berlin focused on the "primary chain of streets Stalinallee—Unter den Linden," as the ceremonial use of the city center and spatial requirements for parades were the driving concern. An official parade route plan was included. The Lustgarten as central square for demonstrations would be the city's architectural high-point, boasting 82,000 square meters (about 20 acres) compared with 50,000 meters (about 12 acres) for Red Square in Moscow, as the document pointed out. Stalinallee, Friedrichstrasse, Wilhelmstrasse, and the Palace Bridge, all on parade routes, were to be widened. The new detailed plan for the Lustgarten area closely resembled Hennig's work (figure 4.4). The grandstand, positioned along the eastern edge of the new square, provided a view of demonstrators entering the square from Unter den Linden. Architectural framing was also considered, as a new government building was positioned behind the grandstand across the Spree, and a new State Opera building and reconstructed Marstall facade would help define the southern edge of the square. On the western edge opposite the grandstand, a monument to Kaiser Wilhelm would be replaced with a memorial for the victims of fascism (the FIAPP-Memorial).[41] On August 15 the Politburo (under SED leadership) approved the "Plan for the New Building of Berlin." The Council of Ministers approved the plan on August 23. *Berliner Zeitung* provided a detailed report on the plan, noting that "artistically valuable parts of the building, such as the Schlüter courtyard and the Eosander Portal," would be preserved for reconstruction on another site.

Several leading architects continued to seek a way to save the palace before the People's Chamber approved the new plans, although in fact this assembly only rubber-stamped SED policy. On August 31, Scharoun sent Otto Grotewohl, an acquaintance of his, a letter and sketches illustrating an alternative plan that would salvage the Schlüter courtyard onsite by incorporating it into a new ensemble. Scharoun's continuing battle to preserve the palace now took on a socialist-realist tone, emphasizing the importance of building upon national traditions.[42] He pointed to its "unique significance," indicating that "spatially and nationally bound [*Volksgebundene*] creative talent responded to contemporary demands in such a way that the result achieved worldwide fame."[43] Scharoun's plan preserved the Schlüter courtyard as a "representative reception area" adjoining the grandstand and helping to define the space. Thus, the new demonstration square and grandstand would be organically combined with one of the greatest examples of national architectural tradition—an astute application of socialist realism.[44]

Before Grotewohl replied, Liebknecht personally consulted Ulbricht on the matter, and reported to Edmund Collein and Walter Pisternik that "the Palace will be torn down and all further measures to this end are to be met. Regarding this affair, the office of Prime Minister, Otto Grotewohl, should only be contacted one more time."[45] That same day, Pisternik wrote to a leading member of the Council of Ministers (which Ulbricht viewed with suspicion) suggesting that the new, big city plan was not as good as the old, small pattern of streets and parcels, whereby the government quarter on Wilhelmstrasse could be expanded north to the Brandenburg Gate. That this might save the Berlin Palace was omitted.[46]

The following day, Grotewohl replied to Scharoun, describing the proposal as interesting but not compelling enough to merit a reversal of the government's decision. The design failed to preserve the artistically valuable exterior, while the courtyard could be placed anywhere in Berlin. Also, the central square would be narrowed, the grandstand was not in position to view demonstrators marching down Unter den Linden, and the structure would detract from the appearance of the city-dominating high-rise planned for the site behind the square. Grotewohl closed with a request that Scharoun reflect on his statements, as he believed Scharoun would come to agree with them.[47] Any sympathy was well concealed by pressure on the architect to drop his protests.

Scharoun received the letter one day before the People's Chamber approved the demolition. He countered Grotewohl's arguments, noting that the palace could have been built on another site, but "the choice of the site, the grandiosity of its implementation and the expressive power of the building have over the course of centuries had the effect that for us today the Palace is only imaginable in its present form and on this particular site."[48] Furthermore, the trees on Unter den Linden would block the view of the demonstrators, until they were near August-Bebel Square, where they would have an "ideal optical connection" to the grandstand in his design. The view of the central building east of the Spree would not be obstructed; rather, the Schlüter courtyard would serve as a "projected post" of the building due to the strong architectural connection. Foreground objects provide a sense of scale to avoid "estrangement of human and building."[49] Finally, Scharoun claimed that any narrowing of the space would not affect its use, and that additional space for "stationary" demonstrators could be established west of the Spree.

Speculation of direct Soviet involvement in the decision to demolish the Berlin Palace appears unfounded.[50] The first record of Soviet consultation occurred in October, when General Sergei Dengin, Commandant of the Soviet Sector in Berlin, informed a German delegation that planning for the Lustgarten had been too concerned with "demonstration-technical questions" and "creating a square for demonstrations" and not enough on "architectural form and planning for buildings."[51] Dengin displayed preservationist rather than iconoclastic impulses, calling for a prompt start to restoration work on the Marstall. Claims later emerged that Grotewohl felt that the resolution should be changed because "everyone has the opinion that it's wrong," but that Ulbricht was unapproachable on the subject.[52]

The extent of opposition to Ulbricht's views within the government is unknown. The official Party line identified the Berlin Palace as an irreparable ruin occupying the center point of the city. This dubious assertion circumvented the theoretical implications of socialist realism and may have mitigated negative public perceptions. Bolz appears to be one of the few people involved who had no objections (see below). Many Communist politicians on the sidelines would have shared Ulbricht's iconoclastic views; however, Ulbricht held ultimate authority, made the decision, and overrode all objections. His shift in terminology from "palace" to "palace-ruin" provided the launching point for a campaign to portray its demolition as an act of historic preservation. Art historian Gerhard Strauss, assigned responsibility for salvaging "artistically valuable parts" of the palace, was allotted just a few months to carry out the work, greatly limiting his effectiveness.[53]

Strauss quietly protested within the Party but appeared in public as a fervent supporter of the decision. He asserted that the palace was the "most meaningful monument of German baroque art and one of the most important monuments of this same art in all Europe."[54] Unlike Ulbricht, Strauss acknowledged that valuable portions were largely intact. Employing socialist realism, he tied artistic achievement to progressive national traditions, declaring that the palace "was created in lasting protest against the small-minded, separatist, dynastic spirit of the Hohenzollerns."[55] The palace's architectural value necessitated extensive preservation, hence demolition could only be justified if the reconstruction of architecturally valuable parts on another site was assured. Strauss presented his case for preservation to Grotewohl, who informed him that the decision to demolish the palace was final.[56]

Berliner Zeitung published plans for the city center on August 23, and representatives of leading cultural institutions were invited to a discussion led by Kurt Liebknecht at the Ministry of Building. Walter Stengel of the Märkisches Museum questioned the democratic nature of the state, as that involved majority rule and no one wanted the palace torn down. Finding no support, Liebknecht ended the meeting. It seemed obvious to many that the culturally invaluable structure was fundamentally intact, not simply a collection of fragments fit for a museum. Many East German state architects, planners, and preservationists reluctantly carried out their duties, while others expressed dissent internally but not publicly. The West Berlin and West German governments did not protest directly as they did not officially recognize the German Democratic Republic, and the West German cultural elite lacked immediate access to the political leadership of the GDR. Hence the press was their primary means of objection.

In September, Strauss posted theses in support of the demolition at Humboldt University, an ex post facto justification for Ulbricht's decision.[57] Strauss deviated from socialist realism regarding the cultural/political meaning of the palace, asserting it was constructed as an expression of Prussian absolutism and not an expression of the nation. It had become a symbol of the "complete decay" of feudal power, a ruin demolished by Anglo-American bombs, in whose facades an expert can make out the work of Schlüter. The German people had a right to give the city center an appearance worthy of the new era, that any restoration would only be a reproduction of Schlüter's work. Thus, "out of respect for the humanistic achievement of the master builder, securing the well-preserved, characteristic details for reuse on another site, but releasing the site by demolishing the Palace, in order to make room for a life-filled, new entrance in the center of Berlin."[58] This statement conflicted with the view of many preservationists, who felt that a reconstruction would be inauthentic, and ignored the potential for on-site conservation. The preservationist was siding with the historic enemy, city planners.[59]

The East German cultural elite, having been lectured on socialist realism, often used it to frame their arguments to save the palace, although in some cases a traditional preservationist stance is evident.[60] Prominent figures as such as Richard Hamann, art historian and national prize winner; Wolfgang Schubert, conservator of Saxon-Anhalt; and Johannes Stroux, president of the German Academy of Science, all wrote letters to Ulbricht praising the artistic value of the palace as separate from the political meanings associated with the time of its creation.[61] They asserted the significance of Schlüter's work for Berlin, Germany, and the world. Schubert and Stroux pointed to the urban design achievement of the palace, linking the medieval core with the Renaissance extension to the west, its style and form corresponding to each. Schubert cited the Fifth Principle of City Planning, which requires consideration for the historically evolved structure of the city to argue for on-site preservation. He argued that the square would lack well-defined edges, was intersected by streets, and was too small for parades of "the grandest style." In Schubert's view, planning must not be hampered by the "passing division of the city," and he recommended two sites in West Berlin. Recognizing the desire for an immense space, he suggested Templehof Field, Berlin's "traditional parade ground." This centuries-old Prussian military drill and parade ground was used by Goebbels in 1933 for a rally of 1.5 million people to celebrate a "Day of German Labor" to supplant working-class May Day celebrations with an event to overcome the "spirit of class struggle"—in the midst of a campaign dismantling the trade unions.[62] Whether or not German Communist politicians were aware of these associations with "reactionary tradition," the field's distance from the urban core precluded any consideration. Alternatively, Schubert also recommended a site somewhere in the devastated area stretching from the Reichstag through Tiergarten and into the Hansaviertel, which was now to be seen as a clean slate—also out of the question because of its location in West Berlin.

Hamann, the most influential of the group, had already visited Grotewohl on August 30. Grotewohl allegedly displayed considerable interest and inquired as to why the specialists had waited so long before coming. In response to dissent within the government, especially Hamann, and to obtain the support of critical GDR intelligentsia, a regional meeting of the Kulturbund was called for September 5 to pass a resolution in favor of the demolition.[63] The members viewed the plans and generally favored demolishing the Berlin Cathedral instead of the Berlin Palace. Yet the cathedral had suffered only limited wartime damage, and Berlin's Christian Democratic mayor had approved RM 975,000 for provisional repairs in 1948.[64] After the division of city government, the Communist Magistrat maintained favorable treatment of Protestant Church structures, contributing additional funding to the medieval Marienkirche, simply stating that it was a "valuable building."[65] In the press, however, they noted its historic significance, its use for religious services, and referred to its artwork depicting the Dance of the Dead to be "noteworthy as a socially critical document from the late Middle Ages."[66] The press attributed the ruin of the historic Parochialkirche to Anglo-American bombs and noted that like many churches, it was being restored by the "democratic Magistrat."[67] To allay any public concerns about the cathedral, *Berliner Zeitung* reported that despite its limited architectural value, it must be restored as it presently was a disgrace to "the representative square of our city and also for the community, no worthy place for church services."[68] Marx had denounced religion as "the opium of the masses" and decades of iconoclasm followed the Russian Revolution, but pragmatism shaped the German Communist state's view of the church and therefore its property.[69] Instead, the ire of Communist politicians was directed at the monarchy.

To influence the Kulturbund, Liebknecht and Pisternik asserted that the palace had been largely destroyed and emphasized "the basic political thoughts behind the planning for Berlin."[70] The "approved" resolution stated that the Berlin region of the Kulturbund greets the government's new plans, "unanimously" rejected the idea of rebuilding the palace, and called for the preservation of the Schlüter courtyard and the Eosander portals on another site. Forced to act behind the scenes, Kulturbund representatives sent an alternative design to Otto Grotewohl locating the demonstration square on the east side of the Spree.[71] Grotewohl did visit the site but concluded that demolition was necessary because of the palace's "ruinous state."[72] Pisternik returned the Kulturbund's plans with a letter declining the proposal due to "city building reasons and other considerations" and reminded them that they knew the government's resolution from the daily newspaper.[73] Hamann obtained an appointment with Ulbricht on September 19, but when the day arrived, he was informed that Ulbricht had to leave for a meeting in Bucharest.[74]

Journalist Helmut Räther hoped to present the arguments of dissenters in a radio commentary, but his supervisor required that Räther first obtain approval from Ulbricht.[75] Ulbricht responded with a letter restricting the program, pointing out that the palace had already been destroyed by "Anglo-American bombers" and suggesting that if Räther would like to organize a protest movement, "then please do it against those who destroyed the Palace through their bomb-terror."[76] Dresden art historian Walter Hentschel devised a set of countertheses to Strauss's and requested they be posted next to his at Humboldt University. Hentschel's arguments occasionally expressed traditional preservationist ideas at odds with tenets of socialist realism.[77] Viewing architecture as heritage of the cultural nation, Hentschel questioned the relevance of political process to cultural production (socialist realism elaborately theorized this relation). Whereas Strauss characterized the palace as product of "serf-slavery," Hentschel pointed out that to the extent this was true, it was truer about the Kremlin, which the Soviet Union carefully tended. Hentschel suggested that the interior be replaced by a "modern creation" and that even if half of the exterior structure had to be rebuilt, this would not be more of a replica than most medieval cathedrals. This would have resonated widely as support for reconstruction as opposed to conservation surged throughout Germany after the war.[78]

Protest in the West often appeared in trade journals and newspapers. The traditional preservationist views that historic architecture possessed a spiritual value to the cultural nation removed from politics predominated. Articles charged that decision-making centered on political rather than art historic reasons, overt iconoclasm to separate the people from their traditions and orient them to Moscow with a "Red Square" in Berlin. They argued that the palace had enduring artistic value for Germany and/or Europe.[79] Ernst Reuter, mayor of West Berlin, was quoted stating that the decision was "typical for the power-holders in the Soviet Zone, and their systematic destruction of all historic-cultural monuments in Germany."[80] The administrative director of state palaces and gardens, Margarete Kühn, viewing the Communists as inherently political thinkers, asserted that there was no political argument for demolition but for preservation because the palace best embodies Berlin's rank as a capital city. She claimed the palace did not need to be rebuilt, simply restored as it was largely intact, thus concerns about originality were unfounded. The building was developed according to the special urban design requirements of the site and would be a "living" part of urban culture only as long as it remained there, emanating "great moral power."[81]

The East German press depicted the demolition of the palace as an act of preservation. This hinged on the illusion that American bombers had already destroyed the palace, and its remaining artistic value survived in disparate fragments. The only viable option was to clear the debris and preserve intact details. Gerhard Strauss was charged with preserving parts of the Berlin Palace possessing "artistic merit." Strauss was a fitting choice as he was not only a devoted Communist but apparently an irresolute preservationist. In a 1948 lecture on historic preservation, he stated: "Ruins are so numerous and so markedly a Hitleresque inheritance, that we not only have the right to dispose of them, but even the duty... it is a sign of progressive, manly courage, when one tears down these 'ruins.'"[82] Nonetheless, he disagreed with the decision to demolish the Berlin Palace and argued internally for an extensive preservation effort. Moving weakly within the narrow range allotted, he achieved the Party's goals: salvaging a few fragments, diverting attention from the demolition, and camouflaging discussion behind a facade of unity.

In late August, Grotewohl ordered Strauss to write up a description of preservation work and cost estimate.[83] Strauss proposed the formation of a "scientific committee," staffed by art and architecture students, to carry out preservation work and field research on the palace.[84] Art historical inventories and archeological work on historic ruins were common throughout Germany at this time, and in West Germany there was some controversy as to whether inventorying served as a "purely scientific undertaking" or as "necrological substitutes for monuments that were quickly disappearing."[85] The group included twenty-five students selected for their skills, with an emphasis on political orientation.[86] Strauss described his plan as the "bare minimum necessary in case of the intended reconstruction," noting that some flexibility was necessary if additional parts prove necessary.[87] The Ministry of Building and the Magistrat did not adopt Strauss's list but specified "the preservation of artistically valuable details (sculptures, Schlüter's courtyard)" and the Ministerrat resolution only stated that "architecturally valuable parts of the Palace should be brought to another site as architectural monuments," with no hint of the reconstruction Strauss had anticipated.

Strauss met with representatives of the Ministry of Building and the Office of Information on August 29 to outline a "systematic" publicity campaign.[88] In every report the ruinous condition of the palace and the necessity of clearing it to build a new city center for "Germany's capital" was to be paired with an example of the preservation of culturally valuable elements, illustrating the government's desire to salvage surviving art and artifacts. "Simple interpretations of the Palace-substance as reactionary architecture" were not acceptable, as this did not correspond to the "objective findings." This offered a defense against charges of iconoclasm and brought the official view in line with socialist realism and traditional preservationism—if one accepted that the palace was an irreparable ruin.

News articles built upon this outline. They attributed the ruinous state of the palace due to "Hitler's war" and "Anglo-American" bombs; having ceased to be whole, its artistic value was lost, except for single, scattered elements. The scientific committee rescued salvageable objects and "scientifically" analyzed the building. The site, the center point of the capital of "all-Germany," would be the focus of a new building effort. Communist utilitarian argument surfaced in claims that the limited funds available must be invested in housing and buildings.[89]

Mayor Ebert's speech to the People's Chamber in support of the demolition provides an excellent example of many of these points. Ebert blamed Hitler, the English, and the Americans for the destruction of the palace and likened this to current US actions, "trying out new methods of annihilating cities and village[s] and murdering old people, women and children in Korea."[90] While capitalists exploited ruins for profit in Heidelberg, the East German government was, in accordance with the teaching of Lenin, clearing away the palace-ruin in order to build a better city for the peaceful future lives of the German people. Ebert claimed that restoring the Schlüter portion alone would cost "more than 30 million marks... we could build very many sunny apartments for the activists and still a few hospitals, of which we are very much in need."[91]

Ebert was far off the mark, as the Ministry of Building estimated the cost of restoring the section attributed to Schlüter at less than DM 9 million.[92] Over DM 6 million were designated for "reconstructing the Lustgarten" as a demonstration ground. Given the price of new construction on Stalinallee, the remaining DM 3 million would provide only thirty-three "sunny apartments for activists," while hospitals were out of the question. The entire palace could have been restored for DM 32 million. The architecturally esteemed Schlüter and Eosander sections, along with the building between the courtyards, could have been restored for approximately DM 15.5 million. Instead, DM 6,065,000 was spent in less than one year to demolish the palace and prepare the new Marx-Engels Square for the May 1 demonstrations in 1951.[93] The demolition was neither an economic imperative nor an act of frugality but a sizable investment.

While demolition work was under way, student groups were given tours of the site and led to develop resolutions. Typically they concluded that the government's decision was an appropriate response to "objective conditions" that would enable the transmission of "undamaged parts of this cultural heritage to later generations." They also called for the speedy approval of a historic preservation law to "guarantee the preservation of valuable cultural heritage in the image of our home (*Heimat*) and... make the preserved treasures of national tradition into a living component of our development striving toward progressive, humanistic goals." The resolution was signed only by the professors but allegedly "unanimously" approved.[94] In contrast to Eastern press depictions of a careful preservation effort, urgency to create space for public ceremonies drove the timing of the demolition. One day after Strauss's preservation plan was presented to Grotewohl, Liebknecht suggested abandoning the program in light of the May Day (parade) deadline. The program could not be completed on time. Any reduction in work would make reconstruction impossible. Instead, he suggested salvaging only those parts listed for display in a museum, concentrating on the Schlüter courtyard and the portal facing the Lustgarten.[95] Whereas the Schlüter courtyard was distinguished for its architectural merit, the portal facing the Lustgarten was notable because Karl Liebknecht had proclaimed a Communist revolution from its balcony in 1918.

On September 7 the apothecary's wing of the palace was detonated, and the building between the courtyards was torn down. Strauss reported that the "substance has been conclusively, scientifically handled."[96] Strauss was verbally informed that his list of items for preservation would have to be further reduced due to temporal constraints. Recognizing that it would be impossible to reconstruct the palace, Strauss suggested that along with museum pieces, "characteristic building parts" could be reused in park design rather than building them into a structure, which "comes close to Grotewohl's idea of conserving and grouping the elements in a sort of architecture museum."[97] This would reduce transport costs, spare building materials, and preserve "cultural heritage as the basis of the development of a new architecture." The proposal fell out of discussion.

A large sculpture of Saint George, the dragon slayer, was removed from the western courtyard and taken to Volkspark Friedrichshain. Strauss considered its creator, August Kiss, to be a "significant sculptor from the late nineteenth century." Yet whether from adherence or sensitivity to Communist iconoclastic tendency, he suggested the removal of the crosses and crown "would not affect the artistic value of the object, but seems desirable in order to exclude a false interpretation."[98] Strauss even avoided naming the referent, other than as a "so-called dragon slayer" or "a mounted knight, who has just conquered a dragon." The sculpture was actually a replica of another of Kiss's works that depicted Saint Michael, patron saint of Germans, slaying a dragon, representing the 1848 Revolution, yet these counterrevolutionary associations were either ignored or unknown.

Grotewohl visited the site on September 13, expressing interest in the extent of the preservation effort. Strauss informed him that because of the deadline, only details could be removed for use in museums. Grotewohl expressed his understanding and requested a revised work proposal by evening. Strauss's list of items for preservation, acknowledged as incomplete, included sculptures, small sections (i.e., 4 square meters) of the ceiling, reliefs, and other details. From Schlüter's still intact marble stairs, only stucco reliefs were marked for preservation.[99] The southwest corner of the palace was detonated on September 15, and preservation work continued.[100] On September 28, Liebknecht, Pisternik, Strauss, and others met at the demolition site and determined that in order to meet the April 30 deadline, there must be a "fundamental change."[101] They settled upon an immediate end to demolition work on the National Memorial, and the transfer of the crane in the Schlüter courtyard to the Lustgarten facade "to remove different portals"—meaning the portal from which Karl Liebknecht proclaimed the revolution.[102] Notice of the "unconditional observance" of the April 30 deadline was repeated.

The Schlüter courtyard would not be saved. The only architectural elements marked for preservation were the portals facing the Lustgarten. Strauss considered Schlüter a leading figure in German architectural history and viewed the courtyard as his "great work."[103] Now it would being razed due to an unwillingness to forgo an expanded Lustgarten for one more year's May Day celebration and to save a portal noteworthy only for its association with Communist memory, rather than artistic value. Demolition continued, section by section from October through December. Casts were taken of some sculptures, a few fragments of Schlüter's sculptures were saved from the southern palace wing Schlüter courtyard, and Schlüter's reliefs from Portal V were removed. Many of Schlüter's fully preserved works and much of the intact structure was destroyed. From the Eosander portion, reliefs and capitals were saved from Portal III. Portal IV fared best as "columns, pilasters, decorative pieces, sandstone blocks and the two other Hermes by Permoser, as well as the so-called Liebknecht Balcony were removed" and stored in Pankow-Heinersdorf until their reuse on the Staatsrat Building (construction period 1962–1964).[104]

The Ministry of Building had intervened to remove a number of architectural elements from the list of items to be preserved, including the Schlüter Portal I, details from the Schlüter courtyard, the marble stairs, and the Eosander stairs. Strauss evidenced his discomfort, sending (rather than destroying) a photograph and negative of Portal I (Schlüter) being detonated to Walter Pisternik with a note stating, "I take it to be appropriate to keep the photo sufficiently safe, which is not possible for myself, here" (figure 4.5).[105] Handwritten on the back of the photo, along with Strauss's signature, "Restricted! Not for publication or other announcement."

The Eastern press gave some attention to salvaged artifacts being transferred to Berlin museums and the palace in Potsdam's Park Sansoussi, but far more to "scientific" research.[106] This approach was a matter of

FIGURE 4.5. Portal I Demolition. Strauss appeared uncomfortable with this image of Portal I (south facade facing Schlossplatz) by Schlüter being detonated, sending it to Pisternik for safekeeping. Gerhard Strauss to Walter Pisternik, November 28, 1950, SAPMO-BA, DH1, 39075. Photographer Unknown.

proven interest, as articles on preservation in nineteenth-century Germany had "often focused more on techniques of classification or restoration than on the finished project... part of a larger cultural phenomenon whereby an industrial age considered technical processes themselves to be of equal or greater concern than their outcome."[107] In the case of the palace, now officially a "ruin," scientific inquiry would both increase and preserve knowledge of the building. Those erasing past achievements were claiming to preserve and further them through science: "In its condition after 1945, the Palace was a dead building. This fact cannot be undone. But just as someone, who does not have the courage to dissect a corpse, cannot become a proper doctor, only someone who can undertake the unpleasant task of examining a deceased architectural monument in the service of science can be called a responsible art historian, even if he had loved this building in all of its magnificence. Or better said: exactly for this reason."[108]

As a final balance, Strauss reported that the scientific committee had transferred "over 8,000 valuable museum pieces" to the head of the Berlin Museum Administration.[109] These "pieces" included sculptures and architectural elements, along with art and craftworks from the palace. In December 1950, Strauss's article, "Historic Preservation on the Palace-ruin in Berlin," in *Planen und Bauen*, stated that a reconstruction of the Schlüter courtyard was intended, even though it had been largely demolished. Strauss claimed success with "450 sets of measurements . . . approximately 2,000 photos . . . and 920 . . . dismantled details."[110] He asserted that the results of the scientific inquiry provided "entirely new views into the history of the construction of the palace," citing some technical details about the construction of the Giant Stairs, and noting that several dissertations would be based on the research undertaken.[111]

To the discredit of Strauss's work, when Hans Scharoun requested emergency repairs for the palace in 1945, he noted that "the architecture . . . is fundamentally intact and with the help of drawings and photographs can be restored archeologically true [and regarding the interior] although all decorations have been photographed down to the smallest details, a reproduction is naturally impossible.[112] Despite the weak harvest of the "scientific committee," the Eastern press found a teachable moment: "The demolition of the Palace-ruin teaches that any historical research on meaningful sites can only be carried out as long as the new construction has not yet begun. Dr. Strauss would like this simple admonition to be punctually heeded, not just in Berlin, but everywhere, because through disregard for research, valuable findings can perhaps be closed off forever."[113] The destroyers had become rescuers to be emulated for their preservation work.

Of the entire preservation effort, the piece that generated the greatest public interest was the Neptune Fountain, a sculpture with little artistic or historic value but considerable popular appeal. In February, Ministry of Building staff suggested that the fountain would disrupt a "unified square design for demonstrations" and must be removed.[114] The following day, the City Planning Commission called for an investigation to determine if the fountain obstructs the flow of demonstrations, and one month later determined that this was the case, necessitating its removal by the Free

German Youth's (Freie Deutsche Jugend, FDJ) Deutschlandtreffen at the end of May.[115] Strauss noted that the fountain was "an object of special affection for the entire population of Berlin" and that "numerous Berliners come walking by the construction site and are concerned about the destiny of the fountain."[116] For these reasons Strauss recommended a public discussion in the media, despite considering the fountain a "late bourgeois product" with little artistic merit that was inappropriate for Marx-Engels Square.[117]

The *Berliner Zeitung* solicited suggestions for a new location for the fountain from the public. Eighteen were reviewed by the City Planning Commission, which selected several sites for further examination.[118] In April 1952 commission members failed to reach an agreement, and called for further discussion with readers in the *BZ*.[119] The results arrived in August, a majority of responses supporting either the location in front of the Märkisches Museum or the Spittalmarkt. The commission resolved to produce "a more precise sculpted model... in order to further work on this question."[120] This small-scale populism was a diversionary tactic, intended to demonstrate state concern for preservation while it demolished the palace. With the conclusion of his work, Strauss wrote to Liebknecht: "You are to be thanked, that out of field of rubble from Hitler's war, the value of our national traditions has been secured as much as possible and is preserved with the future of our people."[121] Given his beliefs about the palace, that Strauss expressed this in a private note could only be explained as an attempt to further his career in an era of Stalinistic repression.

In the Western press the palace still possessed artistic value of global significance. Culpability for the destruction lay primarily with the East German and East Berlin administration and to a much lesser extent with the war. The Eastern "power-holders" were either blindly following a Soviet model for socialist indoctrination through mass rallies and parades and thus were constructing a "Red Square" on the site of the palace, or the Soviets themselves had commanded the demolition with disregard for German history and cultural heritage. Some articles made the accusation of iconoclasm, asserting a broader effort to erase sites of German cultural history.[122] Regarding the end result, the Eastern press purported that the public was "pleased by the grandiose expanse that has been established there by the demolition of the gray Palace-ruin."[123] Western press reports countered: "The observer, frightened by the emptiness of the square, goes back over the bridge."[124] Furthermore, "Communists are trying to outdo their predecessors, the National Socialists," by creating a bigger space for marching the oppressed.[125]

Shaping Marx-Engels Square

Demolishing the Berlin Palace quickly created sufficient space for mass ceremonies, but it would take decades to transform this space into a square enclosed by representative architecture and furnished with commemorative art. During the early years of the GDR, debate centered on several components of the square: (1) a proposed grandstand and Marx-Engels Memorial, (2) a proposed FIAPP Memorial, and (3) the future of Schinkel's German Building Academy (Deutsche Bauakademie).

Grandstand and Marx-Engels Memorial

Soviet leaders viewed large parades on holidays from a grandstand on Red Square, and GDR political leaders were determined to follow suit. The State Building Law of 1950 indicated that rubble from the palace would be used to construct a grandstand on the east side of the square.[126] A provisional grandstand was to be deployed for several years while the final form of the square was determined.[127] Rubble from the palace was carted away during demolition, and in January 1951 the commission determined that an excessive amount of labor would be required to bring it back and then remove it again. Despite this, the impractical proposal returned in March suggesting that the primary motive had been symbolic. The commission once again rejected the idea, noting, "It would not be understood by the Berlin population or by world opinion, if after the clearance of all rubble from the palace, rubble would be piled up once again to form an eleven-meter-high grandstand."[128] The initiative was driven by Erick Honecker, first secretary of the Free German Youth (later first secretary of the SED). Planners successfully appealed to Ulbricht to prevent Honecker from wasting state resources to obtain palace rubble for his seat at the upcoming World Festival of Youth for Peace.[129] Honecker, like many Communists, outwardly accepted socialist realism, which interpreted monarchal architecture as a product of the people, while remaining deeply convinced that it was a symbol of the oppressor.

The Marx Engels Memorial, approved by the Politburo for the site of the demolished National Memorial honoring Kaiser Wilhelm I, soon became entwined with the grandstand project. Ulbricht himself chaired the memorial committee, which included five leading politicians (including Grotewohl, Pieck, and Ebert) and one architect, Liebknecht. The committee determined that Marx and Engels would be realistically depicted in 3.6-meter-tall (about 12 feet) bronze statues with their hands on the *Communist Manifesto* and set on a platform in the middle of the grandstand.[130] Liebknecht requested that this competition be postponed until after the city center design competition, as the architectural form of the square was crucial to the design of the memorial.[131] His appeal unsuccessful, he drafted competition guidelines. The Planning Commission reviewed these and concluded that "the memorial of Marx and Engels... should form the midpoint of the Marx-Engels Square, should dominate it."[132] However, to dominate, the statute would have to be much larger than 12 feet, raising issues of scale that would plague the project.

The Politburo approved competition guidelines in May. Marx and Engels were attributed significance for Germans and all the world's peoples, and their friendship should be expressed. The memorial would signify that Germany had broken with its reactionary past and is following the progressive teachings of the great socialists to a future of freedom, peace, democracy, national unity, happiness, and prosperity. Situated in the center of Germany's capital, the sculpture would help convey the lessons of the great socialists to the German people. Positioned on the West bank of the Spree on axis with Unter den Linden, approaching columns of demonstrators would view the bronze statue and the government high-rise behind it, dominating the city. The grandstand would seat fifteen hundred to three thousand people, with "leading personalities" of the GDR in front of the statue and "guests and delegations" to the left and right. The walls of the side grandstands could be decorated with figures and reliefs depicting the working-class movement.[133] Thus Marx and Engels would occupy the pivotal position linking German working-class history, homage-paying citizens, GDR state leaders, and a dominant government building—a forceful metonymic display of Communist teleology culminating in the GDR.

Oral history suggests that due to an internal dispute between the artists and politicians over the size, form, and placement of the memorial on the extremely oversized square, the competition was suspended.[134] Unmentioned, and equally significant, were conflicting preferences for realism and abstract art. The competition was hardly under way when the internationally recognized German sculptor, Gustav Sietz, expressed frustration with the project parameters to the director of the German Academy of Art.[135] Most of the year, the empty grandstand would act as an oversized base keeping visitors at a distance, whereas an expression of friendship between the men required the sculptures should be human scale and close to viewers, to express "nearness." Socialist realism eschewed modesty, espousing that when individuals associate with grandiose art, they are exalted.[136] Sietz's letter was forwarded to the German Building Academy and while failing to persuade, it doubtless contributed to a loss of confidence in the sculptors. The Politburo quickly terminated the competition and determined that two German artists should be sent to the Soviet Union to study "monumental-sculpture."[137]

Ulbricht wrote the Soviet government on behalf of the Politburo but was ignored. Pieck followed up in November, requesting specific artists known for realism.[138] Pieck then invited seven leading German sculptors for a meeting in December. As an invitation to discussion, Pieck suggested the competition be cancelled as a Soviet would probably emerge victorious, and therefore it would be more expedient to appoint a Soviet sculptor and provide him with a few German assistants. Pieck then asked where the memorial should be placed and who should build it. Sietz emphasized that a good architectural solution was impossible without demolishing the Berlin Cathedral.[139] The cathedral was not valued by architectural historians, and the Kulturbund had recommended demolishing it instead of the palace in 1950 (discussed earlier in the chapter). Given the cathedral's condition and the GDR's politically pragmatic view of religion, Pieck objected, clarifying that it would depend on the political situation and relationship between the state and church. Several of the sculptors refused to work under a Soviet artist, emphasizing the importance of having a German perform this important assignment. Fritz Cremer, another German sculptor of international reputation with considerable Communist political credentials, added that he would not have a Soviet sculptor assist him; Walter Howard followed suit.[140] This apparently had less to do with nationalism and more to do with individual pride and the German modernist tradition of abstract sculpture as opposed to Soviet realism. Pieck informed the artists that he would bring the matter to the Politburo for discussion. The sculptors were charged with developing sketches of their proposed statues of Marx and Engels and would receive a commission.

The Soviets sent two sculptors and arranged for three German sculptors to visit the Soviet Union.[141] In February 1952 the Politburo approved a second competition with the size of the statues increased to 5.5 meters (about 18 feet). The visiting Soviet sculptors toured ateliers and, according to oral history, criticized their German colleagues for their undersized work.[142] However, the sole concern expressed in their report to the Soviet Union was frustration with the German sculptors' "capability" to produce realistic art. As the Germans remained trapped in "formalistic thinking and creating," they recommended that a Soviet sculptor be sent to complete the work. The "battle against formalism" (aka modernism) continued in the GDR.

A second competition was never held. Howard, a "master student" under Sietz at the Academy of Art, was chosen to continue work on the memorial. Though lacking the name power of Sietz and Cremer, he was apparently more willing to comply with politicians' demands and completed a bronze that was cast in late 1956. Still lacking an official plan for Marx-Engels Square, the Ministry of Culture recommended placing the memorial in front of the Palace Bridge across from the Arsenal. The Politburo determined that a committee should investigate the issue and decide whether it was "possible" to place the memorial in Berlin.[143] The memorial was brought into the Capital City Berlin competition in 1958 (see Chapter 2). Gerhard Kroiber's winning entry included the statue in an ensemble with the grandstand and a bridge across the Spree leading to the 150-meter (about 492 feet) high-rise. The 25-meter-high memorial (about 82 feet) would be set in forecourt leading to the building entrance. Again, no building project was realized and therefore no memorial. A more modestly sized Marx-Engels Memorial was finally erected on Marx-Engels Forum behind the Palace of the Republic in 1986. Although the ideological significance of Marx and Engels never wavered, and Ulbricht could have imposed his will to resolve questions of design and location, the indeterminate form of the central square and conflict with artists was sufficient to delay the project for several decades.[144]

FIAPP Memorial

After World War II, groups of former resistance fighters emerged throughout Germany to form committees for Victims of Fascism (Opfer des Faschismus, OdF). In the Soviet Zone the second Sunday in September was declared Memorial Day for the Victims of Fascism, and each year a provisional memorial was constructed on the Lustgarten for the ceremony. Berlin's Communist-dominated committee welcomed non-Communists, West Germans, and West Europeans, and highlighted their participation in the press—a visible manifestation of the proclaimed "antifascist front." At Berlin's first ceremony in 1945, OdF chair Ottomar Geschke (KPD), a former concentration camp prisoner, argued that those who offered the greatest resistance against National Socialism should now have political leadership.[145] Given the strength of Communist opposition, their claims of widespread guilt among Germans and the Leninist principle that a people who cannot be trusted required an "educational dictatorship," Geschke was supporting the case for the less-than-democratic democracy in the Soviet Zone. Yet, during these early years, the event was supported by a broad political coalition and the Eastern and Western press viewed it favorably.[146]

In 1947 the German organization for the victims, the Association of Those Persecuted by the Nazi Regime (Vereinigung der Verfolgten des Naziregimes, VVN), joined the International Federation of Former Political Prisoners of the Nazi Regime (Fédération Internationale des Anciens Prisonniers Politiques du Fascisme, FIAPP). Mayor Schroeder spoke about victims from Berlin, Germany, and the entire world, while Geschke noted the suffering of Jews and called for denazification of the court system.[147] However, with rising political tension, the Socialist Unity Party (SED) began to co-opt the organization and drive out non-Communists.[148] The ceremonies and Eastern press reports reflected these changes, depicting a massive demonstration for peace and democracy that included Western participants despite efforts of reactionary forces to stop them.[149] Western press accused the SED of forcing participation in this ceremony, similar to the Nazis.[150]

At the initial meeting on city center planning on August 5, 1950, the National Memorial was marked for demolition to create space for a new FIAPP Memorial.[151] This equestrian statue, designed by Begas and unveiled in 1897, honored Kaiser Wilhelm I and was not highly regarded by art historians. If left in place, the monarch may eventually have faced off with Marx, Engels, and the seated Politburo during state ceremonies. Geschke and the Berlin VVN leadership condoned the location and agreed to take a position regarding a proposed international competition by the end of August. The competition would be open to citizens of the eighteen nations belonging to the FIAPP, which included Eastern and Western European lands.[152]

The competition was never held. In December 1950 the Politburo decided to locate the Marx-Engels Memorial on the site of the National Memorial and find a new location for the FIAPP Memorial.[153] Six months later, the Politburo targeted the future City Hall Square for the new memorial. The City Planning Commission agreed but recommended Mayor Ebert delay the design competition until after the Central Axis Berlin competition. That competition required the government high-rise to be located on the east bank of the Spree bordering City Hall Square. The design of the memorial was seen to be dependent upon the form of a square, to appropriately convey its meaning and allow "sufficient free space for stationary demonstrations."[154]

Informed of this issue, the Politburo changed the FIAPP Memorial's location to Leipziger Platz, while keeping the competition on track. Thus, in addition to a Thälmann Memorial on Thälmannplatz (Chapter 5), a second monument would espouse the GDR's antifascist credentials even closer to the sector border. This competition was also abandoned. It made little sense due to the absence of a design for Leipziger Platz or any intention to develop one in the near future and the potential to use Thälmannplatz for VVN ceremonies.[155] In fact, the main VVN ceremony was held on Thälmannplatz from 1952 through 1956 and thereafter on Marx-Engels Square. A permanent memorial was never constructed, nor was it included in the guidelines for the 1958 Hauptstadt Berlin competition. Bruno Flierl has suggested that the memorialization of concentration camps in Buchenwald (1958), Sachsenhausen (1961), and Ravensbruck (1959) provided new national centers to commemorate the victims of fascism, explaining why planning for a memorial in the center city was terminated.[156] A second reason had to do with a changing narrative of commemoration. The FIAPP ceremony had increasingly deemphasized mourning and solidarity among diverse persecuted groups in favor of celebrating the triumph of socialism, a role more directly filled by May Day, Liberation Day, and L-L-L ceremonies. Hence state leadership focused on the Marx-Engels memorial for the central square, which was themed as a "forum of the German working-class movement." A memorial for victims had little to contribute to a festive center hosting celebrations of progress and victory.

The German Building Academy

The final focal point of decision-making in this area during the early postwar years involved the German Building Academy, considered by art historians to be a major work by Karl Friedrich Schinkel (figure 4.6). Though it dates to the early nineteenth century (1836), the building is seen as a precursor to modern architecture, because (1) the cubic building presents a duplicate face on four sides instead of a primary facade; (2) the division of the facade and interior axes did not take a rhythmic form but

FIGURE 4.6. German Building Academy. Gerhard Strauss viewed this Schinkel-designed neoclassical building as a precedent for the New German Architecture. He failed to convince, and the structure was ultimately torn down. Landesarchiv Berlin, F-Rep. 290/Fotograf 61-2097.

were partitioned into eight equal sections, resulting in an interior configuration of sixty-four cells, which is visible in the "nonfacades"; (3) the entire building was constructed of brick for fire-safety reasons; and (4) rooms of different sizes were fit into the cellular structural frame as Schinkel had seen in English industrial buildings. Yet articulation and ornamentation of the building's exterior are unmistakably classical.[157]

During World War II, the interior of the Building Academy was largely destroyed, while the exterior suffered moderate damage.[158] The building was ignored until the GDR began planning the city center. Documents from summer of 1950 and early 1951 slated the building for preservation without specifying a future use.[159] Gerhard Strauss saw the building as a launching point for the "new German architecture": "the one object of German architecture, in which Schinkel attempted to unify the possibilities and necessities of construction after the industrial revolution with the requirements of national tradition. Here then, is the beginning of a new realistic art of building."[160] Instead, leading architects drew lessons from Schinkel's more traditional work as the basis for the new German architecture. This was most visible in the preference for the rhythmic articulation, rather than a repetitive pattern that would lend itself more easily to their desired standardization.

Flierl has suggested that rumors about the demolition of the Building Academy began circulating in 1958, possibly originating with the choice to leave its preservation optional in the guidelines for the 1958–1959 *Ideenwettbewerb zur sozialistischen Umgestaltung des Zentrums der Hauptstadt der DDR, Berlin.*[161] The rumors were well founded. Shortly after the competition guidelines were released in October 1958, the Deutsche Bauakademie (DBA) planned for the demolition of the Building Academy "and surrounding ruins."[162] The Politburo's sense of urgency to complete the central axis and shape the central square was noted. Another minor note revealed the intention: "so that the present expanse of Marx-Engels Square is not reduced by the erection of buildings, the ruinous building area west of the Spree canal must be taken up."[163] Dengin's advice to focus on architectural framing rather than numbers of demonstrators went unheeded. The desire for a grandiose space (275,000 persons specified) once again trumped the demand to preserve historic structure. Architects in the design competition viewed the matter differently as forty-four of fifty-six opted to preserve the building. Yet when Gerhard Kosel developed a new plan in 1959, the Building Academy and several nearby structures were removed to make space for a new Foreign Ministry Building enclosing the west edge of Marx-Engels Square.

When the intent to demolish the Building Academy became known in late 1959, East German architects, architectural historians, and preservationists launched an intensive, internal protest. Appeals were directed to Paul Verner, the leading politician on the Commission for Building the Berlin City Center. Strauss, speaking for art historians throughout the GDR, declared the building a "monument to national and international architectural history."[164] As in the case of the palace, an alternative plan demonstrated possibilities for incorporating the structure. Verner ignored the pleas and in December 1959 clarified that a new Foreign Ministry building would be placed on the west side of Marx-Engels Square where the "ruin of Schinkel's Bauakademie will be cleared." In early 1960, West Berlin art historians joined the protest. In late May 1960 city center planners met with leading politicians, including Ulbricht, and the decision for demolition was conclusively affirmed. In early 1961 planners examined possibilities for salvaging part or all of the structure: (1) reconstruct the building on another spot, (2) move it to a nearby site, or (3) save several axes for use elsewhere.[165]

In April 1961 the Politburo noted that a number of architects and art historians spoke out against demolition, but the cost to save the "ruin" and construct a habitable interior was deemed too high at DM 8 million to DM 8.5 million. It would be demolished and "the most valuable parts of the facade" (four bays around the entrance) would be saved and installed in a new building in the future for an estimated DM 6.5 million. Strauss's decade-old warning against saving only the facade due to the significance of Schinkel's work in the interior was ignored.[166] The DM 2 million difference between rehabilitation and preservation on another site could hardly be considered significant, thus the driving factors were disinterest in historic architecture and the rush to shape the new government center.[167]

When construction of the Palace of the Republic fronting Marx-Engels Square began in 1973, considerable theoretical developments had occurred. Emily Pugh indicates its central design motifs, "unity, openness and accessibility, and visibility," reflected new theoretical developments that tied into international modernism and recent scientific inquiry from the fields of psychology, sociology and semiotics that examined the emotional and psychological impacts of urban form.[168] The building could be considered the apex of technological optimism in GDR architecture, with extensive mechanization and a theoretical basis in science not tradition. For instance, one article reported that the great hall's size could be adjusted by remotely moving its walls from a control room. The architect declared that the design of the room had no precedent, but it was "something completely new."[169]

Theory Distorted or a Matter of Emphasis?

After the war, architect Hans Scharoun attempted to fund minimal repairs to the Berlin Palace based on a modernist view of the building as a valuable historical monument and a crucial urban design element. Communist politicians opposed the repairs, an iconoclastic approach, at times directly expressed as opposition to the German monarchy and militarism, and at times concealed by utilitarian arguments pitting spending on monumental structures against housing, as Communists had done since the nineteenth century. The spatial value of sections of the palace for exhibitions, offices, and storage attracted some attention from German Communists, and especially the SMAD, which commandeered the structure after the SPD won control of the City Council. Following the division of the city administration in 1948, Eastern planners and preservationists expressed conflicting views of the palace, continuing a decades-old conflict between the professions and generating uncertainty about its future.

After the Trip to Moscow, planning was officially guided by socialist realism, which valued historic preservation but also called for a large central square for demonstrations. Whereas this theory held the political center to be a broad area, discussion quickly centered on the site of the palace as "the center." In July 1950, Ulbricht announced that the "palace-ruin" destroyed by Anglo-American bombers would be torn down to make room for a new square, thereby denying its existence as valuable architecture and ignoring its political symbolism. Architects protested internally, offering alternative plans that preserved at least part of the palace while providing a large square, but Ulbricht was undeterred. *Neues Deutschland* let slip iconoclastic motives, identifying the building as a reminder of "ignominious deeds." Western assertions that the Soviets were behind the decision appear unfounded. When the Soviets were informed of planning in October, they asserted that much attention had been given to parades and not enough to preservation.

Initial protest came from East German cultural leaders, who attempted to challenge the decision with recently acquired socialist-realist concepts, traditional preservationist arguments, and in one case the need for "democratic" decision-making. Western cultural elites sent appeals solely in the terms of traditional preservationism, while the West Berlin and West German governments remained silent as they did not formally recognize the GDR. Gerhard Strauss led efforts to salvage artistically valuable pieces and document new information about the "ruin." He both employed and contradicted socialist realism and traditional preservationism, while making hearty use of claims to scientific legitimacy, as he attempted to publicly justify the decision and privately appeal it. Granted only a few months, preservation work was extremely limited, although a carefully calculated press campaign presented the effort as a triumph. Tellingly, the artistically valuable Schlüter courtyard was demolished and the balcony where Karl Liebknecht proclaimed a socialist republic was saved. Documentation was largely a public relations farce under the guise of science. Finally, a populist outreach effort over the future location for the artistically and historically insignificant Neptune Fountain served to divert attention from the destruction.

Decades would pass before the new Marx-Engels Square took its final form. During the 1950s attention centered on decisions regarding a new grandstand, Marx-Engels memorial and FIAPP memorial, and regarding the fate of Schinkel's German Building Academy. The grandstand and Marx-Engels memorial project reveal the eagerness of the new state to establish its physical and symbolic presence on the new parade ground in the "center" of Berlin. Yet disputes between German modernist sculptors and German political leaders invested in socialist realism, along with uncertainty regarding the final form of the square, proved intractable. The FIAPP memorial project was received with some enthusiasm during the GDR's early years but was soon abandoned due to redundancy through the memorialization of concentration camps and a state shift from emphasizing victimhood to celebrating socialist victory.

The case of the German Building Academy is emblematic of the gradual shift in East German city building practice that set in during the mid- to late 1950s. According to socialist realism, the building was a prime example of national architectural heritage. Fittingly, it was marked for preservation as one of the buildings enclosing the western edge of Marx-Engels Square in the early 1950s. By the late 1950s the state emphasized economic efficiency, technological progress, and a modernist aesthetic and devalued national architectural heritage. The building was demolished.

5

Wilhelmstrasse

On Downing Street and on Wall Street, one has slowly come to grasp that the times in which one can do business with millions of human lives on Wilhelmplatz belong to the past.

—"Vom Wilhelmplatz zum Thälmannplatz," *Neues Deutschland*, November 29, 1949

WILHELMSTRASSE EVOLVED over several centuries from an upscale residential quarter to the center of German government. This process included a series of changes to the use and symbolic content of its buildings as well as some demolition and new construction. World War II left much of the area in ruins with heavier damage to older, smaller buildings. Though subject to the same ideological currents as other areas in Berlin, decision-making regarding the future of buildings in this area appeared more complicated and at times seem contradictory. Tainted pasts were ignored for some sites and highlighted in others. Some Nazi buildings were demolished, while others came to house important government institutions. Eighteenth-century buildings were demolished here, while they were being restored on Unter den Linden. A square foreseen as an important center of governmental and commemorative activity was fit with a new, representative subway station, before slowly sinking into obscurity.

These peculiarities may result from some of the unique qualities of Wilhelmstrasse. First, few structures were considered important for cultural or artistic history, but many were strongly associated with the more sensitive issue of state history. Second, some structures had great spatial capacity, which had to be considered vis-a-vis their dark pasts. Third, many buildings had complex histories, some of which was well known, and some of which was terra incognita. Fourth, planners who foresaw this area continuing its role as government center were confronted by a state leadership determined that Marx-Engels Square would play this role. Fifth, as East-

West tensions escalated, this street's position near the border made it less appealing to government planners.

Friedrich's Baroque Extension

Wilhelmstrasse and Wilhelmplatz were planned as part of the baroque extension of Friedrichstadt at the beginning of the eighteenth century. King Friedrich Wilhelm I was keenly involved with the planning process that resulted in geometric expressions believed to reflect the holy trinity and the sign of the cross. Three major public spaces would adjoin gates in new customs' walls: the Quarre, the Oktogon, and the Rondell. Wilhelmstrasse stretched from the Rondell in the south to the Quarre (Pariser Platz) in the north, with the section between contemporary Leipzigerstrasse and Pariser Platz being of greatest historical interest.

During the second and third decades of the century, Berlin experienced a construction boom as King Friedrich Wilhelm I offered an array of incentives to those willing to locate there. On Wilhelmstrasse, in particular, the king granted those who had earned his favor construction materials and building lots. The new residences and small palaces would be inhabited by nobility and bourgeois, native Prussians, Hugonauts, migrant south Germans, and one member of the Jewish community. Building facades on the west side of the street concealed extremely deep lots extending to the customs wall and primarily belonged to Prussia's leading statesmen. The smaller lots on the east side were granted to lesser statesmen and notable bourgeois citizens. In 1734 with insufficient new construction to build out the extension, the king provided incentives to manufactories, craftsmen, and professionals.[1] Most of the impact of this policy would occur on and below Leipzigerstrasse. However, a nonpolluting manufactory of gold and silver ornaments for the military and high society was constructed on Wilhelmplatz to finance an orphanage. It was sold to a Jewish resident, who purchased a second lot on Wilhelmplatz for a "Haus der Judenschaft." Also, the Schwerin Palais was built as residence of the Prussian General Schwerin and his brother on a large lot in the northern end of the street.[2]

Following the Seven Years War, Wilhelmplatz was chosen as the site for new statues commemorating Prussian military leaders, primarily because leading statesmen lived in the area. Initially, this included four statues of moderate artistic value honoring fallen generals, and over the next decades two exceptional sculptures by Johann Gottfried Schadow honoring victorious generals were added. Wet Prussian winters began eroding the marble statues, so in the mid-nineteenth century bronze reproductions by Christian Daniel Rauch were placed on Wilhelmplatz and the originals were eventually displayed in the Kaiser Friedrich Museum (Bode Museum). Further military symbolism accrued in 1806 as Napoleon's commandant of Berlin occupied General Schulenberg's palace. Upon liberation in 1815 the three nearby squares were renamed after battles where Napoleon's troops were defeated: the Quarre to Pariser Platz, the Oktogon to Leipziger Platz and the Rondell to Belle-Alliance Platz.[3]

In the late eighteenth century a number of nobles under financial duress sold their palaces to ascendant bourgeois, while remaining aristocrats viewed the newcomers as interlopers. In the 1790s the offices of the second most powerful person in Prussia, the Gross-Canzler and Ministry of Justice, were moved from the Berlin Palace to Wilhelmstrasse 74. King Friedrich Wilhelm III's motives were to establish a separate space for the Gross-Canzler and to "rescue" Wilhelmstrasse, which he saw as part of his heritage. Through the early nineteenth century, the Prussian state continued to expand and depart the Berlin Palace. Wilhelmstrasse was the street of choice as an office holder could obtain a palace with residential space, rooms for offices, and large, representative spaces for meetings—all within walking distance to the Gross-Canzler. In 1819 the foreign affairs minister moved into Wilhelmstrasse 76. Additional ministries and foreign embassies continued to occupy buildings in and around Wilhelmstrasse, such that it became a center of Prussian and international politics by the midcentury. The architecture of the new ministries lacked representative expression, their presence in the "province of royals" viewed as a sufficient demonstration of authority.[4]

In the 1840s hotels and restaurants were opened on Wilhelmstrasse and surrounding areas. The "Hotel Royal" on Wilhelmstrasse was a favorite among visiting diplomats, who often met the king there. The Revolution of 1848 and 1849 centered on the palace, but petitions were evaluated by the government on Wilhelmstrasse. After the Revolution, political functions continued to spread throughout the area. With national unification in 1871, the ministries of the newly formed German government developed from their Prussian predecessors, and the most important new offices were located on Wilhelmstrasse. Renovations, additions, and new construction endowed the street with larger neoclassical structures. Attempts to introduce liberal iconography, typically by adding the female Germania figure to buildings, largely failed. Symbols of monarchy dominated the new structures just as the royal house dominated the constitutional monarchy. The Prussian Gross-Canzler's building was briefly used as the German Chancellor's Office, and Chancellor Bismarck resided at Wilhelmstrasse 76. Adjacent to the Chancellor's office, Vossstrasse was cut through to Königgrätzerstrasse. A few years later the Chancellor's Office was moved to the Schulenberg Palace, facing Wilhelmplatz. The Foreign Office and Finance Ministry also occupied buildings on Wilhelmplatz. Several top Prussian government offices were located on the east side of the street, including the Prussian State Ministries building at Wilhelmstrasse 63-64. The Reichstag was provisionally located in a former porcelain factory on Leipzigerstrasse, before moving to its present location in nearby Tiergarten. In 1875, Kaiser Wilhelm I attended the opening of the Kaiserhof Hotel (Wilhelmplatz), a new center of political activity, most notably where Bismarck hosted the Congress of Berlin in 1878. Renown artists, scientists, and businessmen stayed at the hotel, which hosted events for a wide range of cultural and political groups.[5]

During the Revolution of 1918, political action including demonstrations was split between Wilhelmstrasse, the Berlin Palace, and the Reichstag. On November 9, 1918, Friedrich Ebert and Phillip Scheidemann negotiated with Max von Baden over the Kaiser's resignation in the Chancellor's Office. Scheidemann addressed a crowd from the office's window but later proclaimed the new republic from a balcony of the Reichstag. A few hours later, Karl Liebknecht proclaimed a doomed Free Socialist Republic of Germany from the window of the palace. Nonetheless, the new constitution was signed in Weimar to associate with the center of the German humanist tradition rather than the Prussian militarist tradition and to maintain a safe distance from the clamorous streets of Berlin. The government institutions of the Weimar Republic went into existing buildings on Wilhelmstrasse for pragmatic reasons and, arguably, a desire to enhance the standing of the new democracy by associating it with the Prussian state. However, the relationship to this tradition was quite ambivalent. The government determined that monarchal symbols would be removed from public buildings, except where they were inseparable from the building or had significant artistic value.[6]

These exceptions allowed many buildings to retain these symbols either for art-historic reasons or under their guise. Some buildings faced iconoclasm, such as the Prussian State Ministries building. In the early 1920s the Prussian minister president sought to remove reliefs of Prussian

FIGURE 5.1. Reichschancellery (view from Wilhelmplatz). Critics considered the modernist extension to the Reichschancellery (center) to be a successful architectural mediation between the baroque Schulenberg Palace (Old Reichschancellery) to its north (right) and the neoclassical structure to its south (left). The statue in the foreground depicts Prussian Field Marshal Jacob Kieth. BA, Digital Picture Database, Bild 146-2006-0097, Sammlung von Repro-Negativen, Kurt Breuer, Spring 1939.

kings and other monarchal symbols and by the mid-1920s this had been completed. The Chancellor's Office was extended to the south with a competition-winning design by Eduard Siedler, described by the state secretary as bringing the "spirit of the new times" while respecting Wilhelmstrasse (figure 5.1). Critics saw a successful mediation between the neoclassical building to the south and the baroque palace to the north; conservatives condemned its modernist appearance as "factory-like," which was later repeated by Hitler, although it would blend with works that Albert Speer added in the ensuing decade. The Kaiserhof continued hosting sundry affairs during this era, notably the founding of Luft Hansa, two meetings of the Jewish Museum Association, Adolf Hitler's taking up residence, and the Nazi Party occupying the top floor as their Berlin headquarters.[7]

Regarding the Nazi's assumption of power, Goebbels wrote: "It is almost like a dream. Wilhelmstrasse belongs to us." National Socialist

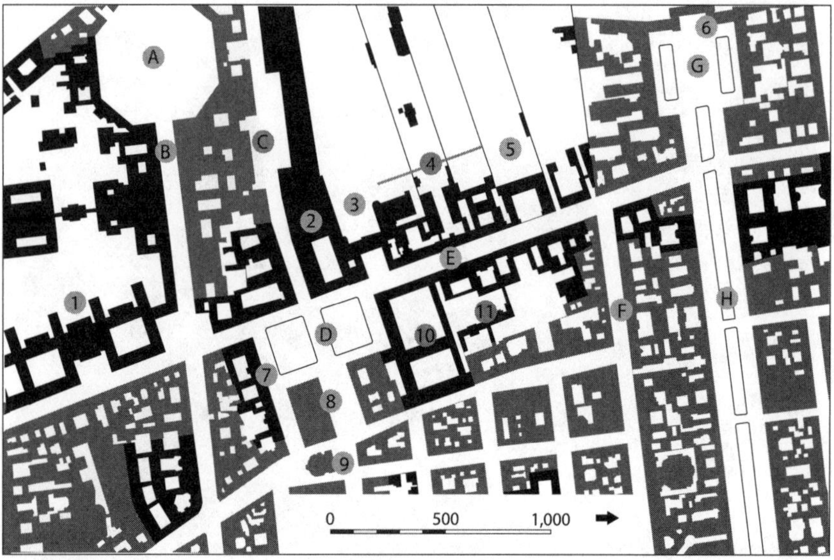

FIGURE 5.2. Map of Wilhelmstrasse, 1930s. Government buildings are shown in black. In general, the small, closely packed, irregular-shaped courtyards indicate older, smaller buildings. Streets and Plazas: (A) Leipziger Platz, (B) Leipzigerstrasse, (C) Vossstrasse, (D) Wilhelmplatz (later Thälmannplatz), (E) Wilhelmstrasse, (F) Behrenstrasse, (G) Pariser Platz, (H) Unter den Linden. Significant buildings: (1) Ministry of Aviation, (2) Hitler's Chancellery, (3) Reichschancellery (Schulenberg Palace), (4) State Department (occupied three buildings), (5) President's Office (Schwerin Palace), (6) Brandenburg Gate, (7) Ministry of Finance, (8) Kaiserhof Hotel, (9) Holy Trinity Church, (10) Ministry of Propaganda, (11) NSDAP offices. Map adapted from "Plan der Wilhelmstrasse aus dem Jahre 1936" und "Der Bereich Wilhelmstrasse und Voßstrasse… 1939," in Demps, *Berlin-Wilhelmstrasse*, 7, 8. Cartography by Paul Stangl.

(NSDAP) party and state officials concentrated their offices on the street and initiated major changes (figure 5.2). Whereas the German Empire's main parade grounds were Unter den Linden and Templehof Field, the NSDAP concentrated parades and rallies on Wilhelmstrasse and Wilhelmplatz. The Nazi era began with a torchlight procession by the SA, the SS, and the Stahlhelm through the Brandenburg Gate, across Pariser Platz, and down Wilhelmstrasse to the Chancellor's Office, informing adjacent embassies and the rest of the world that a significant political shift had occurred. Hitler, greatly concerned about establishing the proper relationship between himself and the masses, found existing windows and balconies either too far or near the street, too concealed or open, or lacking appro-

FIGURE 5.3. Ministry of Aviation. This sprawling structure with two thousand rooms extends down Wilhelmstrasse (left) and Leipzigerstrasse (right). It is organized around three closed and five open courtyards, with a primary forecourt ("court-of-honor") opening onto Wilhelmstrasse (visible as gap to left). BA, Digital Picture Database, Image 146-1979-074-36A, Sammlung von Repro Negativen, Otto Hagemann, December 1938.

priate architectural form. Hence a new balcony was added to the recent Chancellor's Office extension. One story above street level on a platform of great solidity, his upper torso and face visible, Hitler observed frequent parades while being photographed for the world press. Flags, previously used to signify the presence of a building's owner, now covered facades creating a dynamic atmosphere on the staid, old street. Wilhelmplatz, officially declared the center of political events in the capital, was renovated as a space for political assemblies. To create space for political rallies and parades, the gardenlike baroque square's trees, commemorative statues, and the U-Bahn pergola were removed and the surface was paved.[8]

Increased state centralization required additional office space, including the occupation of numerous existing buildings by Party and state and the construction of several large buildings on Wilhelmstrasse, each in an austere neoclassical style. The Propaganda Ministry occupied Schinkel's Ordenspalais on Wilhelmplatz and constructed a very large addition that related to the original in scale and in fenestration proportion and pattern. From the site of the former Prussian War Ministry at the intersection of Leipzigerstrasse, the new Ministry of Aviation building sprawled down Wilhelmstrasse (figure 5.3). The largest office building in Berlin, it con-

FIGURE 5.4. Hitler's Reichschancellery. View of Hitler's Chancellery from the west, looking down Voßstrasse from the corner of Ebertstrasse. The long, shallow forecourt opening onto Voßstrasse is visible as a gap to the right. BA, Digital Picture Database, Image 212-127, Sammlung Ugo Proietti, July 1946.

tained two thousand individual offices and 7 kilometers (over 4 miles) of corridors. Its modernity was celebrated in the press just a few years after the term had been used as a "curse word" by Nazis. The building's footprint followed baroque precedent with wings to the street defining a "court of honor" and a hall of honor on the piano nobile. The press depicted these features as carrying forth Prussian tradition.[9]

A huge addition to the chancellor's office, stretched a full block from Wilhelmstrasse west on Voßstrasse (figure 5.4). The immensity and monumentality of the new chancellor's office had much to do with Hitler's aggrandizement and little to do with functional needs. Whereas the old chancellor's office acquired meaning through Bismarck's prolonged occupation, the new chancellor's office would employ spatial composition and symbolic expression to glorify Hitler as the "working chancellor" and "impress small potentates." In turn, Hitler's importance to the Nazi regime and war crimes were indelibly impressed upon the structure. The infamous Führer's Bunker was constructed under the original Chancellor's Garden, and Gestapo headquarters occupied the former School of Industrial Arts and Crafts on nearby Prinz Albrecht Strasse. In sum, "Wilhelmstrasse had become a place of culprits, political criminals and organized mass murder. . . . Mass murder, war and unspeakable horrors were planned and organized in Wilhelmstrasse."[10]

During World War II, aerial bombing raids and artillery battles on the ground reduced much of Wilhelmstrasse and Wilhelmplatz to ruins. Many premodern, Prussian buildings, such as the old Reichs Chancellery, the Ordenspalais, and the Foreign Office, were little more than rubble, and the Kaiserhof Hotel and Finance Ministry were severely damaged. Numerous other older buildings were damaged beyond recognition. Nazi-era buildings tended to survive the war in better condition.[11]

An Uneasy Balance

In a city decimated by war, Wilhelmstrasse possessed a great deal of easily restorable office space, albeit loaded with militaristic and Nazi associations. German Communists rarely were deterred by this history, often making due with purges of symbolism. While the calculus of place-based meaning, representation, and spatial relations was important, how they were considered did not follow hard-and-fast rules. Instead they appear to have been weighed off, akin to a legal balancing test. Pre-twentieth-century buildings on Wilhelmstrasse, especially those dating to the eighteenth century, were relatively small and often heavily damaged, offering little to an administration in dire need of office space. Also, they were tainted by the Prussian monarchal and militaristic traditions, although less stigmatized by the Nazi past than many newer structures.

Some structures that survived in better condition were reused without any consideration for the Allied Control Council (ACC) directive to "demilitarize" and "denazify." For instance, the palace that had housed the Finance Ministry during the Nazi era was quickly renovated to house the Magistrat's Department of Sozialwesen (Social Services). The former Kaiser's Civilkabinett, which served as NSDAP headquarters after their ascension to power, was converted to a dormitory for Berlin University by the SMAD in 1947, absent any soul searching. The building was not as identifiable to the public as one of Wilhelmstrasse's more notorious power centers and was not built to serve this purpose—seemingly more important than meaning acquired though use. Yet the majority of older structures on Wilhelmstrasse would require significant restoration work to become habitable, or they would have to be demolished before their site could be reused.

In the eyes of German Communists, most of the buildings failed to merit resources for either of these purposes and were therefore left to decay.[12]

The potential reuse of Nazi-era structures was complicated by their greater spatial capacity and better condition, one the one hand, and their direct connection with the NSDAP on the other. The Aviation Ministry was responsible for civil air travel and military aviation, which played a significant role supporting the German Army invasion of Eastern Europe. In 1945 the SMAD ordered the provisional renovation of the former Ministry of Transportation and the Ministry of Aviation as offices for the Deutsche Wirtschaftskommission (DWK), the highest German administrative organization in the Soviet Zone. Any surviving Nazi iconography was removed on command of the victorious allies. At the behest of the Berlin Magistrat, a relief depicting the great generals of Prussian and German history was removed for its militaristic content. Given the structure's immense spatial value, German Communists accepted the removal of iconography and text as sufficient to overcome its past as a Nazi military command center.[13]

Although many nearby structures were cannibalized for materials to restore the Ministry of Aviation, the Nazi-era extension of the Propaganda Ministry was spared as it too offered valuable office space. These offices were the symbolic and functional headquarters of an important ministry in the National Socialist state working to construct a "people's community." This entailed glorification of racial purity and hatred of enemies, especially Bolsheviks and Jews. As such, this ministry was strongly tied to the Holocaust. In contrast, the pre-twentieth-century section of the building that fronted Wilhelmplatz (Ordenspalais) was demolished because it was severely damaged. The Nazi-era section, which survived in better condition, was occupied without discussion of place-based meaning.[14]

Nevertheless, Communists were not entirely comfortable with the origins and history of either the Ministry of Aviation or the Ministry of Propaganda buildings. One is hard-pressed to find mention of their locations in the press, or any reference to their past function, which was not standard practice. For instance, the Lustgarten featured prominently in reports as the site of parades and rallies, often in headlines. On October 7, 1949, the German People's Council constituted itself as the provisional People's Chamber of the new German Democratic Republic in the former Aviation Ministry. *Neues Deutschland* and the *Berliner Zeitung* referred to the site as "the building of the Deutsche Wirtschaftskommission," and the latter went so far as to describe the architecture.[15] The new People's Chamber's offices, located in the Nazi extension of the Propaganda Ministry, were listed as "Mauerstrasse 45." For "as long as this state existed, there was deliberate confusion about the place where its formation was carried out."[16]

Hitler's Chancellery, the most notorious building on Wilhelmstrasse and sole building representative of a state organ built by the Nazis, survived the war in a heavily damaged state.[17] Restoration was never considered. Shortly after the war, Berliners stole metal and wood parts and peat roof insulation, and the Magistrat salvaged materials that were in short supply. The Soviet commandant ordered the removal of marble and limestone plates from the interior, which were reused in Soviet war memorials in the Tiergarten and in Treptow. A few years later, some was used in the Kaiserhof subway station (later Thälmannplatz, now Mohrenstrasse), echoing Moscow's luxurious stations.[18] Additional material from the Chancellery was used in a variety of applications throughout the city including the People's Theater and Humboldt University.[19] By the end of 1948 little more than a shell remained, which could have been restored for use as another "unnamed" office building. Instead, the Soviet commandant ordered its demolition, perhaps the only case in which they intervened in Berlin to efface a structure for its symbolism.[20] Direct association with Hitler proved too nefarious a memory to overcome.

The SMAD also ordered the destruction of bunkers in this area. In 1945 one detonation damaged the ruin of the Holy Trinity Church to the extent that it later had to be torn down. In 1948 the Soviets ordered more demolitions, but the German administration lacked equipment and explosives and feared endangering other buildings. In response, the SMAD required only that the structures be made unusable. Hitler's bunker was noted as being destroyed, but in 1988 it was discovered that it had only been blocked off.[21]

Wilhelmstrasse in the GDR

With the founding of the East German state, Wilhelmstrasse briefly became the focus of planning efforts. In *Berlin-Wilhelmstrasse*, Laurenz Demps argues that this area was intended to be a new East German center of government with the central square for state-run parades on Wilhelmplatz, enlarged through the demolition of the Ordenspalais. This idea was allegedly abandoned, however, when the streets proved too narrow to accommodate massive parades during the Deutschlandtreffen in May 1950. Indeed, the Magistrat's Building Department appears to have assumed this would be the government center. Yet soon after the GDR's founding, jurisdiction over all planning in Berlin had been granted to the Ministry of Building (Ministerium für Aufbau, MfA), which was only beginning to shape its ideas about the city. The shift of the main government center away from Wilhelmstrasse resulted from the MfA's socialist-realist planning efforts and Walter Ulbricht's ideas about Berlin—evidence indicates that the alleged parade jam-up never occurred.[22]

It is logical that Magistrat planners intended Wilhelmstrasse to be the government center because of its existing monumental buildings and concentration of administrative functions. The former Aviation Ministry, renamed the House of Ministries, contained many leading administrative offices. The former Prussian Chamber of Deputies on Prinz Albrecht Strasse became Prime Minister Otto Grotewohl's office. A former bank on Wilhelmplatz became the Guesthouse of the Government of the GDR, and the former Propaganda Ministry housed the provisional People's Chamber. Yet Communist uneasiness with Wilhelmstrasse's past, already evident in their effacement of iconography and buildings, continued as they selectively engaged place-based meanings. Wilhelmplatz became the focus of an effort to symbolically rehabilitate the government quarter for the new German state by evading recognition of the militaristic and Nazi past and taking steps to eradicate evidence of it, while inscribing symbols of the German socialist past. On November 30, 1949, a state ceremony rededicated Wilhelmplatz as Thalmannplatz in honor of the iconic Communist leader Ernst Thälmann. The press elaborated on the change "From Wilhelmplatz to Thälmannplatz" in an article by that name. A narrative of German exceptionalism portrayed the area as the center of militaristic reactionary tradition extending from the "Prussian militarists" through the "Nazis."[23]

Prussia's wars and plundering raids had been planned in the buildings lining the square. Rather than honoring "artists or scientists," the statues that had been erected here commemorated Frederick the Great's generals, who carried out the Seven Years War "at the expense of the people." The "bad tradition" initiated by the Prussians carried in to the Nazi era, when ploys "hatched in the conference rooms of the Kaiserhof [were] turned into dreadful reality" across Wilhelmplatz in the Chancellor's Office, making those two hundred steps "the most criminal path" of German reactionary forces. During World War II, barbaric Western allies bombed working-class residential areas before turning attention to the government on Wilhelmstrasse, where the war had been organized. The tone was one of achievement, as though bombing buildings had cleansed the city of a burden. In fact, the war had not erased the past. Many older buildings existed in a ruinous state, their demolition or restoration yet to be determined.

"A new spirit" was coming to Wilhelmstrasse with the "bright white of the People's Council building" shining across the square as citizens cast a hate-filled glance at the last rubble of the Chancellor's Office being packed into trains.[24] The article failed to mention that the People's Council met in the Nazi Propaganda Ministry extension or to provide the former identities of other buildings occupied by the government. The square's future name derived from a different facet of the nation's past: Communist Party chairman and parliamentarian, Ernst Thälmann. He had been arrested and imprisoned for more than eleven years before he "was cowardly murdered by the fascist power-holders on Wilhelmstrasse." A new era of German politics was emerging, in which diplomats based on Thälmannplatz would have the "lofty assignment of securing peace and establishing friendship" between Germans and other nations. The name "Wilhelmplatz" and the militaristic policies associated with it were being relegated to "oblivion," which should be noted on "Wall Street and Downing Street"—presumably the true command centers of the West that may face similar fates.

While the MfA-organized Trip to Moscow was under way in May 1950, the Magistrat obtained approval for a DM 1 million restoration of the decimated Thälmannplatz subway station (formerly Kaisershof Station), the last station to be reopened. A "worthy, simple form" would be required as this would be the entrance to Thälmannplatz with the future Thälmann memorial, forming the heart of the government quarter. Retail and advertisements would be excluded, and marble from Hitler's Chancellery would cover walls and columns, which along with other artistic work accounted for 40 percent of the budget.[25] When the station opened in August, the press touted its completion in 108 days and made no mention of the source of the marble.[26] If Communist decision-makers felt some satisfaction in reusing materials from the Chancellery, they withheld it from the public, declaring that the last marble plates arrived from Thuringia just in time to complete the project. Instead, reports on the dedication ceremony emphasized its destruction by "Anglo-American bombs," and the links between the Communist past, the new German state, and progress in reconstruction. The wife and daughter of Thälmann, the martyred "great German labor leader" murdered in a concentration camp, were joined by the twenty youth who would operate the station. The station was decorated with greenery, flowers, and the flags of the GDR, the workers' movement, as well as the "youth of the city of Berlin" (FDJ). The district mayor expressed the gratitude of Berliners for the support of the "government of our republic."

In July, Magistrat planning director Brockschmidt was directed to "coordinate" planning with the Ministry of Building. He identified fourteen areas in "urgent" need of a plan. The first project he listed was the design of Thälmannplatz, which could be further expanded onto the grounds of the Chancellery and Transportation Ministry if they were torn down. Next came the design of Thälmannstrasse, and third, the choice of location for the Ministry of Transportation. Fourth, was the "design of the government quarter" surrounding Thälmannstrasse. The Lustgarten was unmentioned.[27] Though the Ministry of Building had supported the creation of Thälmannplatz, the Trip to Moscow ensured that city planning would begin from scratch according to socialist-realist principles. The Soviets had emphasized the importance of identifying the "city center," which must include a main square for parades and demonstrations. In fact, the idea of demolishing the palace for a "parade forum" had already been expressed in 1949 and the main ceremonial activities in East Berlin centered on the Lustgarten since the end of the war.

Likely Lothar Bolz and/or Walter Ulbricht had already set their sights there rather than Thälmannstrasse. In July, with the approval of a five-year plan to finance looming construction, the development of a city center building plan became a pressing priority. Hence Brockschmidt sent his plans to Bolz, and the next day Ulbricht negated them by announcing plans to demolish the palace for a new central square on the Lustgarten and palace site. In August the Plan for the New Building of Berlin specified that Thälmannstrasse would include "embassies and government buildings" and the main representative government building would occupy Marx-Engels Square. Thälmannstrasse was slated for widening to enhance its role feeding marching columns onto Unter den Linden, but this was soon deemed unnecessary as the Palace Bridge limited the flow of demonstrators headed to Marx-Engels Square.[28]

The design of Thälmannplatz and the Thälmann Memorial were to be developed through a competition with guidelines written prior to the Trip to Moscow when modernist principles predominated. The 1940s extension to the former Propaganda Ministry was to form the north and east sides of the square and contain government administrative offices.

FIGURE 5.5. Wilhelmplatz to Thälmannplatz. With the demolition of the Ministry of Propaganda's wings fronting Wilhelmplatz and Wilhelmstrasse, the square was expanded to the north. The remaining rear and side wings now fronted the plaza. BA, Digital Picture Database, Image 183-S87231, *Allgemeiner Deutcher Nachrichtendienst—Zentralbild*, Rudolph, August 1949.

The south side was to be enclosed by a future building and on the west side, the Chancellor's Office ruin would be demolished, making room for a "parking lot or green space." Just south of Thälmannplatz, the "most important east-west thoroughfare solely for automobile traffic" was planned, an expressway following Vossstrasse.[29]

The jury was primarily composed of political leaders, headed by Otto Grotewohl and Walter Ulbricht, but also architects including Hans Scharoun (figure 5.5). The competition concluded in April 1950, and a public exhibition was held in the recently founded Academy of Art on Robert-Koch Square. The competition results were to be announced on May 31, while the cornerstone-laying ceremony was planned for August 18, the sixth anniversary of Ernst Thälmann's murder. The sculpture was to be located in the center of the square, which would provided partial physical and visual obstruction of parades and rallies. In August the Plan for the New Building of Berlin placed the memorial on the west side of Thälmannstrasse, according to Liebknecht, "probably approximately on the site of the former Chancellery."[30] This both cleared the square for parades and placed a symbol of Communist martyrdom astride the former epicenter of Nazi rule.

The Politburo acknowledged the winning entry by Ruth Hähne but did not find the result sufficient to approve construction. The Planning Commission began preparation for a limited competition to develop a new plan for Thälmannplatz, a design program for a new Ministry of Foreign Affairs building on Thälmannplatz, and a site plan for Thälmannstrasse. The second competition was never held and previous winning sculptors, René Graetz and Ruthild Hahne, were commissioned to further develop a model. Visiting Soviet artists informed President Pieck that the sculpture had a poor relationship to the square, criticized Graetz for formalistic rather than realistic thinking, and suggested the possibility of another competition.[31] This same issue of Soviet realism versus German modernism had plagued the effort to create a Marx-Engels Memorial (Chapter 4). Eventually Graetz withdrew and Hans Kies eventually replaced him. A new directive required the sculpture to consist of a group of workers being led by Thälmann, a concept mentioned during Pieck's meeting with Soviet sculptors, likely reflecting on Hähne's entry in the first competition.[32]

In 1952, Politburo leaders made Thälmannplatz the site of a major state ceremony, moving commemoration for the victims of fascism there from August-Bebel Square, and visiting the artists' atelier to offer advice.[33] Plans for a FIAPP memorial on Marx-Engels Square had been abandoned. Placing the "remembrance for the victims of fascist terror" on Thälmannplatz fit changes in the political context and the ceremony. By the 1950s this day of remembering victims increasingly emphasized resistance and fighting against Hitler and for the "bright socialist future," with remembrance of Thälmann playing a larger role.[34] In fact, the Politburo approved measures at Buchenwald to honor Thälmann but no one else persecuted there.[35] The initiation of a "purge of cosmopolitanism" led to the arrest of many Jewish Communists and the flight of others. Soon, the Persecuted by the Nazi Regime (Vereinigung der Verfolgten des Naziregimes, VVN) was disbanded in favor of a state-run Committee of Antifascist Resistance that excluded Jewish voices from organizing the ceremony. The centrality of Thälmann, the German martyr-hero, would highlight resistance and fighting for German socialism and diminish "lost causes such as the Jews."[36] This reinforced Thälmannplatz as a space of commemoration, akin to the cemetery in Friedrichsfelde. In the summer of 1952 the City Planning

Commission agreed on a plan for the square that built over Vossstrasse and included a green space enclosed by buildings behind the memorial.[37] In October the Politburo approved a program to develop the memorial, including determining the final form of the square, providing a studio for the artists, and developing a press release plan.[38] The new city center plan of April 1953 shifted the green space north of Vossstrasse and proposed a new building across the western edge of the former Thälmannplatz site, creating a traditional square.[39]

Little progress occurred before planning efforts were complicated by the Uprising of June 17, 1953. East German citizens occupied the space in front of the House of Ministries on Wilhelmstrasse and Leipzigerstrasse. Demps observes: "The government and their employees were hemmed in: out front was the demonstrating People [*Volk*] and behind lay the 'class enemy,' the western sectors of the city, which one could not flee into. The entire problem of the all too western position of Wilhelmstrasse and with that, the planning of it, revealed themselves. This space was no longer secure. Familiar images from these days show Soviet tanks, coming from the west, from Potsdamer Platz, finally driving the demonstrators away from the exposed government buildings."[40] The departure of government and nongovernment functions followed. The Council of Ministers moved to the Altes Stadthaus near Klösterstrasse, the Ministry of the Interior moved to Mauerstrasse, and the student dormitory moved to Biesdorf. However, the House of Ministries, remained in the former Aviation Ministry for the life of the GDR, its immense spatial value outweighing concerns about its proximity to the border.[41]

Despite uncertainties resulting from the impacts of the uprising and annually increasing tensions along the border, Thälmannplatz was not immediately abandoned. Annual ceremonies for the victims of fascism were held there until being returned to August-Bebel Square in 1956.[42] Planning for the memorial continued as well. In November 1954 a Soviet sculptor visited the atelier, questioned the "artistic qualifications of comrades Hähne and Kies for this giant project" and gave advice on its form. In 1956 a group of architects, representatives of the Ministry of Culture, and leading politicians including Walter Ulbricht and Friedrich Ebert visited the atelier. Soon after, the Politburo resolved that a mock-up of the finished square and memorial be produced.[43] It also specified that the sculptors would be sent to the Soviet Union for four to six weeks to acquire "special knowledge" for the project and appointed a "political adviser" to assist in the design of the memorial. The mock-up of the square never materialized, but a model of the memorial was produced at a scale of 1:10 and placed in storage.[44]

The project disappeared from the files—around the same time ceremonies were removed.[45] Delay was sufficient that attention was diverted for a new round of planning for Berlin with a focus on Marx-Engels Square and the second phase of Stalinallee. Instead of Thälmannstrasse, Friedrichstrasse, a shopping street, now drew attention as the primary north-south axis in the area, reflecting the state's new focus on consumer goods (see Chapter 6).[46] Thälmannstrasse and Thälmannplatz were ignored. Thälmann remained an important figure in Communist memory, and in 1980 a memorial was constructed in the working class district of Prenzlauer Berg on Griefswalder Street. Allegedly, one major siting factor was that Erich Honecker passed by on his daily commute.[47]

Planners and Preservationists

Despite wartime damage to pre-twentieth-century buildings on Wilhelmstrasse, many remained reparable after the state founding. The new state had little interest in these structures, and many would be demolished in the 1950s, yet discussion and debate over individual buildings reveals highly varied approaches to this heritage. In January 1950, Johannes Stroux, president of the German Academy of Science, appealed to Mayor Ebert to stop demolitions and support preservation.[48] Stroux noted that industrial expansion and war had destroyed many of Berlin's artistically significant buildings and lamented that the remainder now were threatened by German authorities. He blamed the administration for the loss of the Ordenspalais and "almost the entire west side of Wilhelmstrasse." He lauded these buildings' artistic value and posited that their use for progressive purposes was more important than occupancy by Nazis.

In July 1950, Brockschmidt informed Bolz that future planning efforts required decisions regarding the demolition or preservation of buildings on Wilhelmstrasse.[49] In August the new city plan foresaw the eastward extension of Fränzosische Street to relieve traffic on Unter den Linden, which would require the demolition of the architecturally and historically valuable Schwerin Palace. Plans to widen Thälmannstrasse and to widen and/or reconfigure Vossstrasse would require additional demolitions, a continuation of the battle between planners and preservationists that extended back to the late nineteenth century. In the summer of 1951, with labor and equipment available upon completion of the palace demolition, ruins on seven Thälmannstrasse properties were torn down and cleared, including eighteenth-century residences that had never been used for political purposes.[50] Plans to widen Thälmannstrasse had been abandoned, but restoring these structures was likely seen as an unnecessary drain on resources. German Communists saw little value in historic buildings and preferred to envision a "new Berlin." Despite the socialist-realist tenet of preserving heritage, they only began restoring buildings on Unter den Linden after Soviet prodding, and they viewed Thälmannstrasse as the tainted center of reactionary power. Among the structures razed, the Civilkabinett is noteworthy, as it had been in use by the Magistrat, apparently rehabilitated despite having served as Nazi Party headquarters.

In contrast, just one floor of the Kaiserhof hotel hosted the Nazi Party during the Weimar Republic, yet it was demonized by the Socialist Unity Party (SED). Hotels are the quintessential provisional space, and the Kaiserhof's prominent clients endowed it with a range of associations with Berlin, German, and European history. For German Communists, its enduring meaning came from the NSDAP. Communist leaders would have remembered the Nazi use of the hotel well, but as most were jailed or fled after the Nazi seizure of power, they did not directly experience Hitler's building program. Furthermore, a wide swath of the public was aware of *Vom Kaiserhof zur Reichskanzlai*, Goebbels's journal on the Nazi ascent to power.[51] The structure would likely have been torn down due to its ruinous state and limited architectural merit, but Goebbels's text had seared the hotel into the nation's memory, sealing its fate. Whereas place-based meaning was generally concealed on Thälmannstrasse, in this case the Communist press expressed their disdain for the hotel as a source of Nazi evil and counterpoint to the new Thälmannplatz.

Unlike the hotel, the residential palace on the south side of Wilhelmplatz had a narrow range of uses, including service to the Nazi-state. The building was occupied by the Prussian Foreign Ministry from the 1820s until the 1880s and thereafter by the Finance Ministry. In the postwar years the building was free from negative connotations because the ministry's leadership adroitly portrayed the institution as the "chief bookkeeper of the nation" removed from politics and the activities of the NSDAP.[52] This image has recently been overturned. The ministry played an essential role in financing the war, in part through the confiscation of property from Jewish Germans and "enemies of the Empire" and the plundering of conquered lands. Thus limited knowledge may have deflected Communist wrath. Contemporary historians are examining this command center in greater depth, uncovering buried layers of the national past and perhaps unintentionally vindicating Communists' stigmatization of the entire area.

The Wertheim Building, a former Jewish-owned department store on Leipziger Platz, presented an entirely different range of issues. In socialist-realist terms the building would seem to have little merit. It was a palace of consumption in a reactionary era, its architecture lauded by modernists as a precursor to their work.[53] In early 1952, Gerhard Strauss praised the structure for building on classical and gothic heritage, but according to socialist realist theory it could have been denigrated as late-bourgois eclecticism.[54] He omitted mention of its importance to German modernists, although he certainly would have known this, and he may have known of the potential threat from the street widening project. The City Planning Commission determined that it must be preserved as it represents the culmination of "Messel's architecture."[55] Their motivation may have been a concealed affection for modernism, or perhaps they recognized it as a significant architectural work regardless of style. They were certainly not deterred by theoretical qualms about style, befitting the preservationist tradition. The German Building Academy considered possible plans for reusing the building, but it was ultimately torn down.[56]

The only significant resistance to demolition centered on the Schwerin Palace, likely due to Stroux's efforts. Stroux appealed to Ebert for the restoration of the palace in 1950, in response to a wave of demolitions in the area.[57] He noted that the Schwerin Palace was the most noteworthy structure remaining. It had been occupied by the first president of Germany, who had strived for a rapprochement between politicians and intellectuals. The iron roof truss and stone sculptures had been removed and the structure condemned as unstable; however, its limited damage was easily reparable. In 1952 the City Planning Commission determined that the Schwerin Palace should be reconstructed on another site, which would be permissible, because Wilhelmstrasse as a historic ensemble no longer existed.[58] Initiatives to demolish the building returned that summer and in 1955 but were successfully opposed by preservationists.[59] In December 1958 the Magistrat considered the possibility of renovating the palace as the Magistrat's guesthouse. However, in 1959 the Magistrat approved its demolition due to the "poor building condition, changes through renovation after 1933, and planned new streets." Their disinterest in historic architecture is implicit. The Kulturbund and prominent scientists protested in vain and in 1960 the building was demolished.

After division, the entire west side of Wilhelmstrasse was razed from Unter den Linden to Leipzigerstrasse as part of the Wall's death strip. The utilitarian spatial demands of international politics trumped all concerns about architecture, place, and street connections.[60]

Navigating Mysterious Layers of State History

Following the war, Soviet and German Communist political leaders continued to use Wilhelmstrasse as a government center. Although many were uncomfortable with its past, the dire need for office space outweighed most concerns. Several Nazi government buildings were renovated and reused, the history of these buildings was concealed, and their iconography removed. At this time the only demolition driven by place-based meaning targeted the Chancellery, which was irrevocably tied to Hitler. Most buildings were left in a ruinous state, and there was no significant activity on the part of preservationists.

With the establishment of the GDR, Magistrat planners focused on reconstructing the government center and providing it with a socialist content. Wilhelmstrasse became Thälmannstrasse and Wilhelmplatz became Thälmannplatz, which would include a monumental Thälmann memorial. The Ministry of Building soon assumed control and redirected building efforts to a new government and city center on Marx-Engels Square but carried the Thälmannplatz project forward to provide a secondary space for ceremonial activity, particularly the annual commemoration of the victims of fascism. The June Uprising of 1953 and the hardening of sector boundaries greatly complicated planning for this area, and the project was never completed. Salvageable historic architecture was demolished due to conflicts with new street plans, general disregard for historic buildings, disdain for the area's past, and preference to expend limited resources on new construction. Examination of individual cases reveals great inconsistency in the basis for decisions to demolish or preserve. The crystalline clarity of socialist-realist theory regarding the interpretation of historic architecture became muddy and confused in the face of pressing demands for space in a street layered with a complex accretion of memory that is still being excavated today.

6

Stalinallee

Stalinallee is the cornerstone for the construction of socialism in the capital of Germany, Berlin. It is the cornerstone insofar as these buildings serve the people, and the architecture embodies the development of the art of city building of the new Germany.

—Walter Ulbricht, general secretary of the Central Committee of the SED, 1952

FOR MORE THAN A CENTURY Berlin's housing reformers concerned themselves with overpriced, crowded, inadequate housing. Wartime destruction greatly exacerbated the situation, leaving the new government to face a tremendous housing crisis. With the establishment of an "antifascist, democratic order" after World War II, they could no longer follow Marx and Engels's precedent of dismissing the failures of housing provision for the working classes as the inevitable product of an unjust capitalist system. Their performance in addressing the housing issue would have considerable political consequences, but they did not look upon this work as a burden. They zealously carried out a planning effort intended to remake the city according to their modernist ideals, to create a new Berlin free from the inequalities and injustices of the past.

Their first effort to construct a "residential cell," the building block of the new city, would occur along Frankfurter Allee. The establishment of the East German state in 1949 allowed for much greater investment in construction but brought a shift to socialist realism as the official paradigm and a halt to construction of the residential cell. Architects and planners willing to at least appear to embrace the new approach were placed in key positions and leapt into their work with revolutionary fervor. Frankfurter Allee, renamed Stalinallee, was the centerpiece of their efforts. Many professionals were deeply concerned with obtaining the best possible design solution but were subjected to great temporal pressure as politicians demanded quick results for display in the press. This approach would crumble in the Uprising of June 1953, which along with shifts in Soviet building practices would prompt an extensive period of reflection and critique, in a continued effort to develop a model solution to the housing issue.

Rise and Fall of a Working-Class District

The origins of Stalinallee lie in a trade route connecting Berlin and Frankfurt an der Oder to the east. In the early eighteenth century, the section leaving the city was transformed into an "Allee" modeled after Unter den Linden with the planning of four rows of lime trees. In the early nineteenth century, "beautiful houses" were built along the street and further out there were slums. With rapid industrialization at the end of the nineteenth century, speculators cleared properties and built large rental barracks (*Mietskaserne*), transforming Friedrichshain into a crammed, working-class district with all of the accompanying ills: overcrowding, poor sanitation, little light and fresh air, poverty, and one-in-three children dying before their first birthday. Reforms toward the end of the century resulted in larger courtyards (in new buildings) and the addition of underground sewage lines, yet well-ornamented facades gave the street an appearance that was not commensurate with the crammed, decaying spaces that lay behind them.[1]

World War II had reduced Berlin's housing stock from about 1.5 million apartments to little more 1 million, and many of these had damaged windows, doors, and roofs. In Friedrichshain the destruction was extensive, surpassed only by that in Mitte and Tiergarten. More than one-fourth of the buildings had been totally destroyed, 68 percent were damaged, and only 41 percent were considered habitable. Many streets were covered with rubble, and Straussberger Platz was buried beneath half a meter (1.6 feet) of rubble.[2] It was here that the Communist leadership would focus their efforts to devise a new approach to the housing question. After the war, Frankfurter Allee quickly became a major focus of the effort to remove rubble and restore damaged apartments, due to its extensive damage and the ambitious work of district mayor Heinrich Starck. An architect by training, Starck joined the Kommunist Partei Deutschland (KPD, Communist Party) in the 1920s and was incarcerated by the Nazis in Sachsenhausen. He organized a competition with Dresden after the war that included considerable public outreach and mobilization of voluntary labor.[3] Preparations for the first winter centered on provisional repairs such as sealing holes in roofs and shattered windows with waterproof cardboard. More substantial repairs followed, but even these were considered provisional.

The same ills that nineteenth-century reformers saw in crowded slums—foul air, lack of sun, lack of daylight, lack of green space, disease, criminality, asocial behavior, and sickly children—were seen by Communists as inherent to the rental barrack and traditional street.[4] Since the 1920s, modernists had proposed breaking up Berlin's courtyards and blocks, and the Athens Charter had specified that unsanitary blocks of housing should be demolished and replaced with green areas containing community facilities. In June 1945 the Planning Collective set the goal of "loosening the blocks" by hollowing their core, opening them into rows of buildings or breaking them into checkerboard or striped patterns with garden spaces or other facilities between buildings.[5] This was viewed as a first step. The time was at hand to overcome the archaic urban form produced by unplanned, chaotic development under capitalism. Several planning documents and press reports indicated that wartime destruction or "mechanical loosening" of the city was an "opportunity" to implement the necessary solution: a new form of city building free from traditional streets and centered on the needs of the working person rather than the privileged.[6] Berlin was to be completely reconfigured.

The Planning Collective's members were trained in modernism and strictly adhered to this paradigm. In August 1945 they made the concept of "cells for living" or "residential cells" central to their work.[7] Each cell would accommodate four thousand residents, which, as Hans Scharoun indicated, approximated the core of the Siemenstadt development (1929–1931).[8] A new highway network would cut Berlin into swaths of land designated as future cells for living, cells for industry and commerce, for work, for agricultural production, or in one case for a college. Residents could access distant cells on highways, and adjoining cells would be connected by bicycle and pedestrian paths over or under the roadways. Cells formed larger groups in a hierarchy, the framework for rationally reordering the metropolis. Economic, social, and cultural facilities would be redistributed according to a demographic analysis and inventory of existing land use patterns, the establishment of a new standard of living, and the spatial requirements of the new planning paradigm. Each cell would include a health-care facility; every four cells would have a primary school; every eight would have a medical clinic with emergency care and a bath house; and every forty would have secondary school and/or higher education and hospital facilities. Schools, formerly crammed into dark courtyards, would be freestanding, open to air and light. The ideas were illustrated in the 1946 exhibition *Berlin Plans.*[9]

In the planners' view the war did not cause the housing crisis but was the capstone of a historical process by which the capitalist system had produced inequalities in all realms of production and distribution. Apartment building had been an "unproductive investment of capital," hence housing reform by the state and cooperatives were of limited consequence. In capitalist speculation, housing was assessed in terms of square feet and price, which resulted in overcrowding. Housing would now be assessed and designed based on a formula linking the number of beds per unit with a minimum floor area.[10] Although these proposals would radically reconfigure the form of the metropolis, they carried forth some traditional ideas about society at a time when the social breakdown of war might have been seen as an opportunity for experimentation. Whereas Hegel and conservative housing reformers viewed marriage and the traditional family with reverence, the *Communist Manifesto* condemned this "bourgeois family" as exploitative. Later socialist thinkers reimagined society, including collective living arrangements that altered responsibilities of women and individual families or in some cases completely eliminated the role of the family.[11]

Notably, German socialist leader August Bebel condemned the traditional family in favor of public management of household duties and child rearing.[12] Yet no such questioning arose after World War II. Instead, the century-old concern with housing for the family unit, shared by conservatives and Social Democrats, became the core of the program. The goal was to provide a separate dwelling unit for every household. Single persons and childless couples, who now constituted a sizable portion of the population, would no longer sublet space from tenants in crowded apartments but obtain units in multistory buildings. Families with children would be placed in small, interlocking L-shaped, single-family houses opened on one side to a garden courtyard with the windowless back of the adjoining unit enclosing this private space—a pattern developed by the Bauhaus during the Weimar era. The interior rooms were closely linked with the outdoor area, "an intimacy between residing in the house and garden that cannot be achieved in other types of housing." Nearly half of the units would be single-family houses, making the city a great deal like a suburban new town.[13] Affordability would be ensured through small lots, small houses, and prefabrication. Five models of prefabricated houses were designed, each allegedly suited for the country whose name it bore: America, England, France, Germany, and Russia. This modest gesture toward normalized relations with occupying powers also offered Berliners, in this hour of despair, an optimistic view of Germany's position in the future world economy; the type "Germany" would relieve the German housing crisis and be exported to help meet the global "need for 100 million housing units."[14]

The exhibit also demonstrated the process of "loosening up" the city with rental barrack block interiors hollowed out and opened up to the street. The planners' long-term goal of eradicating rental barracks was not presented; rather, a mix of new construction with retrofitted old buildings was depicted. However, a model portraying a new residential cell in the Charlottenburg district could only be realized with the demolition of entire blocks in an area that did not suffer nearly as extensively as other districts. Ten-story apartment buildings would be interspersed among groups of three-story row houses and fields of L-shaped single-family houses, maximizing access to sun and air for all residents. New high-speed arterials adjoined the site, but through-traffic could move indirectly across the site.[15]

Once in power, the Social Democratic Party (SPD) replaced Hans Scharoun with Karl Bonatz, who was critical of the Planning Collective's work, but allowed them to continue. Magistrat planners under Heinrich Starck worked out the redistribution of school and health-care facilities and the programmatic and spatial form of residential cells. The school system, seen as favoring the wealthy by privileging high schools specialized in academics, would be "democratized" by combining academic and vocational training on one site and increasing emphasis on the latter. These programmatic estimates provided the basis for a new, three-dimensional model of a theoretical residential cell that adhered to the same principles as the Charlottenburg cell, while offering a larger portion of the site for open space and civic uses.[16]

With a separate eastern Magistrat established in the fall of 1948, Communists had a free hand to pursue their planning agenda. Heinrich Starck, now Berlin's building director, oversaw the development of a program to carry out the conversion of an area along Frankfurter Allee into a residential cell. In November 1949, shortly after the GDR's founding, Starck published an article on the project. Although this modernist idea had been pursued both by Berlins' Social Democratic administration in the 1920s and the NSDAP (the National Socialist German Worker's Party) in the 1930s, Starck presented it as a distinctly Marxist project. Citing Marx, Starck explained that under capitalism, Western European cities bifurcated into a modern city quarters (*Cityviertel*) containing wide streets, palatial edifices for banks and retail stores, and crowded squalor quarters (*Elendsviertel*) of the working people with run-down, overpriced housing. City planning in this era included limited transportation improvements intended to increase the wealth of property owners. Only in a socialist economy could the working people and their needs become the basis for an extensive planning effort, as demonstrated in the Soviet Union. Now, the chaotic development of the old city would be swept away. Starck depicted a three-phase conversion of a site adjoining the S-Bahn tracks that would result in an immense superblock, a "cell" emblematic of the modernist principles previously discussed. The final phase, to be complete in 1975, would eliminate even rental barracks that had survived the war, leaving only new buildings with types correlated to sociological classifications—that is, low-rise, interlocking L-shaped houses for families with children and multifamily houses for others. A monopoly on political power and state confiscation of private land emboldened ideological purists to plan this vast purge of buildings that did not fit their ideals.[17]

A few months previously, however, Scharoun, as director of Berlin's newly formed Institute of Building of the German Academy of Science, was assigned with developing plans for "residential cell Friedrichshain" (figure 6.1). This would contain five thousand residents in nineteen hundred dwelling units on a different site adjoining the southern edge of Frankfurter Allee, which would be converted to a limited-access parkway and renamed Stalinallee. Scharoun wrote that those traveling past would recognize the unity of each cell and sense its successful mediation of the "chaos of the world city and the isolation of the individual." Scharoun's plan exhibited many of the design principles found in previous models, differing primarily in the placement of buildings at irregular angles to increase the sense that buildings and nature organically merge into a "city landscape." A "market square" and a "square of social life" formed the center of the cell, adjoined by a cultural center, restaurant, cinema, outpatient clinic, and other facilities for residents. The existing street network and numerous habitable buildings would be completely eliminated, the exception being a school. The dire housing shortage was no constraint to these immense changes, because Communists viewed the project as a symbol of the new society being constructed.

FIGURE 6.1. Residential Cell Friedrichshain. Sign presenting the plan for the first residential cell in Berlin to the public. Stalinallee runs along the top edge of the site, and a "square of democracy" occupies the center. BA, Digital Picture Database, Image 183-S94252, *Allgemeiner Deutcher Nachrichtendienst—Zentralbild*, Gustav Köhler, March 9, 1950.

Scharoun noted that before 1933 he and other designers had to overcome resistance from the building police, the fire department, and property owners, to create social housing that met basic needs of residents. Since that time, these experiences were built upon throughout the world, but not in Germany. Under the new sociopolitical conditions one could apply the requisite knowledge from collective experiences to rationally plan the new city. In this view planners were restoring the modernist planning tradition that had been severed from its roots in Germany and Berlin. Communist adoption of a form of housing strongly associated with Social Democratic rule possessed symbolic value that could be employed to speak for socialist unity, reinforcing the claims centered on the monument in Friedrichfelde. However, the connection was largely ignored in the press, likely as the Communists had not led the way. Instead, the ability of the new state to provide high-quality housing was celebrated.[18]

To carry out the project, the Magistrat established a "people's own" property administration unit: Heimstätte Berlin under Karl Brockschmidt.[19] Scharoun's plans were reconfigured with a new selection of building types that did not include single-family homes, though in previous planning they accounted for almost half of all housing units. The spatial structure displayed a modest degree of geometry, enclosure of internal spaces, and orientation of buildings to the street, rather than striving toward a "city landscape." Yet here too the existing street pattern would largely be eliminated, and numerous habitable rental barracks would be demolished. A central "square of democracy" would include facilities similar to the earlier plan, plus a "house of democracy" providing office space for political parties and other organizations. Distinguished neither in its form nor scale, this structure lined the southern edge of the plaza, while others were buffered from it by green space.[20] German modernists had always focused on reforming the vernacular city and rejected monumentality, explaining the incorporation of state institutions into a residential cell. A half year later, Brockschmidt would more pragmatically plan for government centralization on Wilhelmstrasse.

In November 1949 the Politburo approved renaming Frankfurter Allee as Stalinallee and a series of "Stalin celebrations" were slated to mark the introduction of the cult of Stalin into East German life. On December 21, Stalin's birthday, a parade accompanied the replacement of street signs and a cornerstone laying ceremony for the first building in Residential Cell Friedrichshain.[21] Yet the form of the new cell was incompatible with Soviet urban theory. Lothar Bolz and Kurt Liebknecht had already tried and failed to convince Grotewohl that the Magistrat was mistaken in choosing to continue the tradition of the pre-Nazi, leftist middle-class. After the cornerstone-laying ceremony, he wrote Mayor Ebert arguing that the four- to five-story buildings reminiscent of the GEHAG and GAGFAH settlements of the Weimar era did not measure up to the project's symbolic importance. Six- to seven-story buildings were required to express the strength of the new state.[22] Bolz made clear the importance of following the example of Moscow and circulated a memorandum on the plan for Moscow developed in the 1930s.[23] Bolz was orchestrating the paradigm shift that would pivot around the Trip to Moscow the following April. Architectural journals began laying the groundwork for the coming paradigm shift, while continuing to report on modernist work in Germany and Western nations. In January an article on rubble use in concrete walls acknowledged the continued development of techniques employed by GAGFAH and examined new building techniques from Western nations

FIGURE 6.2. External Corridor Buildings. This photo of the first new building in the planned residential cell was taken a few days after the dedication ceremony. BA, Digital Picture Database, Bild 183-08289-0001, *Allgemeiner Deutcher Nachrichtendienst—Zentralbild,* Heinz Funck, October 13, 1950.

where modernism was carried forward as potential models. This was followed by an article by Kurt Liebknecht warning that while many GDR architects were dedicated modernists, it was a product of capitalist society. Architects must free themselves from this "formalistic thinking."[24]

The Ministerium für Aufbau (MfA, Ministry of Building) quickly obtained the upper hand over the Magistrat on planning issues, but construction of the residential cell was under way. Liebknecht joined in the fray, demanding that a reporter stop writing about the project. Provoked by Liebknecht and Bolz, Mayor Ebert threatened to take matters to "another level." Bolz warned the mayor not to threaten a minister of the

Republic and advised him to forget the letter. Willi Stoph, director of the Economics Division of the Socialist Unity Party (Sozialistische Einheitspartei Deutschlands, SED), divided responsibility for the project between Brockschmidt, Pisternik, and Liebknecht. Stoph made clear that "representative streets have representative buildings [which] also is valid for apartment buildings." Construction was to be halted, except for the completion of two five-story external-corridor buildings (figure 6.2).[25] Discussion with Stoph also established the building-to-building width of 70 meters (about 230 feet) for Stalinallee, which was expanded to 75 meters (about 246 feet) a few days later.[26] The MfA inquired as to whether the foundations could support taller buildings, but Brockschmidt only replied that the plans had been approved.[27] The topping-out ceremony for the first external-corridor building was held on July 20, 1950. Mayor Ebert declared "every stone that set here is a building stone for peace." Brockschmidt named the construction workers "fighters for peace," contending that this work must never again be destroyed by war and admonishing workers to "defend it with your minds and fists."[28] The celebration coincided with the start of SED's Third Party Congress, at which Ulbricht would terminate modernist planning.

Stalinizing Stalinallee

Just days after the topping-out ceremony, Ulbricht delivered his infamous speech on city building in Berlin at the Third Party Conference. He accused Magistrat architects of wanting to "trivialize the capital of Germany" with low-rise buildings suitable for the outskirts of cities. Berlin traditions should be respected instead of pursuing "cosmopolitan fantasies that one could build houses in Berlin which could just as well fit into the South African landscape."[29] Ulbricht spoke of a "central axis," stretching from Unter den Linden across the "great demonstration square" (future Marx-Engels Square) and Alexanderplatz, where it would turn and proceed along Stalinallee. Metonymically, the East German state would be depicted as the culmination of the German nation: state-produced housing for the masses rooted in "national traditions" was connected to the reconfigured historic center of the German state (Lustgarten becomes Marx-Engels Platz) and further west to the historic center of the nation's high culture (Unter den Linden). In September a Soviet delegate reminded German planners that these "demonstration streets" must be "seen as first rank."[30] The extension of the central parade street through a monumental residential boulevard was standard practice in Soviet city planning, ultimately derived from baroque tradition. The most recent German embodiment of the idea came in Hitler's plans for a gigantic north-south axis in his Capital City, Germania. Thus Berlin's new "central axis" was exactly the type that led Hans Scharoun to reject all axes.

Hermann Henselmann had begun designing "residential city Stalinallee" prior to Ulbricht's speech. He presented a plan in June bearing considerable resemblance to one of Bruno Taut's renderings for Frankfurter Allee from 1946. Evenly spaced, tall apartments were set perpendicular to the street, linked by low-rise commercial buildings parallel to the street that provided (near) continuous frontage. The result was unmistakably modernist in building massing and articulation with weak street enclosure. It not only deviated from the Moscow model but bore great similarity to Weimar-era plans that were being embraced by decimated West German cities.[31] Unsurprisingly, the SED leadership rejected the design as "formalistic," "cosmopolitan," and lacking understanding of the new requirements.[32] The "Plan for the New Building of Berlin" of August 1950 included a schematic proposal for Stalinallee, specifying mixed-use structures at least seven stories high directly adjoining the sidewalk.[33] Henselmann and Rolf Göpfert fleshed out new plans, but these were rejected by the SED's Central Committee.[34]

Difficulties stemming from theoretical conflicts were compounded by material shortages. In September, Magistrat planners met with Soviet representatives who indicated that work on the "demonstration-streets" from Stalinallee through Unter den Linden was top priority. Pisternik informed the Soviets that there was not enough steel, cement, or elevators to build as high as planned on Stalinallee, so some new buildings would have to be located elsewhere.[35] Illjen confirmed that this was preferable to placing inadequate buildings on Stalinallee. At an October meeting the SKK (Sowjetische Kontrollkommission, Soviet Control Commission) questioned whether productivity could be increased on Stalinallee. Liebknecht, who joined Magistrat planners at the meeting, pointed to supply shortages limiting the state's building capacity. The SKK was convinced that apartment repairs must take priority over the new construction program in 1951.[36]

While the Soviets reinforced the imperative of monumental building, leading architects and politicians in the GDR pressed forward with the socialist-realist paradigm. Dissatisfied with current state of design work, Willi Stoph wrote an article in October declaring, "The new building of Berlin is incompatible with the... still deeply rooted 'Heimstätten' and 'GEHAG' ideology and cosmopolitan fantasies."[37] GEHAG, iconic of international modernist affordable housing, perfectly contrasted with Stoph's call for national character. Although "Heimstätte" had varied associations, Stoph linked it with modernism through the Weimar-era housing program and the Berlin Magistrat's pre-GDR housing department. A few days later, Henselmann completed his plan with buildings considerably more luxurious than the external-corridor buildings that lacked even hot water and central heating. The new structures would include "spacious stairwells with elevators, apartments with loggias, fitted kitchens, electricity, central heating/air conditioning and garbage chutes, built-in closets, a hotel for renter's guests in the first floor, and a laundromat." The buildings facing Stalinallee would be richly ornamented, including columns with a white enamel veneer and capitals in gold-leaf.[38]

Apartments ranged between one and four rooms, which in Henselmann's thinking was not to be strictly correlated with family size as the Planning Collective had intended. Instead, he felt that citizens had a right to live according to their "societal contribution"; this belief aligned Henselmann with humanist Marx rather than socialist Marx. With characteristic rhetorical flair, Henselmann maintained that his design expressed "the possibilities of societal riches in a society grounded in peace and care for people [expressed through] all possible civilizing means and the representative posture of the entire building."[39] Yet a modernist sensibility remained with one-story structures linking taller buildings running perpendicular to the street; there was a lack of enclosure. Even the flanking six-story buildings that paralleled the street were too short to meet expectations.[40] In addition, the massing of the structures generated more of a repetitive rhythm than a hierarchical order, which was also true of the facade articulation. The Politburo rejected the plan in January 1951 as it failed to enclose the street and most structures lacked monumentality. A public design competition would be developed by a commission including politicians and architects.[41]

Before the design competition took shape, two seminal projects in the development of a "New German Architecture" were under way: the German Sports Hall (Sportshalle) on Stalinallee and the Weberwiese residential project just south of Stalinallee. The Sports Hall was one of four major projects constructed in Berlin for the Third Weltfestspiel der Jugend

(World Festival of Youth) in August 1951. A prominent location on Stalinallee required adherence to principles of the new architecture. Richard Paulick led the project due to his prior experience designing sports facilities. His first proposal was rejected for modernist leanings, so he devised a more monumental structure. Faced with a shortage of materials and pressing deadline, steel girders from the destroyed central cattle yard were used for the roof. Travertine used to sheath the skeleton was taken from a stockpile that had been accumulated for use in Hitler's "Germania." Paulick personally visited the storage area for the remains of the Berlin Palace, where he hoped to obtain the most valuable parts of the Schlüter courtyard. Casts were taken from four statues and reproductions were erected in front of the Sportshalle in time for the festival. As a monumental building with classical influences, the Sportshalle represents a move toward a "new German architecture."[42]

The cornerstone-laying ceremony was a minor event, yet its limited press coverage pitted peaceful GDR construction projects against Western imperialism: "During the excavation work on the day of the cornerstone laying, the remains of several victims of American terror-attacks on Berlin's women and children during the last war were recovered. They admonish to deploy all power for the preservation of peace. The Sports Hall on Stalinallee will be a symbol of our battle against imperialistic war and for a better future."[43] One month later an article contrasted the construction on the Sports Hall with the construction of bunkers in West Berlin.[44]

Just prior to the opening of the World Festival of Youth, the "first Stalin monument in Germany" was unveiled across from the Sports Hall in a ceremony attended by the GDR's government leadership. Placing a statue of Stalin as leader on a residential street rather than in the political center spoke of his connection to the German people rather than the state. Ulbricht's speech highlighted this, applying the narrative used in commemoration at the Soviet War Memorial in Treptow. Stalin, the Soviet Union, and its army were standard-bearers for world peace, viewed as freeing the German nation from Hitler and fascism and enabling democracy and the founding of the GDR. Furthermore, Stalin had provided advice and economic assistance for the Aufbau and admitted the GDR into the "family of peace-loving nations, who, under the leadership of the Great Soviet Union and its leader Stalin, are fighting for world peace."[45] These words belied the heavy reparations the USSR was receiving. Whether the cult of Stalin made inroads beyond the most dedicated German Communists, the monument and festival made explicit the increasing integration of East Germany into the Communist world.

Before the design competition for Stalinallee, the Berlin SED tasked the three Master Workshops of the newly created German Building Academy with developing plans for a residential area at Weberwiese on the south side of Stalinallee. The project was to provide a model demonstrating the New German Architecture, yet only Paulick's team returned with a design at the deadline in July 1951. The simmering conflict between architects and politicians erupted in the press. *Neues Deutschland* editor Rudolf Herrnstadt personally reported on the meeting in "On Architectural Style, Political Style, and Comrade Henselmann."[46] Herrnstadt criticized Paulick's design as "functionalism" of the sort "built in all capitalist lands by the thousands and tens of thousands over the past decades" . . . "natural products of dying capitalism's greed for profit and disdain for people." "Functionalist" meant that it only took the physical needs of the residents into consideration, whereas building in the "new Germany" should have "beauty and monumentality" in accordance with "greatness of the era and the greatness of the German people." To illustrate this point, he declared that according to "functionalists, the door is an 'opening' for a creature with an average height of 1.75 meters. According to the liberated workers, in contrast, the door, like the facade, like every detail, has to reflect the dignity of the free human." Photos of a Chicago skyscraper and an external-corridor apartment building in Berlin provided negative examples, and an eighteenth-century orphanage from nearby Oranienburg and a socialist-realist apartment building in Leningrad provided positive "humanistic" examples. The lightness and horizontal lines of the new apartment building contrasted with the solidity and vertical articulation of the Soviet example. These forms were believed to reflect the societies that produced them: "The humanistic character of this architecture as a mirror of the increasing strength of socialist society becomes especially clear when this building is compared with the dreary boxes of the American skyscraper." The cellular facade of the "cosmopolitan" Chicago skyscraper lacked "articulation and proportion." It could be built to any arbitrary height or width for any number of people, an "ice-cold economic, political, and technical calculation"; if there were a nuclear explosion, the steel frame would remain and one only need replace the windows and add new renters.[47]

Herrnstadt concluded with strong criticism of the architects, who were considered in the midst of a learning process. Henselmann was singled out for hiding his opinions and talking around questions instead of openly discussing disagreements with the SED, whose task is to "help the artists overcome their misfortune." The artists were directed to work harder to produce a work of such "beauty and power that he take the breath away from the critics of yesterday." In this sense, Henselmann felt threatened and considered emigration but decided to stay as a result of the "relationships of his large family and a nighttime talk with Bertolt Brecht, which committed him to the 'higher goals' of the new society."[48] Within days, Henselmann, Paulick, and Hans Hopp presented revised plans to politicians and the German Building Academy. Henselmann's design was selected for construction and the politicians' warmly affirmed his work, giving him a feeling of acceptance that touched him deeply.[49] Nonetheless, the press made clear the leading role of the politicians in directing the designers: "Only now, through a public discussion on building style held especially in *Neues Deutschland*, has the initiative of the SED's Landesleitung Gross-Berlin succeeded in enabling the architects to work out designs that amount to a decisive change."[50]

The public shaming and tutoring of the state's leading architects sent a clear message to the architectural profession, which was targeted in a comprehensive reeducation strategy led by the German Building Academy.[51] While many viewed the New German Architecture as an imposition and avoided open discussion out of fear, one could either follow along or emigrate.[52] Both were popular choices. Most of the former Planning Collective moved to the West. Those who became leading state architects embraced socialist realism, likely viewing this as a compromise enabling them to continue their efforts to improve housing for the masses under a state supporting these efforts.[53] Socialist realism required the development of progressive national tradition in architecture. Liebknecht's article "The Battle for a New German Architecture" pointed out that the last progressive architectural period in Germany and Europe was the "classicist," which was related to the French Revolution and subsequent democratic bourgeois movement against absolutism. The advance of capitalism in the mid-nineteenth century resulted in a "neogothic, neorenaissance, and neobaroque," finally a "mishmash" of "eclecticism with its senseless piling up of style elements" lacking a "carrying idea." The modernist movement purged eclecticism at the price of banishing art from architecture. The Soviet Union had forged the path forward developing an architecture connected to tradition, "socialist in content, national in form."[54] With this a theoretical quandary emerges: if building techniques and architectural styles diffused and developed internationally, how could there be national traditions?

Gerhard Strauss of the German Building Academy's Institute for Theory conducted architectural seminars throughout the GDR, presenting the socialist-realist perspective on the history of German architecture. In his "Analysis of the Main Phases in the History of German Building," Strauss theorized that buildings in styles found internationally still expressed national identity by (a) reflecting national aspirations, (b) being diffused throughout the nation, and (c) being imbued with established national design characteristics or new design characteristics unique to a nation.[55] Strauss provided examples of how both ornament, construction, and spatial structure of architecture had been imprinted with unique regional features that derived from local vernacular tradition—for example, Hanseatic gothic architecture in which brick tracery derives from half-timbered buildings and spatial layouts derive from country houses. While a great deal of variation is evident in urban building types across Germany, Strauss divided the GDR into just four areas with gothic dominating the Baltic coast, classicism and baroque in Brandenburg and Anhalt, baroque in Saxony, and "regional connections" in Thuringia and Harz.[56] Regional design characteristics are far easier to identify than national, and more important, the *Heimatschutz* movement had framed "authentic" local cultures as the building blocks of the German nation—an idea deeply rooted in the minds of Germans.[57] Hence the solution on Stalinallee was to express "national form" through "Berlin traditions."

Socialist realism posited that architecture must further develop the best cultural heritage of a people, not the commonplace or most frequent.[58] Edmund Collein asserted that the design for Weberwiese tied into the "architecture of historic Berlin residential buildings" and that details from Schinkel's Feilner House in Berlin had been 'critically developed' for its facade." This is evident in the similarity between the window proportions, their division into four panes, the proportions of the panes, and the ornamental element across the base of the windows: terra cotta on the Feilner House and cast iron on the Weberwiese. Henselmann claimed the ornament on the ceramic tiles was derived from old German folk art, making it more "national" than the classical ornament typically used on Berlin architecture. Also, setting a colonnade into a recess in the center of a facade appears both in Weberwiese and several Schinkel designs.[59]

While reliefs on Berlin's classical architecture contained mythological figures, the Aufbau provided the content for reliefs on Weberwiese—that is, solidarity between intellectuals and workers, the latter including a rubble woman and two laborers under scaffolding.[60] At Henselmann's request, Berlin Communist writer Berthold Brecht was happy to design an inscription for the entrance to the high-rise. Yet, another Brecht quotation would appear in its entrance: "Peace in our land, peace in our city, so that you may well house, those who have built you!" This was inscribed on a large black marble portal removed from Hermann Göring's former residence, Karinhall.[61]

Ulbricht visited the Weberwiese high-rise in January 1952, noting its "great meaning for the development of our architecture."[62] He commended Henselmann for building on "the work of the great German master builders" and setting a precedent for the rest of Stalinallee. The press attributed the engagement of tradition to architectural details.[63] While this was evident in several ways, even Berlin's rental barracks embraced classical ornamentation, and their windows bear some resemblance to those of the Feilner House in form and proportion. The focus on facade details as a means of engaging national tradition—warned against by Hopp during the Trip to Moscow—resulted in similarity to both the "progressive" and "regressive" urban inheritance. This was unnoticed or ignored. Yet a strong counterimage to the rental barracks was attained by a break with tradition: the composition of building volumes along a street overlooking an existing meadow and absence of cramped courtyards (figure 6.3).

Workers who distinguished themselves with their performance were chosen to receive apartments. Ebert portrayed the project as evidence of Soviet support for the GDR and the German people, in contrast to American imperialism in West Berlin—a common trope at the time. He emphasized that rents would be 25 percent lower than in West Berlin, that the high-rise symbolized the will to battle for a pleasant, peaceful life, and that the war plans of West German chancellor Konrad Adenauer and the US High Commissioner for Germany, John McCloy, would not prevent this.[64] The article, "Those Who Build Apartments, Build no Barracks," reported sympathetic statements from West Germans, one asserting: "For me, Berlin's new building is the symbol of a speedy beginning of a new building of all Germany."[65] The topping-out ceremony of one building was completed early in time for Stalin's birthday as a "thank you to the Soviet people and their wise leader Stalin, who have created the opportunity for

FIGURE 6.3. Weberwiese Model. Walter Ulbricht gestures toward a model of the Weberwiese project. The structures designed by Henselmann appear to the right and bottom, and one of the external corridor buildings lining Stalinallee is to the left. BA, Digital Picture Database, Bild 183-12896-0003, *Allgemeiner Deutcher Nachrichtendienst—Zentralbild,* Horst Sturm, December 9, 1951.

us to have such a building (program)"; the article described the buildings as "residential palaces."[66]

The building's luxuries—stone and ceramic facade, marble lobby, and spacious apartments filled with the latest modern gadgetry—that is, electric stoves, intercom to entrance, garbage chutes, and so on—were depicted as evidence that "the societal changes of the German Democratic Republic, the rule of the people [and] the bright accessible future that lay before us."[67] Western press assertions that the apartments on Weberwiese were built for politics not people (seeming to imply that West Berlin housing and Marshall Plan support were divorced from politics) were met with claims of unfairly high Western rental costs that left many new apartments empty or occupied by the wealthy.[68] Other articles commonly depicted poor housing conditions in West Berlin; one suggested that looking west, "there too, our Berlin must be rebuilt. The capital of Germany should—like the high-rise on the Weberwiese—express the richness of the German people living and working in peace."[69]

The first renters were given their keys in a public ceremony on May Day 1952, and throngs came for open house tours, "where a few years ago, in the hail of bombs from American flyers, apartments went up in flames and sank in debris and ashes, new buildings are created, light, sunny apartments for happy, productive people."[70] Ebert countered Western assertions that only party bosses would live in the high-rise, listing the names, professions, and addresses of future tenants. Although unstated, "party bigwigs" would obtain suburban villas and, more important, propaganda value depended on real workers occupying the housing. While the modern outfitting of the apartments and aesthetically pleasing facade spoke well of the new state's concern for the workers, construction was constrained by the price. The cost of DM 90,000 per unit was nine times more than the Ministry of Building's targeted price limit of DM 10,000.[71] A small fraction of the poorly housed masses would receive luxurious apartments. Henselmann asserted that the building is "not just for the hundreds who will live there, nor just for the thousands who will occasionally use the stairs and elevator of this building, but also the hundreds of thousands, who will walk past this building on the street." Yet for the majority of Berlin's workers suffering substandard conditions in the ruins and basements of war-damaged rental barracks this would offer little consolation. Socioeconomic inequality was facilitated not through salary but state decision-making in assigning housing. Marx grappled to reconcile individualism and equality in his theoretical works. Here, the former was heavily favored as a consequence of the socialist-realist paradigm.

In January 1951 the Politburo established a committee of prominent architects and politicians to develop guidelines for an urban design competition for Stalinallee. In April guidelines were released by the Berlin Magistrat, which officially hosted the competition. The "architectural solution for the New Building of Berlin appropriate to its meaning as the capital of Germany" would express the "the fight for a peace-loving, democratic, united Germany."[72] The guidelines attempted to express all-German aspirations, while retaining Communist control. The competition was open to architects living in all of Berlin and in the GDR. However, no Western representatives were on the jury, which included GDR state architects and local politicians with Mayor Ebert as chair. The absence of leading GDR officials was intended to provide an appearance of local control.

Planning for a residential cell had followed modernist precedent in the statistical determination of the optimal mix of land uses, departure from traditional urban form, and development of standardized, technologically advanced construction techniques and rationalized building processes. In contrast, Stalinallee competition guidelines treated land use in a cursory manner, specified traditional masonry construction, and called for the conservation of existing urban fabric: connecting streets and infrastructure would be preserved, existing buildings could be incorporated as a provisional measure, and a nearby park and cemetery would be linked with a new green space. Concepts espoused during the design process for the Weberwiese were written into the guidelines. "Formalism" as a "symptom of the decline of imperialism" was to be rejected in favor of a "critical appropriation of... the cultural heritage one's own people... in contrast to the cosmopolitan view, which [serves] American ideas of world rule." Designers would draw upon the "best building traditions of Berlin"—in particular, "Schlüter, Knobellsdorf, Gilly, Langhans and Schinkel," renowned classical and baroque architects who had worked in Berlin. Unworthy local traditions were to be avoided, including residential cell Friedrichshain, where buildings were "mechanically lined-up." To the contrary, buildings should "have well-structured volumes and special emphasis will be placed on the formation of architectural details (balconies, loggias, bay windows, cornices, entrances, windows, bases, etc.)."[73]

Instead of a residential cell bordering a traffic artery, the new unit of development would be the traditional street, but this did not mean the return of rental barracks, described as "a disgraceful blot in the urban fabric of the capital of Germany." Architects were given a free hand to raze structures that survived the war to make room for new buildings. "Residential high-rises" with "representative stores of greater than regional significance" on the ground floor would dominate the south side. Two large cinemas, and some restaurants and cafes, would appear primarily on the north side. Stalinallee was both "the most important traffic artery in Berlin," as well as "an architectural axis of special importance." It would be "the most important street in the eastern area of the city for marching to rallies and demonstrations in the city center and for the traditional march to the graves of the great socialists at the central cemetery in Friedrichsfelde." Monumentality would be achieved by increasing the width between building lines to 75 meters (246 feet), establishing a minimum building height of eight stories, and requiring traditional architectural design.[74] Though unstated, this form derived from baroque urban design, the "primary straight street" that Berlin's planners had worked to incorporate since the late nineteenth century.

Of forty-six submissions the jury eliminated twenty-seven at its first meeting on August 27, with cursory commentary, generally indicating low-quality architecture and/or urban design. Some submissions were derided for modernist notions—that is, similarity to the "backwards residential complex." At the second session nine more entries were removed for similar reasons, such as resemblance to "cubic buildings of the new objectivity" or "GEHAG style."[75] Despite plans for ten awards, the jury determined that only five designs met the criteria and none was completely satisfactory. These five were credited with providing a "fundamental step forward to the Sixteen Principles of City Building in the battle for a new German architecture," although for different aspects.[76] First prize went to the collective headed by an outsider, Egon Hartmann of Weimar, which effectively handled architecture and urban design for the entire project area. Second through fifth prizes were awarded to leading Berlin architects. The German Building Academy's Master Workshops III & II, headed by Paulick and Hopp, respectively, Architectural Collective Kurt Souradny, and Brigade Kurt W. Leucht. Henselmann and his Master Workshop I did not submit a design.[77]

The top designs for Stalinallee included strong street enclosure with spatial variation from changes in building line (or setback) accentuated by differences in building height. Some were lauded for creating a block structure extending into the existing neighborhoods, while others came up short with these adjoining areas resembling modernist residential cells (linear buildings set in open space). Although the New German Architecture derived from design theory developed in Moscow, imitating urban and architectural forms from Moscow was not desirable. For this reason, Leucht's project was criticized for not tying into "national and special Berlin traditions."[78] Dürth, Duwel, and Gutschow describe the formal properties making this design imitative of Soviet architecture (modeled on Gorki Street) and present evidence that this was the basis of the jury's decision.[79] Their observations are exceptional, as contemporary Western criticism ordinarily dismisses the distinction, depicting socialist realism as a Soviet style, labeled "Stalinist," or in Germany, "wedding-cake style." The facile denigration of socialist realism is unsound, as "national architecture" had been actively pursued throughout nineteenth-century Europe.[80] Socialist realism was presented as a method. How one engaged national traditions would be left to architects and theorists, who faced a double dilemma in attempting to follow Soviet example to develop German traditions without being imitative of either.[81] The question is how effectively the buildings on Stalinallee met the theoretical criteria.

The eastern press framed the competition as an all-German effort and continued the populist "democratic" rhetoric deployed for the General Building Plan of 1949. *Berliner Zeitung* announced the results in September 1951 under the heading, "The German People Are Building a New Capital: The Working People Themselves Are Deciding What Will Be Built / Happy People Want to Live in a Beautiful City." Another article was titled, "Help Us—To Shape Our Berlin." Models of the winning designs were on display in an exhibition by the "democratic Magistrat" in the Berolina House on Alexanderplatz. The public was invited to fill out a survey and to make suggestions for the "new building of the representative street of the German capital." Readers' suggestions would be sent to the collective of architects that, "at the suggestion of Mayor Ebert, are working out a further plan, combining the advantages of the individual designs." While local government appeared to lead planning, the GDR was credited, as the Five-Year Plan enabling the German people "for the first time in its history... to decide for themselves what should be built and how it should be built."[82] In this, the "new democratic Berlin" provided a marked contrast with "capitalist Berlin" in which the "rental barracks became a disgraceful blot on the city." The proficiency of East German professionals and construction workers was also acknowledged, as were the "uncountable, voluntary hours of work" by Berlin residents.

Looking behind this image of a harmonious, democratic effort, however, a different picture emerges. First, the Politburo exerted control over the planning and design process, operating behind the scenes through a committee chaired by Walter Ulbricht.[83] Durth, Düwel, and Gutschow noted that "the politicians, among other things, even decided on architectural details. Of the 12,000 visitors to the exhibition, only 455 Berliners participated in the survey, which had no further recognizable effect on the further course of planning.[84] Second, Berliners' "voluntary" hours of work were a source of strain that resulted in conflict at the topping-out ceremony and would continue to build until the events of June 17. Finally, the state was becoming increasingly concerned about the emigration of professionals to the West.

Upon invitation from Mayor Ebert, the five prize-winning architects spent much of September in a village near Berlin, Kienbaum, to collectively develop a final design. Herbert Nicolaus and Alexander Obeth point to an ensuing dispute over control of the project as the established architects of the DBA viewed the competition winner, Egon Hartmann, as an upstart outsider. The confrontation centered on the key section of the project, Straussberger Platz. Hartmann, at odds with DBA architects and under pressure from a closing deadline, gave up his concept for Straussberger Platz in favor of Paulick's circular plan, which required the demolition of an existing church and factory. When the deadline arrived, the architects had produced a plan that Hans Gericke later criticized as a composite of elements from the winning designs, lacking significant further development (figure 6.4).[85]

Discussion of Berlin and German architectural traditions seems to have been focused heavily upon ornament and even more so on window design. These issues came to the fore at Kienbaum, prompting the architects to visit Schinkel's Feilner House in Berlin. Perceiving that the windows were too narrow, they decided to develop an alternative solution. Ulbricht was particularly enthused about window design, and Bolz noted his strong stance regarding windows at a meeting on city building. Apparently, Ulbricht indirectly assigned Henselmann with developing a catalog of typical window sizes and structures for Berlin. Liebknecht, who later acknowledged the importance of windows to Ulbricht, published an article in *Neues Deutschland* extolling the traditional vertical window over modernist, horizontal windows.[86] The article elicited many letters in disagreement, mainly from architects, hence Liebknecht responded in *Deutsche Architektur*. He elaborated on the impact of window size, form, and placement for interior lighting and facade composition. This latter role was especially crucial as windows formed a placid, rhythmic backdrop for more prominent elements (balconies, loggias, bay windows, etc.), which together formed a monumental effect that expressed the "humanistic Stalinistic idea of care for people."[87]

The Kienbaum Plan was presented to the Politburo on November 16, 1951. Heinz Auspurg, who had represented the team of Karl Souradny, recalled direct intervention on the part of Ulbricht:

> Pieck, Grotewohl, Ulbricht, and others were present. Ulbricht led the discussion and he went berserk from the start, "The architecture is not fitting." . . . he showed us pictures of Gorki-Prospect and said, "This is how it has to be." Indeed, Pieck and Grotewohl tried to placate [Ulbricht] and suggested that he should also listen to the

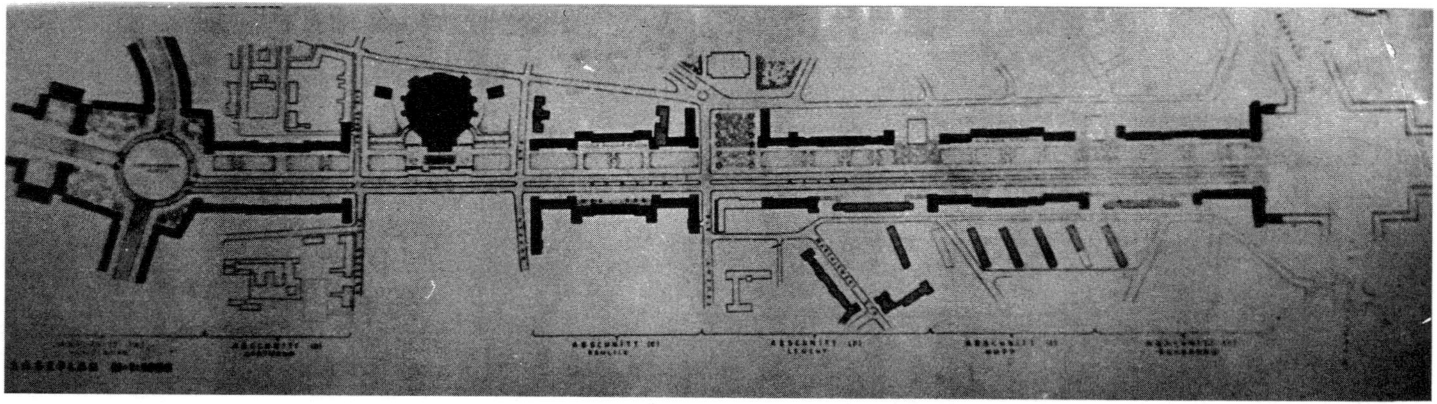

FIGURE 6.4. Stalinallee Plan. Plan from the exhibition *Im Kampf um eine deutsche Architektur*, which opened in November 1951. At the left, section A, is Henselmann's "spade plan" for Straussberger Platz, which was modified before construction. The large structure on the north side (top) between section B and C is the Sports Hall. The two lighter-colored buildings on either side of D-south are the recently constructed external-corridor buildings. Section F ends at the start of Besarinplatz. BA, Digital Picture Database, Bild 183-12930-0006, *Allgemeiner Deutcher Nachrichtendienst—Zentralbild*, Heinz Junge, December 11, 1951.

architect's arguments. Yet no one contradicted Ulbricht.... We were sent home and had to revise the designs and present them again later.[88]

Ulbricht did not share the jury's sensitivities about imitating Moscow.

The presentation followed the street, east to west, from Besarinplatz to Straussberger Platz, the high point of interest. Hartmann recalled that Straussberger Platz's simple round form and symmetrically arranged high-rises corresponded to the politician's ideas, and they were "visibly satisfied." Paulick sensed the affirmation for his plan, when Henselmann—who had not participated in the effort—approached the wall. One by one, he turned over boards and explained his own plans for Stalinallee.

He got the last frame with a perspective of Straussberger Platz and placed it directly in front of Pieck. There was a large fountain the middle of the plaza. Water fountains splashed around a monumental sculpture of a group full of fighting spirit and confident of victory. As a finale Henselmann posed in the same position as the sculptures. He bent his knee slightly, placed one foot a large step forward, balled his fist, stuck his arm in the air and said, "Sch—Sch—stürmische Jugend"! [passionate youth]

This appearance carried the politicians away in a storm of excitement. "As though electrified," Ulbricht, Pieck, and Grohtewohl sprang up. Pieck, likewise stretched both hands up in the air, and waving at Henselmann with them, he called loudly, "Hermann, Hermann, you build Straussberger Platz." Later meetings had an "almost celebratory" air.[89]

The Politburo resolved that the plans should be presented on December 5. Henselmann was assigned Straussberger Platz, section A; Hartmann, the adjacent section B; Richard Paulick, section C; Kurt Leucht, section D; Hans Hopp, section E; and Karl Souradny, section F, adjoining Besarinplatz. The Politburo approved the new designs subject to minor revision except for Souradny's section, which, being too "schematic," required extensive changes.

A few weeks later, a Soviet delegation including the chief architect of Moscow, Alexander Vlasov, and the vice president of the Soviet Academy of Architecture, Sergei Tchernychev, critiqued the projects upon invitation. Meeting Pieck and Liebknecht, they delivered "extensive criticism." Tchernychev pointed out the psychological effects of streets and architectural ensembles, such as to depress, overwhelm, or terrify. A street bearing the name of Stalin "must express the idea of humanity.... It must express concern for the people. This architecture must be a friend to the people." Apart from Orwellian doublespeak, the Soviets offered specific suggestions applying principles of neoclassical urban design: greater unity between the north and south sides of the street, additional building around the Sports Hall to maintain enclosure of the street, and an appropriate accent across from the planned cinemas. They proposed planting thirty- to forty-year-old trees in front of the external-corridor buildings to camouflage them and plantings on the north side of the street. Revised plans published a few weeks later reveal considerable adjustments relative to their input.[90]

Considering the socialist-realist imperative that art serve cultural and political indoctrination and the presence of bas-reliefs and sculptures on Berlin's historic architecture, it is logical that a commission was formed to develop a plan for art on Stalinallee. Under the leadership of Kurt Junghans (of the DBA), the commission made recommendations for the street from Alexanderplatz to Lichtenberg Station. The section from Alexanderplatz to Straussberger Platz would illustrate the "German people's battle for liberation," including all major wars from 1815 through World War II, when the Red Army liberated the nation from fascism and into the current battle for national sovereignty. Straussberger Platz would depict "Stalin and Germany," including liberation, German-Soviet friendship, and help from the Soviet Union in economic, political, and cultural reconstruction. Straussberger Platz to Besarin Street was meant to illustrate "socialist friendship," including friendship among nations, athletes, youth, workers, and Germans in East and West. The section from Besarin Street to Stalinallee Station would be themed "forward to the construction of socialism," including developments on Stalinallee, which extended beyond construction to "national defense, cultural facilities, battle for peace."[91] From Stalinallee Station to Lichtenberg Station, "the fame of labor" would include "the activist movement, heroes of work, progressive technicians and doctors, artists and scientists, people's own businesses, the great plans, improvement of production and life, and vigilance."[92]

Along the lines of national history writing, the national past was reduced to a battle for liberation seemingly exonerating the German people from all culpability. The path of national progress continued into the contemporary era by allying the GDR with the Soviet Union and socialist states, striving for national unity and peace while preparing for a defensive war, glorifying labor of all forms, and constructing a socialist state and society. The leading architects of Stalinallee had no qualms about the commission's message, yet turf defense came to the fore as they sought to retain in-house control over all aspects of their buildings. In February 1953 the

FIGURE 6.5. The New Apartment. Richard Paulick explains his design for Block C-North at the exhibition in the Sports Hall for the film *Die Neue Wohnung*. BA, Digital Picture Database, Bild 183-17346-0009, *Allgemeiner Deutcher Nachrichtendienst—Zentralbild*, Hans-Günter Quaschinsky, November 26, 1952.

Department of Fine Literature and Art of Central Committee of the SED, led by Herrnstadt and Ebert, reviewed the proposal and declined, eventually removing responsibility from the commission.[93]

Ulbricht's personal interests prompted undue focus on windows, but the popular and professional press gave a great deal of attention to overall facade composition. This may have been related to the fact that the field of architecture was dominated by modernists, who had eliminated ornament to focus on structural and spatial aspects of buildings. Socialist realism, like modernism, embraced new developments in these latter areas. However, the press's emphasis on facade design based on artistic rules of classical composition created a flashpoint, hence the Trip to Moscow and the "formalism debate." In fairness to socialist-realist theory, the entire design should be assessed (figures 6.5 and 6.6). Was Stalinallee "national in form and socialist in content"? Nicolaus and Obeth note that Stalinallee's designers pinned examples of Berlin's historic architecture to the walls and credit them with tying into Berlin architectural traditions. They both

FIGURE 6.6. E-North (eye-level view). This view from the sidewalk highlights Stalinallee's role as a shopping street and reveals a degree of plasticity in the facade that is less apparent in images attempting to show entire buildings on Stalinallee. BA, Digital Picture Database, Bild 183-20497-0012, *Allgemeiner Deutcher Nachrichtendienst—Zentralbild*, Günter Weiss, July 23, 1953.

praise and criticize the functional and aesthetic efficacy of architectural and urban design, as did the East German architectural press, which viewed the project as a step in a larger process to develop the new German architecture.[94] These qualities are only discussed below as pertinent to the claim to build upon national tradition.

The baroque origins of Stalinallee as a boulevard or "primary straight street" are evident in similarity to Berlin's most renowned examples, Unter den Linden and Wilhelmstrasse. These are similar in length, yet much narrower. At 75 meters (246 feet), Stalinallee came closer in scale to the 60-meter-wide (about 197 feet) Gorki Street in Moscow, which the Communists had widened to several times its original size. This precedent is clear, but was Stalinallee intended to emulate or perhaps one-up Moscow, or were both building on baroque precedent—the Champs Élysées falls between the two streets in width.[95]

Indeed, Stalinallee's cross streets, squares, changing building lines, and heights create a rhythm, but on a much larger scale and with more regularity than Berlin precedents.[96] Stalinallee's green median and larger green area on the north side could be seen as variation of the planting strips on Unter den Linden. The German Sports Hall and two "planned cultural buildings," like the diminutive Neue Wache, stands free surrounded by open space, inverting the relationship found on the rest of the streets where building walls shape spaces. Straussberger Platz and Frankfurter Gate were conceptualized as gateways terminating grand axes, similar to the three squares of the eighteenth-century baroque extension. The buildings on Stalinallee are considerably taller and immensely longer than those on Unter den Linden, to obtain a strong sense of enclosure on the much wider street. Elements of Berlin planning tradition are translated into a more regular pattern and considerably larger scale. This was viewed as part of an uplifting monumentality expressing the ideals of the new state as "concern for the people" and a framework for state parades, as prescribed in Moscow and reflective of Soviet tradition.

Nicolaus and Obeth offer a detailed analysis of how and why large structures were broken into smaller volumes. The massing of the buildings was developed in response to the block's characteristics or location on the street, including (a) enclosing a square, (b) mediating excessive block length, (c) establishing a connection across a significant gap in the building wall (the external corridor houses, the sports hall, and planned cultural buildings), and (d) transitioning into a square.[97] The squares were a matter of particular interest. Henselmann reworked the design of Straussberger Platz over a period of several months with input from the Politburo, visiting Soviet architects, Richard Paulick, and in a last round of criticism, Walter Ulbricht, who was dissatisfied with the facades.[98] Most concerns centered on the spatial form of the square. Henselmann conceptualized the design of Straussberger Platz as entry to the city center through a synthesis of the traditional elements of "gate" and "tower." Berlin's eighteenth-century squares were located just inside city gates.

On Stalinallee, towers accentuate the transition in lieu of a gatehouse. The original plan (that won over the politicians) with two emphatic towers flanking a trapezoidal space, seemed too much a stopping point. The final design included two major towers on the city center side, two minor towers on the other side, with gently curving building lines in between, obtaining the desired balance between axial movement and repose (figure 6.7).[99] Unlike traditional squares that served as a gathering space, this was a node along a path to the political center. In fact, the paired tower elements of Straussberger Platz closely resemble examples of socialist-realist architecture in Moscow.[100] For Frankfurter Gate at the western terminus of Stalinallee, Henselmann placed two slender towers capped by tall cupolas and ruminated on the significance of the tower and the gate in Germany. *Berliner Zeitung* compared these to several cupolas in Berlin, while contemporary sources pin them to the cupolas atop the iconic churches on Gendarmenmarkt, likely due to their proportions and symmetrical pairing.[101]

Nicolaus and Obeth note that the extremely long buildings in sections C and E, monumental expressions made possible by closing off adjoining streets, are divided into three volumes as typical for Berlin residential buildings around 1800.[102] Several other midscale features are noteworthy. Avant-corps, found on numerous buildings in Berlin, appear on several Stalinallee buildings, modifying their volume and accentuating the ends of these long structures. While Berlin's classical architecture displays impressive porticos, the element is largely omitted on Stalinallee. The exception is C North, where a portico marks the central entrance, transitioning between the immense structure and the human being. Several passageways linked Stalinallee with existing streets behind the new structures. Passageways leading to courtyards were ubiquitous on Berlin's rental barracks and appeared on the Berlin Palace and State Library. However, on Stalinallee and in Moscow they led through long buildings to

FIGURE 6.7. Straussbergerplatz to Frankfurter Gate. The northeast corner of Henselmann's design is evident in the foreground, and the towers of the Frankfurter Gate are in the distance. The asymmetrical layout allows the wide pedestrian promenade and green strip on the north side to remain in the sun, while the southern sidewalks are shaded. BA, Digital Picture Database, Bild 183-51895-0006, *Allgemeiner Deutcher Nachrichtendienst—Zentralbild*, Hans-Günter Quaschinsky, December 1953.

existing urban fabric rather than internal courtyards. The scale, massing, use of similar architectural elements (avant-corps, passageways, loggias, and balconies) on buildings in Moscow and Berlin give them a degree of similarity, yet their formal characteristics often distinguished them. For instance, passages in walls framed by avant-corps are found on Stalinallee and on Gorki Street in Moscow but with marked differences in shape, scale, proportions, and ornamentation.

Attention to style, facade composition, and ornament was perhaps a fitting focal point for tying into tradition, as their relationship to other Berlin architecture is easier to perceive than for larger-scale elements. Nicolaus and Obeth observe that ornamentation, the pattern of solid and void, and its relationship to the entire building along with the predominantly symmetrical structure of buildings together create a characteristic Berlin rhythm.[103] The tripartite structuring in base, body, and cornice is fundamental to classical facade design. The "balustrade-cornice," which appears on numerous buildings on Unter den Linden, specifically the Zeughaus (the Arsenal), reappeared in various forms on Stalinallee—some close to the classical model, others stylized or simplified.[104] Ornament tied into Berlin classicism and, in places, neogothic and baroque.[105] Window form and ornamental forms were often directly inspired by Schinkel's work, particularly the Feilner House. The choice of cladding material, primarily white ceramic tile to provide a cheerful countenance, had been employed in the USSR. Although this specific material was new in Germany, terra cotta ornament was not, and Stalinallee architects were inspired by its use on the Feilner House.[106] In contrast to Nicolaus and Obeth's views, Durth, Düwel, and Gutschow critically assess the architects' relationship to classical heritage as "playful lightness," "almost neglectful" with forms varied almost to abstraction. The exception, Hans Hopp (section E), "cited historic repertoires with great familiarity" due to his academic training.[107]

The spatial arrangement of rooms and utilitarian spaces within the apartment buildings and individual room size and form was also a matter of considerable attention. The goals of offering sizable rooms and bringing direct sunlight into at least a portion of all individual units were defined in opposition the memory of crammed, gloomy rental barracks. The kitchen was a matter of particular interest. Rental barrack kitchens were all-purpose rooms for cooking, eating, socializing, children playing, bathing if possible (apartments had no bathrooms), and sometimes doubled as workspace and/or sleeping areas. August Bebel's 1879 rethinking of the role of women in socialism dismissed the private kitchen as outdated, a factor in the confinement of women in traditional roles. Weimar-era social housing ignored this precedent, in favor of Taylorist-inspired modernity, the "Frankfurter kitchen"—a small galley configured to the smallest detail to minimize the movements of the housewife.[108]

GDR architects either ignored or were unaware of Bebel's challenge, adapting the Frankfurter kitchen with no mention of its origins. *Berliner Zeitung* declared the "residential kitchen" inadequate for "modern progressive people," as the housewife lost time traversing the large room in the course of work. Alternatively, the "cooking kitchen" was just 6 square meters (almost 20 square feet), and the "eating kitchen," including a small built-in table with seating was 9 square meters (almost 30 square feet).

The public was invited to vote for the kitchen they liked best; however, they were guided by the article, which declared, for instance, that working people preferring the old kitchen possessed "outdated consciousness." Nonetheless, feedback indicated that housewives wanted "freedom of movement," the possibility of eating breakfast in the kitchen, and a place for children to eat under the mother's supervision. Many buildings on Stalinallee offered an "eating kitchen," and on Straussberger Platz, Henselmann resolved the issue with a working kitchen largely open to an adjoining "seating area," a layout attributed to a Soviet model.[109]

Though modernism was derided, elements of this tradition continued to influence the designers in other ways too. The spatial composition of buildings is closely related to structural possibilities, and in order to reduce design and construction costs, the state explored development of building types with standardized components. The 1950 Building Law specified that to building faster, cheaper, and better, standardization and prefabrication would be necessary as a step toward the industrialization of construction. Despite some effort to make progress in this area, the capacity for industrialization was minimal. Efforts to prefabricate parts off-site met with little success, although the first prefabricated concrete structural components were employed in 1952. An unbridgeable gap emerged between expectations set by publications revealing, neoclassical apartments with modern amenities and MfA-dictated cost per unit of DM 10,000. In an attempt to overcome deficiencies, resources including building equipment would be brought from around the country, and mass voluntary labor would be mobilized in the National Building Program. Efforts to standardize building types continued under the leadership of Otto Engelberger (DBA), who noted that his experience with GAGFAH in the 1920s strongly shaped his work in the 1950s. Thus, while modernist housing had been rejected, it continued to influence the spatial and structural design of the New German Architecture.[110]

The Trip to Moscow focused on streets, squares, and unified urban form, yet Soviet planners acknowledged some value in the "residential cell" as a planning unit similar to those used in the Soviet Union. However, Berlin planners' were informed that their modernist cells were problematic for their internal focus, isolation, and equality of size. To maintain a real city, they must be integrated into a continuous urban fabric and sized according to their site and location.[111] Soviet theorists had in fact transformed the modernist "residential cell" into the "residential complex" to support socialist-realist urbanism. Large blocks of 9 to 15 hectares (about 22 to 37 acres) would allow sufficient open space and facilities for daily needs, reduce unnecessary cross streets, and guarantee a good form for the adjoining thoroughfare.[112] East German planners adopted the term "residential complex" as a unit of development in the Sixteen Principles of City Building. In fact, similarity to the residential cell was sufficient to elicit occasional confusion. During the Stalinallee design competition, one plan was derided for similarity to the "backward residential complex." Given the emphasis on streets and squares, Engelberger warily noted that Soviet planning did not exclude a comprehensive mix of land use in ensembles, suggesting that "socialist residential complexes" be developed for the GDR.[113]

In 1953, *Deutsche Architektur* dedicated an article to residential complexes, illustrating design principles with Moscow's proposed Frunze Quay. The large site included abundant internal walkways and green space of modernist layouts, yet these were axially ordered, well-defined spaces, and large, representative structures lined the main street.[114] Kurt Junghans's 1954 brochure illustrated another significant difference from residential cells, as major shopping streets would form a seam between complexes.[115] Henselmann, in response to the first sections of Stalinallee being cut off from adjoining urban fabric, designed the Frankfurter Gate section with more frequent connections and asserted that this was the dialectical resolution of the contradiction between street and *Hinterhof* (rear courtyard) of capitalist Berlin. This should not be dismissed as mere rhetoric, as dialectics appears to have been central to his thinking.[116]

In some ways, Stalinallee's neoclassical architecture tied into Berlin tradition, giving it claim to being "national in form." In other ways it resembled Soviet socialist-realist architecture, hence the derogatory "Stalinist" and "wedding-cake style" labels. Aspects of German modernist housing were present in less visible ways, although concealed in architectural discourse, as this would acknowledge elements of unacceptable "formalism." The ideas of the new society, including "care for people," were ubiquitous in discourse about Stalinallee and present in various ways in its design: access to sunlight and air, room size, monumentality as a stimulus to optimism, and modern appliances, among other features. Similarly, the street's role as an outdoor promenade and shopping street was celebrated as an achievement of the East German state, while its purpose as a frame for state parades was withheld from the publicity campaign.

The National Building Program

In 1952, Stalinallee became the focal point of the GDR's new National Aufbauprogram (National Building Program) to implement plans for East German cities.[117] Progress on Stalinallee was imperative for the new state to show it could effectively solve the housing issue, "to overcome the rental barracks as expressions of the capitalist era, and... to form a new countenance for East of Berlin through a grandiose building idea."[118] Along with overcoming the past, the program was intended to outperform the capitalist West. The United States provided massive financial support for housing in West Germany, which was highlighted in a design competition for cost-effective housing. Marshall Plan funding also supported a range of exhibitions on American life, including the Marshall House Pavilion in West Berlin (1950) with a "family" of local actors displaying domestic pleasure in Western housing. The exhibit drew tens of thousands of West Berliners per week, and an estimated fifteen thousand visitors from East Berlin.[119] To counter this, the National Building Program would offer an "exciting example of peaceful construction and show the population of West Berlin and West Germany, the performance workers are capable of, when they are freed from imperialists and not subjected to the command of Anglo-American governors."[120]

A massive public relations effort would juxtapose populist rhetoric with SED and state slogans to mobilize public enthusiasm and attract voluntary labor. Public participation and its lionization in the press would assist in the "battle for peace, the battle for the unity of Germany, the battle for the unity of Berlin and the battle for a rapid increase in production" and portray the democratic, humanist nature of the state. As Fulbrook indicates, this era of *Aufbau* offered a new beginning to a population that included many who were disillusioned with the results of Nazism and war. Many were already disillusioned with the SED, but the newly established GDR had no track record and could attempt to win support through an appealing new vision for Berlin and Germany.[121]

A National Committee for Building the German Capital comprised of an equal number of cultural and political figures from East and West Germany would play a largely symbolic role, as the program would be implemented by a staff of seven under guidance of the Politburo. Lacking West German participation, a number of East German committee members were struck from the press release to maintain a better balance: twenty members from the GDR, ten from the Federal Republic of German (FRG), ten from West Berlin, and ten from East Berlin. The Politburo outlined an intensive press campaign that would precede the launch of the program on January 2, 1952. Yet popularization of the effort had already commenced shortly after its provisional approval. Jendretsky's appeal "For the Building [*Aufbau*] of Berlin" was published in a *Neues Deutschland* on November 25 and reprinted in *Berliner Zeitung*. The article challenged Berliners as well as Germans from East and West to contribute by appealing to their pride as a people. Any German citizen could enter the housing lottery for one of a thousand apartments through one hundred half shifts of labor or by contributing 3 percent of their income for one year, which would be returned with 3 percent interest between 1956 and 1958. Most labor would be provided by Berlin construction workers with temporary assistance from construction workers from other parts of the GDR. Voluntary labor would provide a crucial service clearing rubble. An exhibition showing the history of German architecture and construction through its present practice in Germany "in the example of the new building of Berlin" would be shown at a site on Stalinallee. To encourage "collaboration of the West German population," West German workers and architects would be invited to submit comments and suggestions. Finally, the national committee would communicate with the government and people of West Berlin to encourage their participation and coordinate an effort for the new building in West Berlin.[122]

On November 29, *Neues Deutschland* alleged that the proposed program found "unanimous approval," publishing letters from West Berlin residents expressing the ideas of the SED in the language of the SED.[123] Enthusiastic responses came from two women's organization in West Berlin that nonetheless were associated with the SED. One reported that salvaged building material was sent to armament factories in the West, not like "the democratic sector, where it is used to build an economy that works for peace." Several letters from West Berlin residents were published. One woman indicated that her first husband was murdered by fascists and expressed dismay at seeing "fascist powers" spreading in West Berlin; this is her incentive to participate in "the great building of our Berlin and thereby stand up for peace." She greeted Wilhelm Pieck's invitation for West German president Theodore Heuss to reestablish talks on unity (which Heuss declined) and concluded that "the unity of Germany must and will be fought for."

As directed by the Politburo, the *Berliner Zeitung* began near daily reportage on Stalinallee, associating the project with national unity and peace, claiming public support from East and West Germans, asserting that the SED was representing the interests of the population, and depicting enthusiasm for labor. The populist veneer was captured in "To Müller, Meier, Schulz, to Everyone! How do These Apartments Please You? We still have Time for Discussion."[124] Letters from readers were published along with short responses to their concerns. One questioned the new apartments' monumentality, suggesting that in light of recent German history more modesty was appropriate. The response indicated that the moral question lay in who the architecture serves, not its size: "All great architecture was representative. What matters is who is being represented [and] by what means. Louis XIV said, 'I am the state.' This was represented in the Palace of Versailles. We say, 'We are the state.' It is an issue for our society to develop an architecture that can stand next to the baroque in artistic merit." Several readers were concerned about a lack of sunlight due to the "narrow" windows. Hopp personally responded, indicating that the form of the windows was based on Berlin tradition and that by pairing the windows, sufficient light would be obtained. None of the questions revealed design weaknesses requiring changes—at least according to the provided responses. While a few Berliners' suggestions would have a modest impact (see kitchen discussion), criticism from Soviet advisers would result in significant changes, thus the "democratic" planning process fit Fulbrook's "participatory dictatorship" model.[125]

With the launch of the National Building Program, three means of political agitation were pursued: on-site political education for construction workers and voluntary labor, organized site visits for West Berliners, and continued press coverage across the GDR. According to the SED, workers' ideological awareness was crucial for the construction of socialism and could motivate them to work harder, increasing productivity. The program achieved results. Along with paid labor, more than four million hours of voluntary labor doing rubble removal was obtained for various motives, including access to consumer goods, entry in the housing lottery, a sense of dignity through labor, contributing to a better city/society, and a sense of camaraderie. After nine months it was reported that "954,461 enthusiastic Berliners and helpers from the GDR have performed 1,062,227 construction [*Aufbau*] shifts. 31,712,419 bricks have been obtained for the new building. 951 tons of usable steel, 7,055 tons of scrap, and 143,375 kilograms of nonferrous metals have been salvaged out of the rubble. 557,907 cubic meters of rubble have been transported away. 60,000 cubic meters of rubble was used to fill cellars."[126]

The Free German Youth (FDJ) spread mason's apprentices throughout Stalinallee with concentrations at several "youth construction sites." A 1952 internal report boasted that one hundred of five hundred apprentices on Block E-South had joined the FDJ, and eleven had decided to join the People's Police.[127] In 1994 one former FDJ apprentice recalled being trained with great care and concern, an experience that ranked among the best in his life. The ideological orientation of youth was a matter of special attention, to "win them over to the construction of socialism."[128]

The construction site also provided opportunity to rehabilitate the image of the Soviet Union. Soviet-developed "three-man" and "five-man" systems of masonry—inspired by capitalist Taylorism, as condoned by Lenin—were introduced to increase productivity but also demonstrated the "leading role of the Soviet Union."[129] These methods enabled the skilled mason to simply set bricks in place and make final adjustments, while unskilled and semiskilled assistants spread mortar and supplied bricks. Berlin masons were very skeptical, so the SED orchestrated a well-publicized demonstration by an expert Soviet mason. Thereafter the Society for German-Soviet Friendship assembled and deployed a group of former prisoners of war, who had experienced these methods in the Soviet Union.

The "activist and competition movement," based on a Soviet model, was another means of increasing productivity and producing "new consciousness." Competitions began with an appeal by a person, brigade, or entire company, as directed by the party or trade union. Activists set a standard under "artificially produced optimal work conditions" or perhaps even fabricated results; in one case, workers claimed to achieve over ten times their quota. The results were publicized and, in response, another brigade would exceed the new quota and the best worker was honored. Next, quotas were raised for all workers, though the basis for meeting them was often not provided. Since 1948, the model had been applied in factories and mines in the Soviet Zone to the dismay of workers, including Communists, who resented it as a program of labor discipline. They shunned model workers and at times engaged in slowdowns and other forms of resistance, as they had through the history of the socialist movement—except they were now pitted against a state run by a socialist party.[130]

By April 1952 the government recognized that far too few apartments were being produced and initiated an activist campaign on Stalinallee. The firm IG Holz called a competition for "the Red Banner of the Stalinallee" to be organized by the SED, the Society for German-Soviet Friendship, and the Construction Workers' Union. The new masonry technique was disseminated through booklets, demonstrations, and schooling. Progress was displayed by on-site sign-boards, reporting on daily tasks, weekly and monthly quotas, and actual achievement. More than 250 brigades joined the competition with new winners each month. There were also a number of smaller competitions such as Brigade of Outstanding Quality and Best Construction Management Collective. Through fifty-four competitions in 1952, a little over half of the twenty-three thousand workers on Stalinallee participated, which increased production as well as accidents, while reducing quality. In April, DBA president Kurt Liebknecht called for each architectural collective to appoint one member to engage in public outreach as this had been neglected and would improve design work. He knew the effort was not possible due to the tremendous temporal pressure, thus it was likely for public relations.[131]

High cost remained a problem. Each apartment unit was estimated to cost DM 40,000, four times those in the external-corridor buildings, although half as much as those in the Weberwiese. The budget of the entire National Building Program in 1952 was estimated at DM 180 million. The Berlin Magistrat was to provide DM 24 million, the lottery DM 118 million, and various other fund-raising activities, the remaining 38 million. Western press accusations that East Berliners were forced to contribute to the National Building Program could have been dispelled had the SED been willing to admit that it came up far short of the goal. By June 1952 the lottery only brought DM 42 million, and other means brought an additional DM 10 million. Planners faced a budget reduced to DM 106 million for the year. This meant a maximum of 2,650 new apartments for a district in which the majority of the population was living in substandard conditions.[132]

Great temporal pressure in the design and construction process resulted in problems from the outset. DBA staff more than doubled, yet drafting work fell behind schedule. Hopp later noted that it was difficult to design a foundation and basement without a clear image of the building up to the attic. Repeated accusations of poor productivity directed at workers (lacking proper ideological motivation) concealed "poor organization on the construction site, as well as missing material and tools. Thus, construction workers viewed the [competitions] as a method to intensify work when tie ups occurred." Such an ambitious schedule in face of dire material provisions due to war and a foreign occupation (Soviet) that drained material resources as reparations had no chance of running smoothly.[133] In sum, construction workers' identification with their project may have been ideologized to an extent, but resentment was an increasing by-product of pressure and blame. How much material gain was obtained through political agitation and publicity is not known, but it was a motivating factor in obtaining volunteer labor, reinforcing the convictions of Communists, helping to convince non-Communists to join the National Building Program, and in some cases to join the SED

A limited number of West Berlin residents were able to directly experience the construction site through tours organized by the East German government in early 1952. Reports on the tours were sent to the SED's Central Committee including Walter Ulbricht, revealing high hopes of impressing Westerners. By bringing East Berliners and West Berliners together, the tours were understood as support for the "Germans at one table" motto, propagated by Otto Grotewohl to bring leading East German and West German politicians together to discuss reunification. West Berlin participants, mostly construction workers, architects, and housewives, were accompanied by a small number of East German activists, who opened dialogue about the new buildings and life in East Berlin, while avoiding volatile political issues. Statements by guests revealed suspicions about the governments of the GDR and Soviet Union. However, they appeared genuinely interested in the building projects, which elicited many positive responses, even among skeptical guests. Subtle and less-than-subtle connections between the policies of the East Berlin and East German governments and the positive aspects of the planning and building efforts were established by the activists.[134]

Voluntary rubble-clearance crews left some of the greatest impressions on visitors, who believed that workers had been forced or pressured into participation. To remedy this, tour buses would stop and allow the visitors to talk with workers, who convinced them of their belief in working for a better future. One report happily recounts how West Berliners in the lead tour bus picked a location to stop, and although the workers were unaware they were talking with Westerners, they provided answers superbly fitting the interests of the East German state. Given the repressive political conditions and excessive ideological agitation, it would have been surprising if anyone diverged from the party line.

Visits to a furnished apartment also proved successful, especially with housewives. The floor plan, built-in kitchen cabinets, and price repeatedly evoked positive responses. The price for a comparable apartment in West Berlin was much more expensive, and on several occasions West Berliners involved in building and planning correctly pointed out that the rental costs bore no relation to the construction costs. Guides suggested that property and buildings were owned by the people, meaning "state-owned," which eliminated speculators and "construction hyenas." This belies the fact that rental prices bore no relation to construction costs, which meant that a small percentage of the population received new, high-quality apartments while the majority resided in ruinous, aging buildings. Nevertheless, the tour guides claimed this as evidence that the saying, "The human stands at the center" is not just propaganda. One group of housewives suggested that the apartments were for "SED bigwigs," but when allowed to visit a unit, the worker's story and simple furniture convinced them otherwise. Regarding the New German Architecture on the Stalinallee, West Berlin architects agreed that pursuing the tradition of Schinkel and Knobellsdorf was appropriate. One suggested that just as Prague has a distinctive architectural character, Berlin too must preserve its architectural countenance. The architects were generally impressed with the new buildings, especially Paulick's design.[135]

These tours had limited impact due to the small number of visitors accommodated. It is reasonable that the opinions expressed in the reports were largely true and that many visitors were genuinely convinced that a more humane city building effort was being carried out in East Berlin. However, as these visitors were open enough to the "East" to take the tour, it is unlikely they were representative of West Berlin as a whole. At a minimum, the process provided feedback identifying which aspects of the project could most effectively appeal to Westerners. A number of Westerners and far more Easterners visited the Stalinallee exhibition in the German Sports Hall. On October 27, 1952, West Berliner Irma Schütter became the five-hundred-thousandth visitor.[136] The first section of the exhibition presented a history of building from antiquity to the "age of exploitation" under capitalism, including rental barracks and skyscrapers. The second section focused on building under socialism, "buildings of peace," with large images of "families in new comfortable apartments" and statistics on the latest development.[137]

The greatest audience for the National Building Program would be obtained through the popular press. Reportage was intended to obtain public support for the program, prompt the contribution of labor and finances, and illustrate the progressive role of the East German state in building a new society and addressing the present political situation. Articles appeared in *Berliner Zeitung* on a near daily basis in early 1952, eventually slowing down to several per week. Newspaper reports could be divided into two categories: (1) frequent progress reports (at first daily, later weekly) that were largely apolitical and served to draw public interest and identification with the new buildings, and (2) major events with highly visible political content to ideologize public identification with the project. The program was depicted as a nonpartisan, all-German effort contributing to peace and the unity of Berlin and Germany, demonstrating the closeness of the Berlin Magistrat and Berliners, and tying nationalist sentiment to East German and Soviet proposals for reunification. The governments of West Berlin and West Germany were depicted as hindering progress, preparing for war, and building new housing that was too expensive for working people. Ardent popular participation in the National Building Program would be needed for its success, enabling progressive forces to work to improve their material condition.[138]

The construction effort, involving ten thousand construction workers and forty-five thousand volunteers, was ceremonially initiated on January 2, 1952, in the presence of Walter Ulbricht, Otto Grotewohl, Lothar Bolz and Friedrich Ebert. On January 3 the *Berliner Zeitung* reported an "atmosphere of confidence and joy" on the first day of the National Building Program. Hans Jendretsky spoke to the workers in nationalist tones: "The great work that we are beginning today on the new building of a beautiful German capital will present the entire world with a testimony of the deep longing for the unity of our fatherland, which includes the unity of Berlin. Along with this, the start of this extraordinary building effort is a declaration for peace." Jendretsky reiterated this last point stating that it is "better to shed 1,000 drops of sweat than one drop of blood." Bolz, of the Ministry of Building and chair of the National Committee, personally worked on rubble removal and spoke, portraying the building effort as uniting the state and the people in a move toward a peaceful future as a united nation.[139]

The cornerstone-laying ceremony for Stalinallee was held on February 3, 1952, the seventh anniversary of the heaviest bombing of Berlin during the war, which killed 2,893, injured 1,934, and left almost 120,000 homeless.[140] The East German press would claim 52,000 deaths and printed a narrative highlighting American bombing of apartments and families, including a mother and child melted in the flames.[141] The National Committee appealed to all Berliners and Germans, in particular the political leaders of East Berlin and West Berlin, to make February 3 the memorial day for devastation into a Day of Building (Aufbautag) for all of Berlin, expressing "the indomitable will of the Berlin population to lead the German capital out of ruins and into a happy, peaceful future." Mayor Ebert (of East Berlin) welcomed the suggestion and agreed to meet, while "Mr. Reuter [Mayor of West Berlin] and the West Berlin City Council" did not respond. Apart from a refusal to be co-opted, they did not officially recognize the GDR.[142]

Berliner Zeitung reported on the ceremony in the article "On Sunday Berlin Met on Stalinallee." Apprentices participated in the ceremony. One felt fortunate for being able to "reach for hand tools in the National Building Program," while West German youth were reaching for draft notices. He lauded the relationship between the youth and "our government" and declared that Stalinallee "bears the name of the best friend of the German People." Grotewohl read a document, cosigned by Bolz (representing East Berlin) and a Hamburg architect (representing West Berlin), that would be enclosed in a case set into the foundation wall. The document emphasized that the building effort was contributing to peace and national liberation and that "the German people are taking the matter of preserving peace in their own hands and will go to the extreme to defend it"—foreshadowing the upcoming establishment of the People's Police in the Barracks.[143]

The article reported that thousands of Berliners had worked on the rubble removal and heard the cornerstone-laying ceremony via radio broadcast. "Thus, February 3, 1952 has become a day of optimism and belief in a better future," the article concluded, "in which February 3, 1945 may not be repeated." A second article claimed widespread support for the memorial day and the National Building Program among people in West Berlin, despite hindrance from the authorities. Allegedly many West Berliners were working on Stalinallee, while others laid wreaths on sites of ruins in West Berlin. Support was also claimed from religious groups as crosses and commemorative symbols were set in front of a few churches, although the SED did not have a monopoly on the memory of the bombing. The GDR's depiction of a broad-based movement rooted in humanistic values was intended to broaden support among the working class, following Stalin's dictate to avoid proclaiming the construction of socialism while he used leverage in Berlin and Germany as a bargaining chip with the West.[144]

On May Day attention turned to Weberwiese as Mayor Ebert presented apartments to new residents. Weberwiese continued to appear in the press with visitor's impressions reported in a highly politicized manner.[145] Several topping-out ceremonies on Stalinallee were planned to precede the SED's Second Party Conference in July 1952, which proclaimed the "construction of socialism" in the GDR, prompting a shift in depictions of Stalinallee from "democratic" to "socialist."[146] Ulbricht declared to loud applause that "Stalinallee is the cornerstone for the construction of socialism in the capital of Germany, Berlin." Grotewohl, Ulbricht, Jendretsky, and Honecker attended the topping-out ceremony for the three buildings, and Wilhelm Pieck spoke, lauding construction workers for finishing ahead of schedule and thereby delivering a "blow to the American warmongers and their henchmen in Germany." Apprentices who were leaving for the People's Police were ceremoniously presented with a carbine and a collection of Lenin's works. Socialist ideology, a gun, and a position in the People's Police were a natural extension of construction work on the Stalinallee as part of "fighting for peace and unity."[147]

Rudolf Herrnstadt elaborated on the link Ulbricht established between Stalinallee and the construction of socialism in his speech "The First Socialist Street in Berlin." Herrnstadt drew upon working-class and *Heimatschutz* tradition to express its political significance. Berlin, split by American imperialists, was on the upswing in its "democratic sector," while West Berlin decayed. The SED's construction of socialism provided a path to restore national unity. Stalinallee would endow the city with beautiful, affordable apartments in contrast to expensive "narrow, dark holes" in West Berlin. Stalinallee would provide a "real *Heimat*" that people will love and defend. Unlike the capitalist city of the past, Stalinallee's artistically shaped buildings would be owned by the people, and its apartments would house "people who feel they are ruler of the state, and plan and secure their creative life based on their new socialist consciousness." Stalinallee therefore had a socialist character and provided the cornerstone of a socialist capital of Germany. West Berlin, a hopeless bridgehead of American war policy, impacts its workers with a "regression of consciousness." The American strategists would ultimately fail as Berlin is a powerful industrial center with a strong working-class tradition. The idea that Stalinallee was a first step in the construction of a socialist Berlin would be repeated time and again.[148]

Days later, Pieck presided over more topping-out ceremonies, proclaiming that "display window West Berlin is displaying 300,000 unemployed, 50,000 of which are construction workers. Display window West Berlin shows despair to the youth, because the 'front-city' policy cannot offer them apprenticeships, it cannot provide them with the prospect of an honest, peaceful life. Here, however, we are showing the face of the new, democratic, socialist Berlin." A dinner for the construction workers in the Sports Hall was followed by a Volksfest on the Weberwiese. "The radiant white high-rise building and the surrounding apartment buildings formed the appropriate frame for this festival, which was dedicated to the joy over that accomplished, as well as the happy preview of the future." Various firms were credited with outstanding achievements, and a few outstanding workers were interviewed, as reported in the *Berliner Zeitung.* Multiple paragraphs depicted workers celebrating, and the article concluded that "the construction workers on Stalinallee... would prevent any dirty hand from reaching out after the fruits of our peaceful labor."[149]

The Berlin working-class tradition of festivals in rental barrack courtyards was carried forth in a new, better, socialist setting, though threatened by the declining West, necessitating a militaristic display. Topping-out ceremonies continued through the summer and fall, and articles claimed thousands of West Berlin residents accepted the invitation to visit Stalinallee and listen to addresses by SED leaders. Speeches reiterated central themes on "the first socialist street in Berlin" and international dignitaries attended key celebrations, such as the Day of the Republic, receiving "applause from construction workers and Berlin residents," demonstrating "the close relation between the population of the German Democratic Republic and the lands of the people's democracies.[150]

The second year of the National Building Program was initiated on New Year's Day 1953 with a rally on Straussberger Platz. Jendretsky, with limited feedback from West Berliners, claimed: "Here on this street, tens of thousands of West Berliners have convinced themselves of where the path can lead if the division of Germany and the division of Berlin is revoked." He called on West Berlin's Mayor Reuter to stop the "hate campaign" and warned of diverse spy organizations following the "American model" turning the saboteurs of yesterday into the murderers of today.[151] In ensuing months, regular progress reports portrayed Stalinallee as a bridge between East Berlin and West Berlin.[152] The first renters moved into apartment blocks draped with the state flag and portraits of Stalin and Pieck in a public ceremony including Bolz, minor East German government officials, and a delegation of construction workers and miners from West Germany.[153] The public was invited to discuss the design of the intersection at Stalinallee and Besarinstrasse, the pace of construction increased several times, and the public mourned Stalin's death at the Stalin monument.[154] Meanwhile, in West Berlin, construction workers were treated poorly, apartment design was driven by "greed for profits," and rent increases were threatened.[155]

Underlying this narrative of progress, the relation between society and state was crumbling. The "construction of socialism" proclaimed at the Second Party Conference emphasized the development of heavy industry while neglecting the production of consumer goods, resulting in fewer material benefits for workers. Shelves became emptier, and inflation eroded purchasing power. Workers suffered indirectly from this shift in investment and directly through cost-saving measures such as the revocation of reduced transit fares and private sector employees' food ration cards, which were necessary for such items as butter, margarine, and sugar. Unions independent of the state had been eliminated, and all labor was increasingly subject to comprehensive control. Starting in March 1950 factory workers were subject to wage reductions if they failed to perform, and gradually quotas were increased for workers in all sectors. In its labor practices the GDR followed the repressive tradition of German industrialists, fueling a growing resentment among the working class.[156]

On Stalinallee, efforts to convince workers to raise their production quotas for the long-term benefits of socialism did little more than aggravate workers, who had to deal with shortages of material and poorly functioning machinery. In a display of tone-deafness, the honored three hundred representatives of the working class at the May Day parade carried banners proclaiming, "Raise the Quotas!"[157] As the extent of the crisis became evident, Grotewohl, Ulbricht, and Fred Oelssner were invited to Moscow on June 2, where they were informed that the poor policy-making of the Second Party Conference should be remedied by reduced repression, increased provisions for consumers, and other reforms. On June 11 a set of reforms known as the "New Course" were approved. The word "socialism" disappeared from slogans, and rumors ran wild including speculation that reunification was under way. Despite extensive promises, the SED failed to address the issue of production quotas, leaving workers to contend with one of their greatest grievances.[158]

Workers on Stalinallee began arguing with party functionaries on Friday, June 12, and some left early on Saturday. On Monday a group went on strike demanding a reduction of quotas. The Free German Trade Union Federation (Freier Deutscher Gewerkshaftsbund, FDGB) newspaper, *Tribüne*, defended the increased quotas on June 16, prompting the first major strike. Hundreds marched to Union headquarters on Wallstrasse in order to obtain support from the FDGB leadership. The building was sealed off, so the workers continued to the House of Ministries on Thälmannstrasse. Hours later the Politburo agreed to discuss the quotas with the unions. Workers marched back to Stalinallee, where party functionaries announced the Politburo response. This failed to satisfy the crowd. On June 17 construction workers initiated a strike that soon expanded into a general strike. Several thousand assembled on Straussberger Platz before marching to the House of Ministries. Thousands more joined along the way. Protestors demanded a reduction of quotas, cheaper consumer goods, the resignation of the government, and free elections. Police blocked off the front of the building, and rioting erupted throughout the city center. Demonstrators attempted to storm the House of Ministries. When it became evident that police would fail to contain them, Soviet troops were called in to restore order. The workers had no chance against armed troops and tanks. The Politburo reduced quotas to the level of April 1, and the "New Course," soon went into effect with the goals of increasing the standard of living and improving the state's public image.[159]

The Eastern press framed the march as a legitimate political expression concerning production quotas, blamed "rowdies" from the West for vandalism and violence, and depicted a return to normalcy on construction sites.[160] Workers in the "democratic sector" were returning in "rapidly increasing numbers" and "had recognized that their justifiable dissatisfaction was exploited by criminal elements from West Berlin in the past days for a provocation against the reunification of Germany." Quotes from construction workers were offered as evidence, one declaring: "We want nothing more than to bring our demands to the government. They then agreed lower the quotas according to our wishes.... We don't want anything to do with what occurred on Wednesday due to West Berlin fascist rowdies."[161] One brigade reported that during their absence a cable for a cement-mixing machine had been cut by "paid rowdies"; coworkers who remained on-site reported fending off a group of "youths in Texas-shirts" intent on demolishing the machines. Another article asserted that the majority of Berlin opposed the actions in its headline "Berliners Condemn the Provocation."[162]

Articles published over the next weeks, also supported by interviews, reinforced these ideas and contextualized them in a narrative of fascist terror in peaceful Berlin, now propagated by the West instead of Hitler. Mayor Ebert thanked Berliners for resisting "international warmongers," who through their "front-city policy in West Berlin" want to turn all of Berlin into a "trigger mechanism."[163] A photo of the 1933 Reichstag fire compared the events, both "fascist provocations" in which "the criminals were curbed by the Soviet Army. An accompanying article by author Stefan Heym described the workers as "having behaved as though struck by blindness" to a degree with few historical parallels, such as the effect of Hitler's demagoguery.[164]

Having put down the uprising by force, the Soviet military had contributed substantial damage to its desired image as "friend and helper." To counter this effect, the Eastern press depicted them as rescuers and reported spontaneous expressions of thanks from Berliners. The article, "Berlin Thanks the Soviet Army," reported that Soviet troops were visible in the streets for defense against fascist provocateurs and that many events testify to workers' trust in Soviet soldiers and officers.[165] A few days later, the article "Children Danced Happily with Soldiers" reported on "friendly visits to the Soviet soldiers, who are stationed in Berlin's inner city to protect the population."[166] A more believable narrative acknowledging some mistakes might have been more effective in winning popular support, yet blaming the West fit existing discourse and allowed the state to quickly close off any potentially threatening public discussion. Over time, GDR historians developed an even less nuanced narrative, erasing legitimate protest by workers, blaming the entire event on incitement by Western agents, and crediting East German workers with ending the unrest while downplaying Soviet involvement.[167] In fact, resentment over state actions did not diminish many workers' sense of achievement, aware that they were building without a Marshall Plan while being drained by Soviet reparations. For young workers this sense of pride would contribute to a building sense of identification with the GDR as conditions improved over time.[168]

The events of June 17 forced the SED to rethink its housing program and dramatically alter press releases. Popular resentment over a few workers receiving luxurious new apartments while the majority crammed into war-damaged rental barracks was approached with a supplemental building program involving small-scale housing projects dispersed throughout the Eastern sector and publicly assisted renovation by renters. Stalinallee, the major news item since January 1952, temporarily disappeared from the papers. The provision of consumer goods became the top story. Regular articles on diverse housing projects emphasized the quantity of new and renovated apartments and their equitable distribution throughout the city in a "new path" on housing.[169]

Stalinallee returned to the headlines in August with a visit by Ukrainian construction workers. An article headlined "We Wished That All of Berlin Looked Like Stalinallee" asked, "How could it come to a June 17? . . . How could a part of the workers from the land of Marx and Engels, after having been freed from fascism, once again allow themselves to be taken into tow by fascist provocateurs? That was totally incomprehensible to the workers of the Soviet Union."[170] After this, very little appeared prior to the topping-out ceremony for block G-south in October. The "construction of socialism" was supplanted by a humanistic appeal, absent direct mention of the state, nation, or any political issue. *BZ* reported that construction workers from Stalinallee, "the most beautiful street in Germany," were received by Wilhelm Pieck.[171] "In a friendly and candid conversation," the article stated, "the masons and carpenters described their successes, but also shortcomings and deficiencies which they are still battling against." This personal link between leadership and workers reinforced the state narrative of the uprising and suggested that workers could be heard through peaceful communication. Yet the "new course" was quickly pressed into the old format as another round of "worker-initiated" appeals was staged. All workers on Stalinallee were challenged to join a special Sunday shift to demonstrate "preparedness to support the government's new course with all their energy . . . to improve the lives of all working people."[172] Thereafter, articles on Stalinallee appeared occasionally with little fanfare or political content; the events of June 17 had disrupted the viability of Stalinallee as the GDR's chief instrument of propaganda.

From Straussberger Platz to Alexanderplatz

The events of June 1953 created a crisis of legitimacy for the state, and more poignantly, for the National Building Program. At a conference the day after the "new course" was announced, leading architects and engineers agreed on the necessity of giving "much more attention to the industrialization of building."[173] Despite being part of the official building program, the standardization and industrialization of building weathered the early 1950s as a picayune sideshow, while center stage was reserved for the New German Architecture. Now it began to draw serious attention. The DBA declared that its main task was apartment building, which in the next years would replace the construction of industrial buildings as the government's primary focus. Under capitalism one built at subsistence level, while under socialism one must satisfy the material and cultural needs of the people. Skilled design to maximize the functionality and aesthetics of small apartments was considered important, but industrialization was seen as the primary means to attain housing goals. The development of standard types for buildings, their structural components, and architectural elements was a first step.

Moscow's building program from 1949 to 1951 was taken as a demonstration that the most advanced building technology worked well with established architectural and urban design principles.[174] In fact, the GDR's first experimental large-panel building, constructed in Berlin in 1953, was overlain with a neoclassical facade demonstrating design possibilities but eliminating cost savings over conventional construction.[175] Internal documents reveal considerable concern regarding the economic shortcomings of existing building methods, and the Politburo expressed its dissatisfaction, calling for a new emphasis on technical improvements to reduce costs.[176] In terms of urban design, buildings would be grouped in residential complexes containing a variety of land uses. Moscow's chief architect, Vlasov, clarified that the economic benefits of industrialization were best realized on large sites, hence Soviet interest in large residential complexes like Frunze Quay.[177] Ignoring myriad modernist precedents, including the work of Berlin architects in the 1940s, the residential complex was presented as a Soviet development. The Soviets did introduce a new urban design approach, employing rules of formal composition found in historic ensembles, such as the Platz der Akademie in Berlin and the market square in Pirna.[178]

This uptick of interest in industrialized building appears trivial when compared with the shift that followed Stalin's death. Nikita Khrushchev, in a battle for power with his chief rival Georgy Malenkow, attacked the slow pace of construction; this resonated with the public, thereby strengthening his political standing.[179] At the All-Union Conference of Builders, Architects, and Workers in Moscow in November 1954, Khrushchev denounced the excessive use of capital and labor for "superfluous" architectural elements and details, while the majority of the population had inadequate residences. Housing had been misused to implement urban design plans, while it should have been treated as a consumer good.[180] The "unnecessary use of money" for "architectural decorations and aesthetic ornamentation" and the placement of towers and sculptures on buildings with no basis was unacceptable. Attractive facades should be created through "good proportions of door and window openings, through adeptly distributed balconies, through a correct choice of the surface treatment and color of the cladding."[181] Leading architects, including Mordvinov and Vlasov, who had advised East German architects, were directly attacked. Sakharov was chastised for producing "beautiful silhouettes [when] people need apartments. They are not enthralled by silhouettes, but should live in buildings!" The entire theory of city building was called into question as he accused architects of using "socialist realism" to cloak their misuse of the people's money. He praised the engineer G. Gradow, whose efforts to standardize and industrialize building had been obstructed under the old regime; Gradow called for end to "conservatism in architecture" and for the "mechanization of construction."[182]

The Soviet paradigm shift gave considerable impetus to industrialize construction in the GDR and provided leeway for stifled modernists to express their views. Although modernism was an obvious choice, Khrushchev's program did not exclude other possibilities. For instance, an austere neoclassicism would have fit the program. However, it had been tainted by fascist architecture such as Speer's Ministry of Aviation and had been condemned in East Berlin as a "violation of heritage."[183] Ivan Sholtowski clarified that one must not abandon the classical but abandon the imitation of classical forms and obtain a deeper understanding of its principles.[184] Industrialization would impact urban design as the maximization of economic gains depended on large sites and modular buildings with linear floor plans laid out to suit the turning radius of a crane. Numerous forms were still possible. Sholtowski hinted that planning must entail not just street facades but entire areas, leaving specifics to be developed.[185]

At the request of the German Building Academy, Gerhard Kosel, who had been working on the industrialization of architecture in the Soviet Union, returned to Berlin in October 1954 to take a position at the

Ministry of Building. In December (after Khrushchev's speech) Kosel lectured at the ministry on the need to create a unified set of building elements to enable industrialization. In April 1955 representatives from all branches of the building industry attended the First Building Conference of the GDR under the motto, "Build better, faster, cheaper." Kosel spoke on the importance of developing one set of prefabricated building components that would determine everything from building depth to floor height. Complete standardization would maximize cost-effective production and efficient deployment on building sites.[186] Ulbricht also spoke, declaring that "architecture must be seen as a unity of technology, science, and art" and that the "fundamental task to solve in the building industry is the implementation of the industrialization of construction, which can only be achieved by extensive development of building types."[187] Art was no longer primary but a partner with technology and science. On April 21, 1955, the Council of Ministers shifted state policy, emphasizing industrialization to increase the pace of construction and reduce costs.

The reception of these changes among East German architects was highly variable. Some enthusiastically viewed this as an invitation to return to modernist principles, although it had not been condoned. Others feared a loss of design freedom and believed that standardization would inevitably result in monotony. In fact, the exact message of Khrushchev's speech for theory and practice in the GDR was a matter of considerable confusion and debate, prompting Hans Gericke to address the issue in an article for *Deutsche Architektur*. Gericke criticized numerous projects in the GDR for eclecticism and wasteful ornamentation. Yet, he noted, Khrushchev did not condemn art and tradition. National tradition must be built upon through the artistic application of classical rules of design without excess and without oversimplification. How this would occur was to be determined through an "open battle of opinions."[188] Contemporary research has observed that the commitment to industrialization imposed unavoidable constraints on architecture and urban design, which were now driven by economic and technological concerns: "After the 'great turn' [*grossen Wende*], city building became a technological phenomenon.... Hardly anyone spoke of the traditions of German building arts; economic pressure and techniques of production determined the new elements of design. The technology of the assembly line and the module of the crane radius were determinant.... Concrete plates, hidden behind technocratic formulas, would now determine the building form and apartment plan."[189]

This statement reads history from the final outcome, attributing technology with deterministic power and overlooking potential human agency. The choice was not an "either-or." How building would be industrialized while retaining flexible design possibilities was explored and debated. Initial investigations of the DBA concluded that the technical demands of industrialized building would not constrain planning, as any urban design solution could be attained with the use of some conventional construction to enclose corners.[190] Indeed, the future of building was determined by choices regarding the appropriate balance of artistic goals with technical and economic concerns, the ability of professionals to develop artistic solutions with accepted technical constraints, and a conflict between repressed modernists and committed traditionalists.

Theoretical writings asserted that socialist realism had been misapplied, that economic and technical aspects of building had been neglected in the battle to create a New German Architecture. There would be no return to the "constructivism" of the Weimar era; rather, technologically advanced building techniques would be artistically employed to express social and national ideas.[191] Gerhard Strauss suggested that this required a deeper understanding of national tradition, studying not external form but the principles by which these forms are developed. One must examine how past architecture related function, economics, technology, and form: What is different in the current situation, and given this, what should be modified?[192]

Liebknecht saw little conflict between the forms of national architecture and industrialized building, suggesting that a catalog of prefabricated construction elements could be used throughout the GDR, and a catalog of architectural details would be developed for each of the four regions of the GDR. The mistake on Stalinallee had been the lack of standardization—that is, far too many types of ceramic plate were produced. Instead, a limited number of types of balcony, loggia, and other architectural elements would be used sparingly for good composition.[193] Liebknecht's suggestions were confirmed by engineers in Dresden, who favored trading a little construction time to include a limited number of architectural elements (loggias, balconies, cornices, bay windows) for effective facade composition.[194]

While the focus on "deeper principles" served to obscure de facto abandonment of much recently disseminated theoretical work, Strauss did outline the core problem and hinted at a direction for future study.

He recounted the rhythmic articulation of building facades in different eras, noting for instance that repetition of columns on a Doric temple did not result in monotony. He accepted that prefabricated building facades would have limited plasticity, and he identified precedents that offered solutions, including Islamic architecture and the brick gothic of northern Germany: building proportions, window proportions, and pattern of solid and void on the facade, all accentuated though the use of color. Further interest would be achieved through grouping buildings in ensembles.[195] Junghans condemned Berlin modernists' attempts to relieve monotony in housing estates with arbitrary jogs in building lines instead of effectively shaping spaces. In contrast, standard building types were used during the Renaissance, but these avoided arbitrary irregularities (only breaking their patterns with purpose—i.e. topography, intersecting streets, etc.) to build street and plaza walls. This resulted in great urban spaces such as Place des Vosges and Place Vendome in Paris. Standardization and repetition would enable housing needs to be met in an expression of "care for the people," reflecting the "higher moral quality of socialist housing construction."[196] High-quality urban design would be met by continued application of the traditional street, block, and square.

In practice, matters were proceeding under the guidance of Gerhard Kosel, who was named first deputy of the Ministry of Building. Kosel led the effort to industrialize construction, which was in its infancy. During the late 1950s approximately two-thirds of construction was brick (under rationalized process), 30 percent prefabricated blocks, and only 3 percent large-panel construction. The ministry did not initiate the development of a standard series of large blocks until 1958.[197] To lower costs, apartment sizes were reduced, and a 1962 assessment revealed that cost savings per unit had resulted from the reduction in apartment size and floor heights and the increase in building height—not prefabrication.[198] The effort did not endure through this period due to success but through faith in science, technology, and rationalized procedure. The belief in technological development as a motor of economic and social progress was strongly embedded in Marxist-Leninist thought.[199] Expectations of success placed pressure on architects to find any means of reducing the cost of labor and material. Also, the construction of smaller, less elaborate apartments for a much broader section of the population was not only politically expedient but fit well with scientific Marxist ideas about social equality. Khrushchev's directive tapped these discourses, which had great appeal to

East German leaders seeking to construct socialism and to compete with the West.

In the mid-1950s the state's focus on industrialization slowly crept into the press, whereas other policies that similarly implemented egalitarian ideals received more attention. Press reports informed the public of apartment rehabilitation and infill projects throughout the city (contra previous concentration of effort on Stalinallee), celebrated state facilitation of small cooperatives' building new apartments, and made note of a program to require apartment exchanges (large families were crammed in small units while single people had large apartments).[200] The importance of public input and Berlin Magistrat competence was highlighted, while district offices were sometimes scapegoated. Quantity and cost of units were central. In this regard, the power of standardized floor plans and, secondarily, industrialization (to speed up production and maintain low costs) appeared in small articles, as though easing the public into the idea. Even the shrinking size of new apartments was depicted favorably as a means of achieving the targeted number of housing units in the five-year plan.[201] Qualitative matters were anecdotal, providing access to light and air, feeding coal ovens through the foyer to keep ashes from the living room, or an attempt to dialectically frame the abandonment of ornament on facades as overcoming the baroque and classical failure to resolve the contradiction between economic/functional matters and artistic matters.[202]

Over time, planners and architects delved more deeply into the relation between the theory and practice of urban design regarding industrialized building. Kurt Leucht claimed that if a planner is aware of the technical requirements of industrialized building, he could reach an "optimal result" in urban design. Leucht condemned previous planning as a "falsely comprehended romanticism in city building" with oversized squares, streets, and buildings. He saw not monumentality but a "gigantomania" incompatible with the basic requirements for healthy, functional, beautiful, and economic residences. Three technical requirements would be significant for urban design. First, replacing mixed-use structures with multistory residential buildings accompanied by one- and two-story commercial and institutional buildings would reduce costs 20–25 percent. Instead of "boring street corridors," these different building volumes could be composed in "multifaceted and contrast-rich" development on "people-serving boulevards," while a green buffer from the street would protect from noise and dirt.[203] In fact, a variety of arrangements were possible, but Leucht was concealing modernist ideas with the traditionalist term "boulevard."

Second, the crane moved along a track, which along with adjoining work space, required a minimum of 40 meters (131 feet) between rows of buildings.[204] This distance was appropriate for a boulevard but left wide swaths of open space surrounding the small cul-de-sacs or pedestrian paths running between buildings in residential complexes. Green space had the advantage of being much cheaper than paving, but the gains were only obtained on undeveloped land.[205] Third, enclosed corners at intersections were not economical, as they could be more effectively constructed through traditional masonry and thus were to be eliminated from planning.[206] Romantic and classical urban design relies heavily on enclosed block corners and often emphasized them. Even a few of Berlin's modernist estates used strong corner articulation in their layouts. Yet the slowdown of construction was not considered to be worth the design gains, except for infill buildings on key sites, such as Unter den Linden.[207] The placement of freestanding towers on corners could have been used to retain much of the effect while maintaining the imperatives of industrialization, but this does not appear to have been considered. Henselmann's new plans for Stalinallee reveal the significance of design theory in this regard.

Henselmann vocalized support for the new approach, criticizing recent practice as eclecticism, an inability to address the big ideas of the contemporary era, and formalistic overvaluation of the nonmaterial side of building arts (dialectically viewed as a unity of material and "*Ideel*," or spiritual)—which he then compared with Nazi architecture.[208] In preparation for the SED's Third Party Congress (July 23–29, 1956), the Berlin SED resolved that a residential complex for five thousand people would be built with industrial methods between Stalinallee and Ostbahnhof. Henselmann was assigned with developing a plan for display in the Sports Hall on Stalinallee during the conference. *Neues Deutschland* publicized plans for this "Residential Complex Friedrichshain," explaining that industrialized construction required the separation of commercial from residential structures and no enclosed block corners, while architectural elements such as loggias could connect buildings. The resulting open, airy, and green quarters allow the creation of beautiful views, while building groupings gracefully shape the "city landscape" and invite walking. Henselmann did not acknowledge this as a return to modernism, instead attributing the approach to the new building techniques.[209] Following the exhibition, Henselmann noted in *Deutsche Architektur* that public response centered on practical matters affecting everyday life, such as the separation of traffic from residential areas or the location of different land uses—not whether a particular building type exhibited formalism or constructivism. He suggested that architects and planners needed to refocus their attention on these matters.[210]

Liebknecht commented on Henselmann's plan in *Deutsche Architektur*, acknowledging its contribution to industrialized construction, while offering extensive criticism. The monumental ensembles of Europe's great cities were suitable models for the "capital of Germany," as evident in recent work on Stalinallee, but Henselmann's plan was of "suburban scale." Instead of enclosing streets and squares, an open plan with varying building heights caused an "artistic breech" with Stalinallee and a "step backwards . . . to the external-corridor houses." Liebknecht concluded that a move "forward" required the development of a new paradigm of city building, the development of which would be facilitated by a design competition.[211] Nicolaus and Obeth, in accord with Liebknecht, suggest that Henselmann's plan "could have been a reformulation of the Wohnzelle Friedrichshain" as both dissolved the block in favor of an internal focus with considerable open space, a "park in the city."[212] Yet Henselmann's new plan lacked the large swaths of interlocking, L-shaped, single-family houses, considered an uneconomical use of space. Also, the irregular or "organic" pattern of the modernist "city landscape" had been replaced by geometric regularity and a degree of spatial enclosure as in Frunze Quay. Rather than the weakly defined center of the residential cell, there was fairly strong centralization around a mixed-use core adjoined by a vertically dominant building. However, the axes established by linear, five-story apartment buildings could have been reinforced by the four eight-story towers, but instead these interrupt the axes, breaking up the space. The result imbues an axial plan with a "city landscape" effect—a modernist expression in opposition to monumentality that was in no way influenced by the demands of industrialization. Liebknecht offered extensive criticism of the plan, including the "arbitrary" placement of the towers and concentration of density at the center. He suggested that taller buildings should have been placed to the edge adjoining Stalinallee as a transition (which would have reinforced the strength of the boulevard).[213]

Taking advantage of a thaw in relations, East German and West German architects began collaborating in 1956, bringing the GDR's leading architects in contact with former colleagues and mentors, such as Ernst May. After visiting Hamburg, Henselmann spearheaded efforts to invite Western architects to participate in a design competition for the Fennpfuhl section of Berlin's Lichtenberg district. The competitors included three architects from East Berlin, three from West Berlin, five from the GDR, and five from Hamburg. The modernist paradigm was prominent, and May won the competition with a plan that the jury attributed "clear spatial structuring with few elements." Most winning designs were praised for effective incorporation of green space as a major design element. *Berliner Zeitung*, which had been ignoring the architect's debate and qualitative issues, lauded this "New Modern City District for 20,000 Berliners."[214] The article praised the architects' contributions for their "generous, modern character" and cited Berlin Deputy Mayor Schmidt's suggestion that the all-German competition "confirmed the leading role of democratic Berlin in the planning and rebuilding of the city." West Berlin's *Tagesspiegel* asserted that East German architects were incapable of solving their problems and were seeking help in the West.[215]

Henselmann maintained that the competition had succeeded in establishing a clear direction for city planning in the GDR, leaving only details to be determined, such as how to most effectively incorporate green space and sunlight, and design for the efficient use of cranes. In contrast, many East German politicians viewed the result of the competition as a Western victory. Hans Schmidt of the Ministry of Building, tasked with assessing the competition, suggested that the fundamental similarity to West Berlin architecture and the fact that a West German architect won the competition belies the necessity of a distinction between socialist or capitalist architecture—architectural form reflects society. His criticism of the design included "schematism," the poor fit of the district center into the design, and the placement of the retail center "somewhere in green space."[216]

Along with politicians, some leading architects such as Liebknecht found this reengagement of modernism too extreme a shift from socialist realism. While Khrushchev had spoken of a "peaceful coexistence" with ideological enemies in 1956, tensions had increased in 1957, and Liebknecht made clear there could be no "ideological coexistence" with Western urbanism.[217] May was excluded from further work on the project. To no avail, May appealed for continued collaboration, declining to enter the

West Berlin Interbau (IBA) competition and expressing "no understanding for the oppositional political ideologies to continually lead to greater alienation between the two parts of Germany."[218] Liebknecht advised a critical stance toward adopting technical developments from the West, and a separation of "anarchistic, capitalistic building" as in the Hansaviertel, where international star architects displayed a wide range of forms.[219]

The centrality of industrialized building was assured, but how one designed building and cities (the "ideology of socialist building") remained a work in progress. As proposed residential complexes failed to adequately reflect socialist society, the DBA foresaw a "continuing discussion" of the relationship between theory and practice in "socialist city building."[220] *Deutsche Architektur* published a variety of opinions on successes and failures of recently designed residential complexes, and how "national form" may or may not remain relevant. One article suggested that "national particularity" would be manifest in the arrangement of facilities and residences, the spatial dimension of the urban order—a facile transition from national building to the residential complex.[221] Another saw traditional forms as expressions of other eras and therefore irrelevant to the contemporary situation. A new architectural language for industrialized building would be developed through the principles that guided the development of earlier "national forms." The only direction provided was that the architect proceed dialectically instead of "mechanistic/dogmatically."[222]

Another pointed to the influence of climate in distinguishing architectural forms among nations and suggested that a full solution to the question of national form required assistance from architectural theorists.[223] Other articles condemned the use of monumental scale and ornament for residential buildings, as found in "apartments of the decadent bourgeoisie on Champs Élysées." Instead, residences should be shaped "for beauty, for a quiet and happy family life, for an area undisturbed by noise and the dangers of traffic."[224] Junghans suggested that monumental buildings are defined by their relation to ordinary urban fabric, inevitably reflecting societal relations between the rulers and subjects. Under socialism a new type of monumentality would place equal importance on the individual and society, by placing civic buildings in a quiet, auto-free area in the center of residences.[225] Though modernism was proscribed, some of its core tenets were finding approval, displacing socialist-realist principles.

Richard Paulick's contribution to the "architecture discussion" maintained the importance of national heritage and insisted that Stalinallee was not a "detour" but a direct if flawed path toward a "socialist architectural style."[226] The claim is telling. The inability to theoretically reconcile national tradition with industrialized building in the era of socialist state building and increasing East-West tension resulted in a discursive shift from a New German Architecture to "socialist architecture." State-driven standardization and industrialization of building was understood as central, while a growing technological optimism also became apparent. In December 1957 the Third Congress of the Bund Deutscher Architekten insisted that socialist and capitalist architecture and city planning were incompatible.[227] In ensuing years, attempts to theorize "socialist architecture" and city building were attributed importance but generally offered only core principles and recognized it as a work in progress.[228]

At the SED's Fifth Party Congress, Ulbricht reinforced the importance of architecture expressing the "victorious idea of socialism." In 1959 the DBA published *Der sozialistische Wohnkomplex*, contrasting the social alienation in capitalist cites with the facilitation of community in residential complexes through well-defined "house groups." This idea was already implicit in the Soviet model and expressed in Liebknecht's critiques under the name "residential groups." In 1961, Alfred Kurella, a leading cultural functionary, posited that because socialism was a work in progress and architecture reflects society, "socialist architecture" could only be in a similar developmental stage. Establishing a full theory of "socialist architecture" would hinder its development. National identity remained important but only in the sense that architecture must differentiate itself from the West. The GDR, as the politically progressive state in the German nation, might use the same technology as the West but would differentiate itself through its application, striving to develop a socialist content.[229] Planning for Stalinallee proceeded absent a unified theory—that is, professionals and politicians maintaining their own perspectives on socialist content.

In October 1957 the Central Committee of the SED resolved that preparations for rebuilding the center of Berlin should begin immediately, forcing the design process to proceed before consensus on theory could emerge. Kosel published plans for the city center in *Deutsche Architektur* prior to the start of "Competition for the Socialist Redesign of the Capital of the German Democratic Republic." On the periphery of his plan a series of schematic, long, narrow high-rises ran parallel to Stalinallee.[230] Henselmann viewed this as an incursion. He wrote to Kosel, criticizing his design for focusing on formal composition without thorough consideration for the actual needs of society and copied Ulbricht as arbiter of such conflicts.[231] Soon Henselmann published his own plan for the section of Stalinallee between Straussberger Platz and Alexanderplatz with an entire residential complex on each side of Stalinallee.[232] A series of high-rise towers ran parallel to Stalinallee with a row of lower, multistory slab buildings staggered behind them. Yet the greened setbacks were so large as to present the impression of a parkway rather than an urban boulevard. The remainder of the site was largely pedestrianized green space loosely framed by slab buildings. Henselmann's intent was to create "charming and varied urban space with the most diverse visual connections."[233] He described the results as a "socialist residential complex," yet many of its features derived from the modernist "city landscape" and "residential cell."

In September 1958 the Politburo noted Henselmann had violated procedure by publishing the plan before they approved it. They also disapproved of similarities to Western modernism, one member characterizing it as "the Hansaviertel in East Berlin." The plan was rejected as a "break in the architecture of Stalinallee," and a "petit-bourgeois city in green space," noting that the "garden city and suburban ideology does not correspond to the fundamental ideas of socialist city building: we say yes to the big-city." Ulbricht personally condemned the plan as imitative of West Berlin.[234] The Politburo invited six architectural collectives to participate in a design competition for the area, requiring that Stalinallee function as a thoroughfare and shopping street with no breech of design from the existing section. There would be no high-rise towers, external-loaded corridor apartments or two-story apartments as in Henselmann's design. The requirements of industrialized building were to guide design work; hence separate two-story buildings were to be used for retail. Designs by Edmund Collein's and Werner Dutschke's collectives won the competition. Nicolaus and Obeth reasonably assert these offered no improvement over Henselmann's design; thus the party leadership was punishing Henselmann for his "high-handedness." These two collectives then revised their plans into a new design, which was approved by the Magistrat and published in October 1958 (figure 6.8).[235]

The revised plan displayed considerable detail in choice and placement of nonresidential functions. Those with regional significance were located directly on Stalinallee, while locally oriented functions were located in a greenway toward the center of each complex. Although Liebknecht had criticized May's Fennpfuhl plan for the poor relation between the

FIGURE 6.8. Alexanderplatz to Straussbergerplatz. View toward Alexanderplatz on the south side of Stalinallee provides a sense of the layout of the "residential complex." Visible in the image are Restaurant Moskau (lower right, foreground), new conference center (domed structure in center), and the House of Scientists and Teachers (under construction, top right). BA, Digital Picture Database, Bild 183-B0830-0002-002, *Allgemeiner Deutcher Nachrichtendienst—Zentralbild*, Horst Sturm, August 30, 1963.

scales of "residential group," "residential complex," and surrounding city, improvements in this regard were modest. "Residential groups," intended to provide intimate spaces for communal identity, were weakly defined, although better than at Fennpfuhl or in Henselmann's Stalinallee plan. Staggered building heights were intended to mediate between the differing scales of the city center to one side and residential districts on the other sides, although some gradation across the site would have been more effective. Also, plans for major arterials along the edges left the complexes isolated from the surrounding city as did the residential cells of the 1940s.[236]

Berliner Zeitung reported on the new plan in November 1958, and the concepts of "national tradition," "heritage," and even "Germany" were absent, while "large," "modern," and "Berlin" were prominent. Soviet identity was present with the "special sensation," Restaurant Moscow. The sole reference to existing urban fabric was brief mention that in order to make room for 2,130 new apartments on the first construction site, 380 old apartments would be demolished, for which "no one will cry."[237] In fact, a total of 2,300 old apartments and 153 businesses were demolished to make room for 5,266 new apartments.[238] In terms of net units produced, this effectively doubled the cost per unit of the new housing without considering the additional costs imposed by demolition. Increasing the supply of housing was subsidiary to the completion of the central axis and a representative city center. A new factory to produce components for large-panel components was constructed on the periphery of Berlin, and the first cornerstone was laid on October 6, 1959.[239] Mayor Ebert spoke at the ceremony, repeating the slogan "faster, better, and cheaper." He insubstantially offered that "to build socialistically also means to build so that people are guaranteed to be able to live together in an interesting, culturally rewarding manner."[240] Another article on Stalinallee stated: "In accordance with the theses of the German Building Academy a residential complex should guarantee a healthy life and promote a sense of belonging together under socialism."[241] Presumably Stalinallee would do so, although the precise relationship between the plan and these goals was not elaborated. Instead, programmatic elements and design details were described, often with quantitative accounts spanning from the number of beds in the hotel to the dimensions of the mosaic in Restaurant Moscow. The building-to-building street width of 125 meters (410 feet) was far wider and greener than the first section of Stalinallee, weakening their connection. Stalinallee retained its symbolic importance in this era but would no longer be the focus of efforts to resolve the housing issue in Berlin. The economics of industrialized construction and desire to maximize return on investment meant that most new housing would be built in residential complexes on greenfield sites beyond the urban core.[242]

The new state approach to the housing problem and its depiction in the press were intertwined with two larger societal changes. First, emphasis on scientific-technical progress, theorized by Kosel as a force of production in 1957, became a central feature of the Seven-Year Plan in 1959. Technological advancement and power now permeated public discourse.[243] Second, the state promoted consumerism as a political strategy to demonstrate its competence and combat the appeal of the West. Rationing of consumer goods was replaced with the policy of "1,000 small things," promising an increased standard of living for the new socialist person.[244]

In April 1959 the Politburo published "Tasks of Construction in the Great Seven-Year Plan of the GDR" for the upcoming Third Building Conference. The goal was to overcome the housing shortage by 1965.

Industrialization would be central. Labor productivity would be increased through technical training for industrialized construction and eduction to develop workers' "socialist consciousness."[245] Ulbricht's address posited that in the coming years, industrialized construction would result in a "great upswing" enabling the GDR to "fundamentally overcome" the housing shortage by 1965 with 764,000 new units (approximately 80,000 in Berlin).[246] While Khrushchev had already stated that housing should be treated as a consumer good in 1954, the GDR now fully embraced the idea and focused on the quantity of housing units produced. Second, concern for the quality of housing centered on the floor plans and modern conveniences of apartment units with reduced attention to urban design. The state also continued very modest support for the construction program that had emerged in the wake of the uprising to enable local self-help and cooperative efforts to restore damaged apartment buildings.

Newspaper reports promoted technological advancement as a means to rapid, cost-effective construction that would provide citizen-consumers with decent housing. Reports on the first section of Stalinallee had often highlighted tradition, place, and qualitative aspects, while largely ignoring the use of mechanical equipment, which was present but on a much more limited scale. Now, technological power and quantity of new units produced were focal points. These were linked in articles, even headlines such as "First Assembly Line in Berlin Apartment Building: Every Week 20 Apartments Completed."[247] Human labor remained crucial and highly valued, as evident in the renewed emphasis on socialist competitions, but it was now subservient to the logic of the crane: "The large-panels must roll on... as they are being used, and any idle time is to be avoided."[248] One article explained it this way: "Every hour of the day now counts for a certain number of crane movements [lifting a panel into place and returning], none of which can be missed."[249] The competition and quota system that helped precipitate the uprising in 1953 returned with the observation that the team that most effectively organized that transport and assembly of prefabricated elements would win.[250] The article "One Crane Movement Costs Just 1.17 DM" reported on a brigade committed to reducing the cost of labor per crane movement, which would help to fulfill the state plan and contribute to "educating the workers... in socialist thinking and acting."[251] The mobilization of voluntary labor through the National Building Program continued to play an important role in preparing sites, cleaning blocks and other tasks, but received relatively limited press coverage.[252] While Lenin had embraced Taylorist principles, they were now the celebrated core of the socialist building effort.

The crane and the large panel, the "absolute newest technique in apartment building," became ubiquitous symbols of progress. Construction photos of a crane lifting a concrete panel appeared regularly.[253] The pairing also appeared in diagrams. A stylized crane hoisting a panel appeared on a poster for the building exhibition in the Sports Hall, and an illustration of construction productivity stacked concrete panels into a bar charts, with a crane in the background.[254] Machine power was also celebrated in narrative form, often involving quantitative data about minutia to express objective knowledge and control. One report began with a hayseed visitor observing a rumbling excavator removing "cubic meter after cubic meter of dirt" and inquiring what was being built, thereby inviting an extensive report on construction.[255] Another showed a crane operator and fitter, using the "Rapid V, the most modern crane in the GDR" with "highest concentration... control five ton parts" with "millimeter precision."[256] Their brigade won the title "Brigade of Socialist Labor" and the article elaborated a great deal on their construction process and productivity. The article "Stalinallee: A Giant Moves" dramatically rendered the process of moving the 112 ton crane across Stalinallee with very large photos, an acclamation of machine power.[257] As Kosel had theorized, Ulbricht made official in his speech for the Twelfth Conference of the Central Committee on March 25, 1961: the key to solving the housing issue through industrialized building was "scientific-technical progress."[258]

In these and myriad other examples, Stalinallee was no longer a place built upon national tradition but a space to showcase technological power and construction productivity.[259] This is confirmed by an internal report stating, "the deployment of large panel building in Berlin for construction projects in the continuation of Stalinallee [was intended] to produce a convincing example of the high scientific-technological level in the area of industrialized apartment building."[260] Tradition rarely appeared in the press, and then only to be denigrated: take, for example, the article "BUILD MORE—Without Outdated Tradition." A planner invited more input from future renters, implying that this would break with tradition and enable progress.[261] Another article revealed enduring Communist iconoclastic notions, as stone from the ruins of Wertheim department store, the Berlin Stock Exchange, and the Reichsbank were being reused on Stalinallee. The cannibalization was portrayed as working-class people benefitting from dissembled capitalist antiheritage, with no distinction between a bank that had become a Nazi organ and a department store confiscated from its Jewish owners.[262]

Popular press depictions of the qualitative aspects of new apartments centered on their layout and dimensions, and their modern conveniences—matters secondary to the development of forms built on national tradition in the first section of Stalinallee. They now emphasized the use of technological prowess and quantified, objective knowledge to master the utilitarian, spatial aspects of architecture—that is, floor plan variability, efficiency, and livability. Articles on the "custom apartment" countered concerns about monotony in mass-produced housing. To the contrary, the latest structural technology enabled adroit designers attentive to public input to generate new, high-quality floor plans. The same building shell could include units of variable size and their interiors could be outfit differently, while including modern conveniences and large glass plate windows maximizing the connection to green space.[263] The "life of the housewife" would be "further lightened" through a "built-in kitchen," essentially a watered-down version of the Frankfurter kitchen separated from the dining/living room by the entry foyer; losing the visual connection that Henselmann maintained in the first section of Stalinallee.[264] Although ornament had been eschewed in theory, the boxy, new apartment building included subtle decorative cornice treatment.

New movie theaters and a restaurant planned for Stalinallee were emblematic of the discursive shift (figure 6.9). The first theater was designed as a freestanding structure with an abstract, pure geometry—a tall, ovular theater space intersecting a trapezoidal base with entry hall and service areas. The exact site was irrelevant, its form was derived entirely from the spatial program and new cinema technology.[265] These qualities were highlighted in the press. *Berliner Zeitung* boasted that the "most modern cinema in the GDR" on Stalinallee offered "1,000 seats and all the requirements of the new cinema technology" that would enable a larger screen than previously, its dimensions potentially ranging from 7.30 to 7.88 meters high and 10.22 to 17.35 meters wide. Given this size and variability, the provision of exact centimeters could serve no purpose other than to convey a sense of precision. The large screen, along with skilled spatial layout, was to assure patrons of an optimal visual and acoustic experience from all seats. There would be forced-air heating, air conditioning, and controlled humidity as well as generously sized seats at 52 by 93 centimeters

FIGURE 6.9. View north, across Stalinallee. Restaurant Moskau with Sputnik model appear along the right edge of the photo. Across the street is the movie theater International and Hotel Berolina, named after the city's female symbol. BA, Digital Picture Database, Bild 183-D0927-0016-001, *Allgemeiner Deutcher Nachrichtendienst—Zentralbild*, Rainer Mittelstädt, September 27, 1965.

(conventional seats were 50 centimeters by 80 centimeters). The exterior would harmonize with existing architecture through a ceramic plate finish, a claim made for this entire section of Stalinallee—and in fact, one of the few relationships that could be observed.[266]

Plans for a second movie theater, Kino International, were revealed in 1960, displaying modern structural strength by extending the second floor foyer so that it "hovers six meters over the sidewalk."[267] Technology was celebrated both for what it could provide and for its own sake in purely technophilic expressions. The new Restaurant Moscow complex included a model of Sputnik hovering (on a pole) above the building, testifying to the success of the Soviet satellite that initiated the space race even though ornament had been condemned. A screen framing the space above the entryway was purely decorative, demonstrating the capacity to produce delicate tracery with prefabricated concrete.

An exhibition of Soviet construction machines was held in the Sports Hall on Stalinallee as a "school of modern construction technique," providing "proof of brotherly assistance and close technical-scientific collaboration" between the two nations.[268] Occasional references to the Soviet origins of specific machines in construction articles reinforced the idea.[269]

West Berlin and West Germany regularly appeared in the press for increasing rents, while the US Army constructed luxurious housing for itself at the expense of the German people.[270] As migration to the West reached crisis levels, reports of international groups visiting Stalinallee began to appear.[271] In August 1960, *Berliner Zeitung* reported a West German family resettling in East Berlin, impressed by the quality of their new apartment and astonished at the low cost.[272] In October 1960, *Berliner Zeitung* reported the "quick and unbureaucratic" admission of twelve-hundred Western visitors per day. Foreign visitors were numerous, and many inquired about the quickest way to Stalinallee.[273]

Nonetheless, industrialized building could not stop the exodus from East to West. In February 1961 resentment over these projects' consumption of resources prompted the Council of Ministers to acknowledge the error and guarantee more building materials for individual households to purchase.[274] Yet the press continued to focus on a bright, technologically advanced future with industrialized construction of new housing. On April 12, Friedrichshain's district mayor revealed DM 100 million would be spent on Stalinallee.[275] On April 13, headlines proclaimed, "Triumph in Outer Space, Victory for Communism," as Yuri Gagarin became the first man in space.[276] Early on the morning of April 14, the Berlin Wall was under construction, but the newspaper did not report the event. Stalinallee would have a captive audience.

The Housing Question and Struggles with Design Paradigms

Throughout the period of study, East German politicians aspired to remedy a housing crisis with a building program that highlighted Frankfurter Allee/Stalinallee as a symbolic focal point. Gaining political support and indoctrinating the population was a central goal that would be best attained through effective implementation of the correct ideological and theoretical guidelines. Yet dispute and debate arose, and the official urban design and architectural paradigms underwent dramatic shifts. There are multiple strands of thought in Marxism, different theories of art and urbanism have been derived from it, and leading agents differed in their knowledge and opinions about these. Furthermore, the political, economic, and technological context underwent significant shifts, altering the potential consequences of different approaches. Those with revolutionary fervor would navigate complex terrain.

In the early postwar years the modernist paradigm was widely accepted in East Berlin as the model for housing under a new "democratic" regime. Most German planners and architects were trained in modernist design, and Berlin's renown modernist housing projects had been developed as a remedy to the industrial slums. The Soviet Military Administration (SMAD) remained aloof at this time. Frankfurter Allee was conceived of as an arterial road, which would be adjoined by separate "residential cells," planned in accordance with statistical analysis of social needs and the optimal spatial distribution of population, housing, and services. Representation and monumentality were rejected.

Following the GDR's founding, political leaders made socialist realism official policy and introduced the cult of Stalin. Those resistant to socialist realism were forced to change their views, appear to change them, resign, or emigrate. Those who dissented openly potentially faced more serious means of Stalinist repression, such as Karl Brockschmidt, who was charged with embezzlement and allegedly committed suicide in jail.[277] Frankfurter Allee was renamed Stalinallee and became the model project in developing a "new German architecture." It was hoped that the project would galvanize interest and support from Berliners and Germans, East and West. Stalinallee would no longer be a traffic artery but an urban design element, a traditional street or boulevard. Housing, retail, and entertainment functions were integral, comprising an architectural ensemble built on Berlin traditions. It was both a vernacular space for social and political life and a monumental place representing the nation and the East German state.

The Uprising of 1953 and the Soviet shift to industrialized building created a practical and theoretical crisis for East Berlin city building. The GDR leadership followed Khrushchev's lead with standardized plans, mass-produced components, and the elimination of ornament. This did not preordain a return to modernist architecture and urban design, although some Berlin architects rushed to do so. Henselmann's attempts to design modernist residential cells were rejected by the party leadership for similarity with Western planning. Theoretical debates, "the architecture discussion," endured for several years. Socialist realism was never rescinded, but national tradition began fading from discussion in favor of a "socialist architecture" that remained a work in progress. Ultimately, the state shift to viewing housing as a consumer good and its demands for the building industry to perform "better, faster, and cheaper" empowered Gerhard Kosel, first deputy of the Ministry of Building, to impose his vision. Kosel's theorization of science and technology as productive forces and its translation into practice as the drive to maximize efficiency in construction through extensive rationalization and mechanization shaped design efforts and the new building program.

Hence the requirements of the building crane were prioritized over traditional urban design in an eclectic combination of socialist realism and modernism. Press reports on industrialized construction celebrated the power of technology to produce great quantities of new apartments, while reassuring the public of their quality. Quantified, objective knowledge of how best to shape architectural space replaced a concern for its relation to national tradition. The crane and concrete panel became iconic symbols of this power, Stalinallee a space for their display. Technological optimism was evident in the ubiquitous concern with the latest, most modern developments and enthusiastic speculation about future possibilities. This was explicit above the entrance to Café Moscow, where rejected ornament appeared in a model representing the Soviet Sputnik satellite. In autumn of 1961 a belated de-Stalinzation took place, as the street was named Karl Marx Allee and the Stalin statue was removed.[278]

Despite all these abrupt changes in theory and practice, there was some long-term continuity. Substantively, concerns over residents' access to sun, air, and daylight continued unabated from the 1840s through this period of study. Philosophically, a concern for developing the correct theory and implementing it properly persisted. In the late 1950s, Henselmann sent Walter Ulbricht a copy of an unpublished document explaining his own theory of city building.[279] He continued to struggle over the correct application of dialectics to this issue, as had been done since the Revolution in Russia and since the end of World War II in Germany. His focus reiterated the enduring concerns of Berlin's housing reformers going back to the early 1800s: "It demands a new answer to an old question.... There is the family—narrowest connection of the individual in society. How to connect and how to free the individual and society in urban space? There is the family in the apartment, there are the apartments in the building."[280]

Conclusion

IN THE MID- TO LATE 1950S the end of food rationing led to a precipitous decline in the numbers of East German citizens fleeing to the West.[1] The tide turned again in 1959 as the economy slowed and the collectivization of agriculture exacerbated shortages, forcing the reintroduction of rationing. By the summer of 1961 emigration had reached crisis levels, particularly for the loss of young people. Khrushchev pressured the West for a peace treaty to settle the Berlin Question, spurring a *Torschlusspanik* (terror of the gate closing). On June 15, 1961, Walter Ulbricht hosted an international press conference. When asked about his intentions for the border, he replied: "As I understand your question, there are people in West Germany, who wish that we mobilize the construction workers of the capital city of the GDR to erect a wall. I am not aware that any such intention exists. The construction workers of our capital city are occupied primarily with apartment building, and their productive power will be fully employed for that. No one has the intention of building a wall."[2] By early July, with the threat of state collapse looming and President Kennedy's refusal to sign a treaty clear, Khrushchev approved Ulbricht's request to build a wall. Ulbricht himself devised a conceptual plan for what would become his master work. Whereas other projects were touted to the press during the planning phase, here only a small group of trusted former Moscow exiles were allowed in on the secret.

On the evening of August 12, 1961, Ulbricht hosted a dinner for the Council of Ministers at his country house. After 10:00 p.m. he initiated a brief working session to approve a resolution ordering the border to be secured, thereby providing state legitimacy for the action.[3] A few hours later, barbed wire was rolled out along the sector border, ending an exodus that exceeded one thousand people daily. This was the first iteration of a barrier that would evolve over decades into a massive concrete wall and death strip. *Neues Deutschland* published the resolution, which offered an explanation for the measures.[4] Under the "mask of anti-Communism," West Germany and "front-city West Berlin" were continuing the militaristic, imperialistic goals of the Third Reich. They were systematically preparing for civil war, terrorizing East German citizens who visited. Peaceful citizens of West Berlin were welcome to travel in the East, but "agents of West German militarism" would not be permitted to enter. Securing the border would maintain peace, protect the GDR and its capital city, Berlin, and guarantee the security of other socialist states.

Accordingly, it came to be deemed the "antifascist, defensive wall," although the Stasi noted that East Germans knew it was intended for them.[5] Indeed, Ulbricht had spoken openly of this purpose at a Warsaw Pact meeting in early August.[6] Many East German citizens were filled with rage and hate but dared not express themselves. In public one saw only "depressed, resigned faces." On September 2, Ulbricht initiated a second phase to construct a concrete wall. He acknowledged that the city building program would have to be scaled back to complete this task, and in fact residents occupying apartments along the wall would have to be relocated. The GDR would continue to shape the city to express its ideals and influence the population, but this massive, concrete incision through the city would provide a colossal counterpoint to East Berlin's touted "socialist" building projects.

Cultural Memory, Politics, and the Interpretation of the Urban Landscape

Throughout this period, political and cultural elites actively shaped the physical and symbolic attributes of the urban landscape due to a belief that it had important impacts on society. Details of the debate over the city reveal that these leaders' motives and understanding of how the urban landscape was significant cannot be reduced to a simple statement. Yet, given the continuity of cultural memory carried in various discourses, there was a strong tendency for discrete social groups to share common views. As reconstruction progressed, the flow of social and political events wrought changes that would alter how these groups viewed and acted on the cityscape.

The Soviet Military Administration (SMAD), German Communist political leaders, non-Communist German political leaders, and the German cultural and technical elite each displayed a great deal of internal unity in their view of the city, and there were often considerable differences between these groups. This was evident in their frameworks for interpreting meaning in the urban landscape and their valuation of specific cultural identities. The impact of key discourses upon these interpretations has been emphasized, but this is not to imply that the city was shaped by structural forces independent of human agency. Rather, intragroup commonalities and points of difference in these matters derive from the choices of individuals with regard to these broader frameworks.

First, all discourse is the product of human effort. The theories that had the greatest impact in East Berlin were developed and applied through individual and group effort. Most individuals in each group drew from the same frameworks for interpreting the city, hence they often agreed about the proper course of action. The frameworks themselves were developed through very different processes, but at some level human decision-making was always involved. Socialist realism emerged in Moscow through political conflict over architectural and planning styles, extensive design efforts, and theory building involving many people over a prolonged time period. In Berlin it was quickly imposed through the efforts of a few key Germans leaders, suppressing the modernist paradigm favored by most German architects. In the mid-1950s, Khrushchev pushed for the industrialization of building, and myriad Soviet and German architects and planners would determine how this would occur, effectively shaping a new paradigm of city building.

Second, the application of these frameworks, even seemingly clear-cut ideologies or theories, requires an act of interpretation that sometimes resulted in differences and debate within groups. For instance, the perception of and disdain for reactionary Prussian/German exceptionalism suggested a purge of symbols of militarism and monarchy, but leeway remained in determining exactly which persons or events should be included. Further questions lingered as to how this iconoclasm would be carried out. The Allied Control Council ordered the disposal of undesirable statues, but if they possessed cultural value, they could be preserved in museums. Given the goal of denazifying the public realm, one might ask why the statues were not subjected to ritualized degradation, such as in the Reformation. Perhaps this was for expediency given the difficult situation, or perhaps a desire to appear more civilized as charges of barbarism have often accompanied iconoclasm.[7] Would removing iconography from buildings rehabilitate them? If not, would they be left to decay, to be cannibalized for material, or to be demolished?

While such decisions were made within the parameters of "denazifying or demilitarizing," they testify to the degree of commitment or enthusiasm found among different persons or groups. Erick Honecker's eagerness to return Berlin Palace rubble to its original site for the construction of a grandstand evidences the depth of his hatred for the German monarchy. New plans faced the same issue. The modernist Athens Charter emphasized the provision of green space in cities, but one still had to decide how much to provide, where to locate it, the exact form it would take, and how to relate it to buildings—and do so with the knowledge that limited resources would limit the extent to which this could be done. Socialist realism demanded that new structures build on classical tradition, but how this would occur led to a prolonged design process, involving criticism and at times open conflict. Many discourses, even theories of city building with a clearly defined ideal urban vision, leave open matters of emphasis and possible conflict between statements. While Ulbricht had nearly singular focus on parade routes and the largest central square possible, Soviet advisers believed too much attention had been given to parades. They emphasized the need for historic preservation in its own right and to save buildings to architecturally frame the central square. One Soviet adviser found the plans too "Prussian," indicating a need for more dispersed small squares for relaxation. Justification for all of these views could be found in the Sixteen Principles.

Third, individuals make choices regarding the interpretation of complex place-based meanings that may testify to competing pasts or tap multiple discourses. For instance, Ulbricht's insistence that the palace be demolished for Marx-Engels Square was a form of iconoclasm, heavily influenced by a negative view of German exceptionalism and a concealed materialist view of buildings as expressions of their owners, while ignoring socialist realism. Regarding the Neue Wache and the Arsenal, planners accepted the socialist-realist imperative of preservation and adaptive reuse, but concerns over the buildings' military origins resulted in some uncertainty and delay in determining their new content. Several buildings on Wilhelmstrasse had been used as residences, and by various forms of government from democratic to totalitarian, offering numerous pasts for consideration.

Fourth, individuals may defy direction provided by discourses for personal reasons, with costs or benefits to the parties involved. Hermann Henselmann's delay in fully engaging socialist realism sparked a conflict with politicians that led to his public shaming and his own consideration for emigrating West. In contrast, architects' inclusion of limited modernist influences in their designs for Stalinallee did not elicit a response, likely because the buildings' defining features adhered to politicians' notions of how they should appear. Wilhelm Pieck's design for the Socialist Memorial in Friedrichsfelde deviated greatly from the classical tradition as expressed in Soviet memorials. No one voiced criticism, likely due to his political power and moral authority regarding the issue, and perhaps because the site was removed from the city center.

Fifth, given great concern over the political impact of decisions regarding the urban landscape and their depiction in the press, individuals sometimes chose to ignore accepted discourses. Although Pieck viewed the Communist Party as the culmination of working-class political history, his memorial proposal included a nonhierarchical depiction of Social Democratic and Communist martyrs until the division of the Berlin Magistrat. In another case, GDR leaders began supporting the renovation of historic Protestant churches in 1949, although Marxism stood opposed to religion. GDR leaders had a more complicated relationship with the church stemming from political opportunism. Finally, material needs and constraints forced a degree of pragmatism that could limit the impact of concerns over ideology. For instance, plans to replace all of the "old Berlin" with a modernist "new Berlin" quickly proved to be utopian. Former Nazi structures on Wilhelmstrasse were reused because they offered large amounts of much needed office space, even though Communist leaders were not comfortable with their histories.

The case studies covered in this book demonstrate how meaning was conveyed through the urban landscape. The content and significance of any site were nearly always derived from the triad of place-based meaning, formal and spatial relations, and representation (iconography and text), however, with vastly different levels of importance attached to each depending on the site and who was viewing the site. For instance, on the one hand, the iconography on Hitler's Chancellery was intolerable and quickly removed, yet the site's place-based meaning was so repulsive that this could not rehabilitate the structure and it was demolished. On the other hand, the Ministry of Aviation had immense spatial value and undesirable but less repulsive place-based meaning, hence a purge of iconography was deemed sufficient to allow its occupation by government. Communists did not approve of the image of Bismarck for display in public space, while non-Communists argued that a small statue partially concealed by trees would be acceptable. The architectural value (spatial properties) of the Schwerin Palace and to a degree its place-based meaning were valued by historic preservationists, while politicians viewed all buildings on Wilhelmstrasse as tainted by reactionary place-based meaning. In contrast, planners prioritized the spatial value of the site for a road extension, devaluing the architectural aspect. Shortly after the war, German Communists valued the Arsenal on Unter den Linden for its spatial capacity to hold exhibitions, although its origins and long use for militaristic purposes tarnished its image. With the adoption of socialist realism, they were required to prioritize its value as architectural heritage, yet they remained uncomfortable with its place-based meaning. There are myriad cases throughout this book that testify to the persistent importance of these three factors, and great differences in the importance attached to each factor for a given site at a given moment.

Memorials, monumental architecture, vernacular buildings, public spaces, and city plans were not treated in the same manner due to differences in how they were understood to convey cultural meaning. Memorials exist as testimonies to specific cultural memories, typically honoring persons, groups, and/or events. Due to this specificity, they are often targeted in periods of great cultural and political change. After World War II, for instance, a great number of Berlin's existing memorials were removed and new major memorials were constructed. Though memorials typically have a fixed set of referents, these may be interpreted in different ways. Hence there were myriad conflicts regarding memorial construction at the revolutionaries' cemeteries. Furthermore, memorials can be designed to limit or expand semantic flexibility, the latter being attained through several techniques at the Soviet Memorial in Treptow, maximizing its appeal to more than one group and in more than one era.

Monumental architecture typically serves cultural or political functions of collective importance and aggrandizes them through spatial and formal properties, iconography, and text. Thus such architecture may contain specific referents like memorials but it has much greater pragmatic value for human activity. Daily use and special events gradually build on these structures' place-based meaning. For instance, the Berlin Palace was occupied by the Prussian-German monarchy for centuries, ever-deepening the association. Some buildings are used for changing purposes over time, adding new layers of memory and complicating interpretations of their significance. On Unter den Linden the Neue Wache was built as a guardhouse and later used as a war memorial. GDR architects seeking to preserve the building as architectural heritage carefully considered each when deciding on a new "content." On Wilhelmstrasse several structures began as private residences for aristocrats, then for ascendant bourgeois, then served governmental purposes during the eras of the Prussian monarchy, the German constitutional monarchy, the democratic Weimar Republic, and the Nazi era, making it difficult to attribute just one meaning. Buildings have greater utilitarian spatial value than memorials, which overcame the taint of place-based meaning for some large Nazi-era buildings on Wilhelmstrasse. The removal of unacceptable iconography and text was deemed sufficient to reuse, if not fully rehabilitate these buildings.

Vernacular buildings and spaces are constructed to serve the citizenry in their everyday lives, although they too can acquire considerable cultural meaning over time. This often occurs on a neighborhood or district level. *Heimatschutz* advocates attributed cultural value to all human settlement and in special cases considered them to be national heritage, such as Sparrows Alley in the Fischerkietz. In socialist realism the vernacular was devalued as a precedent, in favor of the monumental, leaving little in the way of Sparrows Alley's demolition. Building types may also accrue meaning, regardless of their specific site. Berlin's rental barracks, for example, were considered by German Communists to be a testimony to capitalist exploitation of the working class. They were also viewed as a formal and spatial problem requiring remediation. Yet their sheer numbers and utilitarian value meant that they would largely be restored rather than removed. They were valued homes to many residents, and GDR policy came to include funds for rehabilitation. Over time criticism in the press tapered off. On occasion, a specific vernacular structure may acquire widely recognized cultural meaning for its use or events that occurred there, such as the Kaiserhof Hotel. Its partial occupation by the Nazi Party imbued it with as much symbolism as structures built by the NSDAP.

City plans may propose changes to any of the above elements but for broad areas and generally with little detail. They are usually only partially implemented over long periods of time. For these reasons the public and even professionals normally have limited awareness of how past plans shaped their city. This partially explains why the cultural meaning of large-scale plans is often seen as highly malleable, as in the case of postwar modernist plans. The paradigm was relatively new, rejected tradition, and had only been applied on a limited scale in Berlin during the 1920s. Although Nazi planners made some use of modernism, the spotlight shone upon Albert Speer's plans for a monumental Welthauptstadt Germania, designed according to traditional baroque principles. In contrast to modernism, socialist-realist plans tied into classical tradition that some German Communists associated with Hitler, that Soviet advisers related to a broader European past, and that Western critics panned as a Soviet expression—in this case the breadth and depth of the paradigms' history enabled one to select from different pasts for flexibility of interpretation. Yet, at some level, socialist realism would always be recognized as the Soviet approach to the classical past imposed in East Germany by the SED.

An Emphatic Statement

Walter Ulbricht and leading German Communists' interest in the cultural meaning and political potential of the cityscape was expressed in myriad ways. Extant discourses and the triad of place, space, and representation have been used throughout this book to examine how they interpreted it. This is not to infer that this analysis has captured the totality of their views and thoughts about the city. For instance, it is noteworthy how often a large sweeping gesture was sought: modernist plans that reconfigured the entire city structure; demolishing the Berlin Palace to create a massive space for demonstrations larger than Red Square; designing a monumental "central axis" running more than 6 kilometers (3.7 miles) through the city center; Stalinallee's great breadth, length, and building height; Gerhard Kröber's winning city center plan praised for its "grand scale"; a proposed government high-rise with the state emblem visible in all directions and illuminated at night; and proposals for giant Marx-Engels memorials. The size of some projects can be ascribed to a socialist-realist emphasis on monumentality. However, when one views the array of projects calling out to be seen and to impress, they testify to the Communist need to stake a claim to legitimacy in a bold manner and of Ulbricht's obsessive competition with the West.

Two moderately sized memorials add another dimension to this observation: the temporary International Federation of Former Political Prisoners of the Nazi Regime (Fédération Internationale des Anciens Prisonniers Politiques du Fascisme, FIAPP) memorial on the Lustgarten, a massive cube in relation to nearby humans, and the Socialists' Memorial in Friedrichsfelde, centered on a twenty-ton, rough-hewn stone. This desire for solidity, or the impression of solidity, seems to complement the desire for grand gestures. All sought to firmly anchor Communist identity in the urban landscape. The Communists' long history of persecution culminating in their virtual elimination by the Nazis, including the arrest, torture, and murder of many leaders who did not flee, would have provided a tremendous sense of insecurity. Gigantism, solidity, and weightiness could be seen as responses to these memories. Ironically, the ultimate statement of the East German regime in Berlin's urban landscape, the Wall, imposed unprecedented immensity and solidity as a barrier to contain its population.

The Berlin Wall began as the most utilitarian of structures, created to restrict the movement of people. The GDR's building program continued to work toward meeting housing needs and construct new government buildings and monuments proclaiming the legitimacy of the state, but the Wall would testify against them. Perhaps for this reason, the Socialist Unity Party (SED) did not permit its residents to photograph the Wall.[8] While state propaganda had claimed that construction on Stalinallee was contributing to peace, it made a more dramatic claim for the Wall, as having "rescued peace in Europe."[9] In fact, it did place on hold the diplomatic jostling, ultimatums, and threats of war between the Soviets and the Western allies over the seemingly intractable Berlin Question. The official state narrative declared that the Wall created a "harbor in which the socialist project would be secure from the storms of competition between the systems," and eventually the superiority of socialist relations of production would triumph.[10] In time, the structure would become a "global icon," symbol of the Cold War and likely the most recognized feature of Berlin.[11] For decades it did harbor the socialist project of the GDR. Then, on November 9, 1989, the Wall was breached, gradually vandalized, and demolished—and its fragments commodified.

Many precedents exist for the drive to monumentality, size, and solidity. Hitler's Germania far exceeded any expression of gigantism in the GDR. According to Speer, the immensity was intended not only to glorify the nation but to convey the strength of Hitler himself, to feed his pride.

Speer believed this to be a consistent feature of newly acquired wealth, pointing to examples in totalitarian and democratic systems in antiquity.[12] Looking past Hitler in Germany, Marx had observed the bourgeois striving to fix a cultural and political order amid the vital chaos its economic system generated. Notably, this included a considerable amount of building, "and the self-consciously monumental character of so much of this building—indeed, throughout Marx's century, every table and chair in a bourgeois interior resembled a monument—testify to the sincerity and seriousness of this claim. And yet, the truth of the matter, is that everything the bourgeois society builds is built to be torn down."[13] As Marx put it: "All that is solid melts into air."[14] Prior to 1989, Marshall Berman suggested that this could apply to a Communist society, too—although speaking on a theoretical level and not about actual governments.[15] Indeed, the GDR, several of its most gigantic monuments, and the Wall itself have dissolved.

Yet cultural memory is not swept away. The stream of debates, histories, traditions, and practices threading through the entire existence of the GDR continue today, and in places they powerfully intersect with the urban landscape. Debates over the future shape of the city are conducted with considerable public attention to obtain "appropriate" solutions in terms of urban design and national memory and identity. Critics have not questioned the earnestness of this pursuit but its apparent lack of theoretical sophistication.[16] They condemn a "primitivist jargon of authenticity" in a "frenzied search for symbolic meaning and fixed interpretations."[17] Those who embrace postmodern relativism rarely shy away from the stance of enlightened viewer to "objectively" delegitimize perspectives other than their own. Even pure relativism, such as Jameson's assertion that "the spatial unconscious can associate anything with anything else," offers little when facing Hitler's Chancellery, the primary meaning of which is fixed and non-negotiable for the vast majority of Europeans.

Whether the goal is to facilitate understanding across horizons of meaning for those employing a hermeneutic approach, to spur active memory work for adherents of postmodernism, or simply to increase the productivity of dialogue for pragmatists, more consideration could be given to clarifying the discourses underlying contemporary debates, along with analysis of their limitations, liabilities, and potential. German politicians may adhere to some of the core assumptions of nineteenth-century preservationists, and there may or may not be a valid basis for this approach. The same is true for the application of concepts derived from postmodern theory. "Places of learning" can offer rich experiences engaging visitors to explore meanings, but they are neither neutral nor completely open-ended, nor should they be. They frame issues and one can always step outside the frame to examine its construction. Interpretation can never be forfeited entirely to the viewer, and the illusion of doing such should be avoided. In this sense, the proclamations and manifestos of modernists and the scientistic laws of socialist realism were advantageous, not as truth but for providing a stance and clear direction, a basis for interpreting sites and for critiquing those interpretations.

The Communist Legacy in Berlin

After reunification, the City of Berlin and the German government quickly initiated an effort to rename East Berlin streets to reflect the "democratization" of political life. A debate emerged between conservatives who wanted to erase symbols of the "Stalinist legacy" that included Soviet symbols and those of German socialism. Others agreed regarding Soviet and East German state symbols but wanted to preserve symbols of German socialism, especially those associated with antifascist resistance. The status of such particular individuals as Karl Marx, Clara Zetkin, Rosa Luxemburg, and Karl Liebknecht became the focus of heavily politicized debate and compromise. Sections of streets named for Marx (former Stalinallee) and Liebknecht closest to the city center were renamed, again indicating a dynamic involving symbolism and spatial relations.[18]

Although the Socialists' Memorial was no longer part of an official state ceremony, a massive procession of diverse left-wing groups treks to Friedrichsfelde each January, while right-wing counterprotesters menace from the sidelines, police separating the groups. The memorial has been left untouched as a burial ground and site of memory for leftist dissent and opposition.[19] The Memorial of the March Revolution has become the site of contestation with far-left parties battling to retain the "red sailor" and asserting its significance for both revolutions. The more centrist Paul Singer Society has proposed that the site become a national memorial and opened a temporary exhibit on the history of the 1848 Revolution and a "learning place" for democracy.[20]

Since reunification, Berlin has officially adopted "critical reconstruction" as official guidelines for city planning, emphasizing that new development must respect the historic structure of Berlin. Regulations place considerable constraint on urban design, while allowing flexibility in architectural style at most locations. This is similar to the traditionalist planning of the early GDR, although more flexible, without a teleology and highlighting the identity of Berlin rather than the nation. The approach has generated considerable criticism among professionals, academics, and journalists for a range of reasons, including allegations of appropriating victim status for Germans. Nonetheless, the critical reconstruction is part of an internationally popular neotraditionalist movement.[21]

Karl Marx Allee was intermittently used for state ceremonies after 1961. During the onset of the 1989 march to Friedrichsfelde, dissenters were apprehended at Frankfurter Gate. Since reunification, the buildings have been preserved at considerable expense given their poor construction, especially the attachment of ceramic plates to the facade.[22] Nonetheless, Star architects Phillip Johnson and Aldo Rossi have both praised Stalinallee as an urban design element.[23] Recently, Berlin architect Hans Kohlhoff contrasted Stalinallee with today's "inhibited social housing behind a forced packaging of science-fiction motifs or Styrofoam classicism."[24] Kohlhoff charges that social housing should make a bold statement for democracy. All of these architects value Stalinallee's form as a traditional boulevard, while Kohlhoff also admires the grand vision and public building effort that created it.

Beginning in 1990, advocates for restoring the Berlin Palace argued its importance for urban design and for its cultural symbolism, "healing wounds" and restoring the heart of the city. A period of protracted contestation ensued over various issues. Some from the East and West argued for a complete or partial preservation of the modernist Palace of the Republic, built by the GDR on the site of the former palace. Some viewed a replica as inauthentic or questioned whether a building could serve the intended symbolic purposes and sought a solution with a more provocative relation to cultural memory. In the postwar era some West Germans embraced the idea of engaging memory through "open wounds" in the cityscape. Leaving a void on the palace site would serve this purpose. After protracted contestation the Bundestag resolved that the Palace of the Republic would be demolished and a replica of the Berlin Palace's exterior would be constructed. This new Humboldtforum will open as a center for culture and the arts in 2019.[25]

Key historic buildings on Unter den Linden were saved from decay by the introduction of socialist realism and continue to undergo renovations and maintenance. Nevertheless, the interior of the Neue Wache underwent one more controversial change when Helmut Kohl ordered the replacement of the East German memorial with a Kollwitz Pieta to the dismay of many on the left.[26] On Wilhelmstrasse spatially valuable structures such as the Ministry of Aviation continue to be used as office space. In 1996 the Topography of Terror Foundation opened an exhibit including thirty stations with photographs and text examining Wilhelmstrasse's past.[27] Finally, while most of the Wall has been removed, a small section has been preserved and transformed into a memorial commemorating the division of the city and "victims of Communist tyranny." The site includes a documentation center and chapel to replace a church that had been demolished when the Wall was constructed.[28]

Communist building projects emerged within a web of discourses rooted in the past and extending into the present. For this reason the postreunification drive to efface evidence of the Communist past was soon met with opposition from the East and West. "Communism" would only be neatly extracted from some sites, such as the Palace of the Republic and Marx-Engels Square. While many streets names honoring socialist and Communist leaders were removed, others were preserved, particularly those named for antifascists. Debate and compromise often led to the reinterpretation of sites. Sometimes this involved physical changes, such as the learning center at the Cemetery of the March Revolution, the new memorial inside the Neue Wache, the stations on Wilhelmstrasse, or the memorialization of a portion of the Wall. In other cases, sites were physically unchanged, but their status was altered by other means. The state no longer organizes marches to Friedrichsfelde in January, but an array of extreme leftist groups does. Stalinallee is no longer depicted in the press as national architecture or a great socialist street. It has been denigrated as wedding-cake architecture and renamed Karl Marx Allee but also restored as heritage expressing both socialist-realist and older planning traditions.

Despite Stalinist crimes, German Communist heritage in Berlin is not without nuance. Contemporary debates and practices continue to determine how this heritage will be expressed in the urban landscape. Underlying this contestation, the dynamic of place, space, and representation impacts efforts to constitute meaning, facilitate or discourage action, and engage or deny the importance of links between cultural memory and contemporary society. Memory and history are not simply imposed in the urban landscape—they are also shaped by it.

Notes

Introduction

Epigraph: Karl Marx, "The Eighteenth Brumaire of Louis Bonaparte," in *Die Revolution* 1, trans. Saul Padower, https://www.marxists.org/archive/marx/works/1852/18th-brumaire, accessed November 10, 2016.

1. Lothar Bolz, File note, November 18, 1949, Stiftung Archiv der Parteien und Massenorganizationen der DDR im Bundesarchiv (hereafter SAPMO-BA), H1/44476. Unless otherwise noted, in this book all translations from the original German into English are by the author.

2. Davie Atkinson and Denis Cosgrove, "Urban Rhetoric and Embodied Identities: City, Nation, and Empire at the Vittorio Emanuele II Monument in Rome, 1870–1945," *Annals of the Association of American Geographers* 88, no. 1 (1998): 28–49; Kenneth Foote, *Shadowed Ground: America's Landscapes of Violence and Tragedy* (Austin: University of Texas Press, 1997); Rudy Koshar, *From Monuments to Traces: Artifacts of German Memory, 1870–1990* (Berkeley: University of California Press, 2000); Brian Ladd, *The Ghosts of Berlin: Confronting German History in the Urban Landscape* (Chicago: University of Chicago Press, 1997); James Young, *The Texture of Memory: Holocaust Memorials and Meaning* (New Haven: Yale University Press, 1993); and Robert Taylor, *The Word in Stone: The Role of Architecture in National Socialist Ideology* (Berkeley: University of California Press, 1974). For an overview of literature on public memory and commemoration and the material environment, see Kenneth Foote and Maoz Azaryahu, "Toward a Geography of Memory: Geographical Dimensions of Public Memory and Commemoration," *Journal of Political and Military Sociology* 35, no. 1 (2007): 125–145.

3. Regarding street names, see Maoz Azaryahu, "Street Names and Political Identity: The Case of East Berlin," *Journal of Contemporary History* 21, no. 4 (1986): 581–604; Maoz Azaryahu, "The Power of Commemorative Street Names," *Environment and Planning D: Society and Space* 14, no. 3 (1996): 311–330; and Duncan Light, Ion Nicolae, and Bogdan Suditu, "Toponymy and the Communist City: Street names in Bucharest, 1948–1965," *Geojournal* 56,

no. 1 (2002): 135–144. Regarding architecture, see David Harvey, "Monument and Myth: The Building of the Basilica of the Sacred Heart," *Annals of the Association of American Geographers* 69, no. 3 (1979): 362–381; Barbara Lane, *Architecture and Politics in Germany*, 1918–1945 (Cambridge, MA: Harvard University Press, 1968); Taylor, *Word in Stone*; and Lawrence Vale, *Architecture, Power, and National Identity* (New Haven: Yale University Press, 1992).

On public spaces, see Linda Hershkovitz, "Tiananmen Square and the Politics of Place," *Political Geography* 12, no. 5 (1993): 395–420. Regarding historic preservation, see Rudy Koshar, *Germany's Transient Pasts: Preservation and National Memory in the Twentieth Century* (Chapel Hill: University of North Carolina Press, 1998); and Joshua Hagen, "Historic Preservation in Nazi Germany: Place, Memory, and Nationalism," *Journal of Historical Geography* 35, no. 4 (2009): 690–715. On city planning, see Stephan Helmer, *Hitler's Berlin: The Speer Plans for Reshaping the Central City* (Ann Arbor: University of Michigan Press, 1985); and Wolfgang Sonne, "Specific Intentions—General Realities: On the Relation between Urban Forms and Political Aspirations in Berlin during the Twentieth Century," *Planning Perspectives* 19, no. 3 (2004): 283–310.

4. Maoz Azaryahu, "The Purge of Bismarck and Saladin: The Renaming of Streets in East Berlin and Haifa, a Comparative Study in Culture-Planning," *Poetics Today* 13, no. 2 (1992): 351–367; Maoz Azaryahu, "German Reunification and the Politics of Street M Names: The Case of East Berlin," *Political Geography* 16, no. 6 (1997): 479–493; Maoz Azaryahu, "The Politics of Commemorative Street Renaming: Berlin 1945–1948," *Journal of Historical Geography* 37, no. 4 (2011): 483–492; Jeffrey Diefendorf, *In the Wake of War: The Reconstruction of German Cities after World War II* (Oxford: Oxford University Press, 1993); Jennifer Jordan, *Structures of Memory: Understanding Urban Change in Berlin and Beyond* (Stanford: Stanford University Press, 2006); Ladd, *Ghosts of Berlin*; Emily Pugh, *Architecture, Politics, and Identity in Divided Berlin* (Pittsburgh: University of Pittsburgh Press, 2014); and Karen Till, *The New Berlin: Memory, Politics, and Place* (Minneapolis: University of Minnesota Press, 2005). Till also has examined commemoration and architecture; see Karen Till, "Staging the Past: Landscape Designs, Cultural Identity, and Erinnerungspolitik at Berlin's Neue Wache," *Ecumene* 6, no. 3 (1999): 251–283; and Florian Urban, *Neo-Historical East Berlin: Architecture and Urban Design in the German Democratic Republic 1970–1990* (London: Ashgate, 2009).

5. On a building or a site, see Michael Cullen and Uwe Kieling, *Das Brandenburger Tor: Ein deustches Symbol* (Berlin: Berlin Edition, 1999); Regina Müller, *Das Berliner Zeughaus: Die Baugeschichte* (Berlin: Deutsches Historisches Museum, 1994); Renate Petras, *Das Schloss in Berlin: Von der Revolution 1918 bis zur Vernichtung 1950* (Berlin: Verlag für Bauwesen, 1999); and Christopher Stölzl, ed., *Die Neue Wache Unter den Linden: Ein Deutsches Denkmal in Wandel der Geschichte* (Munich: Koehler & Amelang, 1993). Regarding a street ensemble, see Laurenz Demps, *Berlin-Wilhelmstrasse: Eine Topographie preussisch-deutscher Macht* (Berlin: Ch. Links Verlag, 1996); and Herbert Nicolaus and Alexander Obeth, *Die Stalinallee: Geschichte einer deutschen Strasse* (Berlin: Verlag für Bauwesen, 1997).

On theoretical issues, see Werner Durth, "Von der Auflösung der Städte zur Architektur des Wiederaufbaus," in *Städtebau und Staatsbau im 20. Jahrhundert*, ed. Gabrielle Dolff-Bonekämper and Hiltrud Kier (Munich: Deutscher Kunstverlag, 1996); Jorn Düwel, *Baukunst voran!: Architektur und Städtebau in der SBZ/DDR* (Berlin: Schelzky & Jeep, 1995);

Bruno Flierl, *Gebaute DDR: Über Stadtplaner, Architekten, und die* Macht (Berlin: Verlag für Bauwesen, 1998); Simone Hain, *Archeologie und Aneignung: Ideen, Pläne, und Stadtfigurationen: Aufsätze zur Ostberliner Stadtentwicklung nach 1945* (Berlin: Leibniz-Institut für Regionalentwicklung und Strukturplanung, 1996); Thomas Topfstedt, "Die nachgeholte Moderne: Architektur und Städtebau in der DDR während der 50er und 60er Jahre," in *Städtebau und Staatsbau*, ed. Dolff-Bonekämper and Kier, 39–54; and Werner Durth, Jorn Düwel, and Nicholas Gutschow, *Ostkreuz: Personen, Pläne, Perspektiven*, vol. 1, *Städte, Themen, Dokumente*, vol. 2, Architektur und Städtebau der DDR (Frankfurt: Campus, 1998).

6. Koshar, *From Monuments to Traces*, 10.

7. See Dennis Cosgrove and Stephan Daniels, eds., *The Iconography of Landscape: Essays on the Symbolic Representation, Design, and Use of Past Environments* (Cambridge: Cambridge University Press, 1988); and *James Duncan, The City as Text: The Politics of Landscape Interpretation in the Kandyan Kingdom* (Cambridge: Cambridge University Press, 2004).

8. This broad, holistic view of space is derived from Edward Relph, "Geographical Experiences and Being-in-the-World: The Phenomenological Origins of Geography," in *Dwelling, Place, and Environment: Towards a Phenomenology of Person and World*, ed. David Seamon and Robert Mugerauer (New York: Columbia University Press, 1985), 15–31. Regarding human perception of space, see Christian Norberg-Schulz, *Intentions in Architecture* (Cambridge: Massachusetts Institute of Technology Press, 1968). For a detailed examination of formal and spatial relations, see Francis Ching, *Architecture: Form, Space, and Order* (Hoboken: John Wiley & Sons, 2014).

9. Relph, "Geographical Experiences," 26.

10. Alois Riegl set out the distinction between intentional and unintentional monuments, the latter being vernacular sites deemed worthy of preservation for their evocation of cultural memory due to historic value or age value. See Alois Riegl, "The Modern Cult of Monuments: Its Character and Its Origin" (1903), trans. Kurt W. Forster and Diane Ghirardo, *Oppositions* 25 (Fall 1982): 21–51. In fact, there is considerable ambiguity between the "vernacular" and the "monumental" and their relationship is quite complex; see Paul Stangl, "The Vernacular and the Monumental: Memory and Landscape in Post-War Berlin," *Geojournal* 73, no. 3 (2008): 245–253. Regarding Rothenburg, see Joshua Hagen, "The Most German of Towns: Creating an Ideal Nazi Community in Rothenburg ob der Tauber," *Annals of the Association of American Geographers* 94, no. 1 (2004): 207–227.

11. Foote, *Shadowed Ground*, 33.

12. John Starrels and Anita Mallinckrodt, *Politics in the German Democratic Republic* (New York: Praeger, 1975), 298–299.

13. Ibid, 40.

14. Mary Fulbrook, *The People's State: East German Society from Hitler to Honecker* (New Haven: Yale University Press, 2008), viii–xii.

15. Katherine Pence and Paul Betts, eds., *Socialist Modern: East German Everyday Culture and Politics* (Ann Arbor: University of Michigan Press, 2007); Mary Fulbrook, *Anatomy of a Dictatorship: Inside the GDR 1949–1989* (Oxford: Oxford University Press, 1995); Fulbrook, *The People's State*; and Mary Fulbrook, *Dissonant Lives: Generations and Violence through the German Dictatorships* (Oxford: Oxford University Press, 2011). A variety of factors impacted

those who were won over for socialism during the Aufbau period, including, "a major drive to win over the hearts and minds of youth to build a 'better future' precisely in the sense intended by the communist regime." Fulbrook, *Dissonant Lives*, 334.

16. Koshar, *Germany's Transient Pasts*, 29.

17. Ibid., 24–25.

18. Thomas Lekan, "The Nature of Home: Landscape Preservation and Local Identities," in *Localism, Landscape, and the Ambiguities of Place*, ed. David Blackbourn and James Retallack (Toronto: University of Toronto Press, 2007).

19. Diefendorf, *In the Wake of War*, 51.

20. Lekan, "Nature of Home"; and Diefendorf, *In the Wake of War*, 67–74.

21. For an overview of the history of science, including the issue of whether there exists one or several sciences, see Thomas Kuhn, *The Essential Tension: Selected Studies in Scientific Tradition and Change* (Chicago: University of Chicago Press, 1977).

22. Richard Olsen, *Science and Scientism in Nineteenth-Century Europe* (Urbana: University of Illinois Press, 2008).

23. Regarding variations in modernity, see Peter Taylor, *Modernities: A Geohistorical Interpretation* (Minneapolis: University of Minnesota Press, 1999).

24. Kitty Newman, *Macmillan, Khrushchev, and the Berlin Crisis, 1958–1960* (London: Routledge, 2007), 69.

25. Friedrich Engels quoted as epigraph in Ernst Engelberg, *Bismarck: Das Reich in der Mitte Europas* (Berlin: Siedler, 1993).

26. George Steinmetz, "German Exceptionalism and the Origins of Nazism: The Career of a Concept," in *Stalinism and Nazism: Dictatorships in Comparison*, ed. Ian Kershaw and Moshe Lewin (Cambridge: Cambridge University Press, 1997), 251–284. Given the Marxist origins of the idea of a "normal" bourgeois revolution, it is unsurprising that many of those who has espoused these views over the past half-century were Communists.

27. Alexander Abusch, *Der Irrweg einer Nation: Ein Beitrag zum Verständnis deutscher Geschichte* (Berlin: Aufbau Verlag, 1947).

28. Similar narratives would be developed and debated in considerable detail from the 1960s through the 1980s by Western historians as the Sonderweg thesis. In recent decades some of the key concepts applied in the theory have been discredited, but the theory has been adapted and continues to attract interest. Many Germans, representatives of neighboring countries, and historians continue to examine Prussian state history for links to Nazism. See Gavriel Rosenfeld, "A Mastered Past? Prussia in Postwar German Memory," *German History* 22, no. 4 (2004): 505–535; and William Hagen, "Descent of the Sonderweg: Hans Rosenberg's History of Old Regime Prussia," *Central European History* 24, no. 1 (2001): 24–50.

29. Alan Bullock, *The Humanist Tradition in the West* (New York: W.W. Norton, 1985).

30. Lloyd Easton and Kurt Guddat, introduction in *Writings of the Young Marx on Philosophy and Society* (Indianapolis: Hackett, 1967), 1–34.

31. Harald Bühl, Dieter Heinze, Hans Koch, and Fred Staufenbiel, *Kulturpolitisches Wörterbuch* (Berlin: Dietz Verlag, 1970), 212–221; and Gertrud Schütz, Waltraud Böhme, Marlene Dehlsen, Hartmut Eisel, Andrée Fischer, Gerhard König, Margot Lange, Renate Polit, and Hans Reinhold, *Kleines Politisches Wörterbuch*, 3rd edition (Berlin: Dietz Verlag, 1978), 355–356.

32. Manfred Jäger, *Kultur und Politik in der DDR, 1945–1990* (Cologne: Edition Deutschland Archiv, 1995), 1–12. Furthermore, a number of the German Communist cultural elite were enthusiasts of this tradition, even if it had stemmed from the bourgeois.

33. Andreas Hillgruber, *Deutsche Geschichte 1945–1986: Die "deutsche Frage" in der Weltpolitik*, 8th ed. (Stuttgart: W. Kohlhammer Verlag, 1983).

34. Wilhelm Pieck, "Reden und Aufsätze: Auswahl aus den Jahren 1908–1950," in *Berlin 1952*, vol. 1 of Gerhard Kiederling, ed., *Berlin 1945–1986: Geschichte der Hauptstadt der DDR* (Berlin: Dietz, 1987), 48.

35. Christoph Klessmann, *Die doppelte Staatsgründung: Deutsche Geschichte, 1945–1955* (Bonn: Bundeszentrale für politische Bildung, 1991), 139; and Eric Weitz, *Creating German Communism, 1890–1990: From Popular Protests to Socialist State* (Princeton: Princeton University Press, 1997), 343.

36. Karl Marx and Friedrich Engels, *The Communist Manifesto* (Chicago: Charles H. Kerr & Company, 1906).

37. Jan Kandiyali, "Freedom and Necessity in Marx's Account of Communism," *British Journal for the History of Philosophy* 22, no. 1 (2014): 104–123.

38. Friedrich Geist and Klaus Kürvers, *Das Berliner Mietshaus 1862–1945* (Munich: Prestl, 1984), vol. 2, 437–463.

39. Wilhelm Riehl, "Die Familie," vol. 3 of *Naturgeschichte des Volkes als Grundlage einer deutschen Social-Politik* (Stuttgart and Augsburg), 1855, cited in Nicholas Bullock and James Read, *The Movement for Housing Reform in Germany and France, 1840–1914* (Cambridge: Cambridge University Press, 1985), 76.

40. Marx and Engels, *Communist Manifesto*, 56.

41. Friedrich Engels, *Zur Wohnungsfrage*, trans. Clemens Dutt as *The Housing Question*, London, n.d.), 46, quoted in Bullock and Read, *Movement for Housing Reform*, 50. Beginning in the late 1860s, many bourgeois reformers and economists independently came to view the property issue as central to the housing crisis, as financing through public mortgage banks enabled large-scale speculation that amounted to monopoly control over land supply. Bullock and Read, *Movement for Housing Reform*, Chapter 7.

42. August Bebel, *Die Frau und der Sozialismus* (Zurich: Verlag der Volksbuchhandlung, 1879).

43. Geist and Kürvers, *Berliner Mietshaus*, vol. 2, 102–121.

44. Bullock and Read, *Movement for Housing Reform*, Chapter 12.

45. Schütz et al., *Kleines Politisches Wörterbuch*, 551. The distinction between socialist and communist political parties emerged during World War I with the latter favoring the violent seizure of power. Regarding the distinction between socialism and communism as types of human society, more variability appears. The Marxist-Leninist view is used throughout most of this book, as it is essential to clearly delineate the perspective of the East German state and relate it to broader discourses. Stalinism, as a doctrine, was never acknowledged during this period of study; however, the Western definition of a "cult of Stalin" is unavoidable, as is the use of "de-Stalinization," which followed his death.

46. Jäger, *Kultur und Politik*, 6–28.

47. Alexandra Richie, *Faust's Metropolis: A History of Berlin* (New York: Carrol & Graf Publishers, 1998), 646.

48. Starrels and Malinckrodt, *Politics in the German Democratic Republic*, 40.

49. Maoz Azaryahu, *Von Wilhelmplatz zu Thälmanplatz: Politische Symbole im öffentlichen Leben der DDR*, trans. Kersten Amrani and Alma Mandelbaum (Gerlingen: Bleicher, 1991), 135, original edition (Tel Aviv: University of Tel Aviv, 1988); and Jan Behrends, Dennis Kuck, and Patrice Poutrus, "Thesenpapier: Historische Ursachen der Fremdenfeindlichkeit in den Neuen Bundesländern," in *Fremde und Fremd-Sein in der DDR: Zu historischen Ursachen der Fremdfeindlichkeit in Ostdeutschland, Berlin*, ed. Jan Behrends and Thomas Lindenberger (Berlin: Metropol, 2003).

50. Politbüro des Zentralkomitees der Sozialistische Einheitspartei Deutschlands (hereafter, Politburo), resolution from July 11, 1050, Stiftung Archiv der Parteien und Massenorganizationen der DDR im Bundesarchiv (hereafter SAPMO-BA), DY30-50.

51. Katerina Clark, *Moscow, the Fourth Rome: Stalinism, Cosmopolitanism, and the Evolution of Soviet Culture, 1931–1941* (Cambridge, MA: Harvard University Press), 131–132.

52. Magdalena Droste, *Bauhaus 1919–1933* (Cologne: Taschen, 2002).

53. Charles Édouard Jeanneret-Gris, *The Athens Charter*, trans. Anthony Eardley (reprint, New York: Grossman Publishers, 1973; Paris: La Librarie Pion, 1943).

54. Norman Fainstein and Susan Fainstein, "City Planning and Political Values," *Urban Affairs Quarterly* 6 (1971): 341–362.

55. Jörg Haspel and Annemarie Jaeggi, *Housing Estates in the Berlin Modern Style* (Munich: Deutscher Kunstverlag, 2007), 16.

56. Herbert Nicolaus and Alexander Obeth, *Die Stalinallee: Geschichte einer deutschen Strasse* (Berlin: Verlag für Bauwesen, 1997), 25.

57. Haspel and Jaeggi, *Berlin Modern Style*; and Wolfgang Schäche, *75 Jahre GEHAG 1924–1999* (Berlin: Gebr. Mann Verlag, 1999), 20–30.

58. Barbara Miller-Lane, *Architecture and Politics in Germany, 1918–1945* (Cambridge: Harvard University Press, 1968); and Schäche, *75 Jahre GEHAG*, 99–104.

59. Diefendorf, *In the Wake of War*, 118.

60. Ibid., 113–125.

61. Anders Åman points out that the materials, technology, and labor skills for modern architecture were in short supply in the Soviet Union. Also, architecture was viewed as a political contribution to building socialism, and classicism was more popular with the general public and more capable of expressing political sentiment. See Anders Åman, *Architecture and Ideology in Eastern Europe during the Stalin Era: An Aspect of Cold War History* (Cambridge: Massachusetts Institute of Technology Press), 50–55.

62. Karl Schlögl, *Terror und Traum: Moskau 1937*, 3rd edition (Frankfurt am Main: Fischer, 2016): 60–85.

63. Jörn Düwel, *Baukunst voran!: Architektur und Stadtplanung im ersten Nachkriegsjahrzehnt in der SBZ/DDR* (Berlin: Schelzky & Jeep, 1995), 24–25.

64. Simone Hain, *Reise nach Moskau* (Berlin: Institut für Regionalentwicklung und Strukturplannung, 1995).

65. Paul Stangl, "Restoring Berlin's Unter den Linden: Ideology, World View, Place, and Space," *Journal of Historical Geography* 31, no. 2 (2006): 352–376.

66. Gianfranco Caniggia and Gian Maffei, *Interpreting Basic Building: Architectural*

Composition and Building Typology, trans. Susan Jane Fraser, rev. Karl Kropf and Brenda Sheer (Florence: Alinea, 2001).

67. Evidence of German Communist iconoclasm is presented throughout this book. For an overview of the term *iconoclasm*, its history, nuances, and diverse means by which it can be carried out, see Dario Gamboni, *The Destruction of Art: Iconoclasm and Vandalism since the French Revolution* (London: Reaktion, 1997).

68. Paul Zucker, "An Aesthetic Hybrid," *Journal of Aesthetics and Art Criticism* 20, no. 2 (1961): 119–130.

69. Albert Speer, *Inside the Third Reich: Memoirs by Albert Speer*, trans. Richard and Clara Winston (New York: Collier, 1970).

70. Angela Arnold, *Bruch Stücke: Trümmerbahn und Trümmerfrauen* (Berlin: Omnis, 1999), 18; Diefendorf, *In the Wake of War*, 3–17; Geist and Kürvers, *Berliner Mietshaus*, vol. 3, 46–180; and Richie, *Faust's Metropolis*, 587–603.

71. Matthias Menzel, "Die ehemalige Innenstadt," May 26, 1945, diary entry quoted in Geist and Kürvers, *Berliner Mietshaus*, vol. 3, 173; Joachim Näther, "Berlin 66: Die Wandlung einer Stadt, 1966," SAPMO-BA, DH2 (K4) II/07-2/20; and Joseph Orlopp, *Zusammenbruch und Aufbau Berlins: 1945/46* (Berlin: Dietz Verlag, 1947).

72. Orlopp, *Zusammenbruch und Aufbau Berlins*, 12.

73. Jörg Friedrich, *Brandstätten: Der Anblick des Bombenkrieges* (Berlin: Propyläen, 2003), 189.

74. "Aus Trümmern wird Beton," *Tägliche Rundschau* (hereafter *TR*), May 4, 1946; and Diefendorf, *In the Wake of War*, 30–36.

75. Berlin Magistrat, Resolution, May 25, 1945, Landesarchiv Berlin (hereafter LAB) 100, 758.

76. "Brillen Unerwünscht," *Berliner Zeitung* (hereafter *BZ*), December 5, 1945.

77. Berlin Magistrat, Resolution, May 25, 1945, LAB 100, 758.

78. Arnold, *Bruch Stücke*, 48.

79. Over time, more machinery became available, and the nature of the effort was transformed.

80. "Schutt wird Strassenpflaster," *TR*, February 19, 1946.

81. "Berliner die beim Aufbau sind," *Der Kurrier*, September 28, 1946.

82. Since the beginning of the rubble-removal process, the Magistrat saw itself compelled to dispose of as much rubble as possible inside the city and as near as possible to the site of damage. See Reinhold Linger, "Die Unterbringung unverwertbaren Trummerschuttes in Berlin als Problem der Stadtplanung," *Planen und Bauen* 4, no. 5 (1950): 158–162.

83. "Auch Schutt kann nützlich sein," *TR*, April 13, 1946; and "Hau-ruck: Die Westhafen Melodie," *Telegraf*, August 9, 1946.

84. "Wohin mit der Schutt," *Nacht Express*, September 10, 1947.

85. "Schuttbeseitgung Schafft Gemüseland," *Nacht Express*, September 26, 1946.

86. "Schutt wird Strassenpflaster," *TR*, February 19, 1946.

87. "Tempelhof verbessert Anlagen," *Neue Zeit*, March 12, 1947.

88. Arnold, *Bruch Stücke*, 22.

89. Otto Grotewohl, Minutes from meeting on May 17, 1946, quoted in Simone Hain,

Archeologie und Aneignung: Ideen, Pläne, und Stadtfigurationen: Aufsätze zur Ostberliner Stadtentwicklung nach 1945 (Berlin: Institut für Regionalentwicklung und Strukturplannung, 1996), 62.

90. For a poem that is emblematic example of this tone, see "Komm und hilf mit!," *Deutsche Volkszeitung*, November 29, 1945. Also see "Nazismus schlug den Kontinent in Trümmer: Friede und Demokratie sind Grundlagen seiner Wiedergeburt," *BZ*, May 28, 1945.

91. As quoted in "Der Oberbürgermeister spricht," *BZ*, May 21, 1945.

92. "Neues Leben Blüht aus den Ruinen," *BZ*, May 21, 1945.

93. See "Premiere der Trümmerbeseitigung," *Nacht Express*, June 30, 1946; "Humboldhain wird zum Humboldtberg," *Neues Deutschland* (hereafter *ND*), May 5, 1946; and caption to photo of caved-in subway tunnel, *TR*, May 9, 1946.

94. Jeffrey Herf, *Divided Memory: The Nazi Past in the Two Germanys* (Cambridge: Harvard University Press, 1997). For a rare example of the popular press linking the actions of the German people to the destruction of their cities, see the reprint of a speech by Mayor Werner: "Der Wiederaufbau Berlins," *TR*, May 3, 1946. This section has not discussed Nazi flak towers, as they belong to the military tradition rather than the vernacular. Too immense to remove, they were demolished, covered with rubble, and landscaped. The well-known tower in Volkspark Friedrichshain was left partially protruding as the amount of rubble available nearby was overestimated. One planner, in a rare connection to the Romantic tradition, suggested this might remind Berliners of "past evil times." See Berlin Magistrat, Hauptamt für Hochbau, file note, February 3, 1947, LAB-110-1174; and Linger, "Die Unterbringung," 158–162.

95. The 1946 exhibition *Berlin baut auf*, reporting on rubble removal and construction progress, was limited to the eight Soviet-controlled districts with no mention of the Western sectors. See "Berlin Plant," *BZ*, August 14, 1946.

96. "Ein Kleiner Unterschied," *Vörwarts*, February 11, 1947. Also see "Zehn-Minute-Verkehr auf der Trümmerbahn," *TR*, November 28, 1947.

97. "Deutsche Demokratische Republik Gegründet," *BZ*, October 8, 1949.

98. Harry Schurdel, "Die Hoheitssymbole der Deutshen Demokratischen Republik," in *Parteiauftrag: Ein neues Deutschland: Bilder, Rituale, und Symbole der frühen DDR*, ed. Dieter Vorsteher, catalog for the exhibition in the German Historical Museum from December 13, 1996, to March 11, 1997, p. 57.

99. "Als Berlin aus Trümmern aufstand," *BZ*, May 7, 1950.

100. Walter Ulbricht. *Das nationale Aufbauwerk und die Aufgaben der deutschen Architektur*. Speech delivered at the inaugural ceremony for the opening of the Deutsche Bauakademie on 12 August 1951. (Berlin: Amt für Information der Regierung der Deutschen Demokratischen Republik, 1951).

101. The tension-raising events included the SED's poor electoral showing in October 1946, the failure of the Moscow Conference (March 10–April 24, 1947) and simultaneous development of the Truman Doctrine, and especially the Marshall Plan (announced on June 5, 1947).

1. Landscapes of Commemoration

Epigraph: "Die deutsche Regierung dankt Stalin," *BZ*, May 7, 1950, p. 1.

1. Regarding the French perspective on Prussia, see Henning Köhler, *Das Ende Preussens in französischer Sicht* (New York: De Gruyter, 1982).

2. Engels, as quoted in an epigraph in Ernst Engelberg, *Bismarck: Das Reich in der Mitte Europas* (Berlin: Siedler, 1993).

3. Alexander Abusch, *Der Irrweg einer Nation: Ein Beitrag zum Verständnis deutscher Geschichte* (Berlin: Aufbau Verlag, 1947).

4. Regarding the shift to "national history writing" in the GDR, see Azaryahu, *Von Wilhelmplatz zu Thälmanplatz*, 135.

5. Azaryahu, "Power of Commemorative Street Names," 311–330.

6. Azaryahu, *Von Wilhelmplatz zu Thälmanplatz*, 69–71; and Azaryahu, "Power of Commemorative Street Names."

7. Azaryahu, "Power of Commemorative Street Names," 486–487.

8. Azaryahu, *Von Wilhelmplatz zu Thälmanplatz*, 73; and Azaryahu, "Power of Commemorative Street Names," 487–488.

9. Azaryahu, *Von Wilhelmplatz zu Thälmanplatz*, 71–76, 133–134.

10. Ibid., 135–136. Regarding the role of nations in world historical progress, see Schütz et al., *Kleines Politisches Wörterbuch*, 597–603.

11. Albrecht Lampe, *Berlin: Kampf um Freiheit und Selbstverwaltung, 1945–1946* (Berlin: Heinz Spitzing Verlag, 1961), 366.

12. Allied Control Council (ACC), "Directive No. 30, Liquidation of German military and Nazi memorials and museums," May 13, 1946, in *Amtsblatt des Kontrollrats in Deutschland 1945–46*, 154.

13. Berlin Magistrat, *Liste von Denkmälern die abzutragen oder zu vernichten sind*, May 18, 1946, Landesarchiv Berlin (hereafter LAB), 100/773.

14. Ibid.

15. Ladd, *Ghosts of Berlin*, 242; and Berlin Magistrat, *Liste von Denkmälern.* During the Weimar era, reactionary political parties invoked Bismarck as their forebear, and Hitler made some use of his myth in speeches, although in changing ways and only to serve his vision of the future. At a minimum, Communist memory of these associations would have helped consolidate their aversion to Bismarck. Contemporary historiography on Bismarck, like that on Prussia, takes a nuanced look at his work, including efforts to maintain a peaceful integration of Germany into the European balance of power. See Engelberg, *Bismarck*; Christoph Nübel, "Der Bismarck-Mythos in den Reden und Schriften Hitlers," *Historische Zeitschrift* 298 (2014): 349–380; and Otto Pflanze, *Bismarck and the Development of Germany*, vols. 1–3 (Princeton: Princeton University Press, 1990).

16. Berlin Magistrat, *Liste von Denkmälern.*

17. Kiederling, *Berlin 1945–1986*, 133–36 and 204–207.

18. Berlin Magistrat, Draft resolution for meeting on June 23, 1946, and June 6, 1947, LAB, 100/793; and Berlin Magistrat, Resolution from meeting on July 7, 1947, LAB, 100/793.

19. Berlin Magistrat, "Verzeichnis der Denkmaler, Embleme, usw., deren sofortige Beseitigung vorgeschlagen wird," Attachment to Magistrat resolution from November 20, 1947, LAB, 100/801.

20. Azaryahu, *Von Wilhelmplatz zu Thälmanplatz*, 135.

21. Ibid., 137–138.

22. Schütz et al., *Kleines Politisches Wörterbuch*, 585.

23. Quote from Michael Ignatieff, "Soviet War Memorials," *History Workshop* 17 (1984): 159; and Kiederling, *Berlin 1945–1986*, 42. Regarding Soviet War Memorials more generally, see Nina Tumarkin, *The Living and the Dead: The Rise and Fall of the Cult of World War II in Russia* (New York: Basic Books, 1994), 101; and Reuben Fowkes, "Soviet War Memorials in Eastern Europe, 1945–1974," in *Figuration/Abstraction: Strategies for Public Sculpture in Europe 1945–1968*, ed. Charlotte Benton (Farnham, UK: Ashgate, 2004), 11–32.

24. Kiederling, *Berlin 1945–1986*, 42.

25. Dimitri Chmelnizki, "Der Kalte Krieg der Monumente," trans. and ed. K. Gimsa, *Der Tagesspiegel*, June 17, 1998, 25, reprinted from *Europa Zenter* (October 1998); and Horst Köpstein and Helga Köpstein, *Das Treptower Ehrenmal: Geschichte und Gegenwart des Ehrenmals für die gefallenen sowjetischen Helden in Berlin* (Berlin: Staatsverlag der Deutschen Demokratischen Republik, 1987), 18–20.

26. Jewgeni Wutschetitsch, "Pamjatnik gerojam-woinam," in *Chudoshinik i shisn* (Moscow, 1963), 187–202, quoted in Köpstein and Köpstein, *Das Treptower Ehrenmal*, 188.

27. Matthew Gallagher, *The Soviet History of World War II: Myths, Memories, and Realities* (New York: Praeger, 1963), 38–51; and Joseph Stalin, *The Great Patriotic War of the Soviet Union* (New York: International Publishers, 1945).

28. Gallagher, *Soviet History*, 15–21; and Benjamin May, "Themes of Soviet War Propaganda 1841–1945," PhD dissertation (New Haven: Yale University, 1957), 107–165.

29. Harald Bühl et al., *Kulturpolitisches Wörterbuch* (Berlin: Dietz Verlag, 1970); May, "Themes of Soviet War Propaganda," 165–225; and Schütz et al., *Kleines Politisches Wörterbuch*, 288.

30. Regarding Soviet consideration for political aims in dealing with invented tradition, see Ignatieff, "Soviet War Memorials." To help mobilize the population during the war, the Soviets had downplayed the "leading role of the Party," and the cult of Stalin was decidedly less prominent. See Paul Stangl, "The Soviet War Memorial in Treptow, Berlin," *Geographical Review* 93, no. 2 (2003): 213–236.

31. Manfred Jäger, *Kultur und Politik in der DDR: 1945–1990* (Cologne: Verlag Wissenschaft und Politik, 1995), 19–20; and Richie, *Faust's Metropolis*, 620–621.

32. Stangl, "Soviet War Memorial in Treptow, Berlin." On May 15, 1945, the SMAD-published *Tägliche Rundschau* (hereafter *TR*) declared in a front-page article that the Soviet Army was not a destroyer but a liberator.

33. See Stangl, "Soviet War Memorial in Treptow, Berlin": "Invading German troops were sometimes welcomed as liberators in the Baltic states and Ukraine, revealing ethnic conflict behind the facade of Soviet identity. Many Soviet citizens were equally terrified of the German invaders and Soviet partisans, as both decimated villages and executed residents for mere suspected collaboration with the enemy. Soviet soldiers suffered abuse from both the Soviet military command and Soviet state; beyond sheer disregard for attrition, returning Soviet prisoners were often branded as traitors and faced the gulag or execution out of suspicion that they had been contaminated by Western ideas. Finally, the Great Purge indifferently consumed soldiers at all levels, Party members and ordinary citizens,

revealing an insidious social atomization and cannibalization driven by an all-corrupting system—and providing an ironic degree of truth to the image of transcended class divisions" (ibid., 222).

34. Clark, *Moscow*, 89–90.

35. Wutschetitsch, "Pamjatnik gerojam-woinam," 61.

36. Red Army relations with Eastern Europe also had a dark side, including the betrayal of the Polish Home Army in Warsaw allowing its decimation by the Wehrmacht, the rape of women, and purges of potential political opponents in newly occupied lands. See Stangl, "Soviet War Memorial in Treptow, Berlin," 223.

37. Regarding German complicity and dissent, see Christopher Browning, *Ordinary Men: Reserve Police Battalion 101 and the Final Solution in Poland* (New York: Harper Collins, 1992); David Crew, ed., *Nazism and German Society, 1933–1945* (London: Routledge, 1994); Daniel Goldhagen, *Hitler's Willing Executioners: Ordinary Germans and the Holocaust* (New York: Knopf, 1996); and Detlev Peukert, *Inside Nazi Germany: Conformity, Opposition, and Racism in Everyday Life*, trans. R. Deveson (New Haven: Yale University Press, 1987).

38. The Soviet military leadership's encouraging soldiers to punish all German people and continued disdain for the German people after the war evidenced a belief that the German people were conquered supporters of Nazism. Richie, *Faust's Metropolis*, 564–657.

39. Herf, *Divided Memory*, 33–35; and Lampe, *Berlin: Kampf um Freiheit und Selbstverwaltung*, 69

40. "Den für das Glück der Menschheit Gefällenen," *TR*, May 9, 1946.

41. "Das deutsche Volk auf dem Wege zur Demokratie," *TR*, November 13, 1945; "Parade am Jahrestag des Sieges," *TR*, May 11, 1946; "Ruhm und Ehre den für die Menschheit Gefallenen, *TR*, May 10, 1947; and "Der Anfang ist gemacht," *Neues Deutschland* (hereafter *ND*), May 9, 1946.

42. "Den Beschützern der Völkerfreiheit," *ND*, May 10, 1949.

43. Ibid.

44. Ibid.

45. "Volkspolizei ubernahm Ehrenwache in Treptow," *Berliner Zeitung* (hereafter *BZ*), May 10, 1950.

46. John Borneman, *Belonging in the Two Berlins: Kin, State, and Nation* (Cambridge: Cambridge University Press, 1992), 16.

47. "Tag der Befreiung in Berlin," *BZ*, May 10, 1951; "Berliner feierten den Tag der Befreiung," *BZ*, May 10, 1952; and "DDR beging den Tag der Befreiung," *BZ*, May 11, 1954.

48. Tumarkin, *Living and the Dead*, 106–113; and Ladd, *Ghosts of Berlin*, 186–187.

49. Koppel Pinson, *Modern Germany: It's History and Civilization* (New York, 1966; reprint, Prospect Heights, IL: Waveland Press, 1989), 80.

50. Roland Bauer and Eric Hühns, *Berlin: 800 Jahre Geschichte in Wort und Bild* (Berlin: VEB Deutscher Verlag der Wissenschaften, 1980), 138; and Winfried Löschburg, *Unter den Linden: Gesichter und Geschichten einer berühmten Strasse* (Berlin: Der Morgen, 1972), 131–132.

51. Bauer and Hühns, *Berlin*, 140.

52. Annamarie Lange, *Berlin, Hauptstadt der DDR* (Leipzig: Brockhaus, 1966), 144.

53. In contrast, contemporary German historiography suggests that the one common denominator among supporters was national unity. This was accompanied by diverse social and political reforms. Democratic reforms were of prominent interest, but the bourgeois demonstrated various degrees of support for democracy, most preferring limited franchise qualified by property or education, or both. In a Marxist-Leninist interpretation, however, "bourgeois democracy" is viewed as a form of democracy serving bourgeois class interests. See David Blackbourn and Geoff Eley, *The Peculiarities of German History: Bourgeois Society and Politics in Nineteenth Century Germany* (Oxford: Oxford University Press): 18–19; German Bundestag, Publications' Section, *Questions on German History: Ideas, Forces, Decisions from 1800 to Present*, catalog to exhibition of the same name, 4th English edition (Bonn: German Bundestag, 1993), 104. Also see Pinson, *Modern Germany*, 80–108; and Schütz et al., *Kleines Politisches Wörterbuch*, 776–778.

54. Pinson, *Modern Germany*, 194–218.

55. Heinz Voske, *Geschichte der Gedenkstätte der Sozialisten in Berlin Friedrichsfelde* (Berlin: Dietz Verlag, 1982), 22.

56. Ibid., 30.

57. "Wie das Ehrenmal entstand," *BZ*, January 15, 1967.

58. Voske, *Geschichte der Gedenkstätte der Sozialisten in Berlin*, 36–37.

59. Ibid., 14; and Richie, *Faust's Metropolis*, 124.

60. Wilhelm Pieck to Emil Brandt, December 1, 1927, Stiftung Archiv der Parteien und Massenorganizationen der DDR im Bundesarchiv (hereafter SAPMO-BA), FBS, 93/1111, Nachlass Wilhelm Pieck 36/611-612, Berlin.

61. Wilhelm Pieck, "Den toten Helden der Revolution," in *Wilhelm Pieck: Gesamelte Reden und Schriften*, vol. 3 (Berlin: Dietz, 1961), 359, quoted in Voske, *Geschichte der Gedenkstätte der Sozialisten*, 148–152.

62. Wilhelm Pieck, File notes, author unknown, undated, SAPMO-BA, FBS, 93/1111, Nachlass Wilhelm Pieck 36/611-612, Berlin.

63. Wilhelm Pieck, File notes, February 3, 1950, SAPMO-BA, FBS, 93/1111, 36/611-612, Berlin; and Voske, *Geschichte der Gedenkstätte der Sozialisten*, 50.

64. Voske, *Geschichte der Gedenkstätte der Sozialisten*, 50.

65. E. F. Werner-Rades, ed., *Reichshauptstadt Berlin* (Berlin: Haude & Spenersche Verlagsbuchhandlung, 1943), 198.

66. Christopher Klessmann, *Die doppelte Staatsgründung: Deutsche Geschichte 1945–1955*, 5th edition (Bonn: Bundeszentrale für Politische Bildung, 1991), 139.

67. Ibid., 135–142.

68. Berlin Magistrat, Resolution from meeting on May 28, 1945, LAB 100/759.

69. There were no significant documents relating to the project in any of the other leading Communists' files, including those of Walter Ulbricht and Otto Grotewohl.

70. This was evident in Pieck's personal visits to the cemetery and his concerted effort to collect the remains of the fallen when possible.

71. Wilhelm Pieck to Karl Maron, December 6, 1945, SAPMO-BA, FBS, 93/1111, 36/611-612.

72. Berlin Magistrat, Resolution from December 17, 1948, LAB, 100/765.

73. "Vom Edenhotel bis zum KZ: Zum Todestag Karl Liebknecht und Rosa Luxembourg," *Der Tagesspiegel*, January 15, 1946.

74. See Gustave LeBon, *The Crowd: A Study of the Popular Mind*, 2nd edition (London: T. Fischer Unwin, 1941), 96. For a similar observation regarding the use of the word in contemporary America, see Gore Vidal, *Inventing a Nation: Washington, Adams, Jefferson* (New Haven: Yale University Press, 2003), 135.

75. "Im Zeichen der Einheit der Arbeiterklasse," *BZ*, January 15, 1946.

76. Similarly, the handshake—a symbol in long-standing use by the SPD but never accepted by the KPD—was co-opted for the new SED party emblem. Gottfried Korff, "From Brotherly Handshake to Militant Clenched Fist: On Political Metaphors for the Worker's Hand," *International Labor and Working Class History* 42 (1992): 70–81.

77. Officially unaffiliated, Werner largely operated as a Communist puppet.

78. Wilhelm Pieck to Arthur Werner, November 21, 1946, SAPMO-BA, FBS, 93/1111, Nachlass Wilhelm Pieck 36/611-612, Berlin.

79. Ibid.

80. Unsigned file note, November 22, 1946, SAPMO-BA, FBS, 93/1111, Nachlass Wilhelm Pieck 36/611-612, Berlin.

81. "Massenaufmarsch der Berliner Arbeiter," *ND*, January 21, 1947.

82. Berlin Magistrat, Resolution from March 17, 1947, LAB, 100/789.

83. "An den Gräbern der Märzkämpfer," *ND*, March 19, 1947

84. Wilhelm Pieck to Herman Matern, July 7, 1947, SAPMO-BA, FBS 93/1111, Nachlass Wilhelm Pieck 36/611-612, Berlin.

85. Project No. 2, unsigned document, December 1, 1947, SAPMO-BA, FBS, 93/1111, Nachlass Wilhelm Pieck 36/611-612, Berlin.

86. Wilhelm Pieck to Karl Maron, December 2, 1947, SAPMO-BA, FBS, 93/1111, Nachlass Wilhelm Pieck 36/611-612, Berlin.

87. *Bericht über die Sitzung des Presigerichts: Wettbewerb Gedächtnisstätte der grossen Sozialisten auf dem Friedhof Friedrichsfelde*, February 15, 1948, SAPMO-BA, FBS, 93/1111, Nachlass Wilhelm Pieck 36/611-612, Berlin.

88. Ibid.

89. "Auf dem Hügel der Freiheit," *Der Sozialdemokrat*, January 10, 1948.

90. "Der 18. März in Berlin: Ein überwaltigenes Bekenntnis zur Freiheit," *Der Tagesspiegel*, March 20, 1948.

91. Max Grabowski to Politburo of the Central Committee of the Socialist Unity Party (hereafter, Politburo), February 2, 1949, SAPMO-BA, FBS, 93/1111, Nachlass Wilhelm Pieck 36/611-612, Berlin.

92. Wilhelm Pieck to Friedrich Ebert, February 23, 1949, SAPMO-BA, FBS, 93/1111, Nachlass Wilhelm Pieck 36/611-612, Berlin.

93. Voske, *Geschichte der Gedenkstätte der Sozialisten*, 72–73.

94. Friedrich Ebert to W. Pieck, March 2, 1949, SAPMO-BA, FBS, 93/1111, Nachlass Wilhelm Pieck 36/611-612, Berlin.

95. Voske, *Geschichte der Gedenkstätte der Sozialisten*, 74.

96. Schwieger to W. Bartel, March 31, 1950, SAPMO-BA, FBS, 93/1111, Nachlass Wilhelm Pieck 36/611-612, Berlin.

97. Wilhelm Pieck to Ebert, September 22, 1950, SAPMO-BA, FBS, 93/1111, Nachlass Wilhelm Pieck 36/611-612, Berlin.

98. Wilhelm Pieck to Karl Glasner, November 15, 1950, SAPMO-BA, FBS, 93/1111, Nachlass Wilhelm Pieck 36/611-612, Berlin.

99. Ulf Ickerodt, "Megaliths, Landscape Perception, and the Bending of Scientific Interpretation," in *Landscapes and Human Developments: The Contribution of European Archaeology*, ed. Kiel Graduate School "Human Development in Landscapes" (Bonn: Dr. Rudolf Habelt, 2010), 77–89.

100. These observations were derived from annual articles on the ceremony over decades. Regarding the dedication ceremony, see: "Weihe eines würdiges Ehrenmals," BZ, January 16, 1951.

101. "Die Opfer des 18. März verpflichten," *ND*, March 19, 1949, p. 4; and "Kranzniederlegung im Friedrichshain," *ND*, March 19, 1950.

2. City Plans

Epigraph: "Berliner werden ein neues Berlin bauen: Oberbürgermeister Ebert stellt den Berliner Aufbauplan zur Diskussion," *Berliner Zeitung* (hereafter *BZ*), July 15, 1949.

1. Clark, *Moscow*.

2. Harold Bodenschatz, *Berlin: Auf der Suche nach dem verlorenen Zentrum* (Hamburg: Junius, 1995), 125–130.

3. Geist and Kürvers, *Berliner Mietshaus*, vol. 1, 464–505. The government negotiated with landowners as development occurred, in cases of conflict, either refusing permitting or giving in to alter street layouts. The Prussian Fluchtliniengesetz of 1875 empowered the police to determine road location, and to construct roads and utilities while passing costs to property owners, and set minimum building standards.

4. Brian Ladd, *Urban Planning and Civic Order in Germany, 1860–1914* (Cambridge, MA: Harvard University Press, 1990).

5. Sonne, "Specific Intentions"; and Harald Bodenschatz, Dieter Frick, Harald Kegler, Hans-Dieter Nägelke, and Wolfgang Sonne, "100 Jahre Allgemeine Städtebau-Ausstellung in Berlin," *Bauwelt* 36 (2010), www.bauwelt.de/cms/bauwerk.html?id=1208143#.U77vk7E2O1l, accessed July 10, 2014.

6. Charles Édouard Jeanneret-Gris, *The Athens Charter*, trans. Anthony Eardley (reprint, New York: Grossman Publishers, 1973; Paris: La Librarie Pion, 1943).

7. Ibid.

8. Diefendorf, *In the Wake of War*, 151–180.

9. This sums up a range of goals held by planners, of which Ladd notes were often a composite including "moral improvement, a cohesive community, order and security (including a contented working class), and an efficiently functioning urban economy. These goals were not entirely separable from one another, but neither were they entirely compatible." Ladd, *Urban Planning and Civic Order in Germany*, 246.

10. Sonne, "Specific Intentions."

11. Diefendorf, *In the Wake of War*, 183

12. Hans Scharoun, "Grundlinien der Stadtplanung," in Minutes of the ninth meeting of the Magistrat Bauwirtschaftsausschuss, April 4, 1946, quoted in Geist and Kürvers, *Berliner Mietshaus*, vol. 3, 232.

13. Ibid., 235.

14. While their work was under way, the Planning Collective came into contact with a group in Zehlendorf working on a transportation plan. This Zehlendorfer Plan was also presented in the exhibition and recommended that Berlin's street network be simplified with a radial pattern of widely spaced surface boulevards carrying citywide traffic, as opposed to the grid of superhighways in the Collective Plan.

15. Hans Scharoun, Undated lecture, quoted in Geist and Kürvers, *Berliner Mietshaus*, vol. 3, 266.

16. Ladd, *Urban Planning and Civic Order in Germany*, 1990.

17. The Athens Charter includes recommendations under the subheadings "dwelling," "recreation," "work," "transportation," and "legacy of history." The first four of these are described as the core of planning and are used as such in the Collective Plan. In my own assessment, twenty-four of thirty (80 percent) of the recommendations are strongly evident in the Collective Plan, while none were contradicted. Six criteria were not apparent in the Collective Plan, due to insufficient detail in the plan and/or subjectivity in the charter's criteria.

18. Geist and Kürvers, *Berliner Mietshaus*, vol. 3, 225–228. The proposed freeways in a greenbelt would require rights-of-way several times wider than those for urban freeways in the United States, which are noted for the extensive damage they caused to American cities.

19. The recommended density is precisely the lower limit specified in the Athens Charter, which also prescribed bands or ribbons of separate land uses tailored to topography as well as nonstop arterials buffered from the city by a greenway.

20. Geist and Kürvers, *Berliner Mietshaus*, vol. 3, 213.

21. Peter Friedrich, "Das neue Berlin und sein Verkehr," *Demokratischer Aufbau* 5 (1946), quoted in Geist and Kürvers, *Berliner Mietshaus*, vol. 3, 228.

22. Geist and Kurvers, *Berliner Mietshaus*, vol. 3, 180–184.

23. Karl Maron, "Unser Berlin," foreword in exhibit catalog *Berlin Plant*, reprinted in Geist and Kürvers, *Berliner Mietshaus*, vol. 3, 184.

24. Doris Müller, Alfred Nützmann, and Katja Protte, eds., *Parteiauftrag: Ein Neues Deutschland: Bilder, Rituale, und Symbole der frühen DDR* (Berlin: Vorsteher, 1996). In fact, this can be seen as an early stage of a Communist technique that would become prominent in the late 1940s and early years of the GDR: utilization of formal characteristics prevalent in the Nazi era to assist indoctrination to socialism.

25. "Rettung der Großstadt: Ausstellung im Weissen Saal des Schloßes," *Tagesspiegel*, August 23, 1946.

26. "Wir bauen das neue Berlin," *Tägliche Rundschau* (hereafter *TR*), August 23, 1946.

27. Ibid.

28. "Die Bauaustellung des Magistrats: Stellungnahme der SPD—Utopische Pläne stiften Verwirrung, " *Der Sozialdemokrat,* September 26, 1946.

29. Scharoun's personal notes, Akademie der Künst, Sammlung Baukunst, Scharoun Collection, reprinted in Geist and Kürvers, *Berliner Mietshaus*, vol. 3, 245.

30. Margret Boveri, "Berlin plant: Werkbund- und Bauhaustradition auf Ruinenfeldern," *Die Wirtschaftzeitung*, December 6, 1946.

31. In this light Karl Scheffler's 1910 statement that "Berlin is a city condemned forever to becoming and never being" comes to mind, as it has been a favorite of urban observers since the Wall fell in 1989. Yet Scharoun's statement, rather than supporting an essentialist view of Berlin, most likely resulted from a reconciliation of modernist rejection of building traditions with a political situation involving foreign occupation.

32. Geist and Kürvers, *Berliner Mietshaus*, vol. 3, 250–251.

33. Karl Bonatz, "Meine Stellungnahme zu den Planungsarbeiten für Gross-Berlin, die ich bei meinem Amtsantritt vorfand," *Neue Bauwelt* 11 (1947), quoted in Geist and Kürvers, *Berliner Mietshaus*, vol. 3, 163.

34. Ibid. Bonatz's focus on aesthetics overlooked impacts on the function of existing neighborhoods. This devastation would soon be demonstrated in US urban freeway building. While Berlin's neighborhoods were heavily damaged and underpopulated, and the plan foresaw their reconstruction as "Wohnzellen," the freeway network would undermine the organic rebuilding and revitalization efforts that were being carried out across the city.

35. "Neuer Plan zum Wiederaufbau Berlins," *Berliner Zeitung* (hereafter *BZ*), December 3, 1947.

36. Geist and Kürvers, *Berliner Mietshaus*, vol. 3, 263.

37. Berlin Magistrat, "Hauptampt für Stadtplanung," Summary of presentation by Planning Collective on May 28, 1949, quoted in Geist and Kürvers, *Berliner Mietshaus*, vol. 3, 259.

38. Ibid.

39. Geist and Kürvers, *Berliner Mietshaus*, vol. 3, 268.

40. Ibid., 258.

41. "Berliner werden ein neues Berlin bauen: Oberbürgermeister Ebert stellt den Berliner Aufbauplan zur Diskussion, " *BZ*, July 15, 1949.

42. Ibid.

43. "Generalplan zum Wiederaufbau Berlins," *Neues Deutschland* (hereafter *ND*), July 16, 1949.

44. "Das neue Berlin," *ND*, July 17, 1949.

45. In a normative view of American democratic planning, experts educate and communicate with the public on planning issues, and in this sense the effort fails. However, there are manifold uses of the term "democracy." Here, the GDR's proclaimed "democratic centralism" may not have been attained, but the public discussion was certainly more extensive than for US planning at the time. For a normative view of democratic planning, see Norman Fainstein and Susan Fainstein, "City Planning and Political Values," *Urban Affairs Quarterly* 6 (1971): 341–362. Regarding use of the term "democracy," see Vidal, *Inventing a Nation*, 135.

46. Simone Hain, "Reise nach Moskau: Wie Deutsche 'sozialistisch' bauen lernten," *Bauwelt* 45 (1992): 9–10.

47. Lothar Bolz, File note, November 18, 1949, Stiftung Archiv der Parteien und Massenorganizationen der DDR im Bundesarchiv (hereafter SAPMO-BA), BA-SAPMO-DH1/44519.

48. Tzschorn, Notes on meeting led by Otto Grotewohl to discuss city building issues, November 18, 1949, in Hain, *Reise nach Moskau,* 19–20.

49. Regarding "technological fetishism," see Åman, *Architecture and Ideology*, 18.

50. Notes on meeting of the MfA, June 3, 1950, reprinted in Hain, *Reise nach Moskau,* 154.

51. Walter Pisternik, Notes on meeting at Soviet Academy of Architecture on April 25, 1950, reprinted in Hain, *Reise nach Moskau,* 108–109.

52. Adrian Forty, *Words and Buildings: A Vocabulary of Modern Architecture* (London: Thames & Hudson, 2000), 165.

53. Manfred Jäger, *Kultur und Politik in der DDR: 1945–1990* (Cologne: Verlag Wissenschaft und Politik, 1995), 38. Also see Ernst Hoffmann, "Ideological Probleme der Architektur," *Deutsche Architektur* (hereafter *DA*) 1, no. 1 (1952): 20–23.

54. Pisternik, Notes on meeting at Soviet Academy of Architecture, in Hain, *Reise nach Moskau,* 108.

55. Ibid., 112.

56. Iwan Scholtowski, "Über die wahre und die falsche Schönheit in der Architektur," *DA* 3, no. 1 (1955): 1–4.

57. Pisternik, Notes on meeting at Soviet Academy of Architecture, in Hain, *Reise nach Moskau,* 109. This is derived from a statement attributed to Stalin ("Culture is socialist in content, national in form"), in Pisternik, Notes on meeting at Soviet Ministry of City Building, April 22, 1950, reprinted in Hain, *Reise nach Moskau,* 101.

58. Schütz et al., *Kleines Politisches Wörterbuch*, 597–603.

59. For Soviet statements on the importance of central streets and squares for political activity during the Trip to Moscow, see Pisternik, Notes on lecture by Victor Baburov at Soviet Ministry of City Building on April 20, 1950, in Hain, *Reise nach Moskau*, 90–95. Socialist orchestration of public celebrations were strictly top-down affairs. The urban population marched along predetermined routes through the center of the city past the socialist leaders while displaying political posters and banners addressing contemporary political concerns along with flags and banners of the government and its institutions. Regarding the contrast between the czarist and socialist city in the Soviet Union, see Kurt Liebknecht, "Neuaufbau in der Sowjetuion," *Bauplanung und Bautechnik* 3, no. 4 (1949): 107–108.

60. Pisternik, Notes on meeting at Soviet Academy of Architecture from April 20, 1950, in Hain, *Reise nach Moskau*, 93.

61. Most early American political leaders did favor rural development due to a fear of the political unrest and mob action in European cities. David Schuyler, *The New Urban Landscape: The Redefinition of City Form in Nineteenth-Century America* (Baltimore: Johns Hopkins University Press, 1986).

62. Pisternik, Notes on meeting at Soviet Academy of Architecture, from April 20, 1950, in Hain, *Reise nach Moskau*, 93.

63. Ibid.

64. Ibid.

65. Not all modernists agreed. Godfrey Samuel of the MARS Group argued for the importance of a city center and central public space for informal gathering and communal expression. Hain, *Reise nach Moskau*, 2553.

66. Ministerrat der Deutsche Demokratische Republik, *Auszug aus dem Protokoll der 38 Sitzung der Provisorische Regierung der Deutsche Demokratische Republik am 23.8.50.*, August 25, 1950, SAPMO-BA, H1, 44476.

67. Ministerrat der Deutsche Demokratische Republik, Ministerialblatt der Deutschen Demokratischen Republik, Sepember 16, 1950, reprinted in Hain, *Reise nach Moskau*, 185–186.

68. Ibid.; Pisternik, Notes on meeting with Soviet Ministry of City Building on April 29, 1950, in Hain, *Reise nach Moskau*, 128.

69. Gerhard Strauss, Deutsche Bauakademie, Institute für Theory und Geschichte, Draft manuscript, "Theoretische Fragen der deutschen Architektur beim Aufbau des Sozialismus in der Deutsche Demokratische Republik," May 5, 1953, SAPMO-BA, DH2 (IV) I/22.

70. Council of Ministers of the GDR, *Ministerialblatt*, September 16, 1950.

71. Pisternik, Minutes of meeting at the MfA, June 2, 1950, SAPMO-Barch, DH 1/44475, in Hain, *Reise nach Moskau*, 153.

72. Heinrich Meier, Notes on meeting at the MfA, June 19, 1950, in Hain, *Reise nach Moskau*, 173.

73. Ibid., 175.

74. Weitz, *Creating German Communism.*

75. Pisternik, Notes on meeting at the MfA on June 3, 1950, in Hain, *Reise nach Moskau*, 150.

76. Ibid., 148.

77. Notes on meeting at the MfA on June 3, 1950, in Hain, *Reise nach Moskau*, 153–160.

78. Ibid., 160.

79. Ibid., 161.

80. Hain, *Reise nach Moskau*, 139.

81. Düwel, *Baukunst voran!*, 60; and Kurt Liebknecht, *Plan des Kampfes um eine neue Architektur*, March 20, 1951, SAPMO-Barch, DH1-38875. Düwel emphasizes the agency of the Central Committee in the process, and it is true they held political authority and helped shape the effort. However, Bolz had already initiated the paradigm shift, thereby placing it on the Party's agenda, and Liebknecht's expertise was essential to provide meaningful form to the discussion.

82. "16 Grundsätze des Stadtebaus," *Baumeister*, October 1950, p. 681, copy of article acknowledged by Pisternik, DH2 (IV) DBA/A34.

83. Lothar Bolz to Otto Grotewohl November 28, 1949, SAPMO-Barch, DH1-39026.

84. Karl Brockschmidt (Berlin Magistrat [hereafter Magistrat], Abteilung Aufbau) to Lothar Bolz, July 6, 1950, SAPMO-Barch, DH2 (K1) A/47.

85. Ministerium für Aufbau (MfA), Institut für Städtebau und Hochbau, *Das Zentrum Berlins*, July 21, 1950, SAPMO-BA, DH2 (K1) A/47.

86. This observation is derived from evidence on the views of Ulbricht and others presented in Chapter 5.

87. Durth, Düwel, and Gutshow, *Aufbau*, 83.

88. Walter Ulbricht, "Die Grossbauten im Fünfjahrplan," speech at the SED's Third

Party Congress on July 22, 1950, reprinted in Geist and Kürvers, *Berliner Mietshaus 1945–1989*, vol. 3, 308–309.

89. The basis of Ulbricht's decision will be taken up in Chapter 5, which focuses on this issue; there were valid arguments to place the square in several areas, according to socialist realism.

90. Ulbricht, "Die Grossbauten im Fünfjahrplan."

91. Pisternik, Minutes of meeting with Walter Ulbricht and others held on August 5, 1950, and August 7, 1950, SAPMO-BA, DH1, 39075.

92. Durth, Düwel, and Gutshow, *Aufbau*, 220–222.

93. MfA, Hauptamt Stadtplanung, *Termin- und Kostenplan für die vorläufige Umgestaltung des Lustgartens,* August 19, 1950, SAPMO-BA, DH1, 39075.

94. "Aufbauplan fur das Zentrum des neuen Berlin," *BZ*, August 27, 1950.

95. Planungkommission Berlin, Minutes from meeting, January 12, 1951, SAPMO-Barch, DH1, 38881.

96. Ibid.

97. Ibid.

98. Herman Henselmann, File note on visit with Professor Baburov, March 10, 1954, SAPMO-Barch, FBS 365/15243.

99. Karthaus to Ministerrat, "Beirat für Bauwesen," October 26, 1955, SAPMO-Barch, DH1, 38927.

100. Durth, Düwel, and Gutschow, *Ostkreuz*, 236–237.

101. Eka Merveldt, "Wie soll die Hauptstadt aussehen?" *Die Zeit*, April 4, 1957.

102. In November 1958, Khrushchev responded to East German concerns, accusing the West of breaking the Potsdam Agreement; he indicated that the USSR was ready to hand full control over East Berlin to the GDR. See Ann Tusa, *The Last Division: Berlin and the Wall* (London: Hodder and Stoughton, 1996), 96.

103. Durth, Düwel, and Gutschow *Aufbau*, 248, suggest that in light of the Hallstein Doctrine (1955), the West Berlin competition's inclusion of East Berlin would have seemed a provocation, a claim requiring some additional substantiation, given recent collaboration between East and West German architects in Fennpfuhl in East Berlin. That had been initiated by professionals, not politicians, and had since dissipated in the face of Cold War tension. This Capital City competition was initiated by West German parliament in a context of growing Cold War tension, and continued East German awareness of city building as a means of asserting state legitimacy and competing with the West. See Chapter 6 in this book for details of this shift

104. "Städtebauliches Program," unsigned document, SAPMO–BA, DH2-DBA/A/305.

105. Ministerrat, "Beirat für Bauwesen," July 30, 1957, file notes, SAPMO-BA, DH2, A/113.

106. Ibid.

107. Ibid.

108. Durth, Düwel, and Gutschow, *Aufbau*, 76.

109. Kurt Magritz, "Die Industrializierung des Bauwesens und die künstlerischen *Aufgaben der Architektur,*" *DA* 4, no. 2 (1955): 49–51; Kurt Liebknecht, "Die Wissenschaft im

Dienste der Industrializierung des Bauwesens" *DA* 4, no. 3 (1955): 103–105; Hanns Hopp, "Tiefere Verständnis für die nationalen Traditionen," *DA* 5, no. 4 (1956): 165–166; and Deutsche Bauakademie, "Die grosse Wende im Bauwesen," *DA* 5, no. 1 (1956): 1–3.

110. Richard Paulick, "Einige Bemerkungen zur Architektur Diskussion," *DA* 6, no. 9 (1957): 479–481.

111. Lothar Kühne, "Zur Begriff sozialistische Architektur," *DA* 8, no. 2 (1959): 63–64.

112. Bund Deutscher Architekten, Entschliessung des III. Bundeskongresses des DBA, reprinted in *DA* 7, no. 2 (1958): 60–61.

113. Kurt Liebknecht, "Grundadressse des ZK der SED An den III Bundeskongress des Bundes Deutscher Architekten," *DA* 7, no. 2 (1958): 59–60.

114. Gerhard Kosel, *Produktivkraft Wissenschaft* (Berlin: Verlag die Wirtschaft, 1957). Kosel later elaborated on his development of these concepts in another book; see Gerhard Kosel, *Unternehmen Wissenschaft: Die Wiederentdeckung einer Idee* (Berlin: Henschelverlag, 1989). In the West science and technology were also prominently situated in a meta-theory of society at this time with "modernization theory." Instead of being a motor toward communism, they led to Western-style democracy and capitalism. See Nils Gilman, *Mandarins of the Future: Modernization Theory in Cold War America* (Baltimore: Johns Hopkins University Press, 2003).

115. Gerhard Kosel, "Aufbau des Zentrums der Hauptstadt des demokratischen Deutschlands Berlin," *DA* 7, no. 4 (1958): 177–182. The plan was developed by Kosel, along with Hopp and Mertens. Years later, Kosel recalled that Henselmann had failed to respond to calls for representative planning of the city center from the SED leadership despite offers of support from the MfA. Henselmann as chief architect of Berlin had remained occupied with piecemeal planning. See Kosel, *Unternehmen Wissenschaft*, 247. Durth, Düwel, and Gutschow later presented Henselmann's view, in which Kosel had developed and published his plan without approval. This, along with criticism of Hermann Henselmann, set off a conflict between Kosel and Henselmann (Durth, Düwel, and Gutschow, *Aufbau*, 242–243). In September, Kosel appeared to obtain favor, as the Politburo criticized Henselmann's plan and noted that he should not have published it without their approval. See Nicolaus and Obeth, *Die Stalinallee*, 275–276.

116. Kosel, "Aufbau des Zentrums der Hauptstadt

117. Herman Henselmann to Gerhard Kosel, March 5, 1958, SAPMO-Barch, FBS 365/15243.

118. Herman Henselmann, "Vom Straussberger Platz zum Alexanderplatz," *DA* 7, no. 8 (1958): 419–424.

119. Politburo, "Ausschreibung eines Städtebau-Ideenwettbewerbes zur sozialistisches Umgestaltung des Zentrums der Hauptstadt der DDR—Berlin," SAPMO-BA, DY30/58. The ideas of "democracy" and "representing all of Germany" did not disappear completely but received scant mention in the competition.

120. Ibid.

121. Durth, Düwel, and Gutschow, *Aufbau*, 250–251.

122. Politburo, "Ausschreibung eines Städtebau-Ideenwettbewerbes."

123. International Style theorists sought to maintain a unified modernist cannon, but it

had become clear that other approaches to modernism were in the works, as exemplified by architects such as Oscar Niemeyer and Eero Saarinen. See Spiro Kostov, *A History of Architecture: Settings and Rituals* (Oxford: Oxford University Press, 1995), 728.

124. Walter Ulbricht, Letter to Gerhard Trötlitzch, August 5, 1959, SAPMO-Barch, NL 182/982, FBS 363/15220.

125. Jury commentary from "Ideenwettbewerb zur sozialistischen Umgestaltung der Hauptstadt der Deutschen Demokratischen Republik," quoted in Durth, Düwel, and Gutschow, *Aufbau*, 256–260.

126. Preisgericht ISUB, Jury commentary to "Ideenwettbewerb 'sozialistische Umgestaltung' Berlins," September 29, 1959, quoted in Geist and Kürvers, *Berliner Mietshaus,* vol. 3, 257–261.

127. "Das neue Zentrum unserer Hauptstadt," *ND*, November 4, 1959.

128. "Kleiner Einkaufsbummel auf grosser Alex-Etage," *BZ*, December 4, 1959.

129. "Utopia oder Berlin von morgen?" *BZ*, November 22, 1959.

130. Durth, Düwel, and Gutschow, *Aufbau*, 271.

131. Ibid., 269.

132. Koshar, *Germany's Transient Pasts*, Chapters 5 and 6.

133. Gerhard Strauss to Committee of the DBA through Henselmann, April 28, 1952, DH2(IV) I-25.

134. Bruno Flierl, Deutsche Bauakademi, Institute for Theory and History, *An Thesen zum Zentrum von Berlin*, November 21, 1959, SAPMO-Barch, DH2(K4) II/07-2/20.

135. "Berlin, wie du wirst Dir verändern," *Freie Welt* 51 (December 17, 1959).

136. "Thesen zur städtebaulichen Grundkonzeption des Stadtzentrums von Berlin," December 1959, in Durth, Düwel, and Gutschow, *Aufbau,* 272–274.

137. Flierl, *An Thesen zum Zentrum von Berlin.*

138. A. Naumov, K. Kriwzow, and S. Speranski, "Konsultatives Gutachten über die schopferischen Vorschläge des 2. Durchgangs der Projektierung des Zentrums von Berlin," February 29, 1960, SAPMO-Barch, DH2-DBA/A/305.

139. Walter Ulbricht, File notes on consultation with "Kommission zum Aufbau des Berliner Stadtzentrums," in Durth, Düwel, and Gutschow, *Aufbau*, 277.

140. Ibid., 281.

141. Ibid.

142. Ibid.

143. Schlögl, *Terror und Traum*, 77.

144. Hermann Henselmann, plans titled "Das Zentrale Gebäude am Marx-Engels-Platz," SAPMO-Barch, DC-20/8913.

145. Pugh (*Divided Berlin*, 166) characterized the television tower as Ulbricht's "monument to the 'scientific-technical revolution.' "

146. "Das neue Zentrum der Hauptstadt," ND, April 21, 1961.

147. "Was sagen die Berliner zum Stadtzentrum?" BZ, 3.

3. Unter den Linden

Epigraph: Lothar Bolz to Otto Grotewohl, Prime Minister of the GDR, November 16,

1950, Stiftung Archiv der Parteien und Massenorganizationen der DDR im Bundesarchiv (hereafter SAPMO-BA), FBS, 123/16322.

1. Bodenschatz, Engstfeld, and Seifert, *Berlin*, 126–127. For comparison with other examples of Renaissance urban design, see Anthony Morris, *History of Urban Form: Prehistory to Renaissance* (London: George Godwin, 1972), 161–163.

2. Waltraud Volk, *Historische Strassen und Plätze heute: Berlin, Haupstadt der DDR* (Berlin: Verlag für Bauwesen, 1980), 9–11, 17; and Martin Wörner, Doris Mollenschott, and Karl-Heinz Hüter, *Architekturführer Berlin* (Berlin: Dietrich Riemer, 1997), 25.

3. Jürgen Tietz, "Schinkels Neue Wache Unter den Linden: Baugeschichte 1816–1993," in Stölzl, *Die Neue Wache*, 17–20.

4. Bodenschatz, Engstfeld, and Seifert, *Berlin*, 133; and Volk, *Historische Strassen*, 19–21.

5. Bodenschatz, Engstfeld, and Seifert, *Berlin*, 133.

6. Volk, *Historische Strassen*, 32.

7. "Grosse Aufraumungsaktion Under den Linden," *Der Morgen*, October 20, 1945; and "Reinmachen Unter den Linden," *Der Morgen*, November 15, 1945.

8. Politburo, *Plan des Neuaufbaus von Berlin*, August 15, 1950, reprinted in Durth, Düwel, and Gutschow, *Ostkreuz*, vol. 2, 220–222.

9. Karl Brockschmidt, Notes on meeting with Soviet Control Commission, October 9, 1950, SAPMO-BA, DH2 (K1) A/47.

10. The interior of the old embassy had been destroyed in the war and the exterior heavily damaged. See Berlin Magistrat, Resolution from July 7, 1947, Landesarchiv Berlin (hereafter LAB) 100/793.

11. Martin Wörner, *Architekturführer Berlin*, 5th edition (Berlin: Dietrich, 1997), 37. The new Soviet embassy was constructed between 1950 and 1953.

12. Brockschmidt, Notes on meeting with Soviet Control Commission, October 9, 1950.

13. Lothar Bolz to Otto Grotewohl, Prime Minister of the GDR, November 16, 1950, SAPMO-BA, FBS, 123/16322.

14. Lothar Bolz to Friedrich Ebert, mayor of Berlin, December 4, 1950, SAPMO-BA, DH1, 39206.

15. Planungskomission Berlin, Minutes from meeting, January 12, 1951, SAPMO-BA, DH1, 38927.

16. "Wettbewerb Zentrale Achse," August 14, 1951, reprinted in Durth, Düwel, and Gutschow, *Ostkreuz*, vol. 2, 231–233.

17. Berlin Magistrat, Resolution, July 7, 1947, LAB 100/793.

18. Kiederling, *Berlin 1945–1986*, 240–241. The Soviets wasted no time initiating their theater program. On May 14, 1945, General Besarin sent a group of German cultural elites on an excursion to survey the condition of Berlin's theaters and to register actors, singers, musicians, and technical personnel. Renovations were quickly under way on several theaters, and on September 24, 1945, the Berlin Magistrat passed a resolution for the restoration of a total of eight theaters for a sum of RM 1,140,000—at a time when obtaining several thousand reichsmarks for architecturally and historically valuable structures was problematic. These spaces also doubled as assembly halls for the Community Party (KPD) and related organizations. See Kiederling, *Berlin 1945–1986*, 94; Schulze, File notes, July 9, 1945, LAB 110/897; Berlin Magistrat, Hauptamt für Stadtplanung, Hauptampt für Hochbau (hereafter BMHH),

unsigned memorandum, October 1, 1945, LAB 110/790; BMHH File note, February 1, 1946; BMHH Report on visit to Metropol Theater, July 26, 1946, LAB, 110/790; and Lampe et al., *Berlin: Kampf um Freiheit,* 355, 365, 375, 397, 404, 416.

19. Politburo, *Plan des Neuaufbaus von Berlin*; Walter Pisternik to Ministry of Education, February 19, 1951, SAPMO-BA, H1, 38615; Planungskomission Berlin, Minutes from meeting, September 18, 1950, SAPMO-BA, DH1, 38927; and Planungskomission Berlin, Minutes from meeting, October 23 1950, SAPMO-BA, DH1, 38927.

20. Kurt Liebknecht, File notes, June 28, 1951, SAPMO-BA, H1, 44476; and Richard Paulick, "Die künstlerische Probleme des Wiederaufbaus der Deutschen Staatsoper Unter den Linden," *Deutsche Architektur* (hereafter *DA*) 1, no. 1 (1952): 30–39.

21. Liebknecht, File note, June 28 1951, SAPMO-BA, H1 44476; and C. Mayer, File note for Lothar Bolz, minister of building, July 9, 1951, SAPMO-BA, H1, 44476.

22. Paulick, "Die künstlerische Probleme," 30.

23. Ibid., 32.

24. Winfried Löschburg, *Unter den Linden: Gesichter und Geschichten einer berühmten Strasse* (Berlin: Der Morgen: 1972), 65; and Wörner, Mollenschott, and Hüter, *Architekturführer Berlin*, 24.

25. Berlin Magistrat, Resolution, July 7, 1947, LAB 100/793; and Durth, Düwel, and Gutschow, *Ostkreuz*, vol. 1, 86.

26. "Neues Theater am Kastanienwäldchen," *Neues Deutschland* (hereafter *ND*), May 13 1947.

27. "60 000 im Haus der Sowjetkultur," *Berliner Zeitung* (hereafter *BZ*), June 27, 1947.

28. "Übergabe des Hauses der Kultur der Sowjetunion und anderer Kulturzentren in deutsche Verwaltung," *ND*, May 24, 1950.

29. Durth, Düwel, and Gutschow, *Ostkreuz*, vol. 1, 86.

30. Since May 1945, Soviet cultural politics had been concerned with transforming the German populace's negative image of the Soviet Union. See Kiederling, *Berlin 1945–1986*, 240–241.

31. Tietz, "Schinkels Neue Wache," 10–21.

32. Ibid., 21–64.

33. Ibid., 75–78.

34. Ibid., 79; and Politburo, *Plan des Neuafbaus von Berlin*.

35. Planungskomission Berlin, Minutes from meeting, August 25, 1950, SAPMO-BA, DH1, 38927; and Planungskomission Berlin, Minutes from meeting September 7, 1950, SAPMO-BA, DH1, 38927.

36. Tietz, "Schinkels Neue Wache," 79.

37. Michealis to Rebetsky, July 14, 1951, SAPMO-BA, DH2 (K1) A/47.

38. Walter Pisternik to Willi Stoph, Member of Central Committee of SED, February 15, 1951, SAPMO-BA, DH1, 39026.

39. Rudolf Michealis, Berlin Magistrat, Abteilung Volksbildung to Gustav Rebetzky, Direktor, Berlin Magistrat, Abteilung Aufbau, July 14, 1951, SAPMO-BA, DH2 (K1) A/47.

40. Regarding this discursive shift, see Herf, *Divided Memory*, 162–167. Regarding Michaelis, see https://libcom.org/history/michaelis-rudolf-aka-michel-aka-hans-bronner-1907-1990.

41. Ernst Hoffman to Walter Pisternik, September 5, 1951, SAPMO-BA, H1, 38881.

42. Tietz, "Schinkels Neue Wache," 80–82.

43. Herf, *Divided Memory*, 175–179.

44. Politburo, Resolution, December 15, 1959, SAPMO-BA, DY 30/59.

45. Ibid.

46. Azaryahu, *Von Wilhelmplatz zu Thälmannplatz*, 135.

47. Politburo, Resolution, December 15, 1959, SAPMO-BA, DY 30/59.

48. "Neue Wache—Mahnmal," *BZ*, February 14, 1960.

49. "Ein Festlicher Tag," *BZ*, May 9, 1960.

50. Ibid.

51. Tietz, "Schinkels Neue Wache," 84–88. The function of the Neue Wache became a subject of renewed debate since German reunification. For an analysis of the negotiation of meaning regarding the Neue Wache during this era, see Till, "Staging the Past."

52. Berlin Magistrat, Copy of excerpt from statement from June 20, 1911, LAB, 110/903.

53. Evidence on the actual decision-making process leading to the Arsenal's reconstruction is especially diaphanous. This section is an interpretation of sometimes dubious accounts in press reports and government records, taking interagency squabbling and political circumstances into account.

54. According to Katz, control of the Arsenal had been turned over to the Planning Department after he convinced "the Allies" to change their plans to demolish the building in accordance with the Potsdam Conference policy that the most significant symbolic sites of Prussian-German militarism be destroyed. See "Noch einmal: Kaninchen im Zeughaus," *TR*, August 14, 1947. In fact, the Allied Control Council did not approve any policy regarding the Arsenal until October, when it determined that its contents must be liquidated. See Regina Müller, *Das Berliner Zeughaus: Die Baugeschichte* (Berlin: Deutschen Historischen Museum, 1994), 252. Ludwig Justi simply notes that the Planning Department "took" the building from his office and refused to return it. See Ludwig Justi to Karl Bonatz, November 28, 1947, LAB 110/903. Given the Soviet interest in exhibition space, and the fact that the Magistrat was engaged in repairs to make the building habitable in the summer of 1945 (Berlin Magistrat, Hauptamt Stadtplanung, *Kostenüberschlag über die notwendigen Baumassnahmen zur Beseitigung Zerstorungen an dem Gebäude des Zeughauses in Berlin, UdL 2*, August 12, 1945, LAB 110/903), along with the SMAD's complete control over the administration of Berlin at that time, it can only be presumed that it arranged for the building to pass control to Katz.

55. Müller, *Das Berliner Zeughaus*, 250–251.

56. Schwenk to Hauptamtes für Hochbau, December 3, 1945, LAB 100/903.

57. Berlin Magistrat, Note on Schwenk's report at meeting, December 10, 1945, LAB 100/761; Listmann to division supervisor, August 22, 1946, LAB, 110/903; and Müller, *Das Berliner Zeughaus*, 251.

58. Müller, *Das Berliner Zeughaus*, 252.

59. Berlin Magistrat, Hauptamt für Stadtplanung, unsigned memorandum, February 6, 1946, LAB, 110/903; Listmann to division supervisor; and Scheper, Letter to division supervisor, Hauptamptes für Hochbau, August 30, 1946, LAB 110/903.

60. Berlin Magistrat, Finanzabteilung, File note, November 30, 1946, LAB, 110/903; and

Ferdinand Friedensburg, Notes from meeting on July 15, 1947 (file dated July 16, 1947), LAB, 110/903.

61. Justi to Karl Bonatz.

62. Friedensburg, Notes from meeting on July 15, 1947 (file dated July 16, 1947), LAB, 110/903.

63. "Kunstwerke im Keller—Kaninchen im Zeughaus," *TR*, August 6, 1947.

64. "Noch einmal: Kaninchen im Zeughaus," *TR*, August 14, 1947.

65. Berlin Magistrat, Resolution, September 8, 1947, LAB, 100/797.

66. Friedensburg, Notes from meeting on November 18, 1947, November 20, 1947, LAB, 100/803.

67. Müller, *Das Berliner Zeughaus*, 258.

68. "Vom Arsenel des Krieges zum Hort des Friedens," *Sonntag*, July 24, 1949.

69. Müller, *Das Berliner Zeughaus*, 260–262 and 288.

70. Ibid., 259.

71. Ibid., 267–272.

72. Ministerrat der Deutschen Demokratischen Republik, "Auszug aus dem Protokoll der 38 Sitzung der Provisoriche Regierung der Deutschen Demokratischen Republik am 23.8.50," August 25, 1950, SAPMO-BA, H1, 44476.

73. Ministerium für Aufbau, Untitled document, undated, SAPMO-BA, DH1, 38927.

74. Kurt Liebknecht, Memorandum on meeting with Walter Ulbricht, September 4, 1950, SAPMO-BA, DH1, 39827.

75. Charles Maier, *The Unmasterable Past: History, Holocaust, and German National Identity* (Cambridge, MA: Harvard University Press, 1988): 124–125.

76. Volk, *Historische Strassen*, 31–35.

77. Ibid., 33; and Planungskomission Berlin, Minutes from meeting, September 18, 1950, SAPMO-BA, DH1, 38927.

78. Volk, *Historische Strassen*, 32.

79. Paulick, "Die künstlerische Probleme," 36.

80. Ibid., 35.

81. Ibid., 36.

82. Sibylle Schulz, "Denkmäler im Stadtbild Berlins," in *Denkmale in Berlin und in der Mark Brandenburg*, ed. Ernst Badstübner and Hannelore Sachs (Weimar: Hermann Böhlaus Nachfolger, 1988): 96; and Stölzl, *Die Neue Wache*, 20.

83. Badstübner and Sachs, *Denkmale in Berlin*, 371.

84. Schulz, "Denkmäler im Stadtbild Berlins," 96–98.

85. Azaryahu, *Von Wilhelmplatz zu Thälmannplatz*, 132.

86. MfA, Hauptampt Stadtplanung, *Termin- und Kostenplan für die vorläufige Umgestaltung des Lustgartens*, August 19, 1950, SAPMO-BA, DH1, 39075.

87. Azaryahu, *Von Wilhelmplatz zu Thälmannplatz*, 142–143.

88. Michael Cullen, *Das Brandenburger Tor: Ein deutsches Symbol* (Berlin: Berlin Edition, 1999), 13–16.

89. Ibid., 39.

90. Helmut Börsch-Supan, foreword in Cullen, *Das Brandenburger Tor*, 9.

91. Jenny March, *Cassel Dictionary of Classical Mythology* (London: Cassel, 1998), 232; and Cullen, *Das Brandenburger Tor* 40.

92. Cullen, *Das Brandenburger Tor*, 51.

93. Ibid., 41–71, 75–82.

94. Ibid., 93–94.

95. Ibid., 85–91.

96. Berlin Magistrat, Resolution, November 12, 1949, LAB, 100/843.

97. Berlin Magistrat, File note, April 5, 1950, LAB, 100/843.

98. Cullen, *Das Brandenburger Tor*, 90–93.

99. Sekretariat des Oberbürgermeisters, File note, February 10, 1951, LAB, 100/843.

100. Friedrich Werner to Walter Ulbricht, January 5, 1951, SAPMO-BA, DH2 (K1) A/47.

101. Otto Gotsche to Kurt Liebknecht, February 7, 1951, SAPMO-BA, DH2 (K1) A/47.

102. Cullen, *Das Brandenburger Tor*, 94–96.

103. Politburo, Resolution, August 28, 1956, SAPMO-BA, DY, 30/56.

104. Cullen, *Das Brandenburger Tor*, 99; Cullen's assertion that the Beautification Plan was a response to West Berlin's IBA is substantiated by examining a copy of the plan published in *BZ*, August 28, 1946: the focus was clearly on sites near border crossings and transportation nodes.

105. Cullen, *Das Brandenburger Tor*, 99–104.

106. Ibid., 103.

107. Politburo, Resolution, September 9, 1958, SAPMO-BA, DY 30/58.

108. "Tor des Friedens ohne militaristische Symbole," *BZ*, September 16, 1958.

109. Ibid.

4. From Royal Palace to Marx-Engels Square

Epigraph: Lothar Bolz, "Program des Aufbaus," speech delivered at the Deutschen Bautagung in Leipzig on March 8, 1950, printed in *Von Deutschem Bauen: Rede und Aufsätze* (Berlin: Verlag der Nation, 1950), 21.

1. Renate Petras, *Das Schloss in Berlin: Von der Revolution 1918 bis zur Vernichtung 1950* (Berlin: Verlag Bauwesen, 1999), 8–30.

2. Alex Zukas, "Workers's Festive Spaces in the Weimar Republic: May Day and the Berlin Lustgarten," *Environment, Space, Place* 4, no. 1 (2012): 48–78; and Petras, *Das Schloss*, 18–19.

3. Petras, *Das Schloss*, 8–36.

4. Ibid., 38–83.

5. Zukas, "Worker's Festive Spaces," 58–59.

6. Alois Riegl, "The Modern Cult of Monuments: Its Character and Its Origin" (1903), trans. Kurt W. Forster and Diane Ghirardo, *Oppositions* 25 (Fall 1982): 21–51; Koshar, *Germany's Transient Pasts*.

7. Koshar, *Germany's Transient Pasts*; Rudy Koshar, "Altar, Stage, and City: Historic Preservation and Urban Meaning in Nazi Germany," *History and Memory* 3, no. 1 (1991): 30–59; Joshua Hagen, "The Most German of Towns: Creating an Ideal Nazi Community in Rothenburg ob der Tauber," *Annals of the Association of American Geographers* 94, no. 1 (2004): 207–227; Joshua Hagen, "Historic Preservation in Nazi Germany: Place, Memory,

and Nationalism," *Journal of Historical Geography* 35, no. 4 (2009): 690–715; and Diefendorf, *In the Wake of War.*

8. Berlin Magistrat, Minutes of meeting, July 23, 1945, Landesarchiv Berlin (hereafter LAB) 100/749.

9. Hans Scharoun, Draft of resolution for Berlin Magistrat, August 15, 1945, LAB 110/910.

10. Berlin Magistrat, Minutes of meeting, August 20, 1945, LAB 100/759.

11. Berlin Magistrat, Minutes of meeting, October 1, 1945, LAB, 100/762

12. Heinrich Starck, 1946, original source not given, quoted in Fritz-Eugen Keller, "Christian Eltesters' Entwürfe für die Erweiterung der Paradekammern und die Kapelle des Berliner Stadtschlosses 1697/98," in *Zeitschrift für Kunstgeschichte* 48 (1985): 541, quoted in Petras, *Das Schloss*, 97.

13. On August 20, 1945, Scharoun requested RM 71,200, and on October 1 he requested RM 45,000. Scharoun protested the diversion of funds to theaters at the Magistrat meeting on August 13, arguing that RM 250,000 had been spent on the Admiralspalast and another RM 300,000 would be given out in the second phase, solely because the project manager "hides behind the Russians at the right times" (Berlin Magistrat, Minutes of meeting, August 13, 1945, LAB 100/759). As would become evident in the early low-cost housing project on Stalinallee, limiting the cost per unit to DM 10,000 proved to be a challenge, thus Scharoun's requested RM 71,000 would barely cover seven new apartments. The argument about difficulties obtaining building materials was valid, but for political reasons; as demonstrated in the case of the Zeughaus, it was nearly impossible to obtain the necessary materials without Soviet support.

14. Berlin Magistrat, October 10, 1947. The Arsenal was also commandeered for exhibition space at this time. Between 1946 and 1948 four exhibitions were held in the Berlin Palace's White Hall: *Berlin plant/erster Bericht*; *Franzosiche Malerei*, on modern French painting; *Wiedersehen mit Museumsgut,* a selected display of art and artifacts from Berlin museum collections; and *Berlin 1848*, depicting the events of the 1848 uprising (Petras, *Das Schloss*, 98–105).

15. Berlin Magistrat, Draft resolution for meeting on October 15, 1947, October 10, 1947, LAB 100/799.

16. As in the case of the Neue Wache, the Communist denial of emergency repairs had led to additional damage.

17. Petras, *Das Schloss*, 109.

18. "Bildersturmer in Berlins Innenstadt," *Der Tag*, May 19, 1949; and "Wird das Schloss Abgebrochen," *Sozial Demokrat*, May 19, 1949.

19. "Berliner werden ein neues Berlin bauen," *Neues Deutschland* (hereafter *ND*), July 17, 1949.

20. Petras, *Das Schloss*, 108–110.

21. Karl Reutti [Karl Rodemann], *Das Berliner Schloss, 1966*, quoted in Petras, *Das Schloss*, 110.

22. Gerd Zuchold, "Der Abriß der Ruinen des Stadtschloßes und der Bauakademie in Ost-Berlin," *Deutschland Archiv* 2 (1985): 178–207.

23. Lothar Bolz, "Program des Aufbaus," speech delivered at the Deutschen Bautagung in Leipzig on March 8, 1950, printed in *Von Deutschem Bauen: Rede und Aufsätze* (Berlin: Verlag der Nation, 1950), 21.

24. Discussion of the center during the Trip to Moscow focused on a broad area rather than a precise point. Soviet advisers pointed out that in Stalingrad a 2.5-kilometer (1.55 miles) strip of land was declared the center. Walter Pisternik, Notes on meeting in Soviet Ministry of City Building on April 20, 1950, reprinted in Hain, "Reise nach Moskau," 90–95. In Moscow the Kremlin could be posited as a precise center point in terms of history, government, and urban design, yet the proposed Palace of Soviets was to be located nearly half a mile away. There, the Cathedral of Christ the Savior was demolished to make room, an additional motive being the anti-Orthodox campaign that predated socialist realism.

25. Laurenz Demps, *Berlin-Wilhelmstrasse: Eine Topographie preussisch-deutscher Macht* (Berlin: Links, 1996).

26. Heinz Habedank, Gerhard Kiederling, Alfred Loesdau, Inga Materna, Hans Meusel, and Wolfgang Schröder, *Geschichte der revolutionären Berliner Arbeiterbewegung: Von den Anfängen bis zur Gegenwart*, vol. 2 (Berlin: Dietz, 1987), map insert between 224 and 225.

27. Bauer and Hühns, *Berlin: 800 Jahre Geschichte.*

28. Stangl, "Revolutionaries' Cemeteries."

29. Pamela Swett, *Neighbors and Enemies: The Culture of Radicalism in Berlin, 1929–1933* (Cambridge: Cambridge University Press, 2004), 56.

30. Bauer and Hühns, *Berlin: 800 Jahre Geschichte.*

31. See Gerhard Strauss, "National Erbe und Neuplanung in deutschen Städtebau," *Deutsche Architektur* (hereafter *DA*) 4 (1955): 160–166. This is also true of Soviet precedent. See note 24, regarding Moscow.

32. The Lustgarten was also a frequent location for other large Communist gatherings at this time.

33. Zukas, "Workers' Festive Spaces."

34. Durth, Düwel, and Gutschow, *Aufbau*, 213.

35. Kurt Liebknecht, Speech given at architecture conference, June 2–5, 1950, quoted in Hain, *Archeologie und Aneignung*, 67–68.

36. MfA, *Das Zentrum Berlins.*

37. Walter Ulbricht, "Die Grossbauten im Fünfjahrplan," speech at the SED's Third Party Congress, quoted in Geist and Kürvers, *Berliner Mietshaus*, vol. 3, 308–309.

38. Hain, *Archeologie und Aneignung*, 68

39. Richard Paulick et al., "Vorschläge für den Bau eines Platzes für zentrale Kundgebungen," July 1950, LAB 110, 11/12, quoted in Hain, *Archeologie und Aneignung*, 68.

40. Kurt Liebknecht et al., "Vorschlag zur Gestaltung des Zentrums der Hauptstadt Deutschlands, Berlin," August 3, 1950, quoted in Durth, Düwel, and Gutschow, *Aufbau*, 217. Hain suggests that after meeting with Ulbricht on August 5, the planners' courage to stand by their convictions seems to have been broken, yet they did muster an effort as late as September.

41. Walter Pisternik, Protocol of meeting with Walter Ulbricht and others on August 5, 1950, August 7, 1950, SAPMO-BA, DH1, 39075.

42. Hans Scharoun to Otto Grotewohl, August 31, 1950, reprinted in Petras, *Das Schloss*, 134–135.

43. Ibid.

44. Yet the proposal was seen as a last-ditch effort at saving the most significant portion of the palace by a man who led the preservation effort just a few years earlier. Scharoun's statements were dually embedded in traditionalist and socialist-realist discourse.

45. Kurt Liebknecht, Memorandum on meeting with Walter Ulbricht, September 4, 1950, SAPMO-BA, DH1, 39827.

46. Petras, *Das Schloss*, 116.

47. Otto Grotewohl to Hans Scharoun, September 5, 1950, quoted in Petras, *Das Schloss*, 135; Walter Pisternik to Staatsekretär Geyer, September 4, 1950, SAPMO-BA, DH1, 38927; and Walter Pisternik to Brockschmidt, September 4, 1950, SAPMO-BA, DH1-38927.

48. Hans Scharoun to Otto Grotewohl, September 6, 1950, reprinted in Petras, *Das Schloss*, 135–136.

49. For this reason, historic preservationists long argued against the disencumberment of monuments. Soviet high-rises overcome the problem of scale and isolation by providing their own "foreground" through large projected sections surrounding their base; Scharoun emulated this form.

50. See Martin Mächler to Kurt Liebknecht, September 1, 1950, SAPMO-BA, DH2(K1) A/47.

51. Brockschmidt, Memorandum, October 9, 1950, SAPMO-Barch, DH2 (K1) A/47.

52. In Petras, *Das Schloss*, 116.

53. Pisternik, Minutes of meeting, August 7, 1950.

54. Gerhard Strauss, "Denkmalpflegerische Arbeiten gelegentlich des erörterten Abbruches des Stadtschlosses Berlin," August 11, 1950, SAPMO-BA, DH2, (K1) A/47.

55. Ibid.

56. Gerhard Strauss to Walter Pisternik, File note, August 23, 1950, SAPMO-BA, DH1-39075.

57. Gerhard Strauss, "Was ist das Berliner Schloss," September 1950, quoted in Petras, *Das Schloss*, 136–137.

58. Ibid.

59. In response to nineteenth-century preservationists "damaging" monuments by attempting to restore them to their original state, Georg Dehio, one of the most influential preservationists in German history, declared, "The first 'commandment' of preservation was 'conserve, do not restore'" (Koshar, *Germany's Transient Pasts*, 32). Both approaches would continue in Germany into the post–World War II era.

60. It can be difficult to separate traditionalist from socialist-realist discourse in the arguments of the cultural elite as their stances toward architecture are somewhat intertwined: both held artistic value to have enduring national significance and political connotations to be ephemeral. Those protesting the demolition would emphasize these points as they recognized iconoclastic undertones in the decision. Socialist realism more elaborately theorized the relationship between culture and politics and the process of change, but this is rarely

identifiable in short statements. Not all efforts to protest the demolition are discussed in this section, as key arguments are repeated.

61. Richard Hamann to Otto Grotewohl, August 30, 1950, reprinted in Petras, *Das Schloss*, 137; Wolf Schubert to Walter Ulbricht, August 28, 1950, reprinted in Petras, *Das Schloss*, 138–139; and Johannes Stroux to Walter Ulbricht, August 29, 1950, reprinted in Petras, *Das Schloss*, 139–140.

62. Moritz van Dülmen, Wolf Kühnelt, and Bjoern Weigel, *Zerstörte Vielfalt, Berlin 1933–1938–1945: Eine Stadt erinnert sich*, 3rd edition (Berlin: Kulturprojecte Berlin GmbH, 2013), 226–231.

63. Petras, *Das Schloss*, 119–121.

64. Berlin Magistrat, Resolution, May 25, 1948, LAB, 100–818.

65. Berlin Magistrat, Resolution, April 28, 1949, LAB 100–837.

66. "Marienkirche wiedererstanden," *Tägliche Rundschau* (hereafter *TR*), October 3, 1948.

67. Untitled photo with caption, *Berliner Zeitung* (hereafter *BZ*), September 16, 1951.

68. "Der Berliner Dom—wie er war und ist," *BZ*, December 25, 1951.

69. Schlögl, *Terror und Traum*, 75–76.

70. Prehm, File note, September 2, 1950, SAPMO-BA, DH1, 39075.

71. Tzschorn to Lothar Bolz, September 11, 1950, SAPMO-BA, DH1, 44476.

72. Gerhard Strauss to Walter Pisternik, September 13, 1950, SAPMO-BA, DH1, 39075.

73. Walter Pisternik to *Deutsche Kulturbund*, September 16, 1950, SAPMO-BA, H1, 44476.

74. Helmut Räther, *Vom Hohenzollernschloss zum Roten Platz: Die Umgestaltung des Berliner Stadtzentrums* (Berlin: Verlag für politische Pulizistik, 1952).

75. Ibid., 35–36.

76. Walter Ulbricht to Helmut Räther, September 18, 1950, quoted in Räther, *Vom Hohenzollernschloss*, 36.

77. Occasionally his views coincided with socialist realism, such as the imperative of building on national culture.

78. Walter Hentschel to Hermann Weidhaas, October 17, 1950, quoted in Petras, *Das Schloss*, 141.

79. See "Angeklagter Andreas Schlüter schuldig—Urteil wird vollstreckt," *Der Tag*, September 3, 1950; "Hofapotheke wurde gesprengt," *Neue Zeitung*, September 8, 1950; "'Fata Morgana,'" *Neue Zeitung*, September 9, 1950; "Bildersturm an der Spree," *Tagesspiegel*, September 9, 1950; and "Damit sie aufmarschieren können," *Neue Zeitung*, September 10, 1950.

80. "Bleibt das Berliner Schloss erhalten?" *Telegraf*, September 2, 1950.

81. Margarete Kühn, "Berliner Schloss vor dem Untergang," October 1, 1950, *Tagesspiegel*.

82. Gerhard Strauss, Notes from lecture, "Kulturdenkmalpflege als neue Aufgabe" at the Kulturbund in Berlin, March 3, 1948, SAPMO-BA, DH2 (K4) I-25.

83. Strauss and the engineer Hermann Weidhaas developed a work schedule based on the availability of labor, finance, and equipment (Walter Pisternik to Karl Brockschmidt, August 31, 1950, SAPMO-BA, DH1, 38927). Strauss's list of details to be removed was not to be found among his files.

84. Gerhard Strauss, "Bericht über die wissenschaftlichen und denkmalpflegerischen Arbeiten bis 30 September 1950," November 8, 1950, SAPMO-BA, DH1, 39075.

85. Koshar, *Germany's Transient Pasts*, 215 and 258.

86. Most belonged to East German political organizations (i.e., Free German Youth, Society for German-Soviet Friendship, Free German Trade Union Federation). Of the two photographers "both were recommended as trustworthy expressly by Dr. Greisler... even though they live in West Berlin. They are both members of the SED" (Gerhard Strauss, Memorandum to Walter Pisternik, September 6, 1950, SAPMO-BA, DH1, 39075). The students were subjected to regular ideological and political discussions and developed "a poster on the demolitions prepared by the Western powers in West Germany" (Strauss, "Bericht über die wissenschaftlichen," November 8, 1950). Control was also extended over the firms carrying out the demolition work—only VEBs (nationalized construction firms) were allowed (Pisternik to Brockschmidt, August 31, 1950, SAPMO-BA, DH1, 38927).

87. Gerhard Strauss to Walter Pisternik, September 1, 1950, SAPMO-BA, DH1-39075.

88. Gerhard Strauss to Prehm, Ministry of Building, September 6, 1950, SAMPMO-BA, DH1-39075.

89. Juencke and Clasen, Untitled resolution, October 20, 1950, SAPMO, FBS, 123/16322.

90. "Lenin und die Schlossruine," *BZ*, September 7, 1950.

91. Ibid.

92. Werner Poppe and G. Thron, "Gutachten über die Wiederaufbaukosten des Berliner Schosses," November 13, 1950, LAB, 110/365. Although Robert Taylor suggested the possibility that in the years prior to its demolition, the palace may in fact have become irreparable (Robert Taylor, *Hohenzollern Berlin* [Ontario: Meany Publishers, 1985]: 35), Poppe and Thron's document demonstrates otherwise. Later estimates would amplify the cost of restoration to as much as DM 50 million ("Museale Auswertung des Berliner Schlosses," *Der Morgen*, February 25, 1951) and assert that even maintaining the palace would cost millions per year ("Dreitausend Baupläne entdeckt," *National Zeitung*, February 25, 1951). In contrast, none of Scharoun's requests for funding to maintain the palace had exceeded RM 100,000.

93. Ministerium für Aufbau (hereafter MfA), Hauptamt Stadtplanung, *Termin- und Kostenplan für die vorläufige Umgestaltung des Lustgartens*, August 19, 1950, SAPMO-BA, DH1, 39075.

94. Juencke and Clasen, Untitled resolution, October 20, 1950, SAPMO-BA, FBS 123/16322.

95. Kurt Liebknecht to Demokratische Frauenbund Deutschlands, September 2, 1950, SAPMO-BA, DH2 (K1) A/47.

96. Gerhard Strauss to Walter Pisternik, September 7, 1950, SAPMO-BA, DH1, 39075.

97. Gerhard Strauss to Walter Pisternik, September 8, 1950, SAPMO-BA, DH1-38927.

98. Ibid.

99. Gerhard Strauss to Walter Pisternik, September 13, 1950, SAPMO-BA, DH1, 39075.

100. Petras, *Das Schloss*, 122.

101. Jahnke, File note, September 28, 1950, SAPMO-BA, H1, 44230.

102. Ibid.

103. MfA, *Termin- und Kostenplan*, August 19, 1950.

104. Petras, *Das Schloss*, 131–132.

105. Gerhard Strauss to Walter Pisternik, November 28, 1950, SAPMO-BA, DH1, 39075.

106. "Es war gar nicht alles Silber," *BZ*, July 2, 1951.

107. Koshar, *Germany's Transient Pasts*, 60.

108. "Kunsthistoriker und Studenten in selbstlosem Einsatz," *National Zeitung*, January 28, 1951.

109. MfA, Hauptabteilung II, "Bericht von der Uberprüfung der Baustelle Schlossruine, Lustgarten," December 12, 1950, SAPMO-BA, DH1, 39075.

110. Strauss, "Denkmalpflege an der Schlossruin in Berlin," *Planen und Bauen* 4 (1950): 384–385.

111. Ibid.

112. Hans Scharoun, Draft resolution for Berlin Magistrat, August 15, 1945, LAB 110/910.

113. "Museale Auswertung des Berliner Schlosses," *Der Morgen*, February 25, 1951.

114. Karl Brockschmidt to Walter Pisternik, February 13, 1951, SAPMO-BA, DH1-38927.

115. Berlin City Planning Commission, Minutes from meetings on February 14, 1951, and March 14, 1951, SAPMO-BA, DH1, 38881.

116. Gerhard Strauss to Berlin Magistrat, Historic Preservation Office, May 23, 1951, SAPMO-BA, DH1, 38927; and Gerhard Strauss to Berlin Magistrat, Historic Preservation Office, May 24, 1951, SAPMO-BA, DH1, 38927.

117. Strauss to Berlin Magistrat, May 24, 1951.

118. Berlin City Planning Commission, Minutes of meeting, September 19, 1951, SAPMO-BA, DH1, 38881.

119. Berlin City Planning Commission, Minutes of meeting, April 16, 1952, SAPMO-BA, DH1, 38881.

120. Ibid.

121. Strauss to Kurt Liebknecht, June 9, 1951, SAPMO-BA, DH2 (K1) A/47.

122. See "Cultural Barbarism," *Telegraf*, September 7, 1950; "Bildersturm an der Spree," *Tagesspiegel*, September 9, 1950; "Zerstörung des Stadtschloss ein Akt vandalismus," *Neue Zeitung*, September 9, 1950; Georg Pless, "Damit sie aufmarschieren können," *Neue Zeitung*, September 10, 1950; and "Früher Lustgarten—Heute Schandflecke," *Tagesspiegel*, March 31, 1951.

123. "Die Geschichte vom versunkenem Schloβ," *BZ*, February 26, 1951.

124. "Es regnet noch immer auf Pergamon," *Kurrier*, March 27, 1951.

125. "Früher Lustgarten—heute Schandfleck," *Der Tagesspiegel*, March 31, 1951.

126. Ministerrat, "Auszug aus dem Protokoll der 38 Sitzung der Provisorische Regierung der Deutsche Demokratische Republik am 23.8.50," August 25, 1950, SAPMO-BA, H1, 44476.

127. Berlin Planning Commission, Minutes from meeting, October 2, 1950, SAPMO-BA, DH1, 38927.

128. Berlin City Planning Commission, Minutes from meeting, March 14, 1951, SAPMO-BA, DH1, 38881.

129. Hans Jendretsky to Erich Honecker, March 19, 1951, SAPMO-BA, DH1, 39026.

130. Berlin Planning Commission, Minutes of first meeting of Marx-Engels memorial committee, February 2, 1951, SAPMO-BA, DH1-38881.

131. Kurt Liebknecht to Wilhelm Pieck, March 24, 1951, SAPMO-BA, FBS 93/1115, NL38 623–628.

132. Kurt Liebknecht, File notes on Berlin City Planning Commission meeting on April 11, 1951, April 12, 1951, SAPMO-BA, DH2, A/107.

133. Politburo, Resolution, May 15, 1951, SAPMO-BA, DY30/51.

134. Bruno Flierl, *Gebaute DDR: Über Stadtplaner, Architekten, und die Macht* (Berlin: Verlag für Bauwesen, 1996): 132. Flierl's insider view holds that a conflict between sculptors and politicians over the size, "artistic form" of the memorial, and its scaled relationship to the oversized square created "irritation and confusion, which could hardly be comprehended from the details in the files. Archival records provide support for Flierl's assertions and provide additional insights to the basis for the conflict.

135. Gustav Sietz to Engel, Director, Deutsche Akademie der Kunst, June 27, 1951, SAPMO-BA, DH2, A/107.

136. See Hain, "Reise nach Moskau."

137. Politburo, Resolution, July 24, 1951, SAPMO-BA, DY30/51.

138. Wilhelm Pieck to the Central Committee of the Communist Party of the Soviet Union, c/o Suslow, November 22, 1951, SAPMO-BA, FBS 93/1115, NL38, 624.

139. Berlin Planning Commission, File notes on meeting with Wilhelm Pieck over the design of a Marx-Engels memorial, December 5, 1951, SAPMO-BA, DH1-38881.

140. Cremer was previously a member of the KPD and recently had an exhibition in West Berlin closed by the police. SED cultural leaders considered him "one of the most capable and recognized sculptors in all of Germany," who had created "representative memorials for the victims of fascism in Vienna and Matthausen." Zentralkomittee der SED Kulturabteilung, File note on sculptors invited to meeting with Wilhelm Pieck, December 4, 1951, SAPMO-BA, NL38, 624.

141. Suslow to the Central Committee of the Communist Party of the Soviet Union, February 9, 1952, SAPMO-BA, FBS 93/1115, NL 38 624.

142. Flierl, *Gebaute DDR*, 132.

143. Ibid., 132–134.

144. Ibid.

145. "Die Toten mahnen die Lebenden," *TR*, September 11, 1945.

146. "Den lebenden zur Pflicht," *Tagesspiegel*, September 24, 1946; and "Die Toten mahnen die Lebenden," *TR*, September 24, 1946.

147. "Die Toten mahnen," *TR*, September 16, 1947.

148. Jörn Schütrumpf, "Besprechungen zwischen ehemaligen VVN-Kameraden… dürfen nicht mehr stattfinden: Antifaschismus in der DDR," in *Parteiauftrag: Ein Neues Deutschland: Bilder, Rituale, und Symbole der früheren DDR* (Berlin: Deutsches Historisches Museum, 1996), 142–152.

149. "Grosskundgebung gegen Faschismus und Krieg," *TR*, September 14, 1948; and "Friedenstaube über den OdF Gedenkkundgebung," *TR*, September 13, 1949.

150. "Befohlene Aufmarsch im Lustgarten," *Tagesspiegel*, September 14, 1949.

151. Pisternik, Minutes of meeting, August 7, 1950.

152. MfA, Hauptabteilung II, Notes on meeting with executive committee of Berlin VVN, August 18, 1950, SAPMO-BA, DH1, 38927.

153. Flierl (*Gebaute DDR*, 131) argues that the decision was prompted by the recent dissolution of the FIAPP, which may have been the case, but the memorial project would continue as would the annual ceremony.

154. Käding to Mayor Fritz Ebert, June 15, 1951, SAPMO, DH1, 39026; and Politburo, resolution, June 12, 1951, SAPMO-BA, DY30/51.

155. Thälmann was an icon for antifascist resistance, heralded in 1951 VVN celebrations; see Herf, *Divided Memory*, 165.

156. Flierl, *Gebaute DDR*, 100.

157. Karl Forssman, *Karl Friedrich Schinkel: Bauwerke und Baugedanken* (Munich: Schnell and Steiner, 1981), 202–205.

158. Berlin Magistrat, Resolution, July 7, 1947, reprinted as attachment on November 17, 1947, LAB, 100–801.

159. MfA, *Der Lustgarten*, August 31, 1950. Regierung der DDR and Berlin Magistrat, Draft guidelines for "Wettbewerb zur Erlangung von Entwurfen fur die Neugestaltung der Strasse Unter den Linden und des Lustgartens in Berlin, der Hauptstadt Deutschlands," January 16, 1951, SAPMO-BA, DH1, 39026.

160. Strauss to Stadtplanungskommission, undated, SAPMO-BA, DH2, (K4) I/25.

161. Bruno Flierl, "Engagement gegen den Abriss der Bauakademie—Bericht," in *Mythos Bauakademie: Austellungskatalog*, ed. Doris Fouquet-Plümacher (Berlin and Munich: Verlag für Bauwesen, 1998), 102–112.

162. Deutsche Bauakademie, Notes on the consultation and draft resolution for the socialist redesign of Berlin, especially the extension of the Stalinallee, October 15, 1958, SAPMO-BA, DH2, DBA, A/305.

163. Deutsche Bauakademie, File note on meeting with the Department of Trade and Provision, Berlin Magistrat, December 19, 1958, SAPMO-Barch, DH2-DBA/A/305.

164. Strauss to Girnus, Gißke and Verner, November 29, 1959, quoted in Flierl, "Engagement gegen den Abriss," 104.

165. Flierl, "Engagement gegen den Abriss," 102–107.

166. Gerhard Strauss to German Building Academy, April 10, 1952, SAPMO-BA, DH2-I/32.

167. Politburo, Minutes of meeting on Aufbau des Stadtzentrums der Hauptstadt der Deutsche Demokratische Republic and attachment "Schinkel's Bauakademie," April 11, 1961, SAPMO-BA, DY30-61 (759).

168. Pugh, *Divided Berlin*, 170–185.

169. "Die Grosse Saal in Palast der Republik," *BZ*, July 10, 1975.

5. Wilhelmstrasse

Epigraph: *Neues Deutschland*, November 29, 1949.

1. Demps, *Berlin–Wilhelmstrasse*, 12–30.

2. Ibid., 16–61.

3. Ibid., 67–71.

4. Ibid., 84–99; and Hans Wilderotter, *Alltag der Macht: Berlin Wilhelmstrasse* (Berlin: Jovis, 1998), 12–20.

5. Demps, *Berlin-Wilhelmstrasse*, 103–139; and Wilderotter, *Alltag der Macht*, 21–51.

6. Wilderotter, *Alltag der Macht*, 51; Demps, *Berlin-Wilhelmstrasse*, 166–169.

7. Angelika Benz, "The Kaiserhof—From Berlin's Premier Address to a Nazi Forum," in *Zerstörte Vielfalt Berlin 1933—1938—1945: Eine Stadt erinnert sich*, ed. Moritz van Dülmen, Wolf Kühnelt, and BjornWeigel (Berlin: Kulturprojekte Berlin, 2013), 222; and Wilderotter, *Alltag der Macht*, 51–61.

8. Demps, *Berlin-Wilhelmstrasse*, 207–224.

9. Ibid., 219–224; Wilderotter, *Alltag der Macht*, 75–83; and Matthew Philipotts, "Cultural-political Palimpsests: The Reich Aviation Ministry and the Multiple Temporalities of Dictatorship," *New German Critique* 39, no. 3 (2012): 207–230.

10. Demps, *Berlin-Wilhelmstrasse*, 207–218, 225–244—citation 228–229; and Wilderotter, *Alltag der Macht*, 71–75. Regarding Hitler's personality cult and its role in supporting Nazi political aims, see Ian Kershaw, *The Hitler Myth: Image and Reality in the Third Reich* (Oxford: Oxford University Press, 2001).

11. Demps, *Berlin-Wilhelmstrasse*, 262–263, 271–272.

12. Regarding the restoration of the Finance Ministry, see Berlin Magistrat, Resolution, November 26, 1945, Landesarchiv Berlin (hereafter LAB) 100, R-762.

13. Berlin Magistrat, Resolution, November 17, 1947, LAB 100–801; Demps, *Berlin-Wilhelmstrasse*, 262–264; Ladd, *Ghosts of Berlin*, 146; and James Corum, "The Luftwaffe's Army Support Doctrine, 1918–1941," *Society for Military History* 59, no. 1 (1995): 53–76.

14. Daniel Mühlenfeld, "Between State and Party: Position and Function of the Gau Propaganda Leader in National Socialist Leadership," *German History* 28, no. 2 (2010): 167–192; and David Welch, "Nazi Propaganda and the Volksgemeinschaft: Constructing a People's Community," *Journal of Contemporary History* 39, no. 2 (2004): 213–238.

15. "Die Erste Deutsche Volkskammer," *Neues Deutschland* (hereafter *ND*), October 8, 1949; and "Deutsche Demokratische Republik Gegründet," *Berliner Zeitung* (hereafter *BZ*), October 8, 1949.

16. Demps, *Berlin-Wilhelmstrasse*, 266.

17. Walter Pisternik to Heinrich Rau, August 17, 1950, Stiftung Archiv der Parteien und Massenorganizationen der DDR im Bundesarchiv (hereafter SAPMO-BA), H1, 38614.

18. Brockschmidt to Bolz, July 6, 1950, SAPMO-BA, H2, HK1.

19. Ladd, *Ghosts of Berlin*, 130–131.

20. Walter Pisternik to Heinrich Rau, August 17, 1950, SAPMO-BA, H1, 38614.

21. Demps, *Berlin-Wilhelmstrasse*, 264.

22. Demps argues this case while acknowledging that no archival or press sources directly substantiate the claim. His primary evidence is the following: (1) several government ministries were located on and around Wilhelmstrasse; (2) the *ND* article examined in the previous section referred to a future with diplomats going into the world from Thälmannplatz; and (3) the demolition of the Ordenspalais greatly increased the size of Thälmannplatz, making it a potential central square for demonstrations. Demps asserts that this idea was abandoned when the square proved too small for mass events at the Deutschlandtreffen

of the Free German Youth celebration in May 1950, and activities were transferred to the Lustgarten, drawing the focus of planners there. This was apparently substantiated later that year when *ND* editor Wilhelm Girnus, in defense of the decision to demolish the palace, informed Richard Hamann that the Deutschlandtreffen had proven that Wilhelmstrasse's narrow streets were inadequately wide to work as the city center. (Wilhelm Girnus, discussion with Richard Hamann, September 1950, quoted in Räther, *Vom Hohenzollernschloss zum Roten Platz*, 14). Girnus's statement was likely a polemical move without foundation. The press did not report any mass events on Wilhelmplatz during the Deutschlandtreffen. To the contrary, the demonstration plan announcing these routes for the "great demonstration of 500,000 young German peace-fighters" marching to the Lustgarten had been published in *ND* on May 18, 1950. Half of the participants marched north on Wilhelmstrasse to Unter den Linden; the other half approached marching south on Friedrichstrasse. On May 31, 1950, *ND* reported that seven hundred thousand participated, filling the Lustgarten and surrounding streets. Moreover, in December 1950, plans to widen Wilhelmstrasse remained as it was a street for monumental architecture representing the state (Kurt Leucht, "Die Neuplanung Berlin," *Planen und Bauen* 4, no. 12 [1950]: 381–383).

23. "Vom Wilhelmplatz zum Thälmannplatz," *ND*, November 29, 1949.

24. Ibid.

25. Regarding Ministerium für Aufbau (MfA) jurisdiction over planning in Berlin, see Lothar Bolz to Otto Grotewohl, November 28, 1949, SAPMO-BA, DH1-39026. On Thälmannplatz station, see Arnold Münter, File note, May 11, 1950, LAB-848

26. "Schönster Bahnhof: 'Thälmannplatz,'" *BZ*, August 19, 1950; and "In 108 Tagen entstand Station Thälmannplatz," *ND*, August 19, 1950.

27. Karl Brockschmidt to Lothar Bolz, July 6, 1950, SAPMO-BA, H2, HK1.

28. MfA, Oberbauleitung für Regierungsbauten, "Liste der Bauvorhaben nach dem Stand vom 24.5.1950," May 24, 1950, SAPMO-BA, H1, 44476; Politburo, Plan des Neuaufbaus von Berlin, August 15, 1950, reprinted Durth, Düwel, and Gutschow, *Aufbau*, 220–222. MfA, Hauptamt Stadtplanung, *Termin- und Kostenplan für die vorläufige Umgestaltung des Lustgartens,* August 19, 1950, SAPMO-BA, DH1, 39075.

29. Demps, *Berlin-Wilhelmstrasse,* 267–268.

30. "Das neue Gesicht der Haupstadt Berlin," *Der Morgen*, August 25, 1950.For information on the jury and the winning design, see Demps, *Berlin-Wilhelmstrasse*, 268–271.

31. Wilhelm Pieck, File note on meeting with Aljoschin and Orlow, February 8, 1952, SAPMO-BA, FBS 93/1115, NL 38-624. Pieck's notes on the meeting consist only of short phrases, such as "53 figures marching," presumably following Thälmann as their leader.

32. Walter Pisternik, File note, September 13, 1950, SAPMO-BA, DH1, 38927; and Walter Pisternik, File note on Planungskomission meeting, November 29, 1950, SAPMO-BA, DH1, 38927.

33. Berlin City Planning Commission, Minutes of meeting, February 27, 1952, SAPMO-BA, DH1, 38881.

34. Herf, *Divided Memory*, 162–167.

35. For instance, in 1953 the Politburo approved measures to memorialize "the death site of Ernst Thälmann," which was the concentration camp Buchenwald. The mess hall was to be

transformed into a permanent exhibition honoring the "patriotic character of the antifascist resistance" and report on Thälmann's life in the camp, "Hitler-fascism," and its successors. The array of groups persecuted here was completely ignored. Politburo, Resolution, July 18, 1953, SAPMO-BA, DY 30/53.

36. Herf, *Divided Memory*, 162–167.

37. Berlin City Planning Commission, Minutes of meeting, August 27, 1952, SAPMO-BA, DH1, 38881; and Politburo, Resolution, June 3, 1952, SAPMO-BA, DY30/52.

38. Politburo, Resolution, October 21, 1952, DY 30/52.

39. Karl Menzel, "Über die wissenschaftlichen Grundlagen für den Neuaufbau Berlins," *Deutsche Architektur* (hereafter *DA*) 3, no. 4 (1954): 145–153.

40. Demps, *Berlin-Wilhelmstrasse*, 282.

41. Ibid.

42. "Aufmarschplan zur Grosskundgebung," *BZ*, September 10, 1953; "Sojas Mutter sprach zur Jugend," *BZ*, September 14, 1954; "Berliner Kämpfer Gelobnis gegen Nazi-Barbarei," *BZ*, September 13, 1955; and "120 000 auf dem August-Bebel-Platz," *BZ*, September 11, 1956.

43. Politburo, Resolution, March 20, 1956, SAPMO-BA, DY30/56.

44. Demps, *Berlin-Wilhelmstrasse*, 283–284.

45. This suggests that the project was no longer a serious concern of the state by the mid-1950s. No concrete plans for Thälmannplatz emerged before the construction of the Wall relegated the area to obscurity.

46. Notes on consultation over the socialist redesign of Berlin, October 15, 1958, SAPMO-BA, DH2, DBA/A/305.

47. Bruno Flierl, "Politische Wandbilder und Denkmäler im Stadtraum," speech delivered at the symposium "Auf der Suche nach dem verlorenen Staat: Die Kunst der Parteien und Massenorganizationen," December 13–14, 1993, in Flierl, *Gebaute DDR*, 100.

48. Stroux to Ebert, January 6, 1950, reprinted in Petras, *Das Schloss*, 134.

49. Brockschmidt to Bolz, July 6, 1950, SAPMO-BA, DH2-A47. Planners still tended to refer to the street as "Wilhelmstrasse" rather than "Thälmannstrasse."

50. Demps, *Berlin-Wilhelmstrasse*, 213, 264, 271–272; and Stroux to Ebert, January 6, 1950.

51. Joseph Goebbels, *Vom Kaiserhof zur Reichskanzlei: Eine historische Darstellung im Tagbuchblätter* (Munich: Zentralverlage der NSDAP, 1941).

52. Christiane Kuller, *Bürokratie und Verbrechen: Antisemitsiche Finanzpolitik und Verwaltungspraxis im nationalsozialistischen Deutschland*, Das Reichsfinanzministerium im Nationalsozialismus series (Munich: De Gruyter, 2013).

53. Robert Habel, "Berliner City-Architektur (1871–1933)," *ICOMOS-Hefte des Deutschen Nationalkomitees* 54, no. 2 (2015): 195–203.

54. Gerhard Strauss, "Die Berliner Bautradition," *BZ*, February 3, 1952. As a step toward modernism, the building retained considerable links to traditional architecture, particularly gothic. See Robert Habel, "Das Warenthaus Wertheim—Eine Inkunable der Moderne," in *Alfred Messel: 1853–1909 Visionär der Großstadt*, ed. Elke Blauert, Robert Habel, and Hans-Dieter Nägelke (Berlin: Staatlichen Museen zu Berlin, 2009).

55. Berlin City Planning Commission, Minutes, February 27, 1952, SAPMO-BA, DH1-38881.

56. Berlin City Planning Commission, Minutes, May 7, 1952, SAPMO-BA, DH1-38881.

57. Stroux to Ebert, January 6, 1950.

58. Berlin City Planning Commission, Minutes, February 27, 1952, SAPMO-BA, DH1-38881.

59. Demps, *Berlin-Wilhelmstrasse*, 286–287.

60. Stroux to Ebert, January 6, 1950; and Stadtplanungskommission Berlin, Minutes, February 27, 1952, SAPMO-BA, DH-1, 38881.

6. Stalinallee

Epigraph: Walter Ulbricht, "Vörwarts für den Frieden, Einheit, Demokratie und Sozialismus," speech at the 2nd Party Conference of the SED, July 9, 1952, quoted in Durth, Düwel, and Gutschow, *Aufbau*, 92.

1. Nicolaus and Obeth, *Die Stalinallee*, 17–24.

2. Ibid., 31–34.

3. Geist and Kürvers, *Berliner Mietshaus*, 278, 281.

4. Nicolaus and Obeth, *Die Stalinallee*, 21–34.

5. Geist and Kürvers, *Berliner Mietshaus*, 284.

6. "Wie werden wir wohnen?" *Neuen Berliner Illustrierte*, September 2, 1946.

7. The Athens Charter had used the term to refer to an individual apartment or dwelling unit, but here it referred to what the Charter considered a "habitation unit," essentially a neighborhood.

8. Scharoun developed the urban design plan for Siemenstadt, designed several buildings, and had resided there. Eberhard Syring and Jörg Kirschenmann, *Hans Scharoun, 1893–1972: Outsider of Modernism* (Cologne: Taschen, 2004).

9. Planungskollektiv, *Berlin Plant/Erster Bericht*, exhibition, 1946, panels reproduced in Geist and Kürvers, *Berliner Mietshaus*, 186–217; and Geist and Kürvers, *Berliner Mietshaus*, 186–203, 284–288.

10. Planungskollektiv, *Berlin Plant*, 207–209.

11. Karl Marx, *Communist Manifesto*. For diverse views of socialist thinkers taking critical views of the family, see Chapter 1 of Richard Stites, *Revolutionary Dreams: Utopian Vision and Experimental Life in the Russian Revolution* (Oxford: Oxford University Press, 1989).

12. August Bebel, *Die Frau und der Sozialismus* (Zurich: Verlag der Volksbuchhandlung, 1879).

13. Planungskollektiv, *Berlin Plant*, 207–209. Units in multifamily housing would range from 25 to 40 square meters (269 to 431 square feet) and comprise 52 percent of the housing stock according to estimated demand. Single-family houses would range from 65 to 80 square meters (700 to 861 square feet) and comprise 48 percent of units.

14. "Wie werden wir wohnen?"

15. Planungskollektiv, *Berlin Plant*, 207–213.

16. Geist and Kürvers, *Berliner Mietshaus*, 272–290.

17. Heinrich Starck, "Berlin plant und baut," *Bauplanung und Bautechnik* 3, no. 11 (1949): 345–355.

18. Hans Scharoun, "Zur Wohnzelle Friedrichshain," November 7, 1949, quoted in Geist and Kürvers, *Berliner Mietshaus*, 297–302.

19. The term *Heimstätte* was associated with programs established in cities throughout Germany after World War I to construct social housing in a time of dire need. Their housing was typically, but not always, single-family in small developments. In Berlin the GEHAG was the best known of these, the letter "h" in the acronym standing for *Heimstätte*. It produced renown modernist developments on the city's periphery, with walk-up apartments as the dominant building type. The program endured through the Nazi era with greater integration into the *Heimatschutz* tradition, including a preference for single-family houses in a traditional style with sloped "German roofs" in small developments. This was set in opposition to the evil big city, yet by the mid-1930s pressing demand necessitated the addition of urban projects. After the war, GEHAG property was divided among the occupying powers. Brockschmidt had worked for GEHAG since 1937 and was placed in charge of its administration in the Soviet sector. See Wolfgang Schäche, *75 Jahre GEHAG* (Berlin: Gebr. Mann, 1999).

20. Heinrich Starck, "Berlins Neuaufbau beginnt," *Demokratischer Aufbau* 1 (1950), quoted in Geist and Kürvers, *Berliner Mietshaus*, 303–304.

21. Politburo, Resolution, December 19, 1949, SAPMO-BA, DY30-49.

22. Lothar Bolz to Otto Grotewohl, November 16, 1950, SAMPO-BA, FBS, 123/16322.

23. Lothar Bolz, Memorandum, "Zur Rekonstruktion Moskaus," December 24, 1949, SAPMO-BA, H1-44476.

24. Robert von Halasz, "Bewährte neue Bauweise," *Bauplanung und Bautechnik* 4, no. 1 (1950): 9–14; and Kurt Liebknecht, "Der Architect beim Aufbau," *Bauplanung und Bautechnik* 4, no. 1 (1950): 15–17.

25. Nicolaus and Obeth, *Die Stalinallee*, 52–58.

26. Walter Pisternik, Minutes of meeting with Will Stoph, March 31, 1950, SAPMO-BA, DH2(K1) A/47. Regarding width at 75 meters, see Liebknecht, Notes on meeting on April 3, 1950, SAPMO-BA, DH2(K1) A/57.

27. Nicolaus and Obeth, *Die Stalinallee*, 57.

28. Karl Brockschmidt, "Der Aufbauplan für die deutsche Hauptstadt," *Demokratischer Aufbau* 10 (1950): 263, reprint, Geist and Kürvers, *Berliner Mietshaus*, 309–310.

29. Walter Ulbricht, "Die Grossbauten im Fünfjahrplan," speech at the Third Party Congress of the SED, quoted in *Neues Deutschland* (hereafter *ND*), July 23, 1950.

30. Kurt Liebknecht, Notes on meeting with City Planning Commission Berlin, Pisternik and Iljen, September 25, 1950, SAPMO-BA, DH2(K1), A/57.

31. Durth, Düwel, and Gutschow, *Ostkreuz*, 188.

32. Nicolaus and Obeth, *Die Stalinallee*, 73.

33. "Aufbauplan fur das Zentrum des neuen Berlin," *Berliner Zeitung* (hereafter *BZ*), August 27, 1950.

34. Nicolaus and Obeth, *Die Stalinallee*, 73; and Durth, Düwel, and Gutschow, *Ostkreuz*, 188.

35. Pisternik, Notes on meeting with Illjen, September 25, 1950, SAPMO-BA, DH2(K1), A/47.

36. Karl Brockschmidt, Notes on meeting with SKK, October 9, 1950, SAPMO-BA, DH2(K1), A/47.

37. Willi Stoph, "Der Aufbauplan Berlins-Angelegenheit der gesamten Berliner Bevolkerung," *ND*, October 20, 1950.

38. Nicolaus and Obeth, *Die Stalinallee*, 74–75.

39. Hermann Henselmann, Undated file note, SAPMO-BA, DH2(K1), A/47.

40. Nicolaus and Obeth, *Die Stalinallee*, 75.

41. Ibid., 76.

42. Ibid., 84–85.

43. "Neue Sporthalle bis August fertig," *BZ*, April 12, 1951.

44. "Straussberger Platz wird nich dunkel," *BZ*, May 13, 1951.

45. "Stalin-Denkmal in Berlin enthüllt," *BZ*, August 4, 1951.

46. Rudolf Herrnstadt, "Über den Baustil, den politischen Stil und den Genossen Henselmann," *ND*, July 31, 1951.

47. Ibid.

48. Werner Durth, Interview with Hermann Henselmann, 1985, quoted in Durth, Düwel, and Gutschow, *Ostkreuz*, 267–268.

49. Nicolaus and Obeth, *Die Stalinallee*, 87.

50. "Unsere Architekten Antworten," *ND*, August 3, 1951.

51. Kurt Liebknecht to MfA, March 28, 1951, SAPMO-BA, DH2 (IV), DBA, A/34; and Nicolaus and Obeth, *Die Stalinallee*, 78.

52. Students from Hochschule für Architektur Weimar to editorial staff of *ND*, August 1, 1951, DH1-38875.

53. Nicolaus and Obeth, *Die Stalinallee*, 110–115.

54. Kurt Liebknecht, "Im Kampf um eine neue deutsche Architektur," *ND*, February 13, 1951.

55. Gerhard Strauss, "Analysen der Hauptphasen deutscher Baugeschichte," undated, SAPMO-BA, DH2-I/32. It is equally valid to emphasize international influences on traditional German architecture—that is, Italy and the Netherlands. See Horst Büttner and Günter Meissner, *Town Houses of Europe* (New York: St. Martin's Press, 1982).

56. Ibid., 201. Strauss's outline later became the basis for a book that provides some additional observations of the imprint of locality and tradition on adopted foreign building styles. See Deutsche Bauakademie, Institut für Theorie und Geschichte, *Deutsche Baukunst in Zehn Jahrhunderten* (Dresden: Sachensverlag, 1953). Tension had emerged in discussion of the regional and national during the Trip to Moscow (Hain, *Trip to Moscow*, 157), although it appears to have been quickly resolved. The acceptance of diverse expressions (i.e., regional) of national identity appears in Kurt Liebknecht, "Deutsche Architektur," *DA* 1, no. 1 (1952): 6–12.

57. For a classic nineteenth-century text expressing this relationship, see Wilhelm Riehl, *The Natural History of the German People*, ed. and trans. David Diephouse (Lewiston, NY: Edwin Mellen, 1990). For a contemporary analysis, see Celia Appelgate, *A Nation of Provin-*

cials: The German Idea of Heimat (Berkeley: University of California Press, 1990); and David Blackbourn and James Retallack, eds., *Localism, Landscape, and the Ambiguities of Place: German-Speaking Central Europe, 1860–1930* (Toronto: University of Toronto Press, 2007).

58. Kurt Liebknecht, "Über das Typicsche in der Architektur," *Deutsche Architektur* (hereafter *DA*) 2 (1953): 1–3.

59. "Walter Ulbricht besichtigte das Hochhaus," *BZ*, January 18, 1952. The author's comparison of Weberwiese with Schinkel's Villa Jenisch, Feilner House, and other works was based on photographs printed in Erik Forssman, *Karl Friedrich Schinkel Bauwerke und Baugedanken* (Munich: Schnell and Steiner, 1981).

60. Durth, Düwel, and Gutschow, *Aufbau*, 312–313.

61. Nicolaus and Obeth, *Die Stalinallee*, 90

62. "Besuch auf dem Weberwiese," *BZ*, January 18, 1951.

63. "Unsere Architekten antworten," *ND*, August 3, 1951.

64. "Richtkrone auf dem Hochhaus," *BZ*, January 20, 1952.

65. "Wer Wohnungen baut, baut keine Kasernen," *BZ*, December 7, 1951. This was reinforced with more quotes in "Ganz Deutschland unterstützt Aufbau Berlins," *BZ*, December 12, 1951.

66. "Richtfest auf der Weberwiese," *BZ*, December 22, 1951.

67. "Grundstein für Hochaus Weberwiese gelegt," *BZ*, September 2, 1951.

68. Ibid.

69. "Unser kleiner Spaziergang zum Hochhaus," *BZ*, April 27, 1952.

70. "Wer wird im Hochaus wohnen?" *BZ*, May 2, 1952.

71. Nicolaus and Obeth, *Die Stalinallee*, 89.

72. Berlin Magistrat, "Wettberwerbes zur Erlangung von Bebaungsvorschlägen und Entwürfen für die städtebaulichen und architektonischen Gestaltung der Stalinallee," April 25, 1951, quoted in Nicolaus and Obeth, *Die Stalinallee*, 94–96. The jury also included local politicians and representatives from local government, political organizations, and the fields of architecture and construction.

73. Ibid.

74. Ibid.

75. Jury commentary quoted in Nicolaus and Obeth, *Die Stalinallee*, 100–104. Durth, Düwel, and Gutschow's (*Aufbau*, 314) suggestion that commentary was "vague and unsure" regarding architecture as it failed to specify the exact characteristics responsible for similarity to modernism in projects being eliminated seems unfounded. The entire project was under extreme temporal pressure, and elaborating on the details of this relationship would have meant diverting precious time to a dead end.

76. Durth, Düwel, and Gutschow, *Aufbau*, 320.

77. "Preisgerichts Wettbewerb Stalinallee: Vorbemerkung zur Bewertung der eingegangenen Entwürfe," August 29, 1951, quoted in Durth, Düwel, and Gutschow, *Aufbau*, 231–233. Although Hartmann did not belong to the inner circle of Berlin's leading architects, he nonetheless ranked among the most successful architects in the GDR, having won prizes in several competitions in a row. The jury reviewed the DBA entries prior to the deadline, and the intention was to present the plans to the Politburo on the eve of the decision. It is not known

whether this occurred, but it seems that advance approval of the SED leadership was sought. See Nicolaus and Obeth, *Die Stalinallee*, 99.

78. "Preisgerichts Wettbewerb Stalinallee," August 29, 1951.

79. Durth, Düwel, and Gutschow, *Aufbau*, 329.

80. This typically involved a style significant to the nation's architectural heritage: Byzantine tradition in Russia, and gothic in France, England, and Germany. In Norway, vernacular architecture (specifically stave churches) formed the basis for the national architecture. See Anders Åman, *Architecture and Ideology in Eastern Europe during the Stalin Era: An Aspect of Cold War History*, trans. Roger and Kerstin Tanner (New York: Architectural History Foundation and the Massachusetts Institute of Technology, 1992; original edition, City, Stockholm, Sweden: Calsson Bokförlag, 1987), 95–96.

81. Temporal pressure made this even more difficult. The most convincing examples of national differences in the same architectural style emerged gradually. For example, gothic originated in "Isle de France" and spread internationally. Had a medieval builder been directed to create an English form of gothic, the task would have seemed formidable and perhaps contrived. Yet over time a particularly English form of gothic developed. In this case, there were no stylistic references to English precedent, but new forms (i.e., fan vaulting) developed in England.

82. "Das deutsche Volk baut eine neue Hauptstadt," *BZ*, September 9, 1951.

83. Nicolaus and Obeth, *Die Stalinallee*, 99–100.

84. Durth, Düwel, and Gutschow, *Aufbau*, 319

85. Nicolaus and Obeth, *Die Stalinallee*, 121.

86. Ibid., 123

87. Kurt Liebknecht, "Zur Frage der Fensterformen," *DA* 1 (1952): 87–89.

88. Interview with Heinz Auspurg, Materials from exhibition, "Die Stalinallee—Architektur und Alltag, 1951," quoted in Nicolaus and Obeth, *Die Stalinallee*, 118–119.

89. In Durth, Düwel, and Gutschow, *Ostkreuz*, 280–281.

90. Nicolaus and Obeth, *Die Stalinallee*, 123–126. A new competition for the intersection of Besarin Street and Warschauer Street was held in October 1952. Though included in the original Stalinallee competition, it was excluded from further planning because of its special significance for urban design and transportation. As a node in a transition to the city center, the square was to be reserved in size and composition. In January 1953, Henselmann was awarded first place in a competition to design the square. See Nicolaus and Obeth, *Die Stalinallee*, 159–161.

91. Durth, Düwel, and Gutschow, *Aufbau*, 365–368.

92. Ibid.

93. Ibid., 364–368; and Nicolaus and Obeth, *Die Stalinallee*, 157–158.

94. Nicolaus and Obeth, *Die Stalinallee*. For an example from an East German architectural journal, see Deutsche Bauakademie, "Auf dem Wege zu einer sozialistischen deutschen Architektur," *DA* 3 (1953): 97–101.

95. In contrast, Hitler's main boulevard was to be 100 yards wide and two-and-a-half times the length of the Champs Élysées (Speer, *Third Reich*, 73–77).

96. Nicolaus and Obeth (*Die Stalinallee*, 222) describe these features, which create a "lively, emotional silhouette."

97. Ibid., 222–228.

98. Ibid., 134–139.

99. Hermann Henselmann, "Aus der Werkstatt des Architekten," *DA* 1 (1952): 156–165.

100. For a comparison, see Düwel, *Baukunst voran!* 36.

101. Nicolaus and Obeth, *Die Stalinallee*, 159–170; and "Baupläne 1954 stehen zur Diskussion," *BZ*, February 15, 1953.

102. Nicolaus and Obeth, *Die Stalinallee*, 222–228.

103. Ibid.

104. Karl Souradny, "Die künstlerishe Gestaltung des Bauabschnittes F an der Stalinallee," *DA* 1 (1953): 6–12.

105. Nicolaus and Obeth, *Die Stalinallee*, 222–228.

106. Ibid., 157.

107. Durth, Düwel, and Gutschow, *Aufbau*, 358.

108. Gerd Kuhn, *Wohnkultur und kommunale Wohnungspolitik in Frankfurt am Main 1880 bis 1930: Auf dem Wege u einer pluralen Gesellschaft der Individuen* (Bonn: Dietz, 1998). In the Soviet Union alternative forms of social organization and communal facilities were experimented with during the 1920s, but under Stalin the family was restored as the core unit for society and housing; see Christine Hannemann, *Die Platte: Industrialisierter Wohnungsbau in der DDR (Berlin: Schiler)*, 50 and 98.

109. "Wir diskutieren jetzt Wohungstypen 1952," *BZ*, June 17, 1951; Herman Henselmann, "Aus der Werkstatt des Architekten," *DA* 1 (1952): 156–165; and Nicolaus and Obeth, *Die Stalinallee*, 240–214.

110. Durth, Düwel, and Gutschow, *Aufbau*, 156–181; and Thomas Hoscislawski, *Bauen Zwischen Macht und Ohnemacht: Architektur und Städtebau in der DDR* (Berlin: Verlag für Bauwesen), 74–82.

Durth, Düwel, and Gutschow, *Aufbau*, 156–181.

111. Walter Pisternik, Notes on lecture by Victor Baburov at Soviet Ministry of City Building on April 20, 1950, reprinted in Hain, "Reise nach Moskau," 90–95.

112. Durth, Düwel, and Gutschow, *Ostkreuz*, 500.

113. Durth, Düwel, and Gutschow, *Aufbau*, 175.

114. Kurt Junghans, "Über die Gruppierung der Wohnblocks in Wohnkomplexen," *DA* 1 (1953): 166–173.

115. Kurt Junghans, Felix Boesler, and Ruth Günter, *Der Wohnkomplex als Planungselement im Städtebau* (Berlin: Henschelverlag, 1954).

116. Nicolaus and Obeth, *Die Stalinallee*, 163–166. Regarding Henselmann's conceptualization through dialectics, see p. 283.

117. *ND* editor Rudolf Herrnstadt was believed to have proposed the program, inspired by the example of Warsaw. Durth, Düwel and Gutschow, *Ostkreuz*, 284.

118. Edmund Collein, "Fragen des deutschen Städtebaus," speech given at the first German Architecture Congress in Berlin, December 1951, quoted in *Fragen der deutschen*

Architektur und des Städtebaus, ed. Kurt Liebknecht and Edmund Collein (Berlin: Henschelverlag, 1952): 16.

119. Regarding Marshall Plan funding and exhibits, see Paul Betts, "Building Socialism at Home" in *Socialist Modern: East German Everyday Culture and Politics*, eds. Katherine Pence and Paul Betts (Ann Arbor: University of Michigan Press, 2008), 96–132. Regarding the influence of American support for housing in West Germany, see Durth, Düwel and Gutschow, *Aufbau*, 340 – 347.

120. Draft proposal for the National Building Program, August 2, 1951, quoted in Nicolaus and Obeth, *Die Stalinallee*, 126–127.

121. Fulbrook, *Dissonant Lives*; and "Nationales Aufbaukomitee gebildet," *BZ*, December 23, 1951.

122. "Nationales Aufbauprogramm Berlin," *BZ*, November 27, 1951.

123. "Einmütige Zustimmung der Bevölkerung zu dem Vorschlag des ZK der SED zum Neuaufbau Berlins," *ND*, November 29, 1951.

124. "An Müller, Meier, Schulz! An Alle!" *BZ*, December 16, 1951.

125. Ibid.

126. "Gruβ deren Erbauern der ersten sozialistischen Strasse Berlins!" *BZ*, September 27, 1952.

127. SED Landesleitung Berlin to Bartel, attached report "Jugendarbeit auf der Baustelle E-Süd," SAPMO-BA, FBS93/1131, Nachlass Wilhelm Pieck, 36/684-686.

128. Nicolaus and Obeth, *Die Stalinallee*, 171–188

129. Regarding Lenin and Taylorism, see Hannemann, *Die Platte*, 36.

130. Weitz, *Creating German Communism*, 350–351.

131. Nicolaus and Obeth, *Die Stalinallee*, 155, 196–198; and Durth, Düwel and Gutschow, *Aufbau*, 170.

132. Nicolaus and Obeth, *Die Stalinallee*, 129–130, 145. Regarding Western press allegations see "Sonderbaustab Berlin beantwortete Frage," *BZ*, February 9, 1952.

133. Nicolaus and Obeth, *Die Stalinallee*, 153, 171–182, 198–99.

134. Biersdorf, Berlin Volkseigene Wohnungsverwaltung Friedrichshain to Central Committee of the SED, February 11, 1952; February 13, 1952; February 25, 1952; and March 3, 1952, SAPMO-BA, FBS, 365/15243. Although the bias of published material was not present, it must be considered that Biersdorf was cautious reporting to his superiors in a Stalinist system.

135. Biersdorf, Berlin Volkseigene Wohnungsverwaltung Friedrichshain to Central Committee of the SED, February 11, 1952.

136. "Patyas Rakosi besuchte die Stalinallee," *BZ*, October 28, 1952.

137. Büsche, Berliner Austellungs und Werbebetriebe, Report on the continual building exhibition on the Stalinalle area on the basis of a request of the Central Committee of the SED, December 12, 1951, SAPMO-BA, DH1-38928.

138. "Wochenbilanz des Berliner Aufbauprogramms," *BZ*, January 11, 1952.

139. "Berlin hat zur Schippe gegriffen," *BZ*, January 3, 1952

140. Geist and Kürvers, *Berliner Mietshaus*, 125.

141. W. Taube, "Am Tor lagen Mutter und Kind...," *BZ*, February 3, 1952.

142. "Für gesamtberliner Aufbautag am 3 Februar," *BZ*, January 29, 1952.

143. "Am Sonntag traf sich Berlin in der Stalinallee," BZ, February 5, 1952.

144. "Der 3. Februar in Westberlin," BZ, February 5, 1952.

145. "Dänischer Besuch in der Stalinallee," *BZ*, May 16, 1952; and "Alle wollen unsere Neubauten besichtigen," *BZ*, May 17, 1952.

146. Walter Ulbricht, "Vörwarts für den Frieden, Einheit, Demokratie und Sozialismus," speech at the Second Party Conference of the SED, July 9, 1952, quoted in Durth, Düwel and Gutschow, *Aufbau*, 92.

147. "Richtkronen über drei Blöcke der Stalinallee, *BZ*, July 13, 1952.

148. Rudolf Herrnstadt, speech quoted in "Die erste sozialistische Strasse Berlins," *BZ*, July 13, 1952. While Stalinallee presented a large step forward in nationalizing private property for public housing, the working people who lived there were anything but rulers of their state.

149. Pieck as quoted in "Jubel unter den Richtkronen der Stalinallee," *BZ*, July 15, 1952.

150. "Stalinallee im Rohbau fertiggestellt," *BZ*, September 28, 1952; and "Freunde besuchten die Stalinallee," *BZ*, October 7, 1952.

151. Jendretsky quoted in "Berlin begann das zweite Aufbaujahr," *BZ*, January 3, 1953.

152. "Von der Begeisterung diktiert," *BZ*, January 7, 1953. A selection of articles are cited to illustrate the press representations, but reports on Stalinallee were much more frequent.

153. As described in "Wohnblocks C- und E-sud werden bezogen," *BZ*, January 8, 1953.

154. "Baupläne 1954 stehen zur Diskussion," *BZ*, February 15, 1953; "Das Bautempo steigert sich wieder," *BZ*, February 27, 1953; and "Gedanken am Denkmal in der Stalinallee," *BZ*, March 8, 1953.

155. "Was die Westpresse verschwiegen musste," *BZ*, March 19, 1953; and "Profitsucht bestimmt Westberliner Baupläne," *BZ*, March 27, 1953.

156. Weitz, *Creating German Communism*, 357–360; and Nicolaus and Obeth, *Die Stalinallee*, 199–200.

157. "Einzigartiges Bekenntnis zum Frieden," *BZ*, May 3, 1953.

158. Nicolaus and Obeth, *Die Stalinallee*, 202–206.

159. Ibid., 208–213.

160. "Mauern der Stalinallee wachsen weiter," *BZ*, June 19, 1953.

161. Ibid.

162. "Die Berliner verurteilen die Provokationen," *BZ*, June 19, 1953.

163. "Berlins Werktätige gingen weiter an die Arbeit," *BZ*, June 20, 1953.

164. Stefan Heym, "Gedanken zum 17. Juni 1953," *BZ*, June 21, 1953.

165. "Berliner danken des Sowjetarmee," *BZ*, June 25, 1953.

166. "Fröhlich tanzten Kinder mit den Soldaten," *BZ*, June 28, 1953.

167. Richard Millington, "Remembering the Uprising of 17 June 1953," in *Remembering the German Democratic Republic: Divided Memory in a United Germany*, ed. David Clarke and Ute Wölfel (Basingstoke, UK: Palgrave Macmillan, 2011), 157–166.

168. Weitz, *Creating German Communism*, 363. Evidence suggests that decades later, those who had ardently supported the regime tended to believe the official narrative, while those who did not felt compelled to avoid speaking of the matter (see Millington, "Remembering the Uprising").

169. The following *BZ* headlines have been translated by the author to illustrate these

points: "More Apartments for Weissensee," July 4, 1953; "48 Million for Apartment Renovations," July 7, 1953; "850 Apartments in District Prenzlauerberg," July 8, 1953; "Further 12 Million for Friedrichshain," July 10, 1953; "More Beautiful Apartments in District Mitte," July 14, 1953; "Playgrounds Missing in District Mitte," July 17, 1953; "Cheaper Apartments Will Also Be Built," July 24, 1953; "Construction Under Way in 1000 Buildings," August 12, 1953; "New Path for the Apartment Administration," September 16, 1953; "Scaffolding, Where One Sees Scaffolding!" August 30, 1953; "39 Apartments Waiting for Renters," September 18, 1953; and "Renters Make Decisions in Their Buildings: The New Path of the Housing Administration/Thousands of Marks Saved by Collaboration," October 2, 1953.

170. "Wir wünschten ganz Berlin sähe aus wie die Stalinallee, *BZ*, August 7, 1953.

171. "Bauarbeiter bei Präsident Pieck," *BZ*, October 11, 1953.

172. "G-sud appeliert an die Bauarbeiter," *BZ*, October 28, 1953.

173. "Mitteilung des Bundes deutscher Architekten," *DA* 2 (1953): 205.

174. Karl-Heinz Schulz, "Aufgaben der Bautechnik im Rahmen der Entwicklung einer realistischen deutschen Architektur," *DA 2* (1953): 202–204.

175. Hannemann, *Die Platte*, 62.

176. Nicolaus and Obeth, *Die Stalinallee*, 264–265.

177. Richard Paulick, "Typus und Norm in der Wohnhausarchitektur," *DA* 2 (1953): 218–225.

178. Schulz, "Aufgaben der Bautechnik im."

179. Hannemann, *Die Platte*, 57.

180. Durth, Düwel, and Gutschow, *Ostkreuz*, 463.

181. Nikita Khrushchev, speech at the All Unions Conference for the Building Industry, quoted in Thomas Hoscislawski, *Bauen zwischen Macht und Ohnemacht: Architektur und Städtebau in der DDR (Berlin: Verlag für Bauwesten, 1991)*, 133–134.

182. Nikita Khrushchev, speech at the All Unions Conference for the Building Industry, quoted in Durth, Düwel, and Gutschow, *Ostkreuz*, 464.

183. Düwel, *Baukunst voran!*, 96–97.

184. Yet he never explained how this might occur. Ivan Sholtowski, "Über die wahre und die falsche Schönheit in der Architektur," *DA* 4 (1955): 1–3.

185. Ibid.

186. Gerhard Kosel, speech at the First Building Conference of the GDR, quoted in Durth, Düwel and Gutschow, *Ostkreuz*, 466–468.

187. Walter Ulbricht, speech at the First Building Conference of the GDR, quoted in Durth, Düwel and Gutschow, *Ostkreuz*, 470.

188. Hans Gericke, "Um den fortschrittlichen Charakter unserer Architektur," *DA* 4 (1955): 328– 330.

189. Nicolaus and Obeth, *Die Stalinallee*, 282. Also see Hannemann, *Die Platte*, 65.

190. Kurt Leucht, quoted in Hoscislawski, *Bauen*, 84.

191. Kurt Magritz, "Die Industrializierung des Bauwesens und die künstlerischen *Aufgaben der Architektur*," *DA* 4 (1955): 49–51; Kurt Liebknecht, "Die Wissenschaft im Dienste der Industrializierung des Bauwesens," *DA* 4 (1955): 103–105; Hans Hopp, "Tieferes Verständ-

nis für die nationalen Traditionen," *DA* 5 (1956): 165–166; and Deutsche Bauakademie, "Die grosse Wende im Bauwesen," *DA* 5 (1956): 1–3.

192. Gerhard Strauss, "Einige Bemerkungen zur architektonishen Form," *DA* 5 (1956): 166–168.

193. Kurt Liebknecht, "Die Bedeutung der Unions-Baukonferenz in Moskau für die Aufgaben im Bauwesen Der Deutschen Demokratischen Republik," *DA* 4 (1955): 50–54.

194. Gerhard Rohn and Fritz Lazarus, "Projektierung von Wohnbauten in Grossblockbauweise," *DA* 5 (1956): 114–117.

195. Liebknecht, "Die Bedeutung der Unions-Baukonferenz."

196. Kurt Junghans, "Das Typisierte Wohnhaus im Strassenbild," *DA* 4 (1955): 25–37.

197. Hoscislawski, *Bauen*, 158–163.

198. Ulbricht initiated the reduction of apartment size at the Thirty-third Meeting of the Central Committee of the SED in 1957. See Hannemann, *Die Platte*, 67; and Hoscislawski, *Bauen*, 262.

199. Hannemann, *Die Platte*, 106–107.

200. For a selection of illustrative articles, see "Mehr Wohnungen durch drei Vorschläge," *BZ*, February 1, 1957; "Bessere Methoden in der Wohnraumpolitik," *BZ*, January 10, 1957; and Wohnraum gerecht zu vertielen fallt Schwer," *BZ*, February 14, 1957.

201. "Eine neuer Wohnungstyp ist zu besichtigen," *BZ*, February 10, 1957; and "Die Zwei-Zimmer-Wohnung ist Trumpf," *BZ*, April 7, 1957.

202. "Zweckmäßiger und billiger bauen," *BZ*, January 22, 1957; and "Berliner Bausaison in allen Stadtteilen," *BZ*, April 6, 1957.

203. Kurt Leucht, "Die Industrializierung des Bauwesens und ihre Auswirkung auf die städtebauliche Planung von Hoyerswerda," *Städtebau und Siedlungswesen* 2 (1955): 63–75.

204. Hoscislawski, *Bauen*, 177–181.

205. This is evident in an infill project by Hochbau Dresden I. See Rohn and Lazarus, "Projektierung von Wohnbauten."

206. Herbert Kuppe, "Zusammenwirken von Städtebau, Projektierung, Typisierung, und Industrializierung für grössere Wohnkomplexe," *DA* 5 (1956): 148–149; and Kurt Leucht, "Die Industrializierung des Bauwesens und ihre Auswirkung auf die städtebauliche Planung von Hoyerswerda," *Städtebau und Siedlungswesen* 2 (1955): 63–75. In a few years some additional impacts of industrialized construction on urban design would be observed, including (1) layouts that minimize the construction of streets for the provision of building supplies and allow several cranes to reach the entire site with two or three passes; (2) minimizing the number of building types to keep components manageable; and (3) keeping gaps between aligned buildings to 20 meters to limit the cost of unused track. See Harald Wohlgemuth and Herbert Spalteholz, "Einige Gedanken über den Einfluss des industriellen Bauens auf die städtebauliche Gestaltung von Wohnkomplexen (Grossblockbau)," *DA* 8 (1959): 600–601.

207. Hans Gericke, "Berlin—Unter den Linden," *DA* (1962): 635–650.

208. Durth, Düwel, and Gutschow, *Ostkreuz*, 470.

209. Herman Henselmann, "Das Wohnkomplex Friedrichshain," *ND*, March 30, 1956.

210. Herman Henselmann, "Einiger Bemerkungen zur Diskussion der Bevölkerung über den Wohnkomplex Friedrichshain," *DA* 5 (1956): 316–321.

211. Kurt Liebknecht, "Einige kritische Bemerkungen zum Entwurf eines Wohnkomplexes," *DA* 5 (1956): 354–355.

212. Nicolaus and Obeth, *Die Stalinallee*, 270; and Geist and Kürvers, *Berliner Mietshaus*, 388.

213. Liebknecht, "Enige kritische Bermekungen."

214. "Neuer moderner Stadtteil für 20 000 Berliner," *BZ*, March 19, 1957.

215. Durth, Düwel, and Gutschow, *Ostkreuz*, 474–480.

216. Geist and Kürvers, *Berliner Mietshaus*, 392–398.

217. Kurt Liebknecht, "Zur Ideologie des sozialistischen Bauens," *DA* 6 (1957): 417–419.

218. Ernst May to Herman Henselmann, July 15, 1957, SAPMO-BA, NL 182/1030, FBS363/15243.

219. Liebknecht, "Zur Ideologie des sozialistischen Bauens."

220. Kurt Liebknecht, "Die Diskussion geht weiter," *DA* 6 (1957): 602–604.

221. Hellmuth Brauer, "Nutzen wir Architekten und Städtebauer die Vorteile unserer Gesellschaftsordnung?" *DA* 6 (1957): 607–608.

222. Peter Bergner, "Über das Problem der nationalen Form," *DA* 6 (1957): 609–610.

223. Gerhard Zilling, "Bedeutet das Industrielle Bauen einen Verzicht auf die Weiterentwicklung nationaler Formen im Städtebau und in der Architektur," *DA* 6 (1957): 610–611.

224. Tage William-Olsson, "Einiges zum Begriff der Monumentalität im modernen Städtebau," *DA* 6 (1957): 16–17.

225. Kurt Junghans, "Zur Monumentalität im Städtebau—ein Erwiderung," *DA* 6 (1957): 422–423.

226. Richard Paulick, "Einige Bemerkungen zur Architektur Diskussion," *DA* 6 (1957): 479–481.

227. Bund Deutscher Architekten, "Entschliessung des III. Bundeskongresses des DBA," reprinted in *DA* 7 (1958): 60–61.

228. Edmund Collein, "Über den sozialistischen Städtebau," *DA* 8 (1959): 495–6; and Herbert Letsch, "Was verstehen wir unter sozilistischer Baukunst?" *DA* 8 (1959): 577–578.

229. Alfred Kurella, "Einige Grundelemente unserer sozialistischen Baugesinnung," *DA* 10 (1961): 1–4.

230. Nicolaus and Obeth, *Die Stalinallee*, 274. Schmidt, Collein, Kosel, and Liebknecht produced a detailed theoretical work on residential complexes, "Der sozialistische Wohnkomplex," published in June 1958. See Geist and Kürvers, *Das Berliner Mietshaus*, 398–401.

231. Durth, Düwel, and Gutschow, *Aufbau*, 242–243.

232. Nicolaus and Obeth, *Die Stalinallee*, 274–276.

233. Hermann Henselmann, "Vom Straussberger Platz zum Alexanderplatz," *DA* 7 (1958): 419–424.

234. Nicolaus and Obeth, *Die Stalinallee*, 275–276.

235. Ibid., 276–278.

236. For planners' design intentions, see Werner Dutschke, "Zwischen Straussberger Platz und Alexanderplatz," *DA* 7 (1959): 539.

237. "So gehts weiter vom Straussberger Platz zum Alex," *BZ*, November 6, 1958.

238. Nicolaus and Obeth, *Die Stalinallee*, 278.

239. Construction would continue until 1965.

240. "Ein Pilsner auf die neue Stalinallee," *BZ*, October 7, 1959.

241. "Berlin, wie wirste dir verändern," *BZ*, January 3, 1960.

242. "684 Wohnungen in Freidrichshain," *BZ*, February 13, 1959.

243. Kosel, *Unternehmen Wissenschaft.*

244. Ina Merkel, *Utopie und Bedürfnis: Die Geschichte der Konsumkultur in der DDR* (Cologne: Böhlau Verlag, 1999).

245. "Aufgaben des Bauwesens im Siebenjahrplan," *BZ*, April 2, 1959.

246. "764 000 Wohnungen werden bis 1965 gebaut," *BZ*, May 8, 1959.

247. "Erste Taktstraße im Berliner Wohnungsbau," *BZ*, April 8, 1959.

248. "Startschuss zum Weiterbau Stalinallee," *BZ*, February 16, 1960.

249. "Turmdrehkräne bewegen sich schneller," *BZ*, September 15, 1959.

250. "Grossblöcke bewegen sich nicht von selbst," *BZ*, August 19, 1959.

251. "Ein Kranspiel kostet nur 1,17 DM," *BZ*, Octobter 11, 1960.

252. Gunter Fischer, "Ist unsere Trümmerfrau noch existent?" *BZ*, May 26, 1960; "Berlin griff zu Schaufel und Hacke," *BZ*, June 9, 1960; and "Kurbeln, Kurbeln! Die Stalinallee ruft uns," *BZ*, October 20, 1960.

253. For instance, see "Zukunftsfrohe Perspektive für Berlin," *BZ*, July 4, 1959; "Interessierte Zuschauer," photo, *BZ*, August 17, 1960; and "Gespräch in der Baubude," *BZ*, September 20, 1960.

254. On the Sports Hall, see Advertisement for Ständige Deutsche Bauaustellung, *BZ*, September 25, 1959. For the construction illustration, see "Mehr-Schneller-Besser-Billiger," *BZ*, May 9 and 10, 1959.

255. "Die Alexanderstraße erhält neues Gesicht," *BZ*, June 3, 1960.

256. "Diskussion auf der Baustelle," *BZ*, December 4, 1960. Also see "Startschuss zum Weiterbau Stalinallee," *BZ*, February 16, 1960.

257. "Stalinallee: Ein Gigant zieht um," *BZ*, January 6, 1961.

258. "Antwort auf aktuelle politische, wirtschaftliche und menschliche Probleme," *BZ*, March 25, 1961.

259. For other examples, see "1787 Wohnungen zwischen Alex und Straussberger Platz," *BZ*, January 6, 1961; and "Geheimnis kurzer Bauzeiten," *BZ*, November 18, 1960. This latter article declared large-panel construction to be the "absolute newest technique in apartment building, proven by work on the newest section of Stalinallee, where the tallest large panel buildings in the world thus far are being erected."

260. Final report of the Komplexbrigade des Zentralkomitees zur Einführung der Grossplattenbauweise in Berlin, October 29, 1959, SAPMO-BA, DH1, 7909.

261. "MEHR BAUEN—ohne überlebte Tradition," *BZ*, November 24, 1959.

262. "'Wertheim in Scheiben' fur den Wohnungsbau," *BZ*, July 5, 1959.

263. Madeleine Grohtewohl, "Wohnungen nach Mass," *BZ*, December 21, 1960; "Ein Grundriss für alle Zwecke," *BZ*, January 17, 1961; and "Jedermanns Wohnung oder... was sagen Sie?" *BZ*, February 7, 1961.

264. "80 000 neue Wohnungen für Berlin bis 1965," *BZ*, May 26, 1959.

265. Udo Schulz, "Geplante Filtheaterbauten in Berlin," *DA* 9 (1958): 492–494.

266. "Modernste Kino der DDR in der Stalinallee," *BZ*, August 24, 1960. This cinema would later be named Kosmos.

267. "Berlin, wie wirste dir verändern," *BZ*, January 3, 1960.

268. "Eine Schule moderner Bautechnik," *BZ*, September 24, 1959.

269. For instance, one article begins describing a worker facing a "rubble mountain," then introduces his "great construction machine of Soviet production"; see "In die Luft gejagt," *BZ*, April 12, 1960.

270. On the increasing rents, see "Die Mieten hoch und höher," *BZ*, May 12, 1960; "Schöneberg beschloβ: Die Miete höher," *BZ*, June 24, 1960; "1½ Zimmer 134,40 WM Miete," *BZ*, August 2, 1960; and "16000 WM für vier Zimmer," *BZ*, March 2, 1961. On the US Army's luxurious housing, see "Besatzerbauten en gros," *BZ*, July 7, 1960.

271. "Schüler aus der Osloer Volksschule Toyen," photo, *BZ*, July 14, 1960; and "Interessierte Zuschauer," photo, *BZ*, August 17, 1960.

272. W. Wenger, "Wir erlebten Überraschungen," *BZ*, August 25, 1960.

273. "Hochbetrieb am Brandenburger Tor," *BZ*, October 9, 1960.

274. "Mehr Baumateriel für die Bevölkerung," *BZ*, February 2, 1960.

275. "100 Millionen DM für Stalinallee," BZ, April 12, 1961.

276. "Triumph im Weltraum Sieg des Kommunismus," BZ, April 13, 1961.

277. Hain, *Archeologie und Aneignung*, 67.

278. Nicolaus and Obeth, *Die Stalinallee*, 283.

279. Hermann Henselmann to Walter Ulbricht, November 28, 1958, SAPMO-BA, NL 182/1030, FBS363/15243.

280. Hermann Henselmann, "Dialektik im Städtebau," undated, SAPMO-BA, DH1-7909.

Conclusion

1. Peter Pulzer, *German Politics: 1945–1995* (Oxford: Oxford University Press, 1995), 101; and Fulbrook, *Divided Nation*, 195.

2. Walter Ulbricht, Press conference, June 15, 1961, quoted in Manfred Wilke, "Der Weg der SED zum Bau der Berliner Mauer," paper presented at the conference "Der Mauerbau: Kalter Krieg, Deutsche Teilung," Berlin, June 16–18, 2011, www.berliner-mauer-gedenkstaette.de/de/der-mauerbau-1961-970.html, accessed March 9, 2016.

3. Wilke, "Weg der SED," 18.

4. Council of Ministers, Resolution, August 12, 1961, reprinted in O. M. von der Gablenz, Hans Kuhn, and C. F. von Metttenheim, eds., *Dokumente zur Berlin Frage: 1941–1962* (Munich: Oldenbourg, 1962).

5. Helge Heidemeyer, "Die Flucht aus der DDR und der Mauerbau," paper presented at the conference "Der Mauerbau: Kalter Krieg, Deutsche Teilung," Berlin, June 16–18, 2011, www.berliner-mauer-gedenkstaette.de/de/der-mauerbau-1961-970.html, accessed March 9, 2016.

6. Wilke, "Weg der SED," 18.

7. Gamboni, *Destruction of Art*.

8. Marion Detjen, "Symbol der Diktatur oder friedensichernde Massnahme?—Die

Mauer als Erinnerungsort in den konkurrierenden Gedächtnissen vor und nach 1989/90," paper presented at the conference "Der Mauerbau: Kalter Krieg, Deutsche Teilung," Berlin, June 16–18, 2011, www.berliner-mauer-gedenkstaette.de/de/der-mauerbau-1961-970.html, accessed March 9, 2016, p. 5.

9. Ibid., 7.

10. Ibid., 8.

11. Axel Klausmeier, "Eine Weltikone als Errinerungsort: Die Gedenkstätte Berliner Mauer an der Bernauer Strasse," paper presented at the conference "Der Mauerbau: Kalter Krieg, Deutsche Teilung, Berlin," June 16–18, 2011, www.berliner-mauer-gedenkstaette.de/de/der-mauerbau-1961-970.html, accessed March 9, 2016.

12. Speer, *Third Reich*, 69.

13. Marshall Berman, *All That Is Solid Melts into Air: The Experience of Modernity* (New York: Simon & Schuster, 1982), 99.

14. Karl Marx, *Communist Manifesto*, 338, quoted in Berman, *All That Is Solid Melts into Air*, 95.

15. Berman, *All That Is Solid Melts into Air*, 105.

16. Susanne Ledanff, "The Palace of the Republic versus the Stadtschloss: The Dilemmas of Planning in the Heart of Berlin," *German Politics and Society* 21, no. 4 (2003): 30–73.

17. Regarding the "primitivist jargon of authenticity," see Lutz Koepnick, "Forget Berlin," *German Quarterly* 74, no. 4 (2001): 343–353. On the "frenzied search for symbolic meaning and fixed interpretations," see Ledanff, "Palace of the Republic," 34.

18. Azaryahu, "Politics of Street Names," 484.

19. Stangl, "Revolutionaries' Cemeteries."

20. "Revolution im Seecontainer," *Der Tagesspiegel*, May 27, 2011.

21. Stangl, "Vernacular and Monumental," 249–250.

22. Nicolaus and Obeth, *Die Stalinallee*, 287–294.

23. Ladd, *Ghosts of Berlin*, 187.

24. Hans Kollhoff, "Wohnungsbau in Berlin: "Wir brauchen eine neue Stalinallee," *Der Tagesspiegel*, March 30, 2016.

25. Ledanff, "Palace of the Republic."

26. Till, "Neue Wache."

27. Helmut Engel and Wolfgang Ribbe, *Geschichtsmeile Wilhelmstraße* (Berlin: Akademie Verlag, 1997).

28. "Die Gedenkstätte Berliner Mauer," www.berliner-mauer-gedenkstaette.de/de/, accessed March 9, 2016.

Index